# FEELING RELIGION

# FEELING
# RELIGION

JOHN CORRIGAN, EDITOR

Duke University Press   Durham & London   2017

© 2017 Duke University Press
All rights reserved

Designed by Courtney Leigh Baker
Typeset in Garamond Premier Pro and Din by Westchester
Book Group

Library of Congress Cataloging-in-Publication Data
Names: Corrigan, John, [date– ] editor.
Title: Feeling religion / John Corrigan, editor.
Description: Durham : Duke University Press, 2017. | Includes
bibliographical references and index.
Identifiers: LCCN 2017027359 (print) | LCCN
2017042415 (ebook)
ISBN 9780822372103 (ebook)
ISBN 9780822370284 (hardcover : alk. paper)
ISBN 9780822370376 (pbk. : alk. paper)
Subjects: LCSH: Emotions—Religious aspects. | Spirituality. |
Secularism.
Classification: LCC BL65.E46 (ebook) | LCC BL65.E46 F445
2017 (print) | DDC 200.1/9—dc23
LC record available at https://lccn.loc.gov/2017027359

Cover art: © Nina Berman / NOOR

TO CARLOS M. N. EIRE

CONTENTS

ACKNOWLEDGMENTS

I AM GRATEFUL to the National Humanities Center, the American Academy of Religion, and Florida State University for their support of a conference held at the National Humanities Center in 2015 during which many of these chapters were first presented. Thanks also to Miriam Angress at Duke University Press for her thoughtfulness, advice, and good cheer in fostering the project, to Karen Carroll for her expert copyediting, and to Susan Albury for seeing it through production. I am especially grateful to two readers for the press for their very careful and detailed reports, full of excellent criticisms and helpful suggestions.

JOHN CORRIGAN

# INTRODUCTION

*How Do We Study Religion and Emotion?*

*Emotion Intertwined with Religion*

In the early twenty-first century, much religion is emotional. We know about the scripture-fueled hatred and anger of religious extremists, the joy of the born-again, religious promotions of hope and compassion, theological conceptualizations of care, the feelings of assurance, and also of emptiness, that are daily enacted in religious settings, the religiously inflected love of nature and a religiously driven fear about the imminent end of the world. Such feelings of religious persons often are worn on the sleeve. But that does not mean those feelings are readily understandable by observers. Emotion in religion, in fact, has been defined for a very long time as essentially resistant to critical probings. It has been cast as irrational and, as such, insusceptible to scholarly analysis. There are reasons for that, having to do historically with parochial efforts to protect both the mystery of emotion and the mystery of religion.

Popular pronouncements of emotion as irrational are equally at home in religious publications and the *New York Times*. Columnist David Brooks, for example, in a *Times* op-ed published in early 2015, attempted an argument about morals that was constructed around such an understanding. Opposing what he called the "secularist" approach to morals and community, he hinged his argument against it on his claim that secularists foolishly believe that human rationality is itself a good enough guide to moral life. We humans, said Brooks, are irrational and emotional: "We are not really rational animals; emotions play a central role in decision-making." Moreover, it is those irrational emotions that are so much needed by all of us as we make our lives together in the world, because they lead us to "self-transcendence" and they make for an "enchanted" world. He concluded by predicting that secularism will never succeed until, in his words, it "arouses the higher emotions."[1]

Ostensibly, there is much in Brooks's piece that resonates with the views of his core readership. Many of them might agree with his characterization of emotions, thinking, "Of course, it's obvious. Emotions *are* irrational. Some *are* 'higher emotions.' An emotional life *is* an enchanted life." For those readers, thinking about emotion, morality, religion, rationality—all those seemingly intertwined topics—presumably takes place within a cocoon of ideological securities and folk wisdom, within a matrix of strongly held ideas about what a person is, what emotion is, and how emotion plays a role in a mysterious process of "transcendence." But conceptualizing the "enchanted life" in such a way is itself a species of magical thinking. Moreover, it is a view that has had its defenders in the academy, as well as its proponents in the popular press. The English anthropologist E. E. Evans-Pritchard, addressing the topic in 1965, criticized some of the best-known scholars in his field—including Émile Durkheim, Marcel Mauss, and Robert Marett, among others—for assuming that the mystery of emotion explained the mystery of religion: "According to Marett, primitive peoples have a feeling that there is an occult power in certain persons and things, and it is the presence or absence of this feeling which cuts off the sacred from the profane, the wonderworld from the workaday world, it being the function of taboos to separate the one world from the other; and this feeling is the emotion of awe, a compound of fear, wonder, admiration, interest, respect, perhaps even love. Whatever evokes this emotion and is treated as a mystery, is religion."[2]

In appreciating both the problems and promise of current research on religion and emotion it is useful to recall that academic investigators until recently tended to protect both religion and emotion from intrusive questions and prying theories. Many scholars who studied religion blanched when their investigation of the role of emotion led them to the doorstep of the question "What is *really* going on here?" They could, after all, be dismissed as *reductionists*, a humanities scare word of the late twentieth century that found particularly good traction within the areas of religious studies and the history of religion. Philosophers, classicists, historians, and literary studies scholars found themselves lost to a similarly discomfiting position, wondering if they could ask "But what is emotion, *really*?" and escape without being accused of betraying the subject. The human subject, that is.

Such concerns about the subject were not trivial. They were not simply anxieties about style points. As Geoffrey Harpham recently wrote, one of the "foundational concepts" of the humanities is "the primacy of the subjective."[3] How far can we analyze, how finely can we parse, how much can we dismantle and reaggregate, detextualize and retextualize, and, ironically, how many veils can we lift before we lose sight of the subject? And if we do, what then? These are questions that are central to the livelihood of the humanities, and they are present in abundance when we study religion and emotion.

Although scholarly reluctance to fully explore the topic of religion and emotion is abating, it has a long history. For centuries, religious writers joined emotion to religion, characterizing both—and especially in their interwovenness— as ineffable, irreducible, and insusceptible to any analysis that potentially would redefine them. Such a claim rings hollow today partly because to an increasing extent we have chosen to take religion as practice and emotion as performance. Neither are mysterious. Both are analyzable. We have the tools to reduce them. But putting aside for a moment what we know about material and visual cultures, the *sedimenti* of scripture, ritual enactments of religious scripts, political power and social force, brain scans, and embodiment generally, we can glimpse how the investigation of religion and emotion was for a very long time narrowed to one thing: what is called *religious experience*. In fact, keeping in mind the pioneering psychological research of the American William James, and his contemporary, the first president of the American Psychological Association G. Stanley Hall, it could be argued that an initial modern paradigm for the study of emotion itself coalesced as an outcome of the studies of religious experience that those two and their followers undertook. Religion was defined *as feeling* for a very long time in the West—namely, by St. Augustine—and in the early days of professional psychological research in America feeling, in turn, was investigated with reference to religion.

The intertwining of religion and emotion was deeply rooted in a Christian anthropology that commended the power of human emotion.[4] That anthropology was made explicit by the German pastor Friedrich Schleiermacher. In 1799 he published the first of several books that both reinforced the emphasis on religious experience as the center of religious life and defined it as emotional in such a way as to isolate religious experience from culture. He argued that religious people—meaning, for him, Christians—experience a "feeling of absolute dependence" that is qualitatively different from all other emotions. He made that feeling the touchstone of religious life. Radically different from other emotions, the "feeling of absolute dependence" was—in spite of Schleiermacher's best efforts to propose otherwise—exempted from the kind of scrutiny that might ordinarily be applied to an investigation of feeling. It was, for him, purely a matter between an individual and God. People report it, he said. And they distinguish it from all else they feel. That was all we could know.[5]

In the critically vibrant scene of the Aufklärung, Schleiermacher's writings were an attempt to respond to what he called the "cultured despisers" of religion. He argued that religion was not what philosophes might put under their microscopes and dissect into surprising bits. It was not philosophy, nor natural science, nor doctrine, nor abstract metaphysical systems. It was emotion, and a kind of emotion so different from others that all the science and philosophy and doctrine that previously had been deployed to define emotions was useless in reaching it. It was, in short, a scheme to protect religion by insulating its center, emotion, from the tides and currents of culture.

Anyone who was inclined to be persuaded to the theological niceties of Schleiermacher's theory of religious emotion likely also would have been happy with the claims of the Scottish philosopher Thomas Brown, who held the chair of moral philosophy at Edinburgh. Brown, son of a clergyman, writing about the same time as Schleiermacher, was an influential thinker in philosophical circles until the late nineteenth century. But more importantly for us, he defined emotion, ostensibly from a philosophical standpoint, as indefinable. "The exact meaning of the term *emotion*," Brown said, "is difficult to state in any form of words." As the historian of emotion Thomas Dixon has observed of Brown's coyness: "Although everyone apparently knew what an 'emotion' was, theorists agreed with Brown that this could not be embodied in any verbal definition. Two hundred years later, we are still living with this legacy of Thomas Brown's concept of 'emotion.'" The Americans James and Hall, in their difficulty defining the emotional experiences of their religious subjects, were psychologists who felt the influence of both Schleiermacher and Brown. They were among the early cohort of what Dixon describes as "psychologists [who] have continued to complain, at regular intervals, right up to the present, that 'emotion' is utterly resistant to definitional efforts. This is hardly surprising for a term that, from the outset, was defined as being indefinable."[6]

While Brown's view remained characteristic of some academic philosophy and psychology, Schleiermacher's theologized take on emotion was more explicitly carried forward by the German historian and theologian Rudolf Otto in the early twentieth century. Otto, writing about "the holy," sought to keep religious feeling, again, out of the laboratories of those who were indisposed to accepting it as ineffable and irreducible. He proposed that feeling involved in religious experience was a "non-rational" thing, and that all that might be managed were some analogies to it—expressed in Latinate words and phrases such as *mysterium tremendum*. Taking religion as sui generis, like Schleiermacher, he took the emotions felt in religious experience as sui generis as well.[7]

The fact is that, for the majority of the intellectual history of the West and until the last century, theological framings of emotional life—including theological language to describe it—profoundly influenced all discussion of feeling. Then, in late nineteenth-century America, by the time of William James, and later, everywhere, as the claims of Schleiermacher and Otto became less persuasive, scholars looked harder at emotion in religion. While not as pointed or ambitious as the research that scholars have undertaken in this century, the twentieth century nevertheless was a time of growing confidence in the susceptibility of emotional life to serious investigation. No one was willing to argue, as many now do, that genetics, nerves, and hippocampi are determinative. But, bit by bit, the *how* of studying emotion and religion became clearer.

Because language about religion, religious experience, and emotion was intertwined, changes in how scholars approached emotion and shifts in how religion was conceptualized took place alongside each other. French historians in the first part of the twentieth century made important contributions to reframing both the practice of emotion in historical settings and the nature of religious life. Because of Lucien Fevre and Marc Bloch and a stream of *annalistes* who followed in their steps, we began to think differently about religious life. The goal of writing *total history* set the tone, but most significant were the redescriptions of the subject matter of religion. The object of study in late medieval and early modern communities became popular religion, also called unofficial religion, and then vernacular religion, *la religion veçue*, and eventually, in an already shopworn expression, *lived religion*. That was a crucial step in the redefinition of religion, and above all, of Christianity, as an object of study. It challenged the tradition of taking religion only as a matter of doctrines, clerics, houses of worship, official religious rituals, and holy calendars. It offered instead a vastly broader view of what people do that is religious.[8] The harvest festivals, the moonlit devil hunts, local dietary guidelines, astrologies, beliefs about the terrain of afterlives, the fleshly signs of sanctity—including bleeding, tears, and the blush: such things mattered. And on an everyday basis, those things sometimes mattered more than what people did on the weekly Christian day of rest. Historian Carlo Ginzburg's Mennochio, the fifteenth-century Italian poster child for such practice of religion, claimed to be Roman Catholic but reported to his inquisitors that he believed various things that had nothing to do with official Catholic traditions and that he felt things differently than the systematic theologies said he should. He was certain that he was a good Catholic, appeared shocked that the church might think otherwise, and yet ended his life at the stake. His report of his understanding of the creation of the world, a cosmology that he trusted was unobjectionably Catholic, was telling:

> I have said that, in my opinion, all was chaos, that is, earth, air, water, and fire were mixed together; and out of that bulk a mass formed—just as cheese is made out of milk—and worms appeared in it, and these were the angels. The most holy majesty decreed that these should be God and the angels, and among that number of angels there was also God, he too having been created out of that mass at the same time, and he was named lord with four captains, Lucifer, Michael, Gabriel, and Raphael. That Lucifer sought to make himself lord equal to the king, who was the majesty of God, and for this arrogance God ordered him driven out of heaven with all his host and his company; and this God later created Adam and Eve and people in great number to take the places of the angels who had been expelled. And as this multitude did not follow God's commandments, he sent his Son, whom the Jews seized, and he was crucified.[9]

The turn to different ways of viewing religion in history took place alongside important developments in philosophical studies about emotion. Emotion was an important part of French existentialist philosophy, and those who were influenced by that philosophy ventured fresh understandings of emotion that challenged previous dichotomies of rational/irrational and emotional/cognitive. In the wake of French existentialists, Robert Solomon and Amélie Rorty, among others, argued for a reconsideration of how feeling and thinking were related, a topic well represented by the title of one of Solomon's many books, *Thinking about Feeling*, which drew together discussion of some themes from his writing over the previous forty years.[10] Solomon, for example, pointed out that persons construct their anger partly out of cognitions about how they were wronged, how awful it was, how the perpetrator was bad. He said, in short, that part of feeling angry was talking oneself into feeling angry. That perspective, as it acquired some academic gravity, was embraced especially by persons working in religious ethics, who were positioned to draw on a deep and rich vein of ethical writing by medieval thinkers, especially Thomas Aquinas, and theologians who followed their leads. In the late twentieth century, scholars such as Diana Cates have interpreted some of those traditions of moral inquiry in ways that demonstrate the reciprocity of emotion and cognition in religious thought. As such, those studies have made strong contributions toward a larger project of situating emotional life within culture, and joining the analysis of religious ideas to the study of feelings.

In the middle of the twentieth century, another important shift in the study of emotion took place as researchers broached the idea that emotion in religious life was something less private than what many had claimed. Many writers, especially those who thought in terms of feeling as *religious experience*, had taken emotion in religion essentially as something so dear that it could not be truly expressed or publicly shared. Scholars began to consider more seriously the likelihood that such feelings were not too profound or precious to suffer investigation. Their approach was to replace the notion of religion and emotion imagined as sui generis with the claim that emotion itself is a construction. That is, they argued that the way persons feel is a product of a social or cultural setting, and, derived from that, that feeling signifies culture. Clifford Geertz began to press the case for a culturally constructed self, and other scholars migrated that approach to the study of emotions. Michelle Rosaldo and Catherine Lutz, among others, argued that emotion, as an integral aspect of self, was constructed within local social and cultural frameworks.[11] Among sociologists, James Averill and Arlie Hochschild were working toward the same conclusions, Hochschild contributing a term of now-proven durability, "feeling rules," to identify cultural expectations for emotional performance.[12] Lutz's evocative book title *Unnatural Emotions* remains most resonant, however. It pointedly expressed the refusal to treat emotions as *given* in nature and therefore refused to accept that emotions were irreducible. In other words, it directly challenged thinking that resisted the critical investigation of emotion. As this view gathered momentum—even in qualified ways—it affected how researchers imagined the study of religion as well as emotion. For if emotions are not natural, and emotions, according to a colossal historical record, are intertwined with religion, then religion itself might not be so hidden after all. It would not be so "wholly other," as Rudolf Otto would say.

The *how* of studying religion and emotion has also been changing because of the influence of research on the human body. Opposite the radical constructivist approach is one that emphasizes biological processes. Researchers have listened to brain scientists and endocrinologists, thought about biochemistry and neurons, adaptation and evolution, and surmised that things might not be as relative and culture-bound as some have thought. Research in the area of the genetics of human behavior, for example, has developed to the point of offering genetic explanations for a wide range of behaviors, including a recent argument, based on a study of seven hundred pairs of twins, for the biological basis of political orientation in America.[13] A groundbreaking book by Robert Fuller exemplifies the extent to which body research is specifically entering historical analysis. Fuller's *The Body of Faith: A Biological History of Religion in America* goes so far as to propose that membership in a religious denomination correlates with genes and biochemistry.[14] Whether you join the emotionally expressive Methodists singing happily about "Jesus Coming in the Air," or the Unitarians, whom Methodists have long criticized for being *unemotional*, it might have more to do with who your great-grandparents were than whether the idea of hellfire resonates. Your feelings might have more to do with a calibration of your peptides than a celebration of your Eastertides.

Scholars have sought ways to combine insights drawn from such biological interpretations with what can be drawn from constructivist theories. While pronounced constructivist or biological theories of emotional life did not invite collaborative scholarship, by the end of the twentieth century, researchers nevertheless were beginning to talk about how both culture and biology shaped feeling in religious life. Much of the discussion of that emergent middle ground now takes place around *embodiment*, a term that has a range of meanings.

One kind of approach to studying the embodied subject is a branch of what has been called *cognitive science*. Religion researchers such as the anthropologist Pascal Boyer, together with other scholars loosely connected across a range of disciplines, have suggested a view of religion as a natural outcome of evolution.[15] In such a view, the emotions associated with religion were derivations from human cognitive processes that operate outside of religion itself. So, for example, one of the things cognitive science concerns itself with is what has been named the "hyperactive agency detection device," a mental mechanism that has evolved, according to some researchers, to detect and assess the activity of agents within a person's environment.[16] Because of the potentially serious consequences of failing to detect a local agent, this mechanism generates false positives; in other words, it leads to perception of agents—or we might even say actants—who are not there. The feelings associated with this process of detection can include fear and surprise, among other emotions. Those feelings arise, presumably, from an embodied engagement with the world—one walks down a dark city street late at night and the gears turning in this mechanism produce recognitions of agents, some of whom are there and some of whom are not. The fact of recognition of agents who are not there, however, suggests that a feeling of fear of a mugger, ghost, demon, or zombie is not directly prompted by something physically present in the environment. For the cognitive science of religion, the middle space between the ordinary physical and the seemingly noumenal in this sort of embodied approach might be further scrutinized for certain things—the spicy smell of ethnic food, the loud clacking sound of elevated trains, the uneven sensation of cobblestones underfoot—in ways that implicate culture. At the same time, this approach would claim that something is going on that is apart from culture. For cognitive scientists, the "hyperactive agency detection device" is one kind of middle ground that might be explored as part of an approach that focuses on embodiment and a potential for the genesis of feelings related to religion.

Another kind of embodiment research in the study of religion and emotion builds on what has been called *affect theory*. Affect theory, simply put, is about what the psychologist Silvan Tomkins and his followers, not surprisingly, call "affects." Notable followers include Paul Ekman, who developed the *facial expression* training sought by police and corporate human resource officers looking for frauds and fakers. The theory asserts that there are nine affects: joy, excitement, surprise, anger, disgust, anguish, fear, shame, dissmell (an impulse to avoid). They are said to be hardwired in all of us. That is, they are viewed, for the most part, as evolutionary adaptations.[17]

Affect theory is not about genes and hormones, and it is not about the mental processes that draw the attention of cognitive science scholars. Rather, in its stripped-down version, it is about bodily postures and movements. It attends to impulsive physical expression. So, affect theorists see in the smile a sign of an affective *fact*, the affect of joy. That joy, displayed on the face, is not something that persons have to talk themselves into. It is a physically embodied emotion, but not one that requires the discourses of culture—however those are defined and displayed—in order to take place (although affect theorists insist that culture matters). As religion and emotions researcher Donovan Schaefer writes in chapter 3 of this book, this approach seeks to discover in affect something of the "pre-discursive materiality of bodies." Or, in the words of affect theorist Brian Massumi, it is an approach which acknowledges that "the skin is faster than the word."[18] This means that, in this kind of research, religious feeling is not necessarily the product of the embrace of doctrines; it is not prompted or formed by cognitions. And yet, such theorists say, it happens oftentimes in collaboration with cultural frameworks that guide feeling. Interpreting writings of affect theorists, feminist film scholar Gail Hamner, in chapter 4, suggests that the shedding of tears, for example, can be "related to but not determined by language and memory," and she offers the neologism "affecognitive" to refer to such events. This is all to say that affect theory, as it has been developing, aims to explore possibilities of speaking about feeling and thinking, biology and culture, together. It is too early to say whether affect theory will deliver. But the animated conversation about affect now coursing through humanities disciplines suggests that scholars are investing in research that they believe will enable more complicated discussions about what feeling has to do with culture, with important implications for the study of religion and emotion.

Scholars currently debate what is meant by affect and emotion; whether that debate will be fruitful is yet to be determined. It is worth noting, however, that, in general, affect theorists focus on preverbal physical response to stimuli while those who research emotion are more inclined to speak in terms of hypocognized/hypercognized feelings. Affect theory, which is only beginning to coalesce, emerged from psychological (but less so psychoanalytic) research and animal studies and has been taken up largely by literary studies and media scholars. Emotions theories—and there are many of them—currently are more important in fields such as philosophy, classics, history, religion, anthropology, and sociology, but not for the same reasons in each of those fields. That said, affect theory and the theorization of emotion remain open-ended scholarly enterprises and while they have proven their analytical utility, both are still developing their distinctive vocabularies and approaches. Some recent efforts to intertwine them in interdisciplinary analyses have evidenced that such projects are promising, but that more generous conversation among different fields of study will be required in order to advance collaboration.

The relation of feeling to culture, the ways that affects as biological facts are related to culture, is a topic of particular interest at this time because of its place within a broader scholarship that has sought to disrupt the traditional separation of *culture* and *biology* into discrete categories. William Connolly's investigation of brain activity and film, Elizabeth A. Wilson's study of biology, psychoanalysis, and affect in conceptualizing feminism, and Felicity Callard and Des Fitzgerald's call for deeper interdisciplinary collaboration among neuroscientists and social scientists all help frame a potential research agenda for the study of religion and emotion.[19]

Constructivist theory, affect theory, embodiment, cognitive science, the *affecognitive*: much is happening in the study of emotion. Because much is happening in the study of religion as well—new theories of what it is and how we study it—scholars who are interested in religion and emotion are inclined to understand that it is necessary to think about how both of those terms are being continuously redefined. Is emotion biological, or cultural, or something in between and if in-between, then how much and what kind of biology are we talking about, and what aspects of culture matter the most? And is religion basically what people do on Sundays, or on Friday nights, or during Ramadan, or is it the way they imagine a cosmos built out of cheese and worms? If emotion is a moving target for researchers, so is religion. That makes studying both together a Heisenbergian challenge. Every time one moves, the other changes. And both are moving. Do we experiment with different ways of understanding each of those elements in the hope that we can guess our way to a combination that delivers some reliable understanding about what they have to do with each other? Or are there some pathways that offer more potential opportunity than others?

The problem of how we study religion and emotion is made more complex by the fact that not all religion is emotional, or at least not as emotional as those traditions (preeminently Christianity) that have been the primary objects of study in the West. Buddhists, especially in Japan, would find David Brooks's promotion of emotion as the foundation for an enchanted moral society uninformed and partisan. For many Buddhists, the spiritual goal of emptiness has no place for a privileging of emotion as the pathway to transcendent order. Buddhists, like all persons, feel. But that is not the spiritual goal, and feeling is not imagined, as Brooks claims, to be a *central* part of moral decision making. Studying religion and emotion sometimes means studying its theological de-emphases.

With that caveat in mind, it is possible to identify several key features of the research that has shaped the study of religion and emotion over the last several decades. There is an emerging scholarly consensus that emotion in religion (1) is not mysterious; (2) can be studied; (3) is about the body and not the transcendence of the body; (4) is about culture but not only about culture; that (5) the distinction between rational cognition and irrational emotion in religion is unwarranted; that (6) spirituality sometimes has to do with feeling and sometimes does not; and that (7) what we mean by religion is entwined with what we mean by emotion—and vice versa.


*Prospect*

The prospect for research on religion and emotion can be improved if it is shaped by several considerations. First, with regard, specifically, to the broader humanities: the study of religion and emotion as a fundamentally interdisciplinary project within the humanities must deepen its engagements with the cutting edges of interpretation *across* the humanities. That means not only continuously incorporating ethnicity, gender, and sexuality into research agendas but seriously engaging the critical literatures in the humanities that have arisen from recent emphases on postcolonialism, capitalism, secularity, and fundamentalisms. Such conversations occasionally have been difficult because much study of religion and emotion has been framed with respect to specifics of personal experience and the seemingly *private*. The conceptual expansiveness and fluidity required to address widely varying social and cultural contexts has not been as well practiced. Prospective leads for this line of research include analyses of the cultural politics of emotion that have been advanced by scholars such as Ann Cvetkovich and Sara Ahmed, as well as Sneja Gunew whose work critically addresses the role of Eurocentric thinking about cognition in emotions research.[20]

Second, the study of religion and emotion must address strange emotions, including what June McDaniel in this volume terms *dark* emotions. Is there a way to move forward that includes opportunities to respond precisely and productively to previous scholarship that emerged out of parochial interests? In other words, can we speak of brain scans in the same breath as Friedrich Schleiermacher's "feeling of absolute dependence"? Are those approaches truly incommensurate, separated by two centuries but more importantly by different epistemologies? The field of the history of emotions has led most who think about these things to conclude that emotions are historicized. But—unless one appeals to a positivist model of *emotional progress*—we risk losing awareness of differences in emotional experiences when compared over time. If we are going to claim that emotional experiences differ from era to era, we need to continue to think about why Schleiermacher could persuade his audience about the existence of a unique emotion that many today would not recognize. In short, this *how* is about taking seriously reports of strange emotions or unfamiliar clusterings of emotions. It experiments with ways to account for them in the analytical and interpretative schemes constructed for the study of religion and emotions over the last few decades.

Third, research is likely to advance by investigating not only the expression of emotion but also the concealment and repression of emotion in religion. Just as scholars in recent decades have been able to build important interpretations of ethnic communities and nations by focusing on repressed memory, so also might the study of repressed emotion lead to new interpretations of religious life. The repression of anger and hatred is important in many religions, and is linked to what cultural commentators since Sigmund Freud and Norbert Elias have thought of as the *civilizing* influence of religion.[21] The cultivation of sorrowful and guilty feelings in some religions can be associated with the diminishment of feelings of happiness. Such emotional dynamics represent a kind of emotional repression, or forgetting, that should be investigated as part of a developing project of the study of religion and emotion.

Fourth, research can attend more closely to conflict. How we study religion and emotion can be better framed with regard to the emotionality underlying religious conflict. There has been much recent scholarly conversation about what emotion has to do with the construction of *others*. Those who are working in religion and emotion can advance that conversation, given that religion is involved in so much conflict worldwide.

Fifth, there are opportunities to advance the study of religion and emotion through a focus on gender. Research on gender and emotion can fruitfully be applied to the study of religion and feminist scholarship, particularly in connection with antiracist theory, offers some promising pathways for research.[22]

Finally, scholarship on religion can inform the broader study of emotion. Religious rituals, material culture, gender orders, and sexual beliefs, as well as the broader interwovenness of religion with economy and politics, are rich areas of study with important potential insights for the study of emotion.

*Ways of Studying Religion and Emotion*

The chapters in this book represent a range of approaches to the study of religion and emotion. This research was originally presented at a conference, "How Do We Study Religion and Emotion?," held at the National Humanities Center in North Carolina in 2015. Each article represents the perspective of a participant in that meeting about the *how* of studying religion and emotion. Accordingly, there is a multiplicity of *hows* represented, some of which comport with or overlap with each other, while others stake out new territories for exploration.

Many who write about emotion make reference to *reason*. Sometimes emotion is contrasted with reason. At other times scholars argue for more complex definitions of reason and especially for nuanced analysis that acknowledges that there are different forms of reason and different ways of talking about it. Moreover, it is clear that conceptualizations of emotion and reason change in relation to one another, emotion appearing differently depending on how one locates it in relation to reason. That issue is central to chapter 1, in which Diana Fritz Cates explores conceptualizations of reason and feeling in Seneca and Aquinas, elucidating how they are intertwined in those writers' thinking about moral action. Cates notes that many challenges confront scholars of religion and ethics who wish to develop accounts of the morality of emotion. She writes about how a fundamental challenge must be met, not only in the context of religious studies, philosophical ethics, and moral psychology, but also in the context of other fields, including the social and natural sciences. That challenge has to do with defining emotion—that is, with communicating to others what scholars mean by the term and understanding what others, in turn, mean by the same or related terms. Her chapter shows, by way of an example from the history of Western religious thought, how difficult it can be to find common definitional ground in the discussion of emotion. An off-kilter exchange that Thomas Aquinas constructed between Aristotelian and Stoic views of the morality of emotion reveals the sort of conceptual mapping that can be required before conversation partners can be confident that, in talking about emotion, they are even talking about the same thing. She demonstrates that there are contexts of scholarly exchange in which deep conceptual analysis cannot always be expected; but *some* attention to definition is always necessary.

The relation of reason—in the form of metaphysics—to emotion likewise is central to chapter 2. For Mark Wynn, a way to bring clarity to the discussion of the place of emotion in religious tradition is to consider how one and the same track of spiritual development may be differently described, depending on whether we adopt the vantage point of metaphysics or experience, including, centrally, emotional experience. To develop his case, Wynn takes John of the Cross and Thomas Aquinas as representatives of, respectively, the perspectives of experience and metaphysics. Wynn argues that if we are to understand the contribution of the emotions to the spiritual life, it is important to see how an account of the trajectory of spiritual development that is cast in emotional terms can be brought into new and deeper focus when it is related to a metaphysical specification of the nature of the spiritual life. Neither vocabulary is reducible to the other. At the same time, neither is entirely detachable from the other: what is said in metaphysical terms in some measure informs and constrains what can be said in emotional terms, and vice versa.

Approaching the topic from a different angle, Donovan Schaefer asks in chapter 3, "What does atheism feel like?" His research is an attempt to address the question asked by Janet Jakobsen and Ann Pellegrini in *Secularisms*: What does secularism feel like?[23] Although atheism and secularism define themselves according to the advance of reason—often with specific reference to the Darwinian revolution's overturning of the anthropocentric cosmos—Darwin's actual situation within the tradition of rationalism is less comfortable. According to Schaefer, it is precisely by drawing lines of continuity between humans and other animals that Darwin shows how human reason must be something that springs up from our bodies, rather than descending from above. Drawing on affect theory and in conversation with evolutionary theory and affective neuroscience, Schaefer suggests that rather than mapping belief and disbelief

onto an emotion/reason binary, we see both religions and the various formations of nonreligion as structures of reticulated emotions. As affect theorist
Lauren Berlant argues, affect theory points in the direction of a "sensualized
epistemology" in which structures of knowledge can be profiled not only in
terms of their propositional content, but in terms of what Raymond Williams
would call the "structures of feeling" they evoke. This is consistent with recent
work in affective neuroscience, such as Antonio Damasio's description of the
"passion for reason"—the affective dimension of knowledge production itself.
Schaefer demonstrates how, from an evolutionary perspective, a return to Darwin's underattended work on emotion can help us map the specific contours of
different atheisms, and he analyzes how early twenty-first-century New Atheism can be studied within this frame. By these lights, disbelief itself impresses
as an animal process, animated by clusters of emotions that become the raw
material for different configurations of power.

Another utilization of affect theory is demonstrated by M. Gail Hamner. In
chapter 4 she attends to the documentary film form in order to examine affect
and the space of religious public cultures. Specifically, her chapter sets out to assess the usefulness of affect theory as a tool for analyzing recent (twenty-first-
century) U.S. documentary films about religion by (1) explicating how the genre
of documentary entails the frame of a particular public culture; (2) examining
how the religion documentaries in question pit rules of emotional propriety
(structure of the public culture) against displays of emotional impropriety (resistance to this structure); and (3) arguing that the disturbance of the operative
norms of emotional display generates circuits of affect that potentially can (work
to) alter the very form of the public culture imaged by the film, especially when
the film maintains what Trinh T. Minh-ha calls an "interval" between truth and
meaning. The chapter recognizes the wide range of contemporary discussions of
affect and emotion and situates itself in the line of Gilles Deleuze, Lauren Berlant, and media theorists such as Tiziana Terranova, Adi Kuntsman, Steven Shaviro, and Zizi Papacharissi, all of whom position affect as a pre-emotional intensity that circulates through public media and, through that circulation, produces
both common experience and further intensifications of affect. The chapter discusses four documentaries about religion (*For the Bible Tells Me So*, *Trembling
Before G-d*, *Jesus Camp*, and *Searching for the Wrong-Eyed Jesus*), and draws on
documentary and film theorists such as Trinh Minh-ha, Eugenie Brinkema, and
Brian Winston to theorize the cinematographic elements of documentary that
both project the boundaries of a specific religious (or national) community and
also show the exclusions wrought by those boundaries as affective indices of unexpected disturbance.

June McDaniel, in chapter 5, observes that there are many ways to study religious emotion. One way is through an anthropological and phenomenological approach centered on observing and describing the emotional and religious
lives of persons. Cautioning that scholars must understand that not all cultures
construct the self and its emotions as do Westerners, and wary of biases embedded in Western scholarship, she reports on religion in Indonesia and the Middle
East in a way that seeks to capture something of the ways that persons in those
places understand their emotions, including their cultivation and display. In the
course of that presentation, she demonstrates how a focus on *dark* emotions—
in contrast to a discussion of *positive* emotions typical of most research—yields
important insights about the role of feeling in religion. McDaniel asks how a
religion is understood within its own cultural context, what it accomplishes for
the people who experience it, and whether there is a cultural value to emotional
experience. She explores the emotions of sorrow, fear, and anger in two cultural
contexts. One is the Shakta tradition of goddess worship in West Bengal, India,
and the other is the Shi'ah tradition of Iran. It is easy to see why religions focus on
happiness, but it is more challenging to understand why they emphasize sorrow.
In both of these traditions, anger and sorrow bring the person close to the deity,
and both are paths of salvation in the afterlife. She examines the *rasa* theory of
emotion in Indian literature, and looks at the works of two Shakta poets. She
then considers literature from Shi'ah Islam, and the virtues of mourning for Husayn. In these religions, the dark emotions unite the worlds, allowing a depth of
insight and compassion that cannot be found through happier forms of faith and
practice.

In chapter 6, Sara M. Ross, a musicologist, likewise reminds us that in considering the different ways that emotions are constructed, expressed, and altered, we do well to bear in mind the interplay between broad historical
tradition and local setting. She points out that Judaism evidences a positive interest in human emotions, and those emotions are portrayed in the scriptures,
such as the Hebrew Bible and Talmud. Ross, however, calls our attention to
another, overlooked aspect of Jewish emotional culture, namely, the role of
music in prompting and channeling feeling. She discusses emotions in Jewish
ritual music, while attending to the question of why musicological scholarship
focuses only on the representation of sentiment in Jewish music. She asks why
there is so much attention to the musical mechanisms employed by composers and performers, but such a shortfall of effort in analyzing the actual emotions felt by human audiences. In this regard, one central question she pursues
has to do with feeling and cognition. Since it is undeniable that the cognitive
sciences can no longer ignore the bodily, social, and cultural dimensions of

cognition as well as the impact of individual experiences on the same, why is it that the study of emotion in Jewish music still disregards the cognitive part in music experience? And what can be gained by overcoming that neglect? Until recently, little has been written about how emotions are actually perceived by the individual worshipper—as well as by the community—during synagogue services in which music plays a central role. Ross offers examples of how emotions are represented in synagogue music, and discusses several methodological challenges in the study of emotions in Jewish ritual music.

Feelings about nature are often interwoven with religious programs of emotion, but how and for what purposes are open questions. In chapter 7, Islamist and environmental studies scholar Anna Gade points out the expectation, fairly widespread across the field called *religion and ecology*, that the world's religions will provide resources to foster environmental care, concern, hope, and so forth—or the reverse, that they have served as obstacles to normatively sanctioned feelings and attitudes. A latent theory of affect rests at the nexus of scholarly fields of religious and environmental studies in this way. Non-academic, and often nonreligious, stakeholders also routinely and similarly cast emotion as religious or moral sentiment cultivated for the sake of the environment within a development industry, global or personal. Sentiment is thus a resource to extract from the world's religious systems, one's own or another's, in order to further environmental goals.

In describing the complexity and turns in that process of aligning religion, feeling, and environment, she juxtaposes American, largely Christian-inflected, views of the environment with those of a Muslim community. The romantic American approach essentializes nature-feeling as definitional to religion, and promoters of a view of world-religious pluralism seek to extend that definition to encompass seemingly cognate sentiments that may support the mission of universalizing environmentalist norms. Reporting on her fieldwork in Indonesia with committed Muslims, she explains how they instead apply *environmental* commitments, framed self-consciously as such, in order to further religious goals. Leaning toward apocalyptic, the feelings of those Muslims about the environment are more oriented to a desire for mercy in the next life than to hope for the resolution of environmental issues in this one. For them, environmental care is cast in service of religious ends rather the reverse.

Jessica Johnson approaches the question "How do we study religion and emotion?" by reflecting on the ways that ethnographic fieldwork at an evangelical megachurch affectively troubled her positionality as a researcher and her identity as a non-Christian. In chapter 8, her discussion of her ethnographic engagement with the Mars Hill Church community in Seattle includes autoethnography that offers a thick description of what she theorizes as the affective labor of coming "under conviction"—an unpredictable bodily process that is difficult to pin down in words and beyond doctrinal understanding. She examines her experience of coming under conviction as social, affective, and embodied, signaling a desire to believe in a pastor with whom she shared no theological or ideological affinity. She subsequently reframes the privileging of language and subject positions of speaker-listener in analyses of the spiritual and political value of conviction. By shifting critical attention from rhetoric and discourse to affect and emotion, she proposes ways for analyzing resonance across hierarchical dichotomies of religious and secular or sacred and profane. The chapter builds on theorizations of affective space, economy, and labor to examine how conviction is manipulated to bodily affect and political effect as emotions such as fear, shame, and paranoia circulate to excite, agitate, and exploit a desire to believe.

Focusing on ritual practice, David Morgan considers in chapter 9 the place of emotion and ritual in social analysis by considering the entangled relationship of religion, sport, and national piety as forms of mediation. The chapter works from Émile Durkheim on emotion and ritual and Benedict Anderson on imagination and cognition toward an integrated treatment of mediation as the aesthetic analysis of thought and feeling. To this is brought an interest in network theory's focus on entanglement as an apt description of social life. Rather than differentiate these three cultural activities as consisting of irreducible essences, the chapter seeks to discern why in fact they so readily overlap and intermingle in practice. Sport, says Morgan, is not modern religion, but a ritual practice that integrates religion and national piety in an amalgam that does cultural work we need to understand better.

Taking as his point of departure a music video issued during the 2012 World Cup, Morgan proposes that a key to understanding some of the emotional dynamics of sport as ritual is to recognize the importance of mediation, which occurs in two different ways: as the ritual itself experienced collectively in person, mediated in the bodies gathered together; and the extended mediation of the event in images, on the radio, on the Internet, or on television. Both forms of mediation make the ritual available to acts of imagination that integrate spectators into social bodies with a keen sense of belonging. The ritual amalgamation of religious faith, fan loyalty, and patriotic sentiment charges competition with a heightened sense of importance. The group's quest for bragging rights, for the right of the superlative, to be *the best*, takes the spectator's experience from ordinary life to a poignant sense of collective consciousness charged with the prospect of exaltation and menaced by the threat of humiliation.

Abby Kluchin returns to affect theory in chapter 10. Bringing a critical eye and a proposal for the usefulness of psychoanalytic theory alongside affect theory, she asks what religious studies has to gain from integrating those two kinds of approaches. For Kluchin, research in the nascent field of affect theory is sometimes constrained by a conceptualization of affect that severely limits possibilities for exploring how affect can be recognized, defined, and discussed in practical, everyday ways. She proposes as a guide to understanding affect Wilfred Bion's classic *Experiences in Groups*, and drawing on that she challenges the emphasis in affect theory on the "the circulation of affects, their hectic Deleuzian traversals of bodies and boundaries," which "seems to preclude the more readily accessible vocabulary of affective contagion *between* subjects, the way that other people's feelings sometimes seem to be 'catching.'" Accordingly, Kluchin resists conceptions of affect as prelinguistic or nonlinguistic or precognitive or noncognitive, or as wholly impersonal. Her central interest is in intersubjectivity, and she argues for a middle ground that does not present an either/or choice between language and bodies. She suggests how religion, considered in affective terms, might look by turning critically to Charles Hirschkind's study of Islamic cassette sermons, and concludes that the Deleuzian strand of affect theory has something to offer religion scholars, but in a qualified way.

Each of these chapters demonstrates an approach to studying religion and emotion. Taken together, they suggest the ways that a great many aspects of religion can be critically explored and creatively interrelated through a focus on emotion. They likewise indicate how research on the emotional aspect of religion generates fresh leads for research into issues that traditionally have attracted the attention of scholars. When we take emotion seriously, metaphysics looks different, and so do ethics, ritual, religious music and poetry, the environment, popular culture, and the secular. We can ask new questions, interweave themes in unexpected ways, and enable innovative critical analysis and theorizing. The study of religion and emotion is an inviting enterprise that already has yielded significant insight into religious belief and practice, and, as it gathers momentum, promises continuing strong returns.

NOTES

While largely written by John Corrigan, this overview is a collaboration among all the authors in this book.

1. David Brooks, "Building Better Secularists," *New York Times*, February 3, 2015, accessed April 14, 2015, http://www.nytimes.com/2015/02/03/opinion/david-brooks-building-better -secularists.html?_r=0.

2. E. E. Evans-Pritchard, *Theories of Primitive Religion* (Oxford: Clarendon Press, 1965), 33.

3. Geoffrey Galt Harpham, "Finding Ourselves: The Humanities as a Discipline," *American Literary History* 25, no. 3 (2013): 22, accessed April 14, 2015, doi:10.1093/alh/ajt027.

4. See essays in John Corrigan, ed., *The Oxford Handbook of Religion and Emotion* (New York: Oxford University Press, 2008), and especially those in part 4 on Augustine, Medieval Mysticism, Kierkegaard, and Jonathan Edwards.

5. Friedrich Schleiermacher, *On Religion: Speeches to Its Cultured Despisers*, ed. and trans. Richard Crouter (Cambridge: Cambridge University Press, 1996), and *The Christian Faith*, English translation of the second German edition, ed. H. R. Mackintosh and J. S. Stewart (London: T and T Clark, 1960).

6. Thomas Dixon, "Emotion: The History of a Keyword in Crisis," *Emotion Review* 4, no. 4 (2012): 340.

7. Rudolf Otto, *The Idea of the Holy: An Inquiry into the Non-Rational Factor in the Idea of the Divine and Its Relation to the Rational*, trans. John W. Harvey (New York: Oxford University Press, 1973).

8. Natalie Zemon Davis, *Society and Culture in Early Modern France: Eight Essays* (Stanford, CA: Stanford University Press, 1975); Peter Burke, *Popular Culture in Early Modern Europe* (New York: New York University Press, 1978); Keith Thomas, *Religion and the Decline of Magic* (New York: Scribner's, 1971); and William A. Christian Jr., "Provoked Religious Weeping in Early Modern Spain," in *Religious Organization and Religious Experience*, ed. John Davis (London: Academic Press, 1982), 97–114.

9. Carlo Ginzburg, *The Cheese and the Worms: The Cosmos of a Sixteenth-Century Miller*, trans. John and Anne Tedeschi (New York: Penguin, 1982).

10. Robert C. Solomon, ed., *Thinking about Feeling: Contemporary Philosophers on Emotions* (Oxford: Oxford University Press, 2004); Robert C. Solomon, *The Passions: The Myth and Nature of Human Emotions* (Garden City, NY: Anchor/Doubleday, 1976); and Amélie Oksenberg Rorty, *Explaining Emotions* (Berkeley: University of California Press, 1980).

11. Clifford Geertz, *The Interpretation of Cultures* (New York: Basic Books, 1973); Catherine A. Lutz, *Unnatural Emotions: Everyday Sentiments on a Micronesian Atoll and Their Challenge to Western Theory* (Chicago: University of Chicago Press, 1988); Michelle Z. Rosaldo, *Knowledge and Passion: Ilongot Notions of Self and Social Life* (New York: Cambridge University Press, 1980).

12. James R. Averill, "A Constructivist View of Emotion," in *Emotion: Theory, Research and Experience*, vol. 1, *Theories of Emotion*, ed. Robert Plutchik and Henry Kellerman (New York: Academic Press, 1980), 305–39; Arlie R. Hochschild, *The Managed Heart: Commercialization of Human Feeling* (Berkeley: University of California Press, 1983).

13. Carolyn L. Funk et al., "Genetic and Environmental Transmission of Political Orientations," *Political Psychology* 34 (2013): 805–19.

14. Robert C. Fuller, *The Body of Faith: A Biological History of Religion in America* (Chicago: University of Chicago Press, 2013).

15. Pascal Boyer, *The Naturalness of Religious Ideas: A Cognitive Theory of Religion* (Berkeley: University of California Press, 1994).

16. On the idea of a hyperactive activity detection device, see Justin L. Barrett, *Why Would Anyone Believe in God?* (Walnut Creek, CA: AltaMira Press, 2004). For broader discussions addressing religion, neuroscience, and emotion, see David Cave and Rebecca Sachs Morris, eds., *Religion and the Body: Modern Science and the Construction of Religious Meaning* (Leiden: Brill, 2012).

17. Silvan S. Tomkins, *Affect Imagery Consciousness*, vol. 1, *The Positive Affects* (London: Tavistock, 1962); and Paul Ekman, *Emotion in the Human Face* (Cambridge: Cambridge University Press, 1982).

18. Brian Massumi, "The Autonomy of Affect," in "The Politics of Systems and Environments, Part II," special issue, *Cultural Critique* 31 (autumn 1995): 83–109. See also Ben Anderson, *Encountering Affect: Capacities, Apparatuses, Conditions* (Burlington, VT: Ashgate, 2014), and Teresa Brennan, *The Transmission of Affect* (Ithaca, NY: Cornell University Press, 2004).

19. William E. Connolly, *Neuropolitics: Thinking, Culture, Speed* (Minneapolis: University of Minnesota Press, 2002); Elizabeth A. Wilson, *Affect and Artificial Intelligence* (Seattle: University of Washington Press, 2010); Elizabeth A. Wilson, *Gut Feminism* (Durham, NC: Duke University Press, 2015); and Felicity Callard and Des Fitzgerald, *Rethinking Interdisciplinarity across the Social Sciences and Neurosciences* (London: Palgrave Macmillan, 2015).

20. Sara Ahmed, *The Cultural Politics of Emotion* (New York: Routledge, 2004); Ann Cvetkovich, *Depression: A Public Feeling* (Durham, NC: Duke University Press, 2012); Sneja Gunew, "Subaltern Empathy: Beyond European Categories in Affect Theory," *Concentric: Literary and Cultural Studies* 35, no. 1 (2009): 11–30.

21. Sigmund S. Freud, *Civilization and Its Discontents*, ed. and trans. James Strachey (New York: W. W. Norton, 1989); and Norbert Elias, *The Civilizing Process*, trans. Edmund Jephcott (New York: Untzen, 1978), originally published as *Über den Prozeß der Zivilisation* (1939).

22. See, for example, Phyllis Mack, *Heart Religion in the British Enlightenment: Gender and Emotion in Early Methodism* (New York: Cambridge University Press, 2008); Susan Broomhall, ed., *Gender and Emotions in Medieval and Early Modern Europe: Destroying Order, Structuring Disorder* (London: Routledge, 2016); John Corrigan, *Business of the Heart: Religion and Emotion in the Nineteenth Century* (Berkeley: University of California Press, 2002); Linda Woodhead and Ole Riis, *A Sociology of Religious Emotion* (New York: Oxford University Press, 2010); and Peter E. Hopkins, "Women, Men, Positionalities, and Emotion: Doing Feminist Geographies of Religion," *ACME: An International E-Journal for Critical Geographies* 8, no. 1 (2009): 1–17.

23. Janet R. Jakobsen and Ann Pellegrini, eds. *Secularisms* (Durham, NC: Duke University Press, 2008).

DIANA FRITZ CATES

# 1. APPROACHING THE MORALITY OF EMOTION
*Specifying the Object of Inquiry*

A good and satisfying human life is marked by virtue. According to the Aristotelian tradition, exercising virtue is not simply a matter of thinking and acting well; it is also a matter of *feeling* well.[1] A virtuous person is disposed, by her own design and prior choices, to be appropriately moved in situations where she notices that her well-being—or the well-being of others for whom she cares—is at stake. A virtuous person has sought and, over time, acquired a second nature, such that she reliably feels the right emotions, toward the right persons, in the right circumstances, with the right intensity, for the right duration, and so on, in a way that coheres with the exercise of additional virtues.

How does one determine which emotions, if any, it is right to feel in a given situation and in what manner it is right to feel them? Are there any universal standards that govern the morality of emotion? Are there, minimally, some limits that can be specified, the transgression of which violate a person's dignity or constitute some other form of moral diminishment? To what extent must emotional appropriateness be assessed from the standpoint of the person in question, in light of the relevant details of her situation? What sorts of details *are* relevant to this kind of assessment?[2]

For Aristotle, right *action* is determined through a process of rational decision making that focuses on what is to be done. Such decision making is to be person-relative and context-sensitive, yet carried out in light of a broadly shared ideal of human flourishing and with reference to what a person of practical wisdom would choose.[3] Perhaps right *emotion* could be determined through a similar process that focuses on what is to be felt.[4] The process of deciding how best to feel would also be relative to particulars, yet undertaken in light of a compelling vision of the good and with reference to what a person of emotional integrity would feel. What makes for a compelling vision of the good when it comes to emotion? How would we identify a person of emotional integrity? What *is* the best way to undergo and deliberately shape the emotions that occur over the course of a life?

Many scholars of ethics, including those who study religious ethics, would like to offer helpful answers to these questions. Surely they are right to argue that the way we feel or fail to feel emotions can have an impact on the moral quality of our lives and communities. Yet persons who wish to analyze the morality of emotion face challenges. This chapter concerns a challenge that must be acknowledged by all who inquire into the emotional dimension of human life, including investigators from the social and natural sciences. It has to do with specifying the object of one's inquiry, namely, *emotion* or a particular, named emotion. Apart from such specification, interlocutors cannot justifiably be confident that, even if they are using the same term, they are referring to the same thing. This chapter shows, by way of an example from the history of philosophy and religious thought, how difficult it can be to find common definitional ground in discussing the emotions. It proceeds by setting the stage with regard to the morality of emotion and then advancing to matters of definition.


*I*

If the best sort of life is characterized by virtue, then it is important to examine the relationship between virtue and emotion. Regarding anger, for example, it seems worthwhile to ask, "Do you do well to be angry?" Is there such a thing as *good anger* or *virtuous anger*?[5]

If one wishes to address such questions in light of historical reflection, then the work of Aristotle is a valuable place to start.[6] If one wishes, in light of the Aristotelian tradition, to consider the influence that religion can have on people's thinking about virtue and emotion, then the work of Thomas Aquinas commends itself. I begin with Aquinas because he offers clear, interconnected accounts of many of the capabilities that characterize moral beings, namely, beings who engage in discursive practices of mutual accountability. Aquinas offers in-depth, formal analyses of the processes of thought, reasoning, deliberation, and choice; the structure of emotion or passion;[7] the means by which good habits of passion can be acquired; the limits to the access that humans have to their passions; the influence that religious faith can have on humans' ways of being moved; and so forth. He also engages earlier thinkers, many of whom participated in philosophical and religious traditions other than his own. Moreover, the ideas of many of his interlocutors, like the ideas of Aquinas himself, continue to have currency today.[8]

In his *Summa theologiae*, Aquinas poses a direct question concerning the morality of the passions: He asks "whether passion increases or decreases the goodness or malice of an act."[9] Consider, for example, an act of beneficence that is in many respects virtuous. Can such an act be made less virtuous by the presence of, say, resentment on the part of the benefactor toward the beneficiary?[10] Aquinas cites Augustine who argues that, yes, passions can decrease the moral value of an act. However, passions do not *necessarily* cause moral diminishment; only unreasonable passions do that.[11] A passion is unreasonable if it reflects indefensible judgments about what is the case and how much it matters—especially if it resists reconsideration and self-correction.[12] Aquinas agrees. Yet he wants to argue further that some passions can actually increase the moral value of an act.[13] Sometimes it is better to act with a relevant passion than to act without it. For example, an act of beneficence that is in other respects virtuous can sometimes be made better by the addition of a corresponding enjoyment of the impression that the other has been benefited.

In arguing for the moral value of acting with relevant passion, Aquinas anticipates an objection on the part of a Stoic.

> As the Stoics held that every passion [*passio*] of the soul is evil, they consequently held that every passion of the soul lessens the goodness of an act; since the admixture of evil either destroys goodness altogether or makes it to be less good. And this is true indeed, if by passions we understand none but the inordinate movements of the sensory appetite, considered as disturbances or ailments. But if we give the name of passions to all the movements of the sensory appetite, then it belongs to the perfection of a human being's good that his passions be moderated by reason. For because a human being's good is founded on reason as its root, that good will be all the more perfect, according as it extends to more things pertaining to the human being. Wherefore no one questions the fact that it belongs to the perfection of moral good that [voluntary movements] of the outward members be governed by the law of reason. Hence, because the sensory appetite can obey reason ... it belongs to the

perfection of the moral or human good that the passions themselves also should be governed by reason.[14]

*Are* passions the sorts of things that can be governed by reason? Are they the sorts of things that can themselves be reasonable?

For Aquinas, yes, some passions are reasonable from the start. They are responses that cohere with defensible judgments about what is happening and how important it is. And some passions that are *not* reasonable from the start are amenable to rational persuasion. Suppose a person feels a passion that she takes to be, in principle, reasonable—for example, fear in the face of danger. Yet she judges that the fear she currently feels is unreasonable. It is too intense for the actual danger posed, and this intensity is making it difficult for her to fulfill her other responsibilities. So she coaches herself into moderating her fear. She is still afraid, but her fear is no longer debilitating. It may even help to motivate appropriate action, such as skillful avoidance. In such a case, a person does more than dispel an unreasonable passion; she transforms a passion into something that is itself reasonable.

How, more specifically, is it possible to make a relatively unreasonable passion more reasonable?[15] As noted above, Aquinas conceives of a passion as a movement of the sensory appetite. Sensory appetite is the power to tend toward or away from objects that strike one as pleasant or painful, helpful or harmful, or the like.[16] Most humans have this power, as do many nonhuman animals. However, because humans also have intellectual powers, which operate in conjunction with our sensory powers, we can do more than be moved by what we sense to be important; we can also observe and assess the way we have been moved.[17] If we judge that the way we currently feel is inappropriate, then we can move ourselves, via the use of our imagination, to redescribe the situation at hand or make some other change, such that we are predictably moved in a different manner. Consequently, we can observe how we (now) feel, assess the success of our efforts, and if necessary further moderate our passion. In short, it is sometimes possible for us to direct ourselves, even as we feel a passion, to feel it in a way that aligns more closely with our best judgment about what a situation requires of us. It is by repeatedly making such choices that virtue is acquired.[18]

As Aquinas anticipates, however, a Stoic would deny that a passion could ever align with a person's best judgment—either by its own impetus or by design. Aquinas has Cicero in mind here,[19] but I want to turn to Seneca, whom Aquinas cites elsewhere, to consider a comparable view. According to Seneca, a passion is itself a form of judgment. Although different passions involve different judgments, which concern different particulars, all passions have something in common: they include an *assent* to the proposition that some object, which has come to our awareness, has the power to affect our well-being and thus our happiness, for good or for ill.[20]

A proposition of this sort often originates as an inarticulate impression. While a person might be quick to put such an impression into words, Seneca thinks that the initial impression is something over which we do not have rational control. It is more like a shiver than a thought.[21] On our way toward feeling a passion, we first experience an incitement in the form of a stirring impression that some object beyond our control bears on the quality of our lives. Then, if we judge this impression to be true, not simply in general, but *true for us*, such that it changes the way we think, going forward, we experience a passion. "A passion does not consist in being moved by impressions that are presented to the mind, but [rather] in [voluntarily] surrendering to them and following up such . . . chance prompting[s]" with a "rushing-forth" of the mind.[22]

Seneca recognizes that it is natural for humans to experience incitements to passion. Even wise people are periodically disturbed or delighted by some of what happens in the world around them.[23] For example, in the wake of a loved one's death, many people form the painful impression that their lives have been damaged. Death is a thief who has robbed them of their happiness. But Seneca insists that all such impressions are mistaken. Virtue alone (that is, our own active exercise of virtue) is the cause of true happiness, and we alone determine the extent of our virtue. "A wise person will lose nothing which he will be able to regard as a loss; for the only possession he has is virtue, and of this he can never be robbed."[24]

No matter what happens to us, and how it initially affects us, we have a choice. We can seek the truth about life or fall prey to false impressions. If we do the latter, we put ourselves in moral jeopardy. Unless we realize what we have done and immediately correct our mistake, the mistake will likely snowball. Before we know it, we will have lost our way. Seneca explains: "For the mind [*animus*] is not a member apart, nor does it view the passions [*affectus*] merely objectively, thus forbidding them to advance farther than they ought, but it is itself transformed into the passion and is, therefore, unable to recover its former useful and saving power when this has once been betrayed and weakened. For . . . [the mind and the passions] do not dwell separate and distinct, but . . . [they are] only the transformation of the mind toward the better or the worse."[25] In this perspective, the part of us that feels a passion (assents to a false impression about the causes of our happiness) and the part that evaluates how we currently feel, in light of what we believe to be true, are the same part; they are aspects of the same, potentially rational mind. Therefore, to assent to a false impression is just to compromise our general mental faculties. It is to weaken our grasp of the truth, diminish our ability to think critically about the impression to which we have assented, and undermine our efforts to determine how best to proceed. A reasonable person does not surrender to mental confusion while supposing that, in a confused state, she will retain the ability to carry out other aspects of her mental life in clear-headed ways.

## II

Aquinas and Seneca appear to disagree about the moral value of the passions partly because they disagree about what the passions are. Aquinas defines a passion as a motion of the soul that human and nonhuman animals can undergo by virtue of their sensory appetite, namely, their power to be moved by sensory images and impressions. Given the basis of *passio* in the Greek *pathôs*, and the way most thinkers before him used these terms, Aquinas thinks it is appropriate to define a passion as an interior motion that is caused by something other than a person's own mind or will. It is a way of being acted upon or moved by a sensible object (one that is capable of being sensed). It is a mode of being passive and receptive.[26]

Seneca also construes a passion as a motion of the soul, but in contrast to Aquinas he construes it as an *active* impulse, which occurs only in potentially rational beings by virtue of their intellectual powers. A passion may be evoked by a sensory impression and related bodily disturbance, but unless and until an intellect is engaged—until the person puts the impression into the form of a thought, takes the thought to be true, and begins to churn out more (confused) thoughts, we do not yet have a passion.[27]

How are we to comprehend the difference between these two thinkers' definitions? Perhaps Aquinas and Seneca are referring to the *same* object, but concentrating on different aspects of it. Aquinas may be right that he and a Stoic have the same range of phenomena in mind, but the Stoic is interested only in extreme, out-of-control cases. Or the Stoic is focusing only on a late stage of a process, the whole of which interests Aquinas. Perhaps the authors are using cognate terms to refer to *different* objects. In that case (to construct an imaginary conversation), maybe one author could specify the object that *he* has in mind when *he* uses the word passion, and ask the other to find a corollary within his own psychology. Then the other could, for the sake of argument, agree to call that corollary a passion while naming what he was originally calling a passion something else. That way each of them would be less likely to become confused about what the other is saying. Then again, perhaps our authors are not using cognates; they are simply talking about two different objects. But Aquinas refers to the Stoic view of the passions, and Seneca refers to aspects of Aristotle's view that Aquinas also holds. There should be a way to read our authors together.

For many reasons, putting Aquinas and Seneca into meaningful conversation is challenging. But so, I think, is putting contemporary accounts of emotion into conversation. For example, in *Upheavals of Thought*, Martha Nussbaum briefly compares her own, modified Stoic account of the emotions with that of neuroscientist Antonio Damasio who, in *Descartes' Error*, articulates a modified James-Lange view, which he links in subsequent work to Spinoza's idea of the *conatus* and connects, all along, to the findings of experimental neuropsychology.[28] In my view, it is difficult to get such a comparison off the ground, given the differences in Nussbaum's and Damasio's terminology, their philosophical orientations, and their primary disciplinary commitments.

Nussbaum holds that an emotion is a thought or, more specifically, an evaluative judgment, which may or may not be accompanied by a feeling—if a feeling is construed as an awareness of a related change in one's bodily state (for example, a sensation of feeling chilled when one judges that one is in danger).[29] Damasio holds that an emotion is itself a change in one's bodily state, of which one may or may not be aware. It is a neurobiochemical process by which an organism registers a disruption of its homeostasis and seeks to reestablish balance.[30] In some cases, an emotion is a process in the brain that tricks an organism into behaving *as if* it were in an altered bodily state, even though it is not.[31] A feeling—more specifically, the feeling of an emotion—is the awareness of a bodily change (or apparent change), accompanied by thoughts and images of particular objects in the situation at hand, which one has learned to associate with that sort of bodily change.[32] Whereas Nussbaum holds that emotions are first and foremost about situations that we judge to be of great importance for our flourishing, Damasio maintains that feelings are "first and foremost about the body." They are interpretations of what is happening in the "theater" of the body.[33]

As we seek to relate these views, it is apparent that we cannot simply equate Nussbaum's emotions with Damasio's emotions or with his feelings (of emotion), for neither emotions nor feelings are construed by Damasio as judgments of an object's value for us. Nor can we equate Nussbaum's feelings with Damasio's emotions or feelings (of emotion) because Nussbaum's feelings are felt sensations of bodily changes, whereas Damasio's emotions are the bodily changes themselves, which may or may not be felt. And Damasio's feelings are fundamentally responses to one's own bodily changes. It is possible, however, to make some useful connections. If Nussbaum's emotion is a thought regarding the significance for one's well-being of a situation in one's life, then Damasio's feeling (of an emotion) can also be construed as a thought—but it is a thought regarding the significance for one's well-being of a felt (or apparent) change in one's bodily state, which one relates, mentally, to the situation that seems to have caused the emotion.

At issue are the necessary and sufficient conditions for properly being said to experience an emotion or a feeling. At issue are also the relationships among the constituent parts of an experience that meets these conditions, including the causal mechanisms by which emotions or feelings are fully constituted. At issue, in addition, is the level of explanation on which one wishes to specify these mechanisms and for what purposes. Rather than address these matters further with respect to Nussbaum and Damasio, I want to return to Aquinas and Seneca. My hope is that by trying to facilitate *their* discussion we can gain insight into how to facilitate current discussions—both academic and inter-personal. Many of Aquinas's and Seneca's ideas still resonate in contemporary scholarship and popular culture. We can therefore clarify some of our own thinking by analyzing their thought.

### III

We can better understand the relationship between Aquinas's and Seneca's definitions of a passion if we unpack the definitions further in the context of the authors' respective philosophical and moral psychologies. As noted, Aquinas characterizes a passion as a motion of the soul that requires the exercise of one's sensory appetite. Sensory appetite is an arcane term, but it is important to our inquiry, so we need to know what it signifies.

The term includes a reference to both the sensory and the appetitive. For our purposes, each of these terms can be understood with reference to its own alternative. First, the sensory implies a distinction between the sensory and the intellectual. For Aquinas, this distinction in turn corresponds loosely to another—between the material and the immaterial. Aquinas argues that sensory operations of the soul, such as passions, are better characterized as operations of the soul-body composite than as operations of the soul per se because they have a material element; they take place (only) in and through changes in the body.[34] By contrast, intellectual operations, such as thinking and willing with regard to the idea of goodness or the concept of God, are better characterized as operations of the intellectual soul alone. In a living human being, intellectual activities are dependent on the tight cooperation of the sensory powers, but they do not have a material element of their own.[35] Taking this tack allows Aquinas to say that an immaterial soul can continue after death to know and love God, even though it must do so in a way that differs greatly from the way a person knows and loves God when her soul is the form of a body.[36]

By saying that a passion has a material element, Aquinas rules out the possibility that the postmortem soul or God (apart from the body of Christ) could experience a passion. Yet Aquinas reads in the Bible about the boundless love of God for humans and the love of humans for God, both in this life and in the next, so he posits an analogue to a passion in the dimension of immateriality, which he often calls an affection (*affectus* or *affectio*).[37] He clarifies that such an affection is best construed as a simple motion of the will.[38] As such, it does not include a corresponding change in bodily state; it does not have a feeling component. However, where there *is* a body, as in the case of a living human being, an (intellectual) affection can be and usually is coupled with a (sensory) passion. Where such coupling occurs, a person can experience an integrated love for God that is both wholehearted and full-bodied.[39]

Seneca, too, distinguishes between the sensory and the intellectual, but he does not link the intellectual with the immaterial. On his view, everything that is real is material; it is a body of some kind.[40] The human soul is a body—in its current form and also after death. Even God, conceived as Nature, Fate, or the unfolding Universe, is a body.[41] Seneca is not worried about how a material postmortem soul could bond with a material deity, for they have been connected all along, much as a limb is related to the body of which it is a part. "And why should you not believe that something of divinity exists in one who is a part of God? All this universe which encompasses us is one, and it is God; we are associates of God; we are God's members."[42]

Regarding the distinction between the sensory and the intellectual, Seneca associates the former not with the material, but with the nonrational and nonvoluntary.[43] He associates the sensory, for example, with the impressions that are preliminary to a passion—impressions that people cannot help but have, at least now and then.[44] He associates the sensory also with nonhuman animals, which are driven by nonrational, bodily impulse and have nothing like the self-directive powers of thought that are characteristic of humans.[45] By contrast, he associates the intellectual with the rational and voluntary.[46] The rational is more precisely the potentially rational, for a thought can be rational or irrational. Likewise, an act of the will can be voluntary or involuntary. Seneca holds that a passion is *caused*, in part, by a nonrational, nonvoluntary impression; but it is *constituted* by a series of intellectual moves, including the thought that a particular item is important for our happiness, a judgment that this thought corresponds to the way things really are, and an eager choice to proceed on the basis of this thought. Although a reader can discern a distinction between the nonrational/nonvoluntary and the rational/voluntary in Seneca's thought, it is important to note that he does not associate these capabilities with different parts of the soul that have, so to speak, minds of their own. More on this point below.

The concept of sensory appetite presupposes, further, a distinction between appetite and its alternative, apprehension. The power of apprehension makes it possible for us to register and process information. Building on the distinction between the sensory and the intellectual, Aquinas argues that humans have powers of both sensory and intellectual apprehension. The power of sensory apprehension makes it possible for us to notice and make basic assessments of sensible objects through the use of our exterior and interior senses.[47] The power of intellectual apprehension makes it possible for us to know and evaluate intelligible objects. It allows us to determine what an object is and judge its relationship to an idea, such as goodness or perfection.[48]

With respect to both the sensory and the intellectual, apprehension is the power to assimilate and assess data. Appetite is something else.[49] It is the power to be moved by that data. It includes, as well, the power to move ourselves relative to that data. Appetite is the power to tend toward or away from objects that we take to be suitable for us or unsuitable, good for us or bad. Our power to be moved and to move ourselves mentally in relation to various objects can play a role in motivating action, but sometimes we are simply moved. Our bearing is changed. In any case, whether we are talking about interior motion alone or interior motion that finds expression in action, we need the concept of appetite to account for it. As Aristotle says, "a mind is never found producing movement without appetite [orexis]."[50]

Building again on the distinction between the sensory and the intellectual, Aquinas argues that humans have powers of sensory appetite and intellectual appetite. The sensory appetite is the power to be moved in body-resonant ways by objects of perception or imagination. This appetite makes it possible for us not only to entertain an image and to judge, on a sensory level, that the object to which it corresponds is, let us say, suitable (both of which are acts of sensory apprehension); the sensory appetite makes it possible for us to be moved. For example, it enables us to be pleased by the object. It enables us also to desire a closer relationship to something that strikes us as lovable.

The intellectual appetite or the will, on the other hand, is the power to be moved by our own intellect. In other words, it is the power to move ourselves mentally. The will is more specifically the power to move ourselves in relation to an idea. The will makes it possible for us not simply to know what an object is and to judge, say, that it is good (both of which are acts of intellectual apprehension); it allows us to affirm the object's value. It allows us also to wish the object well and choose to act in ways that express our wish.

In sum, Aquinas has many options in defining a passion. He chooses to identify it as an object-oriented motion of the sensory appetite. In a human being, it is a way of being moved by an object that we take to be agreeable or disagreeable, attractive or repulsive. A passion has its principal *cause* in an object that appears (to us) to have possible implications for our well-being. It has its *basis* in the experience of being inclined toward or away from that object. Thought can definitely affect the formation of a passion; it can give a passion greater definition through the addition of descriptive detail. But this detail is added to a sensory pattern, which determines to some extent the details that count as relevant.

Seneca does not distinguish formally between apprehension and appetite— that is, he does not regard these as interior acts that are different in kind and associated with different powers of the soul.[51] Accordingly, he does not distinguish between sensory apprehension, intellectual apprehension, sensory appetite, and intellectual appetite. He prefers to characterize the mind or soul as a single power, albeit one with wide-ranging capabilities. On his view, it is best to say that *the mind* puts nonrational and nonvoluntary impressions into the form of explicit thoughts; *it* considers whether these thoughts reflect the way things really are; *it* freely assents to them; *it* becomes increasingly confused; *it* loses the ability to recognize and correct its own confusion; *it* becomes enslaved— until *it* spends itself on some related action and (tragically) is ready to begin the process all over again.[52] In other words, *we* do all these things by virtue of a range of mental capabilities that belong to *us*. These capabilities should not be assigned to different powers of the soul that can act on their own initiative. As Brad Inwood argues, Seneca, like most of the Stoics before him, is best construed as a psychological monist.[53]

Is the disagreement with Aquinas's psychology here anything more than apparent? Aquinas would agree that a living entity has one—and only one—soul. But he does sometimes give the impression that the soul has parts, and some of the parts can, so to speak, make things difficult for the other parts. Following Aristotle, he says that "a power is called political [as opposed to despotic] by which a person rules over free subjects, who, though subject to the government of the ruler, have nevertheless something of their own, by reason of which they can resist the orders of him who commands. . . . The intellect or reason is said to rule the [sensory appetite] by a political power: because the sensory appetite has something of its own, by virtue of which it can resist the commands of reason."[54] What is the significance of the notion that the sensory appetite has "something of its own"?

It is helpful to consider this question in light of a version of psychological dualism with which both Seneca and Aquinas were familiar.[55] Aristotle, for example, writes that there is a rational part of the soul and a nonrational part. That is, there is a part of us that is capable of reasoning; and there is another part that is *not* capable of reasoning, either well or poorly, but is capable of doing other, nonrational things.[56] The rational part of the self includes the power to conceive ideas, reason through problems in light of ideas, and guide other operations of the soul as a parent guides a child.[57]

The nonrational part has two subparts. The operations of the first subpart cannot be altered directly by the power of reason. Aristotle associates this subpart, sometimes called the vegetative, with the power of biological life and growth. We know, for example, that humans cannot simply instruct our bodies to grow taller or shorter (although we can direct ourselves to do things that can have an impact on our height). The operations of the second subpart of the nonrational part are not exactly under the direct command of reason, either. Aristotle associates this part with the power of being moved by sensory impressions—a potential that we actualize when we feel a passion.[58] It is apparent that we cannot, by means of a simple self-command, cause ourselves to feel or stop feeling a passion (as we can direct ourselves, for example, to call a familiar object to mind). However, this part can be responsive to reason in a less direct way. By virtue of our intellectual powers, we can choose to engage our sensory powers in ways that we have good reason to think will cause a shift in an occurrent passion. Thus, for example, we can sometimes stop feeling anger by directing ourselves to take a deep breath and by choosing to picture an offender in a new light. At the same time, we can resist this very effort, as when (what may strike us as) another part of us becomes attached to the anger and will not listen to reason.

Aquinas is attracted to this conception of the soul. His own conception is more elaborate, but it preserves Aristotle's thesis that there is a part of us, most notably a nonrational appetitive part, that can resist our best efforts to quiet or otherwise alter it. For Aquinas, it is helpful to be able to say that we sometimes crave objects and feel compelled by these cravings to engage in activities that we know, in a calmer moment, by virtue of our rational part, are morally wrong. Sometimes the nonrational appetitive part becomes so strong that it not only drives us to commit a wrong action that we later regret; it also warps the way we think about what we are doing, so that we are able to convince ourselves, with the co-optation of our rational part, that what we are doing is not *really* wrong.[59] Or what we have done is not *really* regrettable.

At the same time, however, we are not simply at the mercy of our nonrational part. In other words, we are more than that part. For Aquinas, it is often possible for the rational part to *contain* the nonrational part (at least, to keep it from finding expression in action), as when we exercise what has traditionally been called continence.[60] It is also possible for the rational part, when conditioned by virtue, to train the nonrational part, such that the latter part, too, becomes habituated to virtue. This takes place, again, not by direct command, but by forms of persuasion that engage our sensory powers—most notably our imagination.[61] In any case, our nonrational part *can* become increasingly disposed to respond to sensory stimuli in ways that are consistent with good judgment.[62] Yet it nonetheless retains "something of its own," which allows it periodically to rebel and tear loose from the hold of reason.

It is this sort of view of the self that Seneca is eager to reject. For him, it suggests that there is a part of us, other than our rational part, which has a kind of agency all its own. If this nonrational part subverts the rational part, then we are perhaps more to be pitied than blamed.[63] Aquinas does say, for example, that a vehement passion can indirectly cause us to sin, and when it does, it makes our action less voluntary, reducing somewhat our culpability for the sin.[64] For Seneca, nonrational impulses do not motivate wrong action; poor thinking does. And we are responsible for the course of our own thinking. If we begin to think distorted thoughts, there is nothing within us to hold accountable but our own mental weakness. The option is not to look for a nonrational part to blame, contain, or train, but to strengthen the mind through the pursuit of virtue.[65]

As we have seen, Seneca distinguishes between a nonrational, nonvoluntary aspect of the person, which is associated primarily with the body, and a rational, voluntary aspect; but he denies that the nonrational, nonvoluntary aspect is able, on its own, to "[generate] sufficient motivating conditions" for action.[66] Seneca does not need to admit to psychological dualism to account for experiences such as weakness of will. He can say that what may strike some of us as a nonrational impulse competing with our rational part is better described as one set of thoughts competing with another set of thoughts, where we have not yet sorted out what we are rationally entitled to think about a situation.[67]

Moreover, Seneca disagrees with Aristotle—and he would disagree with Aquinas—that virtue is ever in need of assistance from a nonrational impulse. "Virtue, being self-sufficient, never needs the help of vice."[68] What might seem to some of us like a boost of energy (supplied by a passion) that helps us to get good things done is actually a disruption of the dignified mental calm that ought to characterize our moral decision making. As Seneca explains, " 'Anger,' says Aristotle, 'is necessary, and no battle can be won without it—unless it fills the mind and fires the soul; it must serve, however, not as a leader, but as the common soldier.' But this is not true. For if it listens to reason and follows where reason leads, it is no longer anger, of which the chief characteristic is willfulness. If, however, it resists and is not submissive when ordered, but is carried away by its own caprice and fury, it will be an instrument of the mind as useless as is the soldier who disregards the signal for retreat."[69] At least with respect to anger, Seneca argues that when a person embraces this passion, she may believe that her anger reflects greatness of soul; but in truth it only reveals that she lacks self-discipline.

When Aquinas says that a passion is a motion of the sensory appetite he is thus saying a lot. He is saying that a passion is *not* an intellectual act; it is *not* a mode of thinking, intellectual judging, or willing. A passion presupposes judgments about the significance of events, but most of these judgments are made, at least initially, on a sensory level, which is why nonhuman animals are able to feel core features of many of the same passions that humans feel. One might recall, here, Damasio's point that even below the level of consciousness an organism makes nonrational assessments, as its species has evolved to do, in order to maintain homeostasis. At the same time, Aquinas acknowledges that rational animals tend, while feeling a passion, to think about its object in ways that cause the passion to emerge in a distinctively human form.[70]

Similarly, a passion is *not* a form of apprehension, whether intellectual or sensory; it is not simply a matter of judging something to be important to our well-being. It is instead the interior act of being moved by what we judge to be important. It is *not* a form of self-motion, issuing from the power of choice. It is *not* a voluntary assent to a proposed truth about life. It is something in relation to which we are more passive—although it is possible for us to make choices (both good and bad) in relation to the ways we have been moved. It is possible for us also, by choice, to practice ways of interpreting reality that predictably shape our habits of being moved.

If Aquinas were to search his own psychology for an analogue to what Seneca calls a passion, he might say that a Senecan passion looks partly like an intellectual apprehension (a judgment) and partly like a motion of the will.[71] Given that the latter presupposes a judgment of value, Aquinas might say that a Senecan passion looks most like a motion of the will. Perhaps Aquinas would say, more specifically, that what Seneca calls an *incitement* to a passion (call it a propassion), Aquinas calls a passion; and what Seneca calls a passion, Aquinas calls a *consent* to a passion, typically followed by intellectual desire, both of which are motions of the will. To the extent that these correspondences hold, it should be possible for Aquinas to adopt Seneca's terminology for the sake of further discussion.

However, I think Aquinas would resist this move. First, he would likely say that Seneca's account of the propassions does not do justice to the natural intelligence that many of our reactions to sensory stimuli exhibit. Many propassions (analogue: Thomistic passions) occur because sensory beings are oriented toward the preservation of their lives and the lives of their kin. Sensory beings generally tend toward what strikes them as life-enhancing and away from what strikes them as life-destroying. And often what strikes them as being the case really is the case. Because life is a basic good, on a Thomistic view, judgments regarding what we ought to do when we have the impression that our lives are at stake are *appropriately* informed (but not driven) by how those impressions make us feel.

Second, Aquinas would say that a Senecan passion (analogue: Thomistic motion of the will) is not sufficiently sensory to capture the range of experiences that Aquinas wants to discuss. Aquinas might argue that a Senecan passion cannot simply be *caused* by a disturbing impression, which is supplanted by a false judgment that has no sensory component. Seneca's own, dramatic examples suggest that a passion *includes* a disturbing impression all along. Seneca could reply that the nonrational, nonvoluntary impression that incites a passion remains part of the passion; however, that would appear to make passion something more than a thought. Seneca could say, in response, that thoughts have material properties, some of which we experience as sensations. But Aquinas would want to distinguish different kinds of thoughts and the ways that only some of our thoughts cause us, indirectly, to feel.

Third, Seneca holds that a propassion (analogue: Thomistic passion) is an impression that takes the form of a judgment, which is *by definition* false and therefore not a fitting object of mental assent. For Aquinas, an intellectual-appetitive motion of consent (analogue: Senecan assent) can be justifiable or unjustifiable, just as a sensory-appetitive motion can be worthy or unworthy of consent. Hence, there seem to be many interior motions, which correspond in form to Senecan propassions and passions, that Aquinas thinks it appropriate to feel and affirm, yet Aquinas would find it difficult to discuss in Seneca's terms.

In any case, Aquinas does not offer to proceed with his Stoic interlocutor on the stipulation that a Stoic passion is basically the same thing as a Thomistic motion of the will—or, more specifically, a volitional consent to a Thomistic passion. Nor does Aquinas concede that he could do just as well to talk about Thomistic passions, such as love and hatred, as mere preliminaries to passions. Instead, he holds to a distinction that the Stoics did not make—between intellectual and sensory appetite. He does so because he believes that this is the best way to delineate the kinds of interior motion that are of concern to him, which are notably passive, responsive, and characterized by bodily commotion, but are not for that reason inaccessible to rational reflection and self-direction.

## IV

Aquinas's and Seneca's definitions of the passions are linked to different perspectives on what matters most for human well-being. On Aquinas's view, some contingent items outside ourselves rightly matter to us, in the present life, because they are genuinely good for us. It is partly in being acted upon by suitable items that our potential is actualized—including our potential for being human and for being good. By implication, a lack or loss of objects that we need, in order to realize our potential, is rightly a matter for concern. On this account, the natural and appropriate response to an item that is potentially good for us is to *love* it.[72] Love (*amor*) can refer to a motion of the will or to a passion; here, we focus on the latter. Qua passion, love refers to a pleasing resonance that we can undergo when we apprehend an object as being suitable for us or for someone who is part of us. The passion of love can evolve into something *more* than this; it can serve as the basis for additional passions, such as a desire to gain more of what pleases us and a delight in gaining what we desired.[73] But love is more fundamental than desire or delight, and it does not always give rise to these additional passions.

Along the same lines, some contingent items rightly matter to us because they are, in fact, bad for us. When we interact with them in certain ways, our ability to operate well as rational animals is diminished. On Aquinas's view, the natural and proper response to an item that causes us or a loved one to be diminished is to *hate* it.[74] Here, too, hatred (*odium*) refers to a passion, although it can also, in other contexts, refer to an act of the will. Qua passion, hatred refers to a painful dissonance that we can undergo when we become aware of an object that we regard as unsuitable or harmful to us—capable of hurting us. Hatred can, but does not necessarily, give rise to additional passions, such as aversion, the desire to destroy, or the anger and sadness that accompany *not* being able to avert or destroy what we regard as bad.

It is worth noting in passing that it would be inaccurate on this account (and it is confusing in any case) to refer to love as a *positive* passion and hatred as a *negative* one, as many psychology books do. Love can be on-target or off—depending on the object of our love and the manner in which we love it. It is possible to love the wrong things, such that we are damaged by what we love, as when we love to watch someone bully someone whom we resent.[75] It is possible also to love the right things, but in the wrong way, as when we love helping others, but we sometimes do for them what they could more profitably do for themselves. Similarly, it is possible to hate the right things, such that we are alerted to relevant dangers and reconnected to that which is genuinely good for us, as when we hate that someone is bent on hurting us. But it is also possible to hate the right things in the wrong way, as when our hatred of someone's mean-spiritedness consumes us to the point that we are no longer inclined to find pleasure in what is suitable for us: we forget to love. And it is possible to hate the wrong things, as when we are pained by the prospect of helping someone because we know it will require a sacrifice on our part, and this disturbance keeps us from acting well.

But let us return to Aquinas's view that the passions of love and hatred (resonance and dissonance) are natural and potentially valuable for humans. Seneca would recognize several problems with this view. To begin with, he would say that, indeed, there are many contingent items outside ourselves that can have an impact on the course of our lives. But none of these is properly regarded as good or evil.[76] The only good is virtue, and the only evil is vice. Everything else is indifferent. Nothing beyond our own virtue and vice ought to generate love or hatred in us. It is fine to prefer certain states of affairs over others. It is fine, for example, to prefer being healthy to being sick. Being healthy is more pleasant and leaves us with more energy to fulfill our social responsibilities. But it is a mistake to love health in such a way that we become attached to it and therefore suffer when it departs from us. The truth is that we can be morally good and thus happy regardless of whether we are healthy; indeed, sometimes being sick is preferable—if, for example, it teaches us how best to care for other people who are sick.

In the same vein, Seneca would argue that Aquinas's view makes us out to be more incomplete and vulnerable to fortune than we are—or ought to think that we are. Whatever happens or fails to happen to us or to various people in our lives, we have the ability as rational beings to determine our attitude toward it. Indeed, our attitude, the operation of our mental powers, is the only thing over which we can have control. Our lack of other-than-mental control over things such as health does not make us vulnerable to evil; it simply brings into focus the importance of mastering our own minds. The only rational way to regard matters that are beyond our control, is to *accept* that they are beyond our control and to understand that we would be foolish to link our happiness to them.[77] Interestingly, Nussbaum parts company with the Stoics when it comes to love (for her, love is the judgment that some person, in his or her particularity, is of immense value to me). While her account of the structure of emotion is Stoic, her view of the value of emotion is closer to Aristotle's and thus, by chance, to Aquinas's. She thinks it is *true* that humans do best when we love others, even though our love makes us vulnerable to serious loss.[78]

Regarding future events, these too are beyond our control. On Seneca's view, if we judge that a particular consequence is worth bringing about—because it is an intrinsic good (virtue) or an *indifferent* one that it is reasonable for us to prefer—we might do well to try to bring it about. However, it is irrational to do so without mental reservation—without knowing that our efforts might not yield the consequences we prefer.[79] A wise Stoic says to himself, " 'I will set sail unless something hinders me,' and 'My enterprise will be successful unless something interferes.' "[80] If what we prefer to happen happens, fine. If it does not, so be it. It is irrational to hope that the future will follow anything other than the course that it has been determined, by Fate, to follow.

As a Stoic, Seneca holds that Fate rules the universe, and humans are part of the universe.[81] But I take it that, for him, our choices are nonetheless, to some extent, up to us.[82] That is to say, what we choose to care about and how we choose to act are not fully determined by external causes; they are determined also by the state of our mind, which is internal to us. Granted, the state of our mind is itself the result of antecedent causes, but many of these causes, too, have been internal to us. We have become who we are on account of the way we have chosen to respond to the events of our lives. Nothing outside of us has compelled our internal assent—or compels it now. This is all we need to know to be able, on a Stoic view, to hold ourselves and each other accountable for our actions.[83]

Another problem that Seneca would likely have with Aquinas's view concerns the fact that if we experience love—for Seneca, if we regularly have the impression, make the judgment, and affirm that some object is good for us and we would be incomplete without it—then we will also be subject to hatred. We will regularly have the impression, make the judgment, and affirm that some object is bad for us; it is capable of damaging us directly or by means of something we love. We will thereby tether our happiness to yet another object outside of ourselves. Seneca acknowledges that we cannot avoid *incitements* to hatred. But judging any of them to be worthy of our assent is dangerous, in addition to being foolish. Assenting, for example, to the proposition that *this person has destroyed my chances for happiness* is likely to yield a related proposition that *this person deserves to suffer for what she has done*, and assenting to *this* proposition is likely to yield a desire to injure the offender, which is likely to motivate destructive action. As Seneca warns,

> When once the mind has been aroused and shaken, it becomes the slave of the disturbing agent. There are certain things which at the start are under our control, but later hurry us away by their violence and leave us no retreat. As a victim hurled from the precipice has no control of his body, and, once cast off, can neither stop nor stay, but, speeding on irrevocably, is cut off from all reconsideration and repentance and cannot now avoid arriving at the goal toward which he might once have avoided starting, so with the mind—if it plunges into anger, love, or the other passions, it has no power to check its impetus; its very weight and the downward tendency of vice . . . must hurry it on, and drive it to the bottom.[84]

Anger and hatred are helpfully distinguished, but on a Stoic view, they are also closely related. As passions, both of them have a basis in love, and even love has its basis in ignorance—often willful ignorance—as when we refuse to acknowledge that we are on our own in securing our happiness.

Partly because Aquinas and Seneca disagree about what is worth caring or becoming upset about, they appear to disagree about what a good and happy life *feels* like, in the living of it. For Aquinas, the felt quality of a Christian's life will be shaped by her view of the ultimate end of life. Her eschatological perspective may make some temporal goods seem less important than they would otherwise seem and some evils easier to bear. But we can nevertheless say that, by Aquinas's lights, the best sort of life is a *moving* one. Above all, it is characterized by affection for God, which is usually coupled with a variety of passions, including delight in the perceived goodness of God's handiwork.

I think Aquinas would say that a good and happy life typically feels like sailing a boat under a clear sky, on a variable, but not too tumultuous sea. Such a life will be *up* or pleasant when a person is united with an object that is suitable for her; less pleasant when she realizes that she is at risk of losing that object; *down* when she learns that the object has indeed been lost; agitated when she encounters the factor that took the object from her; *up* when there is a possibility of recovering what she lost; *up* further when she actually recovers it; and so on. Living well will not generally feel like struggling successfully to keep a boat from capsizing, but neither will it feel like holding the boat still, "being never uplifted nor ever cast down."[85] A good life is one in which events happen and passions occur, including disturbing ones; yet they occur in a manner that coheres with our best judgment of what is important in life—or they are brought skillfully into such coherence. Living a happy life will feel like sailing with confidence toward a chosen destination, under sometimes-challenging but mostly manageable conditions, tacking and jibbing as needed to stay the course.

Seneca would argue, to the contrary, that the best sort of life is devoid of relative *highs* and *lows*. Specifically, it is absent the excitements and disappointments that we appear to suffer on account of contingent factors—including what happens to the people we love. Yet a good Stoic life is not dull. It is not without joy, without love and friendship, or lacking in boldness and drive, if these states of mind are properly understood. Senecan *joy* is the (intellectual) experience of the freedom and dignity that accompany being in command of one's own mind.[86] (It is not, as with Aquinas, the experience of uniting with a suitable object that allows us to actualize some of our potential.) Senecan *love* is "kindness and concord," which are the natural expression of a tranquil mind.[87] (It is not the Thomistic experience of resonating with and consenting to an object that we regard as suitable for us—an experience that often, and often appropriately, gives rise to the desire for more.) Senecan *friendship* is active engagement with people who are similarly virtuous, self-sufficient, and free.[88] (It is not a relationship that includes a bond that makes a virtuous person vulnerable to loss and sorrow.) Finally, a good Stoic life is "courageous and energetic [in the face of challenges], and, too, capable of the noblest fortitude, ready for every emergency . . . but without anxiety."[89] (For Aquinas, even the best temporal life will be marked by anxiety because it includes attachments to finite goods, even if these goods are subordinated to God as the highest good. Other animals, too, experience anxiety, and it is good that they do. Their anxiety often assists in their self-preservation; it motivates them to do what they must to stay alive.)

Seneca says that to live well is to experience "something great and supreme and very near to being a god—to be unshaken."[90] I would suggest that, for him, living a happy life *feels* more like rowing a boat with confidence under a clear sky, on a calm, glassy lake. Unexpected disturbances may occur, and the boat may rock, but the disturbances generally pass quickly.[91] If they do not, the wise person takes the waves as an opportunity to test her ability to remain serene under all conditions.[92] Or she navigates the boat to more peaceful waters. There is something exceedingly pleasant, and not the least bit dull, about finding a glassy lake within one's mind and being able to project that calm to others as one works dutifully to benefit the human lot.

*V*

In summary, Aquinas and Seneca define passion differently. They name and organize in different ways the many operations of the soul. They have different ideas about what really matters in life—about what ought and ought not to bother a person. They hold different views about what it feels like to live well. None of these differences is total. There are similarities within the differences. But there *are* differences, and they appear to go all the way down.[93] They appear to have roots in each author's view of the fundamental nature of reality and the point of life. If we elucidate a few aspects of their respective theologies, we might be able to put the differences in their accounts of passion into even better perspective.

According to Aquinas's natural theology, every existing entity is held together, as an individual, and it stands in relation to every other entity, by virtue of a bond that can meaningfully be called love (*amor*).[94] Notice, here, that love can signify a metaphysical bond, in addition to a passional and a volitional bond. Aquinas is sometimes said to characterize the *glue* of the universe as the desire of all things for God,[95] but it is more precisely the appetite (*appetitus*) of all things for God, where appetite includes love, as well as desire and other modes of tending.[96] Love refers to the way that every object stands in relation to other objects that are suitable for it—capable of interacting with it in ways that are beneficial for it.

Humans naturally tend toward what we regard as beneficial and away from what we regard as harmful. To say this is not to say, however, that we cannot make mistakes in sensing or judging what is good for us and what is bad, such that we feel at ease—or ill at ease—when we should not. Even when our beliefs and impressions are correct, we can be weak or pulled in contrary directions by forces within us that our intellectual powers do not completely command. When we are pulled off course, and we choose poorly, particularly in contravention of what we *know* or ought to know is right, we drive a wedge between ourselves and the deepest source of our being and goodness. We fail to operate in a way that is marked by a pleasing awareness of, and a gratitude for, that source. With each wrongful act that we commit, we become further alienated from our best possibilities. We become increasingly disposed to respond to situations in ways that are harmful to others.[97] For these reasons, moral evil and sin are sometimes worth getting upset about.

Sin matters not only to humans, but also to God. According to Aquinas's dogmatic theology, sin and the suffering that it generates matter so much to

God that God chooses to take on the form of a human being in order to address them. In the person of Christ, God suffers because of us, with us, and on our behalf the painful consequences of individual and collective sin. It is partly because Aquinas conceives of human passion in light of the divine Passion that he *must* approve of passions and related motions of the will that conform to the will of God.[98] He must approve of a love for what is genuinely good and, presumably, a hatred for what is bad.

For Seneca, as well, there is a sense in which all things are ordered, fundamentally, toward the good; both worldviews are teleological. But with Seneca, the good is conceived, not as the way things ought to be (as distinct from the way they currently are), or the way things *would* be if it were not for sin. Rather, the good is conceived as the way things really are (as distinct from the way they merely appear to be, to an ignorant or irrational person). For a Stoic, Divine Reason guides all of creation ineluctably toward an ideal of perfection, and specifically human or moral goodness consists in our obedience to this Reason.[99] Such a worldview does not imply fatalism. Our obedience might find expression, for example, in freely chosen actions that are intended to promote virtue and concord for all. However, as noted previously, a good Stoic commits all such actions with reservation.[100] Moreover, she adjusts her intentions, moment by moment, in light of what actually happens, aligning her will with the will of the universe.[101]

Seneca says that a good Stoic dwells, as much as possible, in the *higher regions* of the eternal and stable Mind,[102] partly through the study of philosophy, even if she chooses for ethical reasons to be involved in political affairs. In this preferred mode of existence, a person is confident that if she conceives a mistaken judgment of value, she can correct it; and if she corrects it, it will have no control over her. Inasmuch as she succeeds in the exercise of rational self-command, she is pleased to encounter the beauty and dignity of the eternal law, as well as the beauty, dignity, and freedom of her own mind. This sort of joy is secure; it cannot be lost as other sorts of joy can be lost, for it is not predicated on the fulfillment of a desire for something that we do not already possess. It is simply what we experience when we behave in an upright manner. We can lose our virtue, by our own decisions, but the more virtuous we are, the less likely this becomes. We can lose our minds, say, through illness or injury, but there is no sense in worrying about that. If it happens, it happens. The future will unfold as it will.

Aquinas, too, recognizes higher-order experiences that characterize a person of virtue. He refers to a set of these experiences as affections, an example of which would be a Christian hope in eternal beatitude. Seneca uses the term affection to refer only to false impressions and misleading impulses. As noted above, Seneca and Aquinas do agree that the best sort of life is characterized by joy. It is just that, for Seneca, joy is the awareness of being independently and self-sufficiently in good working order,[103] whereas, for Aquinas, it is the pleasing awareness of having attained, in relation to others, what you rightly love and desire.[104] And, for Aquinas, it is sometimes more suitable to experience hatred and sadness than to experience joy—for example, in the face of undeniable evil.

More could be said about the views of Aquinas and Seneca regarding what it means to respond well, as a human being, to what occurs in life—whether it is best to suffer, for a time, over what one rightly regards as evil or to remain detached and unmoved by contingencies that are not properly characterized as evil. But enough has been said to show that, on a Thomistic view, something of the dynamism of compatibility and incompatibility—resonance and dissonance—reflects the nature of reality. It is part of the way the cosmos hangs together and unfolds over time. Accordingly, feeling comfortable or uncomfortable with, or having mixed feelings about, various objects in one's environment can be part of a human being's natural response to what is real.

For Seneca, passion is something that can, in fact, happen, but when it happens it is a manifestation, not of knowledge (regarding how the world works), but of ignorance and irrationality. There is nothing natural about passion, if by *natural* we mean in accord with and reflective of the Reason that rules the cosmos. The only thing that is natural about the experience of passion is the mental determination to *vanquish* a passion in the defense of human dignity.


## VI

In conclusion, our analysis indicates that if we want to talk about the passions in Aquinas and Seneca, it is not possible to limit ourselves to one concept—whether it be *passio* or *affectus* or something else. Each concept with which we might begin is, for each author, part of a larger constellation of concepts, and each element of the constellation can be understood adequately only in relation to the others. Moreover, each constellation is part of a view concerning the nature of reality and the way humans relate, ideally, to the rest of reality.

Similarly, if we want to construct an argument today regarding the morality of emotion, it will not do simply to stipulate a definition of what an emotion is, anticipating that generous readers will grant our definition and then proceed straightway to engage our argument concerning emotion's moral status. A definition that is robust enough to serve our purposes will likely have built into it assumptions that strike active readers as question-begging. That is, such a definition will likely include assumptions that effectively decide the moral value of emotion before the argument has been made. The same is true for definitions of particular emotions.

Finally, regarding the question of how we study religion and emotion, I hope to have shown that religious thought and ethics, along with philosophy and moral psychology, have much to contribute. It appears that many people share something interesting with Aquinas and Seneca. Our thoughts about what emotions are and how emotions can affect the quality of people's lives are implicitly if not explicitly connected to our views about what is ultimately real. Our thoughts about the emotions are connected also to our perceptions of ourselves and our proper place in society. Analyses of comprehensive worldviews and their social-ethical implications are the bailiwick of religious studies. Even if we are not treating what people may think of as religious emotions, the study of religious thought and ethics is indispensable for the study of emotion.

The study of ideas and how ideas can be expected to inform a person's perspective cannot tell us what actual people, from various historical periods, regions, and cultures, felt or feel in particular circumstances. What people say, write, or do about how they feel is not necessarily a good reflection of how they feel. Nor can we expect people from different cultures, or from different social positions within the same culture, to feel or express their emotions in the same way. It would be odd, however, if we found no significant commonalities among members of the same highly evolved species. In any event, if we hope to find and analyze actual cases of emotion, in history or today, then we need to know what we are looking for, how we will recognize it when we find it, and how we will characterize it in conversation with others, for what reasons. We need to consider matters of definition.

The study of emotion is, of course, multidisciplinary. Emotion is not simply a concept or a mental construction. It is a term that many of us use to refer to a range of phenomena, a set of social practices, or a field of experiences about which we think it is important to be able to communicate. Emotions are evidently shaped by a multitude of factors, from biology and brain physiology, to processes of socialization and acculturation, to the predictable and random events of life, to our gendered and often politicized ways of interpreting those events—all of which can be subjected to different sorts of analysis. Virtually every discipline can be expected to make unique and valuable contributions, as long as those who employ the discipline can specify reasonably well the object of their inquiry.

As challenging as the conceptual and ethical analysis of emotion can be, particularly in the context of the study of religion, it is humbling to know all along that this approach is only one among a wide variety of approaches. The more a particular approach consumes a person's time, the less time there is to consider, let alone master, other approaches. It is difficult to know any discipline well enough to be able to take a justifiable view *within* it, and even if we are able to do this with respect to disciplines other than our own, primary discipline, it is difficult to piece these views together, such that they inform each other all along. Collaboration is essential. My hope is that it will be possible for collaborators to grasp and integrate the best of each other's approaches so as to create insights that can be generated in no other way. Fulfilling this hope will require flexibility of mind and, above all, patience.[105]

NOTES

1. Aristotle, *Nicomachean Ethics*, trans. Terence Irwin (Indianapolis: Hackett, 1985), 1104b3–8; 1107a1–1107b8. For further discussion, see L. A. Kosman, "Being Properly Affected: Virtues and Feelings in Aristotle's Ethics," in *Essays on Aristotle's Ethics*, ed. Amélie Oksenberg Rorty (Berkeley: University of California Press, 1980), 103–16.

2. For example, are race and gender relevant details? In *Black Womanist Ethics*, Katie Cannon argues that black women ought to hold themselves to somewhat different moral standards from the standards that are asserted by white people because the latter standards function to maintain the subjugation of black people (Atlanta: Scholars Press, 1988), 75–76. Consider the purported moral standards for anger. In a white-majority society that is characterized by racism and sexism, some white men believe that, as a group, they *deserve* to be in their dominant position, and it is *right* for them to be angry with people of color and various women who challenge this position. For them, anger can feel like an affirmation of their moral right to rule. Yet some people of color and women think that if it is right for anyone to be angry, surely it is right for *them* to be angry about white male domination. For them, anger can feel like an affirmation of their moral right to dismantle white male privilege. Are these groups of people bound by different moral standards? Or are they bound by the same standard (say, justice) whose demands they interpret and apply differently? What *is* the proper interpretation and application of the standard of justice in cases where differences in social power are notable?

3. Aristotle, *Nicomachean Ethics*, 1106b36–1107a5.

4. One could acknowledge that humans generally have less power to shape their emotions, after the emotions have been evoked, than they have to determine their actions. Yet one could argue that the power of emotional self-determination can nonetheless be significant in many people who exercise it. For further discussion of the possibility of choosing one's emotions, see Diana Fritz Cates, *Choosing to Feel: Virtue, Friendship, and Compassion for Friends* (Notre Dame, IN: University of Notre Dame Press, 1997).

5. William Werpehowski, "Do You Do Well to Be Angry," *Annual of the Society of Christian Ethics* 16 (1996): 59–77; J. Giles Milhaven, *Good Anger* (Kansas City, MO: Sheed and Ward, 1989); and William Mattison, "Virtuous Anger? From Questions of *Vindicatio* to the Habituation of Emotion," *Journal of the Society of Christian Ethics* 24, no. 1 (2004): 159–79.

6. For a discussion of why it is important to analyze contemporary ideas in light of the history of similar ideas, see Jean Porter, "Mere History: The Place of Historical Studies in Theological Ethics," *Journal of Religious Ethics* 25, no. 3 (1998): 103–26.

7. In Diana Fritz Cates, *Aquinas on the Emotions: A Religious-Ethical Inquiry* (Washington, DC: Georgetown University Press, 2009), I argue that, when considering the relevance of Aquinas's ideas for contemporary thought, it is often best to refer to a Thomistic *passio* as an emotion, rather than a passion. Emotion is the more familiar of the two terms, and it may signal better than passion that, when it comes to humans, most ways of being moved on a predominantly sensory level by objects of perception and imagination are informed, all along, by thinking. However, it seems best, here, to use the term *passion* to refer to a Thomistic passio and to the *affectus* of the Stoic because passion may do a better job than emotion in signifying experiences that *can* be intense and, when they *are* intense, can distort a person's thinking. I acknowledge that all such words—passion, emotion, feeling, affection, affect—have different connotations for different people, which is part of the problem I seek to address.

8. As this volume demonstrates, many historical cultures provide resources for the study of emotion. Collaboration is therefore essential for scholars who wish to analyze the best of what people around the world have had to say on the topic. The fact that I begin with Aristotle and proceed to Aquinas does not imply that, in my view, Greco-Roman or Mediterranean or European or Christian approaches ought to set the terms of debate for everyone; it is simply to make my own, limited contribution to the conversation.

9. Thomas Aquinas, *Summa theologiae* (hereafter cited as *ST*), 1a2ae.24 *pr.* 3: "utrum omnis passio addat, vel diminuat, ad bonitatem vel malitiam actus." All references are to the *Latin/English Edition of the Works of St. Thomas Aquinas*, trans. Laurence Shapcote, ed. John Mortensen and Enrique Alarcón (Lander, WY: The Aquinas Institute for the Study of Sacred Doctrine, 2012).

10. *ST* 2a2ae.31.1*ad*2, 31.2.

11. To be clear, there are *some* passions that are always vicious, for Augustine and for Aquinas. An example is envy. "We grieve over a person's good, insofar as his good surpasses ours; this is envy properly speaking, and it is always sinful, as also the Philosopher states (*Rhetoric*.ii.10), because to [feel envy] is to grieve over what should make us rejoice, viz., our neighbor's good" (*ST* 2a2ae.36.2).

12. *ST* 1a2ae.24.1.

13. *ST* 1a2ae.24.3. Augustine appears to make a similar move himself, as Aquinas notes; see *ST* 1a2ae.59.2 *s.c.*

14. *ST* 1a2ae.24.3.

15. For a more in-depth discussion of this question, with documentation, see Cates, *Aquinas on the Emotions*, chap. 9.

16. *ST* 1a.81.1. Keep in mind that *objects* can refer not only to things or persons, but also to multifaceted situations and to aspects of those situations.

17. *ST* 1a.81.2.

18. Aquinas is not limited to the cognitive therapy of the passions. He says, for example, that sadness can be assuaged by tears, groans, sleep, baths, and more, which restore vitality to the body and thus drive out some of the pain of sadness (*ST* 1a2ae.38).

19. *ST* 1a2ae.24.2. See Cicero, *Tusculan Disputations*, trans. J. E. King, Loeb Classical Library (Cambridge, MA: Harvard University Press, 1945). For a discussion of Cicero's account of hatred as inveterate anger, see J. Keith Green et al., "The Nature of the Beast: Hatred in Cross-Traditional Religious and Philosophical Perspective," *Journal of the Society of Christian Ethics* 29, no. 2 (2009): 175–205.

20. Seneca, *Moral Letters to Lucilius*, Loeb Classical Library (1925), accessed July 5, 2016, https://en.wikisource.org/wiki/Moral_letters_to_Lucilius, Letter 75.11–12; *De ira*, in *Seneca: Moral Essays I*, trans. John W. Basore, ed. Jeffrey Henderson, Loeb Classical Library (Cambridge, MA: Harvard University Press, 1928), 2.23.2, 3.5.8–6.1, 8.1; *De vita beata*, in *Seneca: Moral Essays II*, trans. John W. Basore, Loeb Classical Library (Cambridge, MA: Harvard University Press, 1932), 4.1–5; and *De constantia sapientis*, in *Seneca: Moral Essays I*, trans. John W. Basore, ed. Jeffrey Henderson, Loeb Classical Library (Cambridge, MA: Harvard University Press, 1928), 5.4–5. My specification of this proposition reflects the influence of Martha C. Nussbaum, *Therapy of Desire: Theory and Practice in Hellenistic Ethics* (Princeton, NJ: Princeton University Press, 1994), chaps. 9–12.

21. Seneca, *De ira*, 2.2.1. See Brad Inwood's discussion of the multiple meanings of *rational* employed by Seneca and other Stoics, "Seneca and Psychological Dualism," in *Passions and Perceptions: Studies in Hellenistic Philosophy of Mind*, ed. Jacques Brunschwig and Martha C. Nussbaum (Cambridge: Cambridge University Press, 1993), 166–67.

22. Seneca, *De ira*, 2.3.1, 2.3.4, 2.4.1–2.

23. Seneca, *De ira*, 2.3.3, 1.16.7.

24. Seneca, *De constantia sapientis*, 5.4–5.

25. Seneca, *De ira*, 1.7.2–4.

26. *ST* 1a2ae.22.1.

27. Seneca, *De ira*, 2.1.4–5.

28. Martha C. Nussbaum, *Upheavals of Thought: The Intelligence of the Emotions* (Cambridge: Cambridge University Press, 2001), 115–19; Antonio R. Damasio, *Descartes' Error: Emotion, Reason, and the Human Brain* (New York: Putnam, 1994), 131–39; and Antonio R. Damasio, *Looking for Spinoza: Joy, Sorrow, and the Feeling Brain* (Orlando, FL: Harcourt, 2003), 170.

29. Nussbaum, *Upheavals of Thought*, chap. 1.

30. Damasio, *Descartes' Error*, 53–54.

31. Damasio, *Descartes' Error*, 155.

32. Damasio, *Descartes' Error*, chap. 7.

33. Damasio, *Descartes' Error*, 159. In subsequent work, Damasio provides more detail about the difference, in his view, between "a state of feeling" and "a state of feeling made conscious." Damasio, *The Feeling of What Happens: Body and Emotion in the Making of Consciousness* (New York: Harcourt Brace, 1999), 37, 155.

34. *ST* 1a2ae.22.1*ad*3, 22.2*ad*3.

35. *ST* 1a.75.2, 75.5, 77.5; *ST* Suppl. 70.1.

36. *ST* 1a.84.6, 89.1–2.

37. *ST* 1a.20.1*ad*1; 2a2ae.24.1; 1a.57.4; 1a.82.5*ad*1.

38. *ST* 1a2ae.22.3.*ad*3.

39. *ST* 1a2ae.24.3. See Cates, *Aquinas on the Emotions*, 201–2.

40. Seneca, *Moral Letters to Lucilius*, Letter 106.

41. Seneca, *De providentia*, in *Seneca: Moral Essays I*, trans. John W. Basore, ed. Jeffrey Henderson, Loeb Classical Library (Cambridge, MA: Harvard University Press, 1928), 5.7. For more on Seneca's conception of the deity, see Aldo Setaioli, "Seneca and the Divine: Stoic Tradition and Personal Developments," *International Journal of the Classical Tradition* 13, no. 3 (2007): 333–68.

42. Seneca, *Moral Letters to Lucilius*, Letter 92.30.

43. Seneca, *De ira*, 1.1.1–7, 1.10.1–2.

44. Seneca, *De ira*, 2.3.1.

45. Seneca, *De ira*, 1.3.4–8.

46. Seneca, *De ira*, 2.1.4–2.2.2.

47. *ST* 1a.81.3.

48. *ST* 1a.79.8.

49. *ST* 1a.78.1, 80.1. See Aristotle, *De anima*, trans. J. A. Smith, in *The Basic Works of Aristotle*, ed. Richard McKeon (New York: Random House, 1941), 3.9.432a15–433b30.

50. Aristotle, *De anima*, 433a23.

51. See *ST* 1a2ae.59.2.

52. Seneca, *De ira*, 2.1.4–5–2.5.3. The mind is one, just as God is one. In *De beneficiis*, Seneca says, "Whether you speak of nature, fate, or fortune, these are all names of the same God, using his power in different ways. So likewise justice, honesty, discretion, courage, frugality, are all the good qualities of one and the same mind; if you are pleased with any one of these, you are pleased with that mind." *De beneficiis* (*On Benefits*), trans. Aubrey Stewart (London: George Bell and Sons, 1900), 4.8.

53. Brad Inwood, "Seneca and Psychological Dualism," 150–83.

54. *ST* 1a.81.3.*ad*2.

55. See Seneca, *Moral Letters to Lucilius*, Letter 92.1. Psychological dualism differs from metaphysical dualism; the former would characterize the Platonic and Aristotelian views, the latter would characterize the Platonic, but not the Aristotelian (form-matter) view.

56. Aristotle, *Nicomachean Ethics*, 1102a28–1103a1.

57. Aristotle, *Nicomachean Ethics*, 1103a1.

58. Aristotle, *Nicomachean Ethics*, 1102b33.

59. *ST* 1a2ae.9.2, 77.1.

60. *ST* 2a2ae.155.4.

61. Although the sensory appetite is associated with the nonrational part of the soul, Aquinas conceives of it as operating (in the case of at least some passions) on the border between the nonrational and the rational. I would say that he is approaching the idea of a continuum between the lowest forms of the nonrational and the highest forms of the rational. Toward the center of this continuum one can find, in humans, a power of sensory judgment that is so reason-like that it is called particular reason (*ratio particularis*). It is especially *this* power, in conjunction with other interior sensory powers and the power

of universal reason, that enables us to persuade ourselves into different ways of feeling. *ST* 1a.78.4*co* and *ad*5, 1a.81.3.

62. *ST* 1a2ae.57.5.

63. Seneca, *De ira*, 2.13.1.

64. *ST* 1a2ae.77.6.

65. Seneca, *De ira*, 2.12.4.

66. Corinne Gartner, "The Possibility of Psychic Conflict in Seneca's *De Ira*," *British Journal for the History of Philosophy* 23, no. 2 (2015): 223.

67. Seneca, *De ira*, 1.8.7. This is also Chrysippus's view, quoted in Nussbaum, *Therapy of Desire*, 383–84.

68. Seneca, *De ira*, 1.9.1.

69. Seneca, *De ira*, 1.9.2.

70. Consider, for example, the difference between a reactive, aggressive impulse and a desire specifically to punish someone for having treated one unjustly.

71. For further discussion of the meaning of *voluntas* (will) in Seneca, see Brad Inwood, "The Will in Seneca the Younger," *Classical Philology* 95, no. 1 (2000): 44–60.

72. *ST* 1a2ae.27.1.

73. *ST* 1a2ae.25.2.

74. *ST* 1a2ae.29.1.

75. Love and the other passions are deemed right or wrong, on this view, not in themselves (considered as nonrational movements) but in light of whether they are consistent or inconsistent with good judgment—inasmuch as they are "subject to the command of reason and will" (*ST* 1a2ae.24.1). Recall Seneca's statement that an interior motion counts as anger only if it is irrational and beyond our control. For Aquinas, an interior motion to which we bring the power of reason might be affirmed and subjected to the command of our will, such that it expresses our rationality, or it might be such that it is not worthy of being affirmed. In either case it might properly be called anger.

76. Seneca, *De constantia sapientis*, 8.3.

77. Seneca, *De vita beata*. Seneca says, "whoever complains and weeps and moans [about what fate determines], is compelled by force to obey commands, and even though he is unwilling, is rushed none the less to the bidden tasks. But what madness to prefer to be dragged rather than to follow!" (15.6).

78. Martha Nussbaum, *The Fragility of Goodness: Luck and Ethics in Greek Tragedy and Philosophy* (Cambridge: Cambridge University Press, 1986). See Diana Fritz Cates, "Conceiving Emotions: Martha Nussbaum's *Upheavals of Thought*," *Journal of Religious Ethics* 31, no. 2 (2003): 325–43.

79. Seneca, *De tranquillitate animi*, in *Seneca: Moral Essays II*, trans. John W. Basore, ed. Jeffrey Henderson, Loeb Classical Library (Cambridge, MA: Harvard University Press, 1928), 5.4, 13.2. See Brad Inwood, *Ethics and Human Action in Early Stoicism* (Oxford: Clarendon Press, 1985). See also Tad Brennan, "Reservation in Stoic Ethics," *Archiv für Geschichte der Philosophie* 82, no. 2 (2000): 149–77.

80. Seneca, *De tranquillitate animi*, 13.3.

81. Seneca, *De providentia*, 5.6–7: "I am under no compulsion, I suffer nothing against my will, and I am not God's slave but his follower, and the more so, indeed, because I know that everything proceeds according to law that is fixed and enacted for all time."

82. *The Complete Works of Lucius Annaeus Seneca: Natural Questions*, ed. Harry M. Hine (Chicago: University of Chicago Press, 2010), 2.38.3, and Seneca, *Moral Letters to Lucilius*, 107.9–12.

83. For a probing analysis of freedom and determinism in Stoicism, see Susan Suavé Meyer, "Fate, Fatalism, and Agency in Stoicism," in *Social Philosophy and Policy* 16, no. 2 (1999): 250–73. See also Tad Brennan, *The Stoic Life: Emotions, Duties, and Fate* (Oxford: Oxford University Press, 2005).

84. Seneca, *De ira*, 1.7.4.

85. Seneca, *De tranquillitate animi*, 2.4.

86. Seneca, *De ira*, 3.5.1.

87. Seneca, *De ira*, 1.6.1.

88. Seneca, *De tranquillitate animi*, 7.3–4.

89. Seneca, *De vita beata*, 3.3.

90. Seneca, *De tranquillitate animi*, 2.3.

91. Seneca, *De providentia*, 4.6.

92. Seneca, *De constantia sapientis*, 9.4.

93. John P. Reeder Jr., "What Is a Religious Ethic?" *Journal of Religious Ethics* 25, no. 3 (1998): 171.

94. *ST* 1a.20.1ad3.

95. Jean Porter, "Desire for God: Ground of the Moral Life in Aquinas," in *Theological Studies* 47, no. 1 (1986): 48–68.

96. Diana Fritz Cates, "Love: A Thomistic Analysis," in "Love," ed. David McCarthy and Joshua P. Hochschild, special issue, *Journal of Moral Theology* 1, no. 2 (2012): 1–30.

97. *ST* 1a2ae.71.1ad3.

98. *ST* 3a.46.

99. Seneca, *De povidentia*, 5.6–8.

100. Seneca, *De tranquillitate animi*, 3.3.

101. Brennan, "Reservation in Stoic Ethics," 168.

102. Seneca, *De tranquillitate animi*, 2.3; *De ira*, 3.6.1. There is a (Platonic) part of Aquinas that is attracted to this model, especially in view of eternal life, but his theory of knowledge expresses the conviction that, in the present life, all intellectual activities are dependent, in multiple respects, on sensory activities, so it is important to attend to the latter with care.

103. Seneca, *De tranquillitate animi*, 2.4.

104. *ST* 2a2ae.28.1.

105. Special thanks to John P. Reeder Jr., Keith Green, Bill McDonough, Pranav Prakash, and John Corrigan, as well as the other members of the Corrigan research group, for their inspiring conversation and insightful critiques.

MARK WYNN

## 2. METAPHYSICS AND EMOTIONAL EXPERIENCE
*Some Themes Drawn from John of the Cross*

In this chapter, I aim to show how a description of the role of the emotions in the spiritual or religious life may be related to a description of that life which is cast in metaphysical terms. I will develop this account by reference to two sources in particular: Thomas Aquinas, and the metaphysical vantage point on the spiritual life that is developed in his thought, and John of the Cross, whose work provides, I am going to suggest, a kind of emotional and experiential specification of various themes that are set down in a more doctrinal or metaphysical idiom in the writings of Aquinas. While I will be concerned with these two authors in particular, my hope is to illustrate a hypothesis that extends beyond their work: namely, the idea that for a rounded understanding of a given spiritual or religious tradition, we need to make use of two kinds of vocabulary, one metaphysical, and one emotional and experiential. It will be an implication of the view I develop here that if we are to understand the significance of the emotions in the spiritual or religious life, then we need to see how a description of the phases of that life which is cast in emotional terms can be related to descriptions of this same track of development that are recorded in the rather different vocabulary of doctrine or metaphysics. Neither vocabulary is reducible to the other, I will suggest, but equally neither vocabulary is entirely detachable from the other: what is said in metaphysical terms, for example, in some measure informs and constrains what can be said in emotional terms, and vice versa.

I will begin by introducing this distinction between the two kinds of perspective—the emotional and experiential, on the one hand, and the metaphysical, on the other—before examining more closely the work of my two focal authors.

## *The Perspectives of Metaphysics and Experience*

Let us suppose that we can agree on the nature of the world in metaphysical terms (a large assumption, I know!). Supposing that our metaphysical enquiries have run their course, a further kind of enquiry comes into view. For we might then want to ask: What would it be like to inhabit a world so conceived? A rough analogy would be this: suppose that physics succeeds in providing a comprehensive account of the fundamental nature, or microstructure, of the material world. Even if such an account cannot be improved on as physics, it would still leave space for another kind of enquiry that is concerned with the question of what it is like, from a subjective point of view, for human beings, or other sentient creatures, to inhabit a world so conceived. Similarly, even if we have agreement on a given characterization of the world in metaphysical terms, it is a further matter to determine how such a world might be presented to subjects of experience such as ourselves. And it is a further matter, therefore, to determine how such a world might be registered in the emotional experience of the person who is negotiating the various phases of the spiritual life that are implied in this conception of the world.

In this chapter, I will take the work of John of the Cross as an example of the second of these kinds of enquiry, that is, as an attempt to specify what it is like to experience a world that is understood in a certain way in metaphysical terms. Given the particular concerns of this volume, I will be especially interested in what he says about what it is like in emotional terms to inhabit a world so understood. Making this connection is not difficult, since so much of John's description of the spiritual life is emotionally toned. Here is the general picture I am going to present. We can see John as inheriting, from the theological tradition in which he stands, a certain conception of the nature of things; and in his work, he is not, I will suggest, trying to elaborate on—and even more clearly, he is not intending to challenge—that conception in creedal or metaphysical terms. His venture is more a matter of providing, we might say, a set of experiential reports, or a phenomenology, to fit the metaphysics. It is a matter of sketching out a vision of the spiritual life, understood in practical and emotional terms, that can be located within the worldview he has inherited. So let me now develop this idea a little, drawing on John's work. Again, the ultimate object of this discussion is to show how an appreciation of the spiritual or religious life in emotional terms needs to be cognizant of other ways of describing that life, and of the relationship between these various descriptions.

## John of the Cross on the Distinctiveness of the Experiential Perspective on the Spiritual Life

John was, of course, theologically literate. He had received a formal theological training at the University of Salamanca, and it is clear from his writings that he is familiar with central themes in the work of his theological forebears, including, to name one key example, Thomas Aquinas. Let us note one instance where John alludes to the work of Aquinas. In the preamble to the Five Ways, Thomas famously distinguishes between two kinds of proof—what he calls a "demonstratio quia" and a "demonstratio propter quid." The first concerns what we might call an inference to the best explanation—where we postulate a cause to account for the data of observation. The second concerns the case where we already know the nature of a cause, and use that knowledge to read off the character of its effects. Here is how Aquinas develops the point: "Demonstration can be made in two ways: One is through the cause, and is called 'a priori' [*propter quid*], and this is to argue from what is prior absolutely. The other is through the effect, and is called a demonstration 'a posteriori' [*quia*]; this is to argue from what is prior relatively only to us" (*Summa Theologiae* 1a.2.2).[1] Of course, for Aquinas, where strictly philosophical enquiry into the nature of the divine is concerned, we are confined to the route of the demonstration *quia*—that is, we must reason from the observation of various phenomena (those of change, gradation of goodness, and teleological directedness, for example) if we are to know, on philosophical grounds, that there is a God who stands as their source. Now John has inherited this epistemology, and in the passage I am about to cite he is providing, I take it, a kind of experiential amplification of Thomas's remarks. In his text *The Living Flame of Love*, John refers to the "joy" of the "awakened" person, that is, the person who has reached a condition of spiritual maturity. He writes: "Though it is true that the soul here sees that all these things are distinct from God, in that they have a created existence . . . it knows also that God in His own essence is, in an infinitely preeminent way, all these things, so that it understands them better in Him, their first cause, than in themselves. This is the great joy of this awakening, namely to know creatures in God, and not God in His creatures: this is to know effects in their cause, and not the cause by its effects."[2] Two things are worth noting about the relationship between Thomas's account and John's. First, John's account is, I suggest, consistent with Thomas's.

For example, John might have talked of an experiential state that involved direct acquaintance with the divine essence, and had he done so, then his account could not have been reconciled with Thomas's understanding of the limits of human cognitive capacities in this life. But in this passage, he is not doing that, I take it. Instead, his focus is on the possibility of a new way of experiencing not the divine essence, but the realm of sensory things, once creatures are seen from the vantage point of God, or apprehended, we might say, according to a divine scale of values. Rowan Williams, speaking of John's text *The Spiritual Canticle*, where a similar vision of human possibilities is set forth, puts the point in this way: "The sense of God living constantly in the soul, of God's goodness in all things, of the warmth of reciprocal love—all these things of which the *Canticle* speaks at length are described not at all in terms of revelations granted in ecstasy, but in terms of a general disposition of the soul, a regular daily mode of seeing and understanding, a new light on things."[3] So here is one conception of John's view of the focus and emotional tenor of the "awakened" person's experience. In brief, what is distinctive about this person's experience is not that they are in a state of enduring or even episodic rapture, nor that their experience is targeted at a new and metaphysically elevated set of objects. It is, rather, that their encounter with the everyday sensory world is now infused with the "warmth" that flows from their sense of the divine presence in all things. To put the point in John's terms, this is a matter of experiencing ordinary things "in God."

Secondly, while it conforms to Thomas's metaphysics, John's emotional and experiential perspective does not simply recapitulate Thomas's text, but presents its own distinctive account of human possibilities. John makes this clear when he writes in the passage I have just cited that "this is to know effects in their cause, and not the cause by its effects." Here, he disagrees with Thomas verbally, since Aquinas, after all, affirms that we cannot know creatures in God, but have on the contrary to proceed from a knowledge of God's effects to the knowledge of God as the source of those effects. But John's intention is not, I take it, to dispute Thomas's claim that we cannot construct a demonstration *propter quid* when reasoning in natural theological terms, but to distinguish what can be said from the vantage point of natural theology, or metaphysics, and what can be said from the vantage point of our emotional experience. In the realm of experience, even if not in the realm of philosophical argumentation, he is saying, the perspective of something like the propter quid is possible. By tracking Aquinas's form of words in this way, John is, I think, drawing our attention to this distinction of perspectives, and entering a kind of plea for the irreducibility of the experiential perspective to the natural theological or metaphysical perspective. In the "joy" of the awakened person's experience, even if not in metaphysical argumentation, it is possible for a human being to know creatures in God.[4]

In sum, John's experiential account is, I would say, faithful to Thomas's metaphysics, but at the same time, it cannot be simply *read off* from that metaphysics. We have here two vocabularies: a metaphysical vocabulary and an experiential vocabulary, each yielding its own distinctive vantage point on the nature of a universe understood in theistic terms.

## *John of the Cross on the Transition from Earlier to Later Phases of the Spiritual Life*

In the passage I have just cited, John is concerned with the emotional condition of the awakened person. And I will return to what he says about these matters at the close of this chapter. But elsewhere, he also describes the various phases of the spiritual life that precede this condition of spiritual maturity. Here again, it is fruitful to consider the relationship between what he has to say in emotional and experiential terms and what might be said in a more doctrinal or metaphysical idiom. Once more, given John's context, the relevant metaphysical picture of these earlier phases of the spiritual life is provided in the writings of Thomas Aquinas. So let us begin with Aquinas's account of the process of spiritual growth and move from there to consider how John understands these matters, paying particular attention once more to his treatment of the emotional dimension of the spiritual life.

Aquinas had, of course, inherited from Aristotle the idea that there are "acquired" moral virtues, such as justice, courage, and temperance. These virtues are produced in the person by way of a process of habituation. Thus, a person becomes just, for example, by repeatedly doing the just thing, so that doing the just thing becomes for them a matter of *second nature*, with the result that thereafter they do not simply do the just thing, but do it as a just person. Aquinas had also inherited a way of talking about the virtues from his theological predecessors, and following his theological forebears, he thought of the virtues of faith, hope, and charity—these are the "theological" virtues—as produced in the person directly by God, rather than by way of some process of habituation. Aquinas elaborates on these dual traditions by supposing that there is a third category of virtue in addition to the "acquired" moral and the "infused" theological virtues, namely, the category of infused moral virtues. These virtues are concerned with our relations to the created order (hence they are "moral"), but at the same time they have a divinely ordered teleology (for this reason, they are "infused").[5] So they differ from the acquired virtues in terms of their aetiology, and differ from the theological virtues insofar as they direct the person to God not immediately but mediately—that is, via the person's relation to created things.

For our purposes, what matters in this picture is Aquinas's account of the transition from the inculcation of the acquired moral virtues to the receipt of the infused moral virtues. Let us take an example of this development. A person can instill the acquired form of temperance in themselves by their own efforts. And once they have the acquired form of the virtue, then their habits of eating, along with the habits that are implied in the proper regulation of other bodily appetites, will be attuned to the health of the body.[6] But it is a further matter for those habits to be directed toward the end of flourishing in relation to God—for this further goal to be achieved, a more radical "rule" needs to be followed, one that requires not simply, as Aquinas says, that the person's consumption of food "should not harm the health of the body, nor hinder the use of reason" but, in addition, "abstinence in food, drink and the like" (*ST* 1a2ae.63.4).[7] Abstinence should not harm the body—so it is consistent with the rule that governs the acquired form of temperance.[8] But it also involves a more demanding ideal of feeling, thought, and, practice. So here as elsewhere, the infused form of the virtue does not displace the acquired form, but stretches or strengthens it. And this is what we should expect Aquinas to say, given his commitment to the general principle that "grace does not destroy nature but perfects it" (*ST* 1a.1.8*ad2*).[9]

Let us now look at John's description of what is, I take it, this same trajectory of development. Earlier, I discussed John's vision of the spiritual life in his text *The Living Flame of Love*. But of course, he is better known for another work, the *Dark Night of the Soul*. In the *Dark Night*, John charts the bewildering, and at times traumatizing, process whereby the soul is stripped of various egocentric attachments, and brought to the condition of seeing all things in God that he describes in the passage I cited from the *Living Flame*. This process of being drawn away from self-referential kinds of fulfillment has a sensory and also a spiritual phase—in brief, it is necessary for the soul to give up not only disordered attachments to sensory things, but also attachments to things of the "spirit," including such spiritual pleasures as feeling oneself to be the object of divine favor.

So John distinguishes between the sensory and spiritual phases of the night. It is notable that each of these phases has an *active* and a *passive* period. In the first period, the person engages in various spiritual exercises, and takes some satisfaction in their growing competence in the performance of these exercises, while in the second they find that they are increasingly incapable of finding any fulfillment in such exercises, and indeed increasingly incapable of performing them. John describes these emotional changes in a richly textured emotional idiom, but for our purposes just now, what is striking is that his discussion of the movement from the active into the passive phase of the spiritual life seems to map onto Aquinas's discussion of the movement from the cultivation of the acquired moral virtues to the receipt of the infused moral virtues.

As we have seen, the acquired moral virtues are produced by way of a process of habituation. So, here, the person is active in shaping their own character. By contrast, the infused moral virtues are divinely bestowed, and cannot be produced by any human initiative. This is Aquinas's story of spiritual growth, whereby the acquired moral virtues are extended or topped up by the infused. And it is a story told in a metaphysical idiom: what distinguishes the various phases of the spiritual life, given this vantage point on it, are the shifts in the relationship between God's agency and ours. John's account is structurally similar, insofar as he also envisages the *active* night being succeeded by the *passive* night. But once again, John's account cannot be simply read off from a knowledge of Thomistic metaphysics.

There is, indeed, a question about whether John's account of these matters is even compatible with Thomas's. As many commentators have noted, John appears to represent the move to the later phases of the spiritual life in antithetical terms. Hence he writes: "God makes [the soul] to die to all that is not naturally God, so that, once it is stripped and denuded of its former skin, He may begin to clothe it anew."[10] Or again, in a similar vein he writes: "The Divine fire of contemplative love . . . before it unites and transforms the soul into itself, first purges it of all contrary accidents."[11] Here, the spiritual life is taken to comprise two discrete steps: the habits of feeling, thought, and perception that were characteristic of its earlier phase have to be kicked away, it seems, before the person can venture on to the later phase. And it is because there is this intermediate ground, when the habits of feeling and perception that constituted the person's sense of self have gone, but have yet to be replaced by a new, divinely infused sense of agency, that the *dark night* is indeed so dark. It is experienced, in short, not as the progressive refinement and redirection of the core energies of the self, but in terms of the bewildering, excoriating dissolution of the habits that constituted the former sense of self. How can this picture be reconciled with Aquinas's conception of the infused virtues as extending or, as it were, topping up the acquired? Does John's teaching not suggest, rather, that the acquired virtues are first brought to nought, and the person to the feeling of having been abandoned by God—and that it is only then that the infused virtues are communicated to the person?

The contrast between these two pictures—one of incremental growth and the other, it seems, of radical rupture—can be understood, I suggest, in terms of the differences of interest of the two authors. Once again, Aquinas is using a metaphysical vocabulary, which is concerned with variations in the pattern of divine and human action, and using this distinction between two kinds of agency to mark a key transition in the journey to spiritual maturity. This is a story—here as elsewhere in Aquinas—of grace perfecting nature. By contrast, it might be said, a natural reading of the texts from John which I have just cited would suggest that his account is rather one of grace displacing nature. To see that this does not follow straightforwardly, I am going to introduce an example which presents, I think, at least a rough analogy for the kind of emotional disorientation that John is describing.

Let us take the case of a new mother's emerging love for her child. As we all know, such love can be experienced, in some cases, as deeply disorienting. And we might suppose that, at least in part, this is because this love can seem to require, and may really require, a radical reordering, and even uprooting, of established attachments, with the result that the mother's sense of herself comes to be fundamentally redefined.[12] For these reasons, a woman's nascent love for her child can sometimes be registered in experience as bewildering and even as *dark* in something like John's sense. But of course, if the mother is fortunate, she will emerge from this period of darkness; and at that point, in the normal case, she will find that her former attachments have been not so much annihilated as located within a newly ordered pattern of desires and concerns, a pattern that, of course, accords a central place to the needs and interests of the child.

Similarly, I suggest, it may be that John's experiential vocabulary records what it is like, for some of us anyway, to receive the infused virtues, and to be drawn thereby into a deepened love—for God. This development can feel like a breakdown or dissolution of the self. But as the example of the new mother shows, I think, the experiential vantage point on events is compatible with the case where certain underlying habits and concerns are retained, albeit, for a time, those habits and concerns do not manifest themselves in experience.

So far, I have examined two cases where Thomas and John appear to be talking about related matters, while using different vocabularies—to put the point in Aquinas's terms, the first case concerns the possibility of a propter quid knowledge of creatures, and the second concerns the relationship between the acquired and infused moral virtues. In each case, John was surely cognizant of Aquinas's stance, and in each case, his own discussion can be read, I am suggesting, as a kind of exploration of related themes in an experiential idiom. And what John provides, in both cases, is, I suggest, a kind of emotional specification of the metaphysical picture that Thomas presents. More briefly, I am going to take one final example of how John's account tracks without simply reiterating the metaphysical commitments of the tradition within which he is working.

### John and the Platonic Tradition of Metaphysics

It is notable that John makes extensive use of the ancient theological idiom of light. When describing the "dark night," he speaks, for example, of how "the soul suffers great pain when it receives [the divine light] in itself, just as, when the eye is dimmed by humours . . . the assault made upon them by a bright light causes them pain."[13] Similarly, he speaks of the soul that is "assailed" by the divine light as "dark and impure."[14] In these texts, John's use of light imagery signifies that the *darkness* to which he refers is fundamentally a condition of the soul: so far as a person's experience is *dark*, that is attributable to the fact that their "eyes" are "dimmed by humours."

At the same time, it is clear that the emphasis of John's account is not so much on the mind's eye being turned toward the divine light, but rather on that light illuminating the objects that are set before it. Hence he writes of the later phases of the spiritual life: "Since this spiritual light is so simple, pure and general, not appropriated or restricted to any particular thing that can be understood, whether natural or Divine (since with respect to all these apprehensions the faculties of the soul are empty and annihilated), it follows that with great comprehensiveness and readiness the soul discerns and penetrates whatsoever thing presents itself to it, whether it come from above or from below."[15]

Here, the soul's attention is trained not on the light itself, but on the objects that are revealed by the light. To use the language of the passage from the *Living Flame of Love* that I cited earlier, this is a matter of seeing creatures "in God."

Accordingly, there are two striking differences between John's account of the spiritual life and the story of spiritual development that is unfolded in Plato's allegory of the cave in book 7 of the *Republic*. In each case, of course, light imagery is crucial. But whereas Plato envisages the summit of the spiritual journey as a matter of the spiritual adept training their gaze on the sun, and enjoying a clear vision of the sun, for John, it is not so much the Divine Light that is seen, as other things, which come into view insofar as they are illuminated by that Light. And secondly, while Plato's story invites the thought that the sensory world is cave-like (when the adept trains their attention once more on the sensory world, this is likened to a return to the cave), John is clear that if we find the sensory world *dark*, that is not because darkness is intrinsic to it, but because of our own spiritually defective condition. Caves while they remain caves will never be illuminated; but the realm of sensory things, John seems to be affirming, can be illuminated, once the person has been purified by the *night*, so that "whatsoever thing presents itself" to the soul is irradiated by the divine light.

Here again, we find an unfolding of the connection between metaphysical commitments and a conception of human experience. John's imagery, and by implication the phenomenology of the experience to which he is alluding, is different from Plato's; and arguably that difference tracks a difference in their metaphysical convictions. For Plato, the summit of the spiritual life is the vision of the Form of the Good, while for John it is, rather, the reorientation of the will that allows everyday things to be experienced *joyously*, in the *light* of a divine scale of values. And while, for Plato, the everyday world is conceived as a realm of shadows, from which a person might reasonably seek to escape (if not burdened with the responsibilities of the philosopher king), for John that world is not in itself an impediment to relationship to God, but becomes an impediment only insofar as it is the object of disordered desires. Once those desires have been purged, it is possible to see everyday things *in God*, and to rejoice in them so understood. So here again, we find an association between John's Christian metaphysics, which implies a commitment to the goodness of the material order, and his representation of the spiritual life in emotional terms.

### The Experience of the "Awakened" Person

To conclude this discussion, I want to return to the end point of the spiritual life, as John understands it, and to consider more closely the emotional condition of the "awakened" person. Here again, John's perspective and Aquinas's are mutually informing: each enlarges on the other.

As we have seen, John thinks of the condition of the awakened person as a matter of knowing "creatures in God" and finding joy in this knowledge—or perhaps the relevant condition is just a joyous knowledge of creatures in God. This account of the awakened person's vantage point on the realm of everyday objects suggests that it is not just certain items in their environment that are newly experienced, now that they are known *in God*, but creatures in general. This reading of John's remarks coheres with a familiar feature of reports of conversion experience, since such reports commonly involve the idea that the convert enjoys not simply a new proximity to God, but also a new perceptual relationship to the everyday world. William James provides a characteristically clear and insightful discussion of these matters in the *Varieties*. He remarks, for instance, that: "When we come to study the phenomenon of conversion or religious regeneration, we ... see that a not infrequent consequence of the change operated in the subject is a transfiguration of the face of nature in his eyes. A new heaven seems to shine upon a new earth."[16]

Here again, what is striking in these reports is that the appearance of the sensory world in general seems to have changed, so that it is enlivened and charged with a new significance. James cites various examples of this phenomenon, and I will note just two. Here, for example, is Jonathan Edwards, the American divine, writing of his conversion experience: "The appearance of everything was altered; there seemed to be, as it were, a calm, sweet cast, or appearance of divine glory, in almost everything. God's excellency, his wisdom, his purity and love, seemed to appear in everything; in the sun, moon, and stars; in the clouds and blue sky; in the grass, flowers, and trees; in the water and all nature; which used greatly to fix my mind."[17]

Edwards is well known for the care and precision of his theological writing, and we have good reason, therefore, to regard these remarks as a sober report of how the sensory world in general—including trees and flowers and stars—appeared to him following his conversion. In a similar vein, another of James's sources remarks that "natural objects were glorified, my spiritual vision was so clarified that I saw beauty in every material object in the universe."[18]

Drawing on reports such as these, and John's comments in the *Living Flame of Love*, concerning the possibility of seeing creatures "in God," we should suppose that in some central cases, the experience of conversion or of "religious regeneration" involves a change in the person's perception of the everyday world—whereby ordinary objects come to appear newly beautiful and charged with a new significance. The emotional tone of this sort of experience is evidently one of being uplifted, and as John says "awakened"—as though everyday objects are being seen in proper focus for the first time.

This story of the terminus of the spiritual life is rehearsed in the language of emotional experience. In brief, the person's feeling of emotional renewal is said to find a mirroring response, somehow, in the renewed appearance of the sensory world. Thomas's picture of the end point of the spiritual life is not cast in experiential terms. But his category of infused moral virtue provides one way of understanding this shift in the appearances that is reported by John of the Cross and the sources cited by James. To see this connection, let us pause briefly to note two ways of conceptualizing the appearance of sensory things.

Suppose I see a large, fast-approaching dog, and suppose that I am, naturally enough, fearful of the dog. In these circumstances, I will be focally aware of the dog, while various other features of my environment, such as the color of the linoleum floor on which I am standing, are consigned to the periphery of my awareness. Here, the salience of the object in my perceptual field tracks my affectively toned judgment concerning its significance for me (here, this is the fearful judgment that the dog poses a threat to me). And we may wish to say that, in such cases, the feeling of fear is partly constituted by this ordering of the perceptual field.

Let us take a second example. Suppose I discover that the meat I am chewing in fact derives from Shuttlecock, the pet rabbit. In that case, the meat is likely to be newly salient in my perceptual field: I will now be focally aware of the meat. But it is not just that the salience of the meat relative to other objects has changed. Its intrinsic phenomenal feel will also have changed: the meat will now be experienced as revolting. Let us call this feature of the appearance of a thing its *hue*. So in this case, the disgust I now feel is realized both in the heightened salience of the meat in my perceptual field and in the change in its hue. (These developments are, of course, commonly connected: notably, a change in hue will standardly involve a change in salience.) So this is one way of understanding the relationship between a change in the significance of a thing (here, the meat), a change in its appearance (here, a change in salience and hue), and a change in the quality of one's emotional engagement with the world (here, the move to a feeling of disgust).

Now, on Thomas's account, the receipt of the infused moral virtues involves everyday objects taking on a new significance. For instance, for the person of acquired temperance, food is significant insofar as it serves to promote the health of the body. This person habitually consumes food, and habitually desires to consume food, according to the requirements of bodily health. The person of infused temperance shares this pattern of feeling and activity, because the practice of infused temperance involves no harm of the body. But in addition, this person also habitually consumes and desires food according to the requirements of relationship to God. More exactly, I would say, the person's dietary habits are now congruent with the truth that they will one day share in the life of God—but that is a story for another occasion. So, on this Thomistic account of the end point of the spiritual life, insofar as that point consists in the receipt of the infused moral virtues, the spiritually mature person will find a new significance in the everyday world. To take the case of food again, a set of objects that formerly served the end of bodily health will now be drawn into a new and more encompassing teleology, because those objects will now serve in addition the end of relationship to God. The other infused virtues invite a similar story. To take just one example, for the person of infused charity (that is, for the person who has the virtue of neighbor love), other human beings will now assume a new significance, insofar as they are now understood, and experienced, in terms of the truth that we will one day share with them in a deep-seated relationship of friendship, when we participate in the life of God, in the beatific vision.[19]

It follows from this account that the world in general will acquire a new significance in the experience of the person of spiritual maturity: food in general, other people in general and, in sum, sensory objects in general will all acquire a new significance, insofar as all are folded into a new, God-directed teleology. And this is not just a new but a heightened significance: the former significance that was characteristic of the acquired form of the relevant virtue will endure (hence food, for example, will retain its significance as a source of bodily health), but there will now be, in addition, a new kind of significance. (Hence food, for example, will now be ordered not only to the health of the body, but also to relationship to God.)

We can now put together these three blocks of material. John's account of spiritual *awakening* at least implies that religious renewal involves not just a change in the emotional condition of the person, but also a change in the appearance of the world. This association is still more clearly evident in many reports of conversion experiences, such as those documented by William James. (Here is the first theme.) We can understand this shift in the appearance of the world as the product of a pervasive change in the significance of things, where this change is manifested in experience in a pervasive change in the salience and hue of sensory objects. (Here is the second.) And lastly, we can understand this far-reaching change of significance, and the associated change in the appearance of the sensory world, in terms of Aquinas's category of infused moral virtue, since that category allows us to see how everyday material objects may be subsumed within a divinely ordered teleology, so that they bear a new and deepened significance.

The category of infused moral virtue relates with particular directness to John's observations on seeing things *in God*, for there is a ready sense in which the person who has the infused moral virtues will indeed experience everyday things *in God*—because the significance of those things, and their appearance to the person, will now be woven into their relation to God. Here again, we can see how reports of the emotional tenor of a certain phase of the spiritual life can be brought into new and clearer focus when we set those reports alongside a metaphysically ordered account of the spiritual life. It is also true, of course, that this metaphysical account can itself be contextualized and newly understood once we are acquainted with the relevant experiential reports. Here, the metaphysical and emotional narratives are mutually informing: we could put the point by saying that metaphysics without emotional experience is humanly blind, and that emotional experience without metaphysics is cognitively empty. That is to say, by referring to the emotions, we can bring out the human meaning of the metaphysical story, allowing us to see how that story finds expression in the lives of creatures of our particular intellectual and emotional sensibility; and by using metaphysical categories, we can see how the emotional experience of the religiously renewed person is not a matter of mere affect, but instead constitutes a structured appreciation of the ultimate import of the everyday sensory world.

### Concluding Remarks

In this chapter, I have been considering the emotional contours of the spiritual life as they have been charted in one particular tradition of spiritual formation and development, namely, the Roman Catholic tradition broadly construed. Using John of the Cross as an exemplar of this tradition, I have noted how the transition from the earlier to the later phases of the spiritual life, and also the end point of the spiritual life, may be registered in a person's emotional and perceptual experience. I have argued that this story of emotional and spiritual development tracks the structure of another story, involving the same transitions, and the same end point, that can be told in the language of metaphysics. The two vantage points, and two vocabularies, I have argued, are not entirely independent of each other, but neither is one vantage point reducible to the other. Instead, each extends its own distinctive appreciation of the nature and goals of the spiritual life, and each therefore enlarges the perspective of the other.

While we have mostly been concerned here with one tradition in particular, this tradition is representative, I take it, of a larger class of cases. In general, I propose, when we seek to understand the contribution of emotional experience to the spiritual life, we should attend to the complex interplay between metaphysical teaching and records of experience, including emotional experience, that is played out in traditions of spiritual formation and practice. And if we want a rounded appreciation of the role of the emotions in the spiritual life, then we need to see how the references to emotional change that are integral to narratives of spiritual growth are interwoven with other ways of describing, from other vantage points, these same developments. And this is no surprise: for it is of the nature of religious traditions to draw into themselves all dimensions of a human life—emotional, perceptual, intellectual, and practical—so that each is transformed, according to the particular tradition's conception of human possibilities and the goals of a human life.[20]

NOTES

1. Aquinas, *Summa Theologiae*, trans. Fathers of the English Dominican Province (Benziger Brothers edition, 1947), accessed July 1, 2016, http://dhspriory.org/thomas/summa/SS/SS025.html#SSQ250UTP1. All subsequent quotations from the *Summa Theologiae* will be from this source except where indicated.

2. *The Living Flame of Love by Saint John of the Cross with His Letters, Poems, and Minor Writings*, trans. D. Lewis (London: Thomas Baker, 1919). Commentary on Stanza 4, 121.

3. Rowan Williams, *The Wound of Knowledge: Christian Spirituality from the New Testament to Saint John of the Cross* (Cambridge, MA: Cowley Publications, 1991), 187–88.

4. In this respect, the awakened person's knowledge resembles angelic "morning knowledge." See Aquinas's comment on the varieties of angelic knowledge: "Knowledge of the Creator through creatures, therefore, is evening knowledge, just as, conversely, knowledge of creatures through the Creator is morning knowledge." *De veritate* 8.16*ad*9, trans. Robert W. Mulligan (Chicago: Henry Regnery, 1952), accessed July 1, 2016, http://dhspriory.org/thomas/QDdeVer.htm. My thanks to Nathan Lyons for this reference.

5. For the connection between the idea that a virtue is God-directed, or concerned with the person's supernatural end, and the idea that it is produced by infusion, see, for example, *Summa Theologiae* 1a2ae.51.4.

6. Some of the recent literature on habit and habituation in cultural studies and sociology develops a similar perspective. See, for instance, the special issue on "Habit" in *Body and Society* 19 (2013): 3–281. I am grateful to a reviewer for the press for drawing my attention to this connection.

7. Aquinas, *Summa Theologiae*, ed. Thomas Gilby (London: Eyre and Spottiswoode, 1964–74).

8. It is, of course, traditional teaching that abstinence should not harm the body: this is why the infirm and children, for example, are standardly exempted from the full rigors of abstinence. Aquinas affirms this teaching in *Summa Theologiae* 2a2ae.147.4*ad*2.

9. This reading is supported by John Inglis, who remarks: "The infused virtue does not replace the acquired virtue for Aquinas, but rather builds on it." See "Aquinas's Replication of the Acquired Moral Virtues: Rethinking the Standard Philosophical Interpretation of Moral Virtue in Aquinas," *Journal of Religious Ethics* 27, no. 1 (1999): 19. However, I am not sure that Inglis is right to take *Summa Theologiae* 1a2ae.51.4.1*ad*3 as direct support for this position (see p. 20). Here, Aquinas's point seems to be that the repeated performance

of acts that derive from an infused virtue does not produce a further, acquired habit. I am grateful to Michael Lamb for this point.

10. *Dark Night of the Soul*, bk. 2, chap. 13, in *The Essential St. John of the Cross*, trans. E. Allison Peers (Radford, VA: Wilder, 2008), 445.

11. *Dark Night of the Soul*, bk. 2, chap. 10, 433.

12. For a reading of postnatal depression in terms of the experience of loss, see Paula Nicolson, *Post-Natal Depression: Psychology, Science and the Transition to Motherhood* (London: Routledge, 1998).

13. *Dark Night of the Soul*, bk. 2, chap. 5, 417.

14. *Dark Night of the Soul*, bk. 2, chap. 5, 417.

15. *Dark Night of the Soul*, bk. 2, chap. 8, 427–28.

16. William James, *The Varieties of Religious Experience: A Study in Human Nature* (London: Longmans, Green, 1911), 151.

17. James, *Varieties*, 249.

18. James, *Varieties*, 250.

19. See, for instance, this passage, where Thomas is considering whether neighbor love properly extends to the angels: "The friendship of charity is founded upon the fellowship of everlasting happiness, in which men share in common with the angels. For it is written (Mt. 22:30) that 'in the resurrection . . . men shall be as the angels of God in heaven.' It is therefore evident that the friendship of charity extends also to the angels." *Summa Theologiae* 2a2ae.25.10, ellipsis in the original. Charity is strictly a theological rather than a moral virtue, but evidently it has a moral dimension.

20. I would like to thank John Corrigan for the invitation to participate in the workshop "How Do We Study Religion and Emotion?" I am very grateful to John, and other participants in the workshop, and also two referees, for their helpful comments on earlier drafts of this chapter.

DONOVAN O. SCHAEFER

## 3. BEAUTIFUL FACTS
*Science, Secularism, and Affect*

*1: Paper Cuts*

This is a chapter about pages. It is about the way that pages leap to life, and the way that knowledge, far from lying flat on the page, enfolds our hypersensitive bodies, creating registers of meaning that compel passions, compel power, compel bodies to move. When we think about a reader, we think about a sovereign, studious mind, a still body traveling outward to an abstract exterior, then returning for quiet, structured reflection. Instead, I want us to think of the reader as a body enthralled, a body possessed, an addict.

To diagram this vital relationship between the still page and the moving body, this chapter turns to the resources of contemporary affect theory. Affect theory is a movement emerging out of contemporary queer theory and poststructural philosophy that emphasizes the correlations between nonlinguistic forces and power. While late twentieth-century critical theory tended to focus on power as operating through the medium of language, affect theory reasserts the salience of living bodies as nodes for the flows of power. For affect theorists, language is not the currency of power, but *a formation* within a broader, organic network of power coursing through bodies.

Affect theory, then, calls on us to think about pages as things that chain us, that thrill us, that cut us, and make us dance. The affective frame prompts us to think of reading not as a computer program that we run and then switch off, but as what anthropologist Kathleen Stewart would call a "surge" running through us. Within the framework of affect theory, affect animates every aspect of embodied life, including the ostensibly affect-neutral domain of knowledge-production. Even science. Even religious, even secular frames of knowledge about God. Affect theory prompts us to ask not just what we know, not just how we know, but *how knowledge feels*.

Specifically, affect theory asks after the way that the things we know and believe shape the contours of our embodied life—dictating and directing where our bodies go. Not only religion, but humanistic scholarship, science, and secularism itself, I will suggest, are all wrapped up in these processes, channeling and directing landscapes of feeling that are inextricable from structures of belief and disbelief. As a case study, this chapter will turn to the affective agenda of the New Atheism. Where atheists have tended to see themselves as sober philosophers stonily erasing the sentimentality of religious superstition, I want to use the register of affect to ask, instead, the question posed by Janet Jakobsen and Ann Pellegrini at the outset of *Secularisms*, published in 2008: "What does secularism 'feel' like?"[1] These, then, are the pages of a postsecular memoir.


PAGE 1

Page 1039 from David Foster Wallace's novel *Infinite Jest*. Here, Orin Incandenza is talking about his estranged mother, Avril, the former chair of the "Tactical Phalanx" of an organization known as the Militant Grammarians of Massachusetts, alleged to have been involved with the "MIT Language Riots" of 1997 in the novel's alternative-world sci-fi timeline.[2] Orin is describing the mission of the group:

> The M.G.M.s for instance go around to Mass. supermarkets and dun the manager if the Express Checkout sign says 10 ITEMS OR LESS instead of OR FEWER and so on. The year before . . . the Orange Crush people had an ad on billboards and little magazine-fall-out cards that said CRUSH: WITH A TASTE THAT'S ALL IT'S OWN, with like a possessive IT'S, and I swear the M.G.M. squad lost their minds; the Moms spent five weeks going back and forth to NNY City, organized two different rallies on Madison Avenue that got very ugly, and acted as her own attorney in the suit the Crush people brought, never slept, never once slept, lived on cigarettes and salad, huge salads always consumed very late at night.[3]

And long after her militant days are over, Avril is still correcting misspelled signs in the cafeteria at Enfield Tennis Academy.

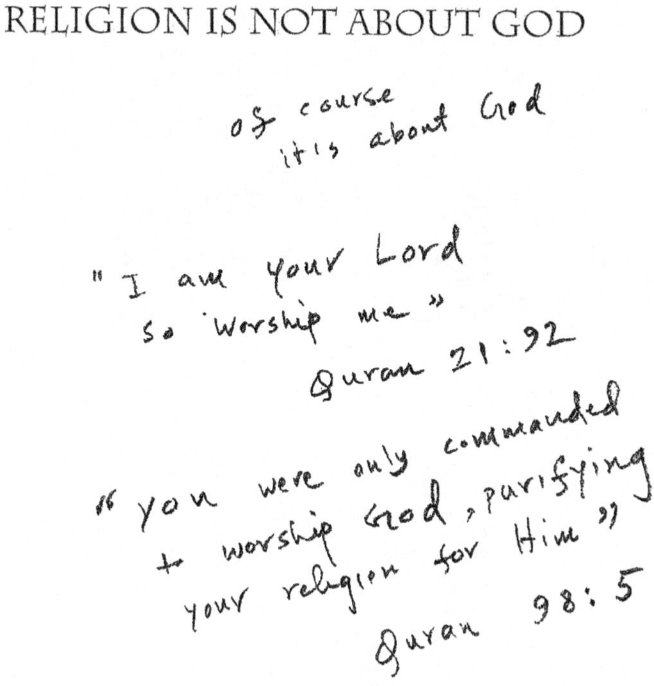

# RELIGION IS NOT ABOUT GOD

of course
it's about God

" I am your Lord
so 'worship me "
Quran 21:92

" you were only commanded
to worship God, purifying
your religion for Him "
Quran 98:5

FIGURE 3.1. Marginalia in Syracuse University library copy of Loyal Rue, *Religion Is Not about God* (New Brunswick, NJ: Rutgers University Press, 2005), i. Credit: Photocopy made by the author of the page from the book as found in Syracuse University Libraries: call number BL53 .R82 2005.

Avril is what Wallace will name, in his essay "Tense Present: Democracy, English, and the Wars Over Usage," a "snoot," "somebody who knows what *dysphemism* means and doesn't mind letting you know it."[4] A snoot is a grammar snob,[5] someone who makes language a justification for a certain exercise of *correctness* in social spaces. A snoot is someone who crosses out typos in books and corrects them. I implicate my own body in this: when I see a mistake on a page, it breaks the flow of my reading, warping my field of vision and pulling my eyes back to it. Especially when the error makes the meaning of a word or sentence truly ambiguous, I feel this strange pulse, this force compelling me to *fix* it, to *correct* it.

That is page 1. It is a page, in a certain sense, about pages, about the fascination that attaches to words, and about the ways that words glitter on the page in different ways for different bodies.

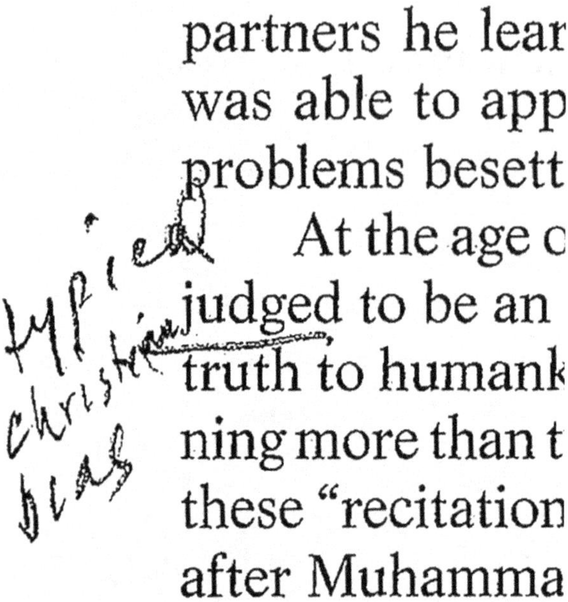

partners he lear

was able to app

problems besett

At the age o

*typical Christian bias* judged to be an

truth to humank

ning more than t

these "recitation

after Muhamma

FIGURE 3.2. Marginalia in Syracuse University library copy of Loyal Rue, *Religion Is Not about God* (New Brunswick, NJ: Rutgers University Press, 2005), 226. Photocopy made by the author of the page from the book as found in Syracuse University Libraries: call number BL53 .R82 2005.

ters worse,

neighbors v

These

*crap* · make perio

solitude. It

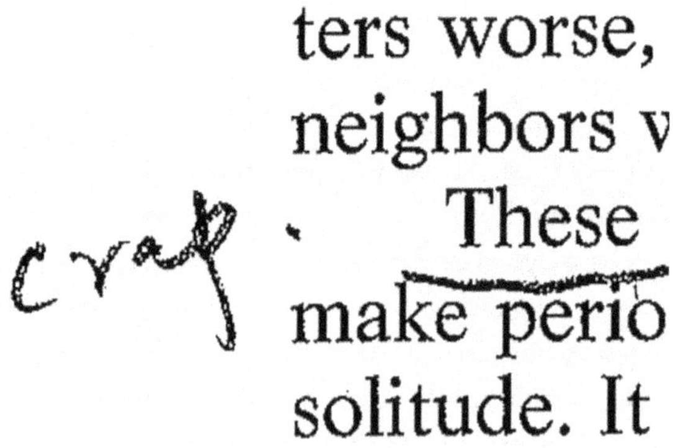

FIGURE 3.3. Marginalia in Syracuse University library copy of Loyal Rue, *Religion Is Not about God* (New Brunswick, NJ: Rutgers University Press, 2005), 228. Photocopy made by the author of the page from the book as found in Syracuse University Libraries: call number BL53 .R82 2005.

PAGE 2

The frontispiece of Loyal Rue's *Religion Is Not About God*, published by Rutgers in 2005.[6] The book has two epigraphs, both from the Qur'an. They read "I am your Lord so worship me" (Surah 21) and "You were only commanded to worship God, purifying your religion for Him" (Surah 98). Also there is a subtitle to the book: "of course it's about God." But although I have not checked, I am almost certain that most copies of this book *do not have* these epigraphs. This is because they are printed on the frontispiece of the Syracuse University library copy of this book *in pencil*, presumably after market.

These amendments to the text go on in the book's chapter on Islam, where the interlocutor takes issue with a number of Professor Rue's claims. What strikes me about these modified pages, scrawled with didactic graffiti, is the sheer *variety* of interventions that the reader makes. Sometimes the reader expands on a point of fact (two sons, four daughters), sometimes the reader corrects a mistake (rightly amending Rue's labeling of Satan as "angel" to "jinn"), and sometimes the reader grows entangled in a snarling polemic, calling Rue's perspective "crap" or "typical Christian bias." Most interesting for our purposes, though, is the *intimacy* between the reader and the pages, an intimacy that seems to decompose the pristinity of the printed words, enfolding them into the reader's *affective* sphere.

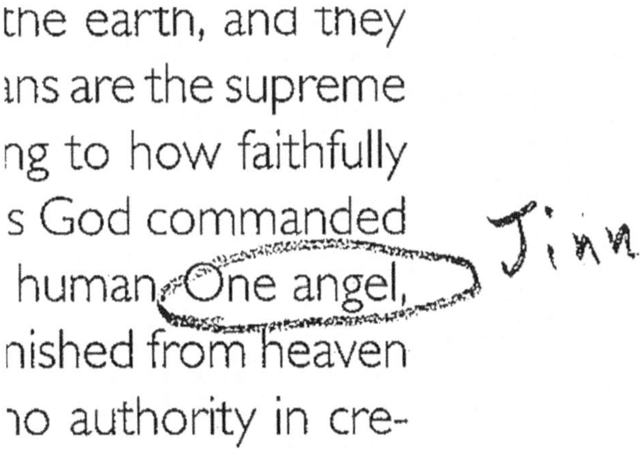
the earth, and they
ıns are the supreme
ng to how faithfully
s God commanded
human. One angel,
nished from heaven
no authority in cre-
Jinn

FIGURE 3.4. Marginalia in Syracuse University library copy of Loyal Rue, *Religion Is Not about God* (New Brunswick, NJ: Rutgers University Press, 2005), 228. Photocopy made by the author of the page from the book as found in Syracuse University Libraries: call number BL53 .R82 2005.

Page 26 of Benjamin Disraeli's published speech on "Church Policy."

> What is the highest nature? Man is the highest nature. But I must say
> that when I compare the interpretation of the highest nature by the most
> advanced, the most fashionable and modish school of modern science,
> with some other teachings with which we are familiar, I am not prepared
> to say that the lecture-room is more scientific than the Church (cheers).
> What is the question now placed before society with a glib assurance the
> most astounding? The question is this—Is man an ape or an angel? (loud
> laughter.) My lord, I am on the side of the angels (laughter and cheering).[7]

These words were spoken by Disraeli in 1863 in the Sheldonian Theatre, at a
meeting of the Oxford Diocesan Society. The lines encapsulate the hardening
reaction, in some quarters, against Darwin's theory of evolution by natural selection, brought to the attention of the public in 1859 with the publication of
*On the Origin of Species*. But what I am interested in is not so much Disraeli's
own view, in which man—for Disraeli is addressing a roomful of men, and
definitely means *men*[8]—is taken as an incorruptible, superlunary being floating
over the earth, the guardian of the sacred texts of civilization. I am interested
in the words in the text that were not actually spoken by Disraeli. These words
record the response of the assembly: "Laughter and cheering."

Why do the members of the Oxford Diocesan Society laugh and cheer when
Disraeli speaks these lines? What does this clamorous, joyful reaction mean for
understanding the relationship between knowledge and feeling? How does it
anticipate future developments in the cross-currents of religion and secularization? And what, pushing this line of inquiry further still, does the *reaction to
the answer* tell us about the question itself? What do we learn about the *kind
of creatures we are*, ape or angel, that we laugh and cheer when we are faced with
what we take to be truth? What does this tell us about *how knowledge feels*? In
this case, religious knowledge?

There is an avenue available, here, for invoking a certain narrative of secularism, a historical drama that casts religion as hysterical—an irrational, emotional
throwback that refuses to leave our threshold even in the Age of Reason. In this
narrative, religious believers are excessively passionate, the cretinous victims of
what arch-atheist Richard Dawkins, in the opening chapter of *The God Delusion* calls the "weakness of the religious mind."[9] In this story, religion is a soft
space, perhaps even a feminine space, that has been insufficiently straightened

out by the instructions of rationality. Contemporary New Atheists, such as Dawkins, frame religion as, essentially, bad science, as emotion masquerading as knowledge. They deploy a binary in which religion is the zone of error, a parcel of feel-good applause lines, and science the space of austere, sovereign reason. In this story, religion *feels*. Science/secularism only *thinks*.

PAGE 4

Volume 15, item 117 of the Huxley papers. Putting the lie to the notion that the New Atheism is particularly new, we must note that this division of the world into the cultures of the rational and the emotional was on display even in Disraeli's time. Another page, another historical scene, also at Oxford, three years before Disraeli gave his speech, another discussion of the legacy of Darwin, now at the Oxford Museum of Natural History. But although the debate concerned Darwinian principles, Darwin himself was not in attendance. The controversy involved, instead, an early champion of Darwin's work, the naturalist Thomas Henry Huxley, and the bishop of Oxford, Samuel Wilberforce. No written record of this debate exists and there is some discrepancy on the particulars,[10] but the most commonly held account reaches its climax with Bishop Wilberforce asking whether we humans claimed ancestry from an ape on our grandmother's or our grandfather's side, to which Huxley responded, as he recounted, in this letter of September 9, 1860: "If then . . . the question is put to me would I rather have a miserable ape for a grandfather or a man highly endowed by nature and possessed of great means of influence and yet who employs those faculties and that influence for the mere purpose of introducing ridicule into a grave scientific discussion—I unhesitatingly affirm my preference for the ape."[11] And how did the assembled attendees at the museum react to Huxley's defense of the new doctrine in the natural sciences? Huxley wrote that, on the conclusion of his remarks, "there was unextinguishable laughter among the people." The "grave scientific discussion" dissolved, at Huxley's prompting, into an uproar, at the climax of which Admiral FitzRoy, who had captained Darwin on his life-altering voyage on the *HMS Beagle* (and who insisted on interpolating his own rogue pages into Darwin's text, offering the rock formations of Patagonia as evidence of the Biblical flood), rose to his feet and marched through the room, holding a Bible aloft and roaring about God's word. And how did Huxley find the whole affair? It was, he wrote, "*great fun.*"[12]

What is interesting, for our purposes, is the way that these parallel scenes, so near in time and space, help illuminate Disraeli's very question: Are we apes, or angels? The traditional secularist narrative commands that religion stay in the fold of the apes: it views religion as animalistic, as driven by passions rather than reasons. Secular science becomes the engine of rationality, the succession of predictable gears that eject us from our obscure, passionate bodies into the ruled pages of the logos. But as Huxley's debate at Oxford shows, *science, too, is wrapped up with emotion*. We are the kind of beings who laugh and cheer not only at religion, but at scientific truths. Far from serenely angelic, the book of reason itself is, somehow, sopping with passion.

PAGE 5

Pages 37 and 38 from Daniel C. Dennett's *Breaking the Spell*, published in 2006.

> We know when eclipses will occur centuries in advance; we can predict the effects on the atmosphere of adjustments in how we generate electricity; we can anticipate in broad outline what will happen as our petroleum reserves dwindle in the next decades. . . . We have avoided economic collapses in recent years because our economic models have shown us impending problems. . . . It has become something of a tradition in recent years for the meteorologists on television to hype an oncoming hurricane or other storm, and then for the public to be underwhelmed by the actual storm. But sober evaluations show that many lives are saved, destruction is minimized.[13]

And he concludes this section saying: "We should extend the same intense scrutiny, for the same *reasons*, to religious phenomena."[14]

Reading this in 2010, I was fascinated by how antiprescient it was, how preposterous this overconfidence in the power of something called reason seemed in the wake of Hurricane Katrina in 2005 or the financial meltdown of 2008. Of course, advances of science have produced means of prediction and control that allow for indispensable, life-saving, and life-enhancing interventions. But to focus only on the web of accomplishments of *reason* without diagramming its limitations, its gaps, its fissures, its fictions, particularly in the wake of such disastrous collapses, tells us something about the way that reason evokes a sometimes unreasonable *passion*. What these pages point to are the way that sometimes our fascination with reason can be *un*reasonable, the way that our *feeling of satisfaction*—what I would even call our pleasure—in the manipulation of words and concepts on the page can lead us to overconfidence in reason's scope—sometimes even to the point of absurdity, as if one addicted.

What strikes me as particularly odd is the way that contemporary atheism, including what Dennett has called the New Atheism, takes on a mantle of Darwinian theory that I think actually cuts against this overconfidence in reason. Darwin was a scientist, but he was a scientist who was interested in complexity and emotion. Darwin tracked our embodied correspondence with animality. He did not see us as determined by clockwork reason.

Although Darwin's interest in emotion has had an impact on a range of contemporary fields, from psychology to zoology, I will focus here on the ways it has been developed in the contemporary project of affect theory. Affect theory helps us understand that pages, words, books, concepts are not just abstract ideas sitting inert in a Cartesian alternate dimension. They are embodied, part of our bodies, ticklish, irritable, erotic, and in every other way affective. Affect theory, I will show, helps us chart the landscape of what Lauren Berlant calls our "sensualized epistemologies"—the way that knowledge feels.[15] By these lights, we will return, at the end of this chapter, to the New Atheism movement, reading its pages again to find them sparking with affects. This chapter makes room for a *different* secularism. To do so, it asks: What are the affective disciplines of secularism—the pastimes of atheism—that give shape to our politics, our practices, and our methods of knowledge production?

## 2: Sensualized Epistemologies: Affect Theory and Cognition

A turn to contemporary affect theory can help us map the bustling nexus of affect and knowledge. I define affect theory very simply, as a methodology that makes affect into the central category in what Michel Foucault calls the "analytics of power,"[16] and I define affect using Lauren Berlant's characterization: it is "sensual matter that is elsewhere to sovereign consciousness but that has historical significance in domains of subjectivity."[17] Affects fuse together to shape the planes of interface between bodies and power. Language, cognition, and *consciousness* are regions of this formation, but far from its totality. According to affect theory, emotional textures must be factored into our accounts of history, politics, culture, relationships, ordinary daily routines, religion, art, and, I would argue, knowledge production itself.

What is affect? Affect theory divides into two branches, which use the term *affect* in different ways. The first is inspired by the French philosopher Gilles Deleuze, and especially Deleuze's reading of the early modern philosopher Benedict Spinoza. This framework understands affect as what I like to think of as the *background noise* of embodiment—out of which the contours of our lives, decisions, and thoughts emerge. Scholars who pursue this branch of affect theory, such as Brian Massumi, Patricia Clough, and Erin Manning, tend to rigorously distinguish affect, singular, from personal emotions, plural.[18]

This branch of affect theory has been criticized by a number of scholars, many focusing on its somewhat hasty use of neuropsychology to back up its reading of Deleuze.[19] I find Sara Ahmed's criticism the most trenchant, however, when she writes that the "analytic distinction between affect [in the singular], and emotion risks cutting emotions off from the *lived experiences* of being and having a body."[20] It is the brush of living bodies against pages that I am interested in here, so I am going to follow a second branch of affect theory, what Ahmed calls "feminist cultural studies of affect." This branch looks at *affects*, in the plural, used interchangeably with *emotions*. This branch comes out of feminist and postcolonial critiques of the Enlightenment model of autonomous human subjects—gendered male—that are defined top down by their rationality. In this undertaking, it links up with queer theory, evolutionary theory, and psychology.

One queer theorist in particular deserves special mention here: this is the late Eve Sedgwick, who in the early 1990s, looking for new resources to explore what she saw as the consummately queer affect of shame, began reading the work of Princeton psychologist Silvan Tomkins. What Sedgwick and her collaborator Adam Frank drew out of Tomkins's 1,300-page magnum opus *Affect Imagery Consciousness* was a new way of encountering bodies within contemporary theory. No longer, Sedgwick and Frank argued, were bodies to be understood exclusively in terms of their production by discursive regimes. The interlacing dynamic between feelings, thoughts, words, habits, images, and sensations—what material feminists and affect theorists would call the *material-semiotic* network—becomes the cradle of subjectivity.[21]

Moreover, they were reluctant to reduce the study of affect itself to an undifferentiated field of background noise. Rather, the turn to affect Sedgwick inaugurated brought the *prediscursive* materiality of bodies, the forces acting on bodies long before and alongside the arrival of *words*, to the fore. "We don't want to minimize," they famously wrote, "the importance, productivity, or even what can be the amazing subtlety of thought that takes this form. But it's still like a scanner or copier that can reproduce any work of art in 256,000 shades of gray. However infinitesimally subtle its discriminations may be, there are *crucial knowledges* it simply cannot transmit unless it is equipped to deal with the coarsely reductive possibility that red is different from yellow is different again from blue."[22] In this *phenomenological* version of affect theory, there are what Sedgwick calls "crucial knowledges" embedded in our prediscursive, emotional realities.[23] I am going to focus in on two facets of affect theory here. First, that affects are epistemic, that they are intertwined with knowledge. And second, that affects are terminal: they serve as ends in themselves.

This first idea, that affects are epistemological, pushes against a Cartesian slant that still afflicts the contemporary intellectual landscape, one that wants to rigidly separate reason from emotion. Tomkins's disciple Donald Nathanson writes that Tomkins saw himself as working in the tradition of Kant, exploring how it was that the human mind "imprinted its shape" on the world through the interlocking dynamics of experience. But whereas, for Kant, these shapes were tantamount to a set of a priori conceptual categories, for Tomkins, the shape was affect. "No matter how reasonable," Nathanson writes, "the engine of analysis is engaged and focused where aimed and sent by emotion; human thought is never dispassionate."[24] In Sara Ahmed's work, this global affectivity becomes the foundation of subjectivity. Every facet of the world makes an *impression* on the bodily horizon. Emotions, for her, are not merely in the world: they make up our *very relation* with the world, *defining* how we experience the world and *redefining* us in the process.[25]

For Ahmed, this *shaping affectivity* extends even into the pages of books, the process by which affectively laden words are *written* on bodies and things—making us into pages etched by the world. She calls this "the emotionality of texts."[26] Carolyn Pedwell expands on this in an essay on the relationship between theory and mood. She points out that readers and texts are always wrapped up in a dynamic swirl of moodiness. Not only do readers always start in a mood that shapes our encounter with texts, "texts themselves exude their 'own' moods, linked to the affective atmospheres of their production and circulation."[27] Texts are technologies for distributing affects, while bodies are landscapes of already existing affect.[28] In conjunction, they form an ensemble of emotional "fluid states produced within wider intellectual and political circuits of feeling."[29] The material-semiotic network of power is rippling with affects.

These insights about the relationship between knowledge production and emotion from affect theory are consistent with perspectives within evolutionary biology. Darwin, too, in the introductory chapter of his *The Expression of the Emotions in Man and Animals*, recognized that affect was the governing force of embodied life, enfolding even our cognitive mechanisms. Seeking to demonstrate that every aspect of human experience can be linked back to animality, he quotes the French psychologist Guillaume Duchenne's thesis in its entirety: "The senses, the imagination, and thought itself—elevated and abstract as we suppose it to be—cannot operate without arousing corresponding feeling."[30] Darwin even noted that thinking often comes with an emotionally indicative facial expression, such as the furrowing of the brow or narrowing of the eyes.[31] For Darwin, a facial expression is always evidence of an underlying emotional process. The fact that thought flickers on our faces demonstrates that cognition is embedded in the same emotional psychic tissue as our other feeling states. The *look* of concentration of a reader buried in a book indicates the organized affective process of cognition.

Affects, then, are everywhere, even sliding off the pages of books. But affect theory offers us a second crucial insight for the understanding of contemporary atheism. Affects are also *terminal*, or, in Sedgwick's vocabulary, "autotelic."[32] Affects are *their own ends*. They are, as I have argued elsewhere, compulsions that need to be understood as driving embodied life without seeking a higher purpose. Their *teloi*, their end points, are embedded inside them. Where the behaviorist notion of "reinforcement," Tomkins wrote, "used motivation as though it were a means to the end of guaranteeing learned behavior . . . this is a craft union's view of the matter, and a particularly American view of it. Everyman is and always has been more interested in just the opposite question— what must he do to guarantee that his life will be exciting and enjoyable?"[33] In other words, where behaviorism sees affect as a *means to an end*, Tomkins insists that affects are the goal, the *endpoint* of *both* thought and behavior.

My favorite example of this is the horror movie: ask anyone and they will tell you that fear is a *bad* emotion. And yet we line up and pay to be scared or saddened or repulsed. As Brian Massumi writes in his analysis of a study showing that viewers preferred the films with the *worst* emotions, "the sadder the better."[34] Pull the frame back and we can see that all movies do this, that film, television, books, perhaps even science itself—are all little apothecaries for the dispensation of affects. The queer critique of affect offered by scholars such as Ann Cvetkovich slices the binary of *good* and *bad* emotions transversally, producing instead a carousel of different emotional patterns that we alternately pursue or are repelled by.[35]

Anthropologist Kathleen Stewart echoes the motif of the everywhereness of affects, suggesting that they are the fibers and tissues of our everyday lives, what she calls, with no dismissive intent, *the ordinary*. "There's pleasure," Stewart writes, "in a clever or funny image, or in being able to see right through things, or in holing up to watch your favorite bad TV show, or spinning classes at the gym, or singing along to loud music in the car. Or the drugs of all kinds."[36] The drugs of all kinds, of course, are David Foster Wallace's territory. It does not take much to see that the 1,079 pages and 388 endnotes of Wallace's *Infinite*

*Jest* are bonded to the theme of addiction. The plot revolves in part around a geopolitical intrigue caused by a short film, *Infinite Jest*, also known as "the Entertainment," which is so fabulously addictive that it paralyzes viewers with pleasure. It is the ultimate *telos*, the ultimate affective enticement, an end in itself, the end of the road for every body.[37]

Wallace's world charts these affective addictions, how we are always embedded in affective relationships with objects. These relationships have varying degrees of elasticity, but they always pull us toward them. Characters become addicted to television, to drugs, to sex, to talking, to violence, to politics, to sports, to AA meetings, and to a long litany of other habits documented on page 202 and continued in endnote 70.

Not to mention, of course, in the case of Avril Incandenza, former chairwoman of the Militant Grammarians of Massachusetts, an addiction to verbal precision. Avril is based on a real person, Wallace's own mother, described in "Tense Present" as "a Comp teacher [who] has written remedial usage books and is a snoot of the most rabid and intractable sort." Affect theory helps us understand this addiction: the promiscuous cross-fertilization between the cognitive, the affective, and the religious. As Wallace writes, "snoots' attitudes about contemporary usage resemble religious/political conservatives' attitudes about contemporary culture," with "a missionary zeal and a near-neural faith in our beliefs' importance."[38] These are more than casual metaphors evoking religion. They indicate how a certain *impulse to correct, to be right*, a fascination with the affects that come off of pages, comes to guide bodies. As I will show in turning to atheism, this is not just an attachment of religion, but of secularism itself.

### 3: New Atheism: The Four Horsemen

By highlighting the inextricability of affect from knowledge production, affect theory, especially in the feminist mode chartered by Ahmed, Cvetkovich, and Sedgwick, offers invaluable resources for responding to Jakobsen and Pellegrini's question: "What does secularism feel like?" This edition of affect theory can help us bring to the surface the different affective agenda on the *color wheel* of secularism. As a case study, I want to turn now to the contemporary New Atheism, which I will explore along two lines: first, the fascination with words on pages as a *passion for reason*, and second, the circulation of what I call the *apocalyptic* affects of fear and scorn. The blending of these affective compulsions produces the palette of the New Atheist formation of the secular.

New Atheism begins in 2003, with the publication of Dennett's *New York Times* op-ed, "The Bright Stuff," calling for solidarity among "brights," those individuals who "don't believe in ghosts or elves or the Easter Bunny—or God."[39] This is followed by a string of best-selling New Atheist books, including Richard Dawkins's *The God Delusion*, Sam Harris's *Letter to a Christian Nation* and *The End of Faith*, and Christopher Hitchens's *God Is Not Great*. In 2007 these four authors gather, in one of the final public offerings of the New Atheist movement, for a roundtable discussion at Dawkins's north Oxford office, which is filmed and made available as a DVD entitled *The Four Horsemen* on Dawkins's website.

There is a basic supposition in the New Atheist rendition of religion—articulated in Dennett's definition of "brights" as "those who don't believe"—that religion is fundamentally cognitive, a question of belief. For Dennett, religion can be slotted squarely into this field of reasons, thoughts, ideas, and concepts. Like any solemn philosopher, his inquiry starts out with a definition: religions, he writes, are "social systems whose participants avow belief in a supernatural agent or agents whose approval is to be sought."[40] Religion is a question of what a thinking subject *thinks* is, or is not, a set of propositions to which the quality of *true* or *false* can be appended. It reflects what Talal Asad has identified as a peculiarly Euromodern, Protestant orientation to religion as "a set of propositions to which believers gave assent, and which could therefore be judged and compared as between different religions and as against natural science."[41] Religion is a data file, a sheaf of pages.

This cognitivist view is one that does not reflect the current state of the conversation in religious studies. Certainly Dennett's account flies in the face of what Manuel Vásquez, in *More Than Belief* (2011),[42] has called the "materialist shift" in contemporary religious studies, which has followed postcolonial critiques of the category of religion to a new attention to the *embodied practices* that make up religion—including the way that words on the page join the material-semiotic network of concepts, bodies, and power. Even Armin W. Geertz, whose research is on the cognitive science of religion, rejects Dennett's version of religion as simply words on the page, disconnected from the lived worlds of religious practitioners. Writing in a rancorous special issue of *Method and Theory in the Study of Religion*—a journal not known for sentimentality toward the category of *religion*—dedicated to *Breaking the Spell* in 2008, Geertz called the book "a catastrophe" and "a disservice to the entire neuroscientific community," a misrepresentation of legitimate work on the cognitive science of religion. His criticism: that Dennett sees the brain as a calculating organ disconnected from the world around it.[43] Dennett himself is aware that this definition is limited. He self-consciously rejects William James's definition of religion, for instance, in that James connected religion to solitary "feelings, acts, and experiences." For Dennett, such solitary, feeling bodies are "*spiritual* people, but not *religious*."[44] But here, too, he lapses into a distinction that most religion scholars would consider to be untenable.[45]

There is a specific intellectual technique at work here: Dennett—and Dawkins, too, with his account of religion as a "God hypothesis"—demarcate the terrain of religion in such a way that it can *only be registered* as a cognitive process, rather than as a hybrid tissue of thoughts, embodied performances, and affects.[46] This is the cognitivist bias in approaching religion: an insistence on viewing religion as a set of propositions that can be assessed as right or wrong, excluding everything that is not on a page.

Darwin would never have made it as a Bright. This is partly because Darwin tends to describe religion in terms of emotion and embodied postures, not in terms of belief.[47] And although he was by no means a Christian, Darwin refused to self-identify as an atheist.[48] This leads us back to a crucial question: Why was Darwin not there in Oxford that day Huxley debated Wilberforce? Why does Darwin not stand and be counted at the academic and cultural battles that are being fought under his standard? Why does he instead allow these skirmishes to be fought by proxies, including Huxley, who became so famous for his pugnacity that he earned the nickname "Darwin's bulldog"?

I would suggest that there is a collective misunderstanding about Darwin in our contemporary age. Although many contemporary atheists hold Darwin up as an emblem of the war against unreason, Darwin was no soldier. Huxley delighted in the intellectual combat that engulfed the English natural sciences academy after the publication of *Origin of Species*—gleefully noting in his review of that book in 1860 that it was considered to be a "decidedly dangerous book" by "old ladies of both sexes," and sneering at the "extinguished theologians [who] lie about the cradle of every science as the strangled snakes beside that of Hercules," effecting his own interweaving of masculinity and rationality.[49] But Darwin shied away from controversy, continuing his experiments at his estate at Down while the intellectual battles raged in the salons and society halls of distant capitals. When Huxley wrote to Darwin describing the Oxford debate, in a letter that has unfortunately been lost, Darwin responded with gratitude, but also admonished his friend, writing "For God's sake remember that your field of labour is original research in the highest and most difficult branches of Natural History."[50] As Darwin's preeminent contemporary biographer Janet Browne writes, "while the *Times* roared against Huxley's support for 'Mr. Darwin's mischievous theory,' the source of the controversy appeared to have strolled into a greenhouse."[51]

But this Darwin who did not go to war was, neither, a bloodless scientific instrument. A contemporary of Darwin's, John Brodie Innes, the vicar in the village of Downe, in his reflections on Darwin shortly after Darwin's death, paints a picture of a scientist whose fascination was not the domination and destruction of his opponents' ideas, but the pursuit of knowledge about the natural world. Innes describes Darwin's relentless policy of truth, recounting an instance

> when a Parish meeting had been held on some disputed point of no great importance, I was surprised by a visit from Mr. Darwin at night. He came to say that, thinking over the debate, though what he had said was quite accurate, he thought I might have drawn an erroneous conclusion, and he would not sleep till he had explained it. I believe that if on any day some certain fact had come to his knowledge which contradicted his most cherished theories, he would have placed the fact on record for publication before he slept.[52]

Although Darwin was fascinated by the push and pull of ideas, he was drawn to the laboratory of their growth and nurturance, not to the scenes (inevitable though he understood them to be) of combat surrounding their propagation.

This depiction of a scientist fretting and exulting in the play of knowledge production is consistent with literary critic George Levine's sketch of Darwin as a body driven by a deep *love* of the natural world and, equally, a *passion for knowledge*, a thirst for scientific discovery. Levine describes reading the *Origin* for the first time through the prism of the expectation of a cold, hard-nosed scientific treatise, and instead finding "a book full of personal warmth, of enormous enthusiasm, of wonder and excitement, all these constrained, of course by a total (and moving) commitment to get the facts right, to build 'one long argument' with precision and fairness and openness."[53] Levine describes Darwin as one who took the exploration of truth in the natural world as an *emotional*— even *religious*—experience. This is why Browne describes Darwin's first project after the publication of *Origin of Species*—the inquiry that would become *Fertilisation of the Orchids*—as affectively saturated: "He had always found the study of plants to be a pleasant combination of relaxation and interest. Whenever he felt over-stretched or ill, a few botanical investigations usually soothed his troubled mind. . . . First and foremost was the feeling that [with the orchids project] he was being introduced to something new and beautiful. Everywhere he spoke of his curiosity about orchids, his appreciation, and how 'very lucky' he was in [encountering what he referred to in an 1861 letter to Asa Gray as] '*beautiful facts*.'"[54] For Darwin, the gleaning of information about the natural world was an encounter with sublime, even healing affects.

In keeping with our starting pages, Darwin's characterization of facts as *beautiful* betrays something about the relationship between affect and emotion, the way that knowledge production is wrapped up with feeling, but also the way that we can become fascinated, even addicted, to a vision of a rationally ordered world. "It is as if," the affective neuroscientist Antonio Damasio writes, "we are possessed by a *passion for reason*, a *drive* that originates in the brain core, permeates other levels of the nervous system, and emerges as either feelings or nonconscious biases to guide decision-making."[55] As Damasio recognizes, brain systems for feeling are *enmeshed* in the machinery of reason. The chessboard of reason, cognition itself, is an affective magnet, pulling us into its waves. Darwin, then, is moved by the passion for reason—the careful study and exploration of the world—but he is not, unlike Dennett, an addict possessed by what Levine diagnoses as the "rage for order."[56] To *reduce* religion to a field where a simplistic set of cognitive heuristics prevail—Is this true or false? Is this right or wrong?—is to succumb to the desire that religion is nothing but words on a page that can be pinned down as a set of rational propositions.

This passion for reason—to varying extremes—is part of how secularism feels. But I think affect theory helps us understand another aspect of the affective profile of the contemporary New Atheism movement, its strong attraction to apocalypticism, the way it compiles emotional registers of fear, anger, and scorn. It is not just that religion is *legible* for the New Atheists, it is also legible as a *mistake*: a mistake made by others. Ahmed writes about how the affects that hover over pages stick to bodies. Language, she writes, "works as a form of power in which emotions align some bodies with others, [sticking] different figures together by the way they move us."[57] Affects help us define an Us against an Other—to be feared or hated. And as Darwin points out, anger is an "exciting emotion," an autotelic affect. "A man when excessively jaded," he muses, "will sometimes invent imaginary offences and put himself into a passion, unconsciously, for the sake of invigorating himself."[58] Chris Hedges writes that New Atheism "reduces the world to a binary formula of good and evil. Religion is a force of darkness. Reason and science are forces of light."[59]

Take one of Dawkins's central screeds in *God Delusion*, in which he invites us to imagine a world without religion, with "no suicide bombers, no 9/11, no 7/7, no Crusades, no witch-hunts, no Gunpowder Plot, no Indian partition, no Israeli/Palestinian wars, no Serb/Croat/Muslim massacres, no persecution of Jews as 'Christ-killers,' no Northern Ireland 'troubles,' no 'honour killings,' no shiny-suited bouffant-haired televangelists fleecing gullible people of their money ('God wants you to give till it hurts')."[60] For Dawkins, religion is tantamount to a violent plague settling on the face of the planet. Nor is this limited to *fundamentalist* religion: "To the vast majority of believers around the world," he insists, "religion all too closely resembles what you hear from the likes of Robertson, Falwell, or Haggard, Osama bin Laden or the Ayatollah Khomeini."[61] As Terry Eagleton writes, there is a willful conflation here of the prominent few with the invisible many.[62] It is as if Dawkins *cannot help himself*—the *temptation* to dismiss the lumpen mass of religious people as zealots who are hazardous to democracy is too incandescent for him to resist.

Robert C. Fuller describes how apocalyptic imagery "mobilizes our physiology and cognition," producing a sort of "tunnel vision" that fixates on safety and survival.[63] Under the pressure of fear, the affectivity intensity of certain pieces of information in the organism's environment shines brightly. As we learned from affect theory, this comes with a certain corollary effect of making the fearsome presence in the environment *desirable*, to the extent that fearful bodies can become *addicted* to their own fearfulness, their own outrage, or their own defiance. Hedges, a former war correspondent, describes this sort of apocalyptic conflict, literally, as a *drug*, one that "instantly reduces the headache and trivia of daily life . . . wiping out unsettling undercurrents of alienation and dislocation."[64] It is also, of course, a motif in *Infinite Jest*. "This is their gift to us," Hal Incandenza realizes, "their *medicine*. Nothing brings you together like a common enemy."[65]

Most troubling, though, is how this gleeful fascination with painting the fearsome Other takes on a decidedly *racial* cast when New Atheists start to talk about Islam. In the *Four Horsemen* video, violent acts are always attached to Islam—the London Underground bombers, Hamas, jihadists. Where Christianity is represented by bumbling pastors to be cheerfully scolded and mocked, Islam is a barbaric tide countenanced with dread. Sam Harris, in particular, asserts a special loathing for Islam, one that goes mainly unchallenged by the other white men sipping drinks beside him in Dawkins's book-lined office. Harris insists, for instance, following Samuel Huntington, that Islam has "bloody borders," and it is only under the historical Islamic caliphates that "Islam can be as totalitarian and happy with itself as possible, and you don't see the inherent conflict and the inherent liability of its creed."[66] Christopher Hitchens adds, "I don't have a difference of opinion with the jihadists. There's nothing to argue with them. There it's a simple matter of I want them to be extirpated. . . . There it's a purely primate response to me, recognizing the need to destroy an enemy to ensure my own survival." At which point Daniel Dennett hastens to clarify that "we find extermination abhorrent."[67] The affective apocalyptic coding of New Atheism becomes most inflamed when it intersects with nonwhite bodies. There emerges a colonialist dichotomy of *white religion* and *brown religion*. White religion is befuddled and foolish, brown religion is terrible and primitive. All religions are equally distasteful, but Islam is first among equals; it is the secret ingredient in the apocalyptic affective gumbo of New Atheism.

This is not to say that the New Atheists are simply *racist*, subscribers to a racist *ideology*. But racist ideological *effects* are an *outcome* of their affective practices, their fascination with apocalypticism, the *affective disciplines* that they cultivate. Sara Ahmed writes that "affect can remake links—it can stick words like 'terrorist' and 'Islam' together *even when arguments are made that seem to unmake those links*."[68] Ideologies, like all formations of *knowledge*, have unexpected dimensions of force coursing beneath and through their pages. Affect theory gives us a window into a new way of understanding ideology, not as a concrete discursive regime, a politics unfolding from a world of colorless pages, but as a contraption of affective practices shaping its knowledge forms. These knowledge-affects *exert their own pull* on bodies. Ideology from this perspective is perhaps best understood as an addiction, an end in itself that makes bodies dance to its tune.

### Conclusion: How Does Knowledge Feel?

Feminist philosopher of religion Kimerer LaMothe has written extensively on how scholarship is guided by our embodied dispositions. She writes:

> The sensory patterns that guide our study can be subtle indeed. A tingle of awe in response to a text or ritual or event impels us to learn more. A wrinkle of confusion troubles us to revisit a mark that remains and ask new questions, gather more data, consult other experts. A surge of excitement pushes us on as pieces of our research start falling into shapes of understanding we have learned to recognize. A sense of ease lets us know that our interpretations are objective or empathetic enough, or will be well received. Such micro-moments in our lived experience, more than our stated principles or procedures, come to define our way of studying religion.[69]

The classical model of rhetoric asks: "How do words on the page use emotions to bring forth an argument?" Affect theory poses the reverse question: "How do the words on the page induce a tissue of ideas, concepts, and beliefs to create emotions?" Pages, reexamined through the multifocal lenses of affect theory, glitter on the page, vibrant with affective power. We see that knowledge—all knowledge—has not only an internal propositional order, but also *a feeling tone*. We can see this, in simplified form, when we look at a book that we have marked up with a highlighter. The maze of color on the page is a low-resolution map of our affective interaction with the printed words, a graphic register of our emotional response to text. We can see it in the way that our pens leap to celebrate or make war in the margins of texts. We can see it in the way that we laugh and cheer when someone recites our knowledge back to us. Our interactions with words on a page are not neutral, as Wallace shows in "Tense Present": we *feel* the fluency of a balanced, well-constructed sentence, just as we feel the binding tension of a glitch in an argument. We feel pulled toward knowledge that organizes the world in ways that mesh with our preexisting affective landscape. As Ahmed suggests, the texts we read become part of our bodies; we feel through them.

The New Atheists call themselves "the Four Horsemen." This self-bestowed title is a dense capsule of the overlapping affects packed into the pages of the New Atheist movement—it is both an apocalyptic fantasy, and a team of white men horsing around with religious texts, mostly oblivious to the way those pages are read, felt, and lived by bodies in the world. But it also points to the undeniable fact, after Darwin, of the animality of our bodies, our proximity to animals, even when we seem to be doing eminently nonanimal things like reading, speaking, or producing transmissible knowledge. Rather than floating angelically over the world of texts, we are lushly connected to it, entangled in it, addicted to it. Its pages are running through our veins. Secularism draws on reason, yes, but reason itself emerges out of the dynamics of sensualized epistemologies. What does secularism feel like? It is a mélange of passions and pleasures, configured differently for different bodies in different times and places.

In keeping with Vásquez's "materialist shift"—the move away from the "suffocating textualism" of earlier approaches which assumed that religions were simply tantamount to worldviews or bundles of beliefs—what affect theory highlights is that neither secularisms nor religions can be flattened down to sets of neutral propositional assertions. In their very practices of knowledge production, they are intimately wrapped up with these sensualized epistemologies. More than just ideas, they are procedures for amplifying the emotional resonance of embodied encounters with things in the world, with other bodies, and with the libraries of murmuring pages that are our worldviews, concepts, and beliefs.

1. Janet R. Jakobsen and Ann Pellegrini, "Introduction: Times Like These," in *Secularisms*, ed. Janet R. Jakobsen and Ann Pellegrini (Durham, NC: Duke University Press, 2008), 1–35, 22.

2. David Foster Wallace, *Infinite Jest* (Boston: Little, Brown, 1996), 288.

3. Wallace, *Infinite Jest*, 1039n234.

4. David Foster Wallace, "Tense Present: Democracy, English, and the Wars over Usage," *Harper's Magazine* (April 2001): 39–58, 41.

5. Either "*Sprachgefühl* Necessitates Our Ongoing Tendance" or "Syntax Nudniks of Our Time." Wallace, "Tense Present," 41n3.

6. Loyal D. Rue, *Religion Is Not about God: How Spiritual Traditions Nurture Our Biological Nature and What to Expect When They Fail* (New Brunswick, NJ: Rutgers University Press), 2005.

7. B. Disraeli, *Church Policy: A Speech Delivered by the Right Hon. B. Disraeli, M.P. at a Meeting of the Oxford Diocesan Society for the Augmentation of Small Living in the Sheldonian Theatre, Oxford, November 25th, 1863* (London: Gilbert and Rivington, 1864), 26.

8. As feminist epistemologists—and especially feminists of color—have pointed out, the preclusion of women from political and intellectual spaces has often been predicated on the notion that women are more emotional than men and therefore cannot be trusted to think clearly about important things. As Lorraine Code writes, "The ideals of rationality and objectivity that have guided and inspired theorists of knowledge throughout the history of western philosophy have been constructed through processes of excluding the attributes and experiences commonly associated with femaleness and underclass social status: emotion, connection, practicality, sensitivity, and idiosyncrasy." Lorraine Code, "Taking Subjectivity into Account," in *Feminist Epistemologies*, ed. Linda Martín Alcoff and Elizabeth Potter (New York: Routledge, 1993), 15–48, 21.

9. Richard Dawkins, *The God Delusion* (New York: Mariner Books, 2006), 18.

10. See Ian Hesketh, *Of Apes and Ancestors: Evolution, Christianity, and the Oxford Debate* (Toronto: University of Toronto Press, 2009), for a breakdown of the clashing reports that have sprung up around the event.

11. *The Huxley Papers*. A Descriptive Catalogue of the Correspondence, Manuscripts and Miscellaneous Papers of the Rt. Hon. Thomas Henry Huxley. Preserved in the Imperial College of Science and Technology, London, by Warren R. Dawson, 15.117.

12. *Huxley Papers*, 15.117. Emphasis added.

13. Daniel C. Dennett, *Breaking the Spell: Religion as a Natural Phenomenon* (New York: Penguin, 2006), 37–38.

14. Dennett, *Breaking the Spell*, 38. Emphasis added.

15. Lauren Berlant, *Cruel Optimism* (Durham, NC: Duke University Press, 2011), 64.

16. Michel Foucault, *The History of Sexuality*, trans. Robert Hurley (New York: Vintage Books, 1990), 1:82.

17. Berlant, *Cruel Optimism*, 53.

18. See, for instance, Brian Massumi, *Parables for the Virtual: Movement, Affect, Sensation* (Durham, NC: Duke University Press, 2002); Brian Massumi, *What Animals Teach Us about Politics* (Durham, NC: Duke University Press, 2014); Patricia Ticineto Clough, introduction to *The Affective Turn: Theorizing the Social*, ed. Patricia Ticineto Clough and Jean Halley (Durham, NC: Duke University Press, 2007), 1–33; Erin Manning, *Relationscapes: Movement, Art, Philosophy* (Cambridge, MA: MIT Press, 2009); Erin Manning, *Always More Than One: Individuation's Dance* (Durham, NC: Duke University Press, 2013).

19. See, for instance, Constantina Papoulias and Felicity Callard, "Biology's Gift: Interrogating the Turn to Affect," *Body and Society* 16, no. 1 (2010): 29–56; and Ruth Leys, "The Turn to Affect: A Critique," *Critical Inquiry* 37, no. 3 (spring 2011): 434–72.

20. Sara Ahmed, "Collective Feelings: Or, the Impressions Left by Others," *Theory, Culture and Society* 21, no. 2 (2004): 25–42, 39n4.

21. Jennifer D. Carlson and Kathleen C. Stewart, "The Legibilities of Mood Work," *New Formations* 82 (2014): 114–33, 116.

22. Eve Kosofsky Sedgwick, *Touching Feeling: Affect, Pedagogy, Performativity* (Durham, NC: Duke University Press, 2003), 114, emphasis mine.

23. See Sara Ahmed, *Queer Phenomenology: Orientations, Objects, Others* (Durham, NC: Duke University Press, 2006), for a discussion of the correlation between the phenomenological tradition in philosophy and the study of affect.

24. Donald L. Nathanson, "Prologue: Affect Imagery Consciousness," in *Positive Aspects*, vol. 1 of *Affect Imagery Consciousness: The Complete Edition*, by Silvan S. Tomkins, ed. Bertram P. Karon (New York: Springer, 2008), xi–xxvi, xii.

25. Sara Ahmed, *The Cultural Politics of Emotion* (New York: Routledge, 2004), 6.

26. Ahmed, *Cultural Politics of Emotion*, 13.

27. Carolyn Pedwell, "Cultural Theory as Mood Work," *New Formations* 82 (2014): 47–63, 48.

28. Donovan O. Schaefer, *Religious Affects: Animality, Evolution, and Power* (Durham, NC: Duke University Press, 2015), 88.

29. Pedwell, "Cultural Theory as Mood Work," 48.

30. In Charles Darwin, *The Expression of the Emotions in Man and Animals* (New York: Penguin, 2009), 336.

31. Darwin, *Expression of the Emotions*, 205.

32. Sedgwick, *Touching Feeling*, 19.

33. Silvan S. Tomkins, *Shame and Its Sisters: A Silvan Tomkins Reader*, ed. Eve Kosofsky Sedgwick and Adam Frank (Durham, NC: Duke University Press, 1995), 51.

34. Massumi, *Parables for the Virtual*, 23.

35. Ann Cvetkovich, *Depression: A Public Feeling* (Durham, NC: Duke University Press, 2012), 2–3.

36. Kathleen Stewart, *Ordinary Affects* (Durham, NC: Duke University Press, 2007), 94–95.

37. Wallace, *Infinite Jest*, 87.

38. Wallace, "Tense Present," 41.

39. Daniel C. Dennett, "The Bright Stuff," *New York Times*, July 12, 2013.

40. Dennett, *Breaking the Spell*, 9.

41. Talal Asad, *Genealogies of Religion: Discipline and Reasons of Power in Christianity and Islam* (Baltimore: Johns Hopkins University Press, 1993), 41.

42. Manuel A. Vásquez, *More Than Belief: A Materialist Theory of Religion* (Oxford: Oxford University Press, 2011).

43. Armin W. Geertz, "How *Not* to Do the Cognitive Science of Religion Today," *Method and Theory in the Study of Religion* 20, no. 1 (2008): 7–21, 9.

44. Dennett, *Breaking the Spell*, 11.

45. See, for instance, the introductory chapter of Courtney Bender, *The New Metaphysicals: Spirituality and the American Religious Imagination* (Chicago: University of Chicago Press, 2010).

46. Vásquez, *More Than Belief*, 185.

47. Darwin, *Expression of the Emotions*, 201–2.

48. Charles Darwin, *The Life and Letters of Charles Darwin*, ed. Francis Darwin (New York: Appleton, 1898), 274.

49. T. H. Huxley, "The Origin of Species," in *Collected Essays* (London: MacMillan, 1896), 2:22–23, 52.

50. Janet Browne, *Charles Darwin: The Power of Place* (New York: Knopf, 2002), 125.

51. Browne, *Power of Place*, 194.

52. John Brodie Innes, "Recollections of J. Brodie Innes," n.d., accessed on August 25, 2015, *Darwin Online*, http://darwin-online.org.uk/content/frameset?pageseq=1&itemID=CUL-DAR112.B85-B92&viewtype=side.

53. George Levine, *Darwin Loves You: Natural Selection and the Reenchantment of the World* (Princeton, NJ: Princeton University Press, 2006), xiii.

54. Browne, *Power of Place*, 166, emphasis mine.

55. Antonio R. Damasio, *Descartes' Error: Emotion, Reason, and the Human Brain* (New York: Putnam, 1994), 245, emphasis mine.

56. Levine, *Darwin Loves You*, 125.

57. Ahmed, *Cultural Politics of Emotion*, 195.

58. Darwin, *Expression of the Emotions*, 81.

59. Chris Hedges, *I Don't Believe in Atheists* (New York: Free Press, 2008), 86.

60. Dawkins, *God Delusion*, 23–24.

61. Dawkins, *God Delusion*, 15.

62. Terry Eagleton, "Lunging, Flailing, Mispunching," review of *The God Delusion*, by Richard Dawkins, *London Review of Books*, October 19, 2006.

63. Robert C. Fuller, *Spirituality in the Flesh: Bodily Sources of Religious Experience* (Oxford: Oxford University Press, 2008), 32.

64. Chris Hedges, *War Is a Force That Gives Us Meaning* (New York: Anchor Books, 2003), 9.

65. Wallace, *Infinite Jest*, 113.

66. Richard Dawkins, Daniel C. Dennett, Sam Harris, and Christopher Hitchens, *The Four Horsemen*, digital video, accessed July 20, 2016, hour 1: http://www.youtube

.com/watch?v=9DKhc1pcDFM and hour 2: http://www.youtube.com/watch?v=TaeJf -Yia3A&feature=relmfu.

67. Dawkins et al., *Four Horsemen*.

68. Sara Ahmed, "Affective Economies," *Social Text* 79, 22 2 (summer 2004): 117–39, 132. Emphasis added.

69. Kimerer LaMothe, "What Bodies Know about Religion and the Study of It," *JAAR* 76, no. 3 (2008): 573–601, 589.

M. GAIL HAMNER

## 4. AFFECT THEORY AS A TOOL FOR EXAMINING RELIGION DOCUMENTARIES

The West moistens everything with meaning, like an authoritarian religion which imposes baptism on entire peoples. —ROLAND BARTHES

*Introduction*

Every fall at Syracuse University, the opening faculty meeting of the College of Arts and Sciences gives space in its agenda for department chairs to read memorials of faculty who have died. Usually this ritual is uneventful, but one September something ruffled the proceedings and that moment has become an instructive frame for my thinking about affect and the space of public culture, that is, the correlations of affect and social form, or how affect moves differently through different genres of space and event (in particular the genre of documentary film that I want to discuss in this essay). As the chair of history read words of recollection and fondness for a dead male colleague, he began to cry. Not only did he cry, but in the face of (or in response to?) the blank, impassive faces before him, this man—a faculty colleague and yet a stranger to me—*apologized* for crying. "I'm sorry," he said, fumbling in his pocket for a tissue to catch the welling tears, "he [the dead man] was a good friend, and I miss him." The gathered faculty remained impassive, the moment flitted by, and the dean efficiently resumed control of the meeting.

It was an odd and squirmy moment. But why? Why should a man crying in remembrance of a dead colleague be disturbing? In the middle of what is at best a banal bureaucratic gathering for the sake of inaugurating the rhythms, obligations, and bickering of yet another academic year, the dean calls for a pause and the entire gathering is given over to funereal oration. And yet it is precisely not a funeral. In fact, most of the folks gathered before the orator not only do not know the remembered dead, they often barely even know the one providing the remembrance. The college bureaucracy carves out space to enact gestures of respect for the recently dead, but only as that space folds smoothly into the impatient boredom of regular business. It is quite simply *inappropriate* to show grief. To put this a bit differently: though the annual ritual of remembrance *gives space* for grief to well up, and though the ritual *requires* department chairs to compose their words in a genre socially programmed to elicit and consolidate grief, the public culture of faculty that frames the space and reception of these *in memoria* actually requires grief to remain hidden, or at least carefully tucked into reasonable administrative competence.[1]

This contradiction between emotional display and the propriety of faculty public culture is itself worthy of reflection, but I am even more intrigued by how the upsetting of propriety generates affective flows that are tangible but barely acknowledged. Grief, here, is both galvanized and doused—both shown and shut down—and through this dynamic interplay of emotion and expectation, the tingling of sensory disturbance patters and skitters among the gathered faculty like mice running through the walls. This kind of transversal, transpersonal affective movement has not historically formed part of social analysis, and so it has been the purview of recent affect theory to call attention to it. In this case, an attention to affect theory can analyze how flows of affect work paraconsciously to strengthen or challenge the norms, rules, and expectations of public cultures. Put more strongly, this essay argues that the tools of affect theory usefully demonstrate how social controversies or group infighting are negotiated not only through rational parsing and appraisal of shared norms and rules but more importantly through the corporeal and intimate affects that, through their circulation, physically constitute, disrupt, and repair the boundaries of a public culture. In fact, it is through what Ben Anderson discusses as "the multiple ways in which affective life is made through processes of mediation" that scholars of culture can better understand the tacitly lived, implicit boundaries that shape and cushion group belonging.[2]

What do I intend by referencing attention to affect as opposed to emotion or feeling? I called the moment of my colleague's improper grief *squirmy* because I was disturbed by the faculty's general lack of overt compassion and support for him, but *squirmy* is not really an emotion. Indeed, the gathered faculty could not share a specific emotional term for the felt disturbance in the room, because what we shared was not a psychological *state* so much as an interpersonal matrix of expectation *in the very moment of its unexpected disruption.* I felt unsettled; that is, I experienced a physiological, sensory response (a *squirm*) that had social and physical form but no proper emotional term because the reality of that response was not *mine alone* but was situational (structural) and transmitted among the gathered faculty (embodied and relational). Clearly, not everyone felt the *same* unsettling. Or rather, not everyone would *conceptualize* the unsettling *affect* in the same way. What I considered to be a lack of compassion others might have considered to be a breach of professionalism, a waste of time, or an understandable but unfortunate awkwardness. These conceptual responses, too, attached diffusely to vague affective orientations that skipped through the structure of that small public culture as indices of unexpected disturbance.[3]

This opening scenario exemplifies the central ideas that will shape my analysis of affects in recent documentaries about religion, including the normative form of public cultures, the display of emotions, and the responsive pattering of affect among the gathered.[4] In setting out to assess the usefulness of *affect theory* as a tool for analyzing recent (twenty-first-century) U.S. documentary films about religion, I will attend to three things in particular. First, the public function of these films, that is, how the genre of documentary refers to and names a particular public culture. Second, how the religion documentaries pit rules of emotional propriety (i.e., the assumed structure of the public culture) against displays of emotional impropriety (i.e., surprising or intentional resistance to this assumed structure) and then correlate these rules and their disturbance with specific religious dispositions and practices. And third, how an enacted disturbance of the operative norms of emotional display generates circuits of affect that both retroactively elucidate those operative norms and also potentially work toward altering the very form of the public culture imaged by the film, especially when the film maintains a looseness between truth and meaning (more on this later). In other words, the power of affect studies for analyzing religion documentaries is its twofold ability to elucidate (1) how some subjects feel, desire, and live on a kind of Möbius strip, positioned at once inside and outside the expected norms of their religious community, and also (2) how those expected norms are themselves affectively constituted. This double mediation then enables audience members themselves to affectively receive and weigh in on the drawing and regulation of those norms.[5]

Delimiting these foci helps me narrow my inquiry from assessing the usefulness of affect theory *in general* to assessing the usefulness of *some* affect theory.

Like theories of religion and theories of documentary film, affect theory is a capacious and multivalent term that canopies an unwieldy set of intellectual genealogies, including approaches that are ontological, sociological, phenomenological, neurological, literary, and political economic. In this essay I attempt to clarify one useful rubric for analyzing affect in film and other media within this wide range of *conversational puddles* about affect and emotion. These puddles do overlap in parts, but the extensive variety of current appeal to affect simply cannot be braided into one, coherent intellectual lineage. Nevertheless, I do think the Foucauldian question of genealogy—transposed in this case to something like: Why is it that we now take affect for granted as a truth of our social being?—is centrally connected to the intensification of visual and social media within neoliberalism (or globalization, late liberalism, metamodernism— whichever term your bailiwick prefers). As Eugenie Brinkema notes in the opening of her recent book, "Is there any remaining doubt that we are now fully within the Episteme of Affect?"[6] It is now commonly accepted by culture and media scholars that we live in worlds that drench us with words and images, the function of which is less to provide comprehensive information or rational argumentation than to provide vehicles for the generation, transmission, and redeployment of affect. Media and communication scholars such as Patricia Ticineto Clough, Alex Galloway, Adi Kuntsman, Zizi Papacharissi, Steven Shaviro, and Tiziana Terranova have made this argument with more expertise than I can marshal, so I will not belabor it. I take as given what Terranova called in 2004 "the interplay of affects and meanings in the constitution of the common,"[7] what Shaviro called in 2010 the "emergence of a different media regime" that organizes media as "machines for generating affect,"[8] what Kuntsman termed in 2012 the "affective fabrics of digital cultures,"[9] and what Papacharissi describes in 2015 as a contemporary structure of feeling that "prompts us to interpret situations by *feeling* like those directly experiencing them, even though, in most cases, we are not able to *think* like them."[10] Within these assumptions about affect and media, I set out to ask about the place of documentary film, and in particular U.S. documentary films about religion.[11]

## What Does Documentary Document?

At first blush, the notion of a documentary film seems both obvious and simple. A documentary film captures reality, right? It *documents* a slice of contemporary society in the etymological sense of providing an official proof, example, or record. The Lumière brothers, for example, famously recorded a train coming into a station, and subsequently produced a film showing a factory at quitting time, when all the workers came flooding out of the factory gates. Today we need only press a button on our cell phones to capture evidence of our travels, of a crime, of the aftermath of a terrorist attack. We also can upload this evidence almost immediately to Facebook, Twitter, email, a *New York Times* comment page, Imgur, and the like. This *mechanical reproduction* of images that Walter Benjamin theorized with such delicacy and sophistication has changed the human experience of art, mutated the human experience of reality, expanded our horizons of expectations about the world beyond our own locality, and fundamentally restructured human consciousness and human sociality. What we see through publicly mediated images is what we *take to be true* about the world: just compare the conversational buzz about Michael Brown or Tamir Rice with that about Eric Garner. We *saw* Garner's murder. It was captured for us on video and it was played (at least in New York) on the nightly news.[12]

Over the century of film history, however, and while the production and uses of documentary film have varied greatly, documentary film has always fallen into the category of art more than journalism. A recent author of an introductory guide to documentary film echoes many textbook commentators when she underscores the obvious but often elided fact that "documentaries are *about* real life; they are not real life."[13] The genre's so-called father, John Grierson, famously defined documentary in 1932 as "the creative treatment of actuality,"[14] and an attempt to "fashion" a slice of reality for the sake of developing a "clearly defined social purpose."[15] As another example, Trinh T. Minh-ha's influential essay "Documentary Is/Not a Name" opens with the salvo, "There is no such thing as *documentary* . . . despite the very visible existence of a documentary tradition."[16] Trinh admits that her assertion is as basic as the fact that a name is not the thing named, but her essay adds two important layers to this insight that enable me to address and summarize the conundrums of documentary filmmaking, and to move fairly quickly to affect.

First, Trinh notes the difference between truth and meaning: "What is put forth [in film] as truth is often no more than *a* meaning." This small distinction, like the small correction—"not reality but *about* reality"—evokes all the distance and slippage of representation, the entire history of changing techniques of images production, techniques that have developed step by step, of course, with changing cultural signs for what counts as *real*. Because all images are framed, angled, and dated, they also necessarily embed a particular perspective, if not an intentionally crafted bias. But while filmmakers now take for granted the uncontrollable blurring between perspective and bias, between an image and its range of meanings, Trinh remains concerned that documentary is received and accepted as a tight imbrication of meaning and truth. She advocates resisting the expectations of the documentary genre by filming in ways that maintain the "interval" between truth and meaning, "without which meaning would be fixed and truth congealed."[17]

Second, Trinh is concerned that the tendency to tightly bind truth and meaning in documentary film constructs an epistemology that supports and rewards imperial, racial, and/or monetary power. In the case of religion documentaries we should add doctrinal, legal, and social power to the list of concerns. Trinh is especially troubled by the legacies of colonialism whose political dominations are sustained by the epistemologies of naming. When we capture reality, she asserts, we capture and name the bodies and lives of so-called *Others*. We bind them to truth and to the meanings that we place on them or pull from them. I would add that we also bind ourselves, because soldering truth to meaning allows very little pliability in our sense of who we are as individuals or as members of the public culture evoked by the documentary. As a corrective, Trinh's own documentary filmmaking keeps open a floating interval between truth and meaning, and thus encourages the play of difference and the ethical dance of learning what matters to the Other (and what the Other matters to).[18]

Trinh notes specific cinematic practices that have built up the genre expectations of documentary film and thus led to the easy binding of truth to meaning. After Foucault, we can think of these cinematic practices as "technologies of reality."[19] These techniques generate the familiar *style* of documentary film and produce a kind of *documentary effect* in viewers; they form the language or conventions of documentary film that are so familiar they have become invisible as aesthetic techniques.[20] Technologies of reality include "personal testimony" where members of the film's public culture are shot in close-up or full shot as they tell their stories; "expert testimony" where religious, academic, political or other salient subcultural authorities are filmed (also typically in close-up) as they provide needed commentary; a "plain folks" technique where the camera seems spontaneously or randomly to solicit opinions from everyday people; and the "bandwagon" technique where the montage of perspective and image "conveys the message that 'everybody is doing it, why not you?'"[21] Again, it is important to hold in mind that documentaries deploy these technologies of reality in order to craft a specific argument or social purpose. Trinh's concern is less the fact that the stakes of this social purpose will always supersede the film (just as reality itself exceeds its capture on film) than whether the techniques are hegemonic in their epistemology, that is, whether the linkage they conscript between truth and meaning has any room to breathe.

Twenty-first-century documentaries about religion align well with the general accountings of Grierson and Trinh.[22] These films rely on technologies of reality to forward specific arguments (meanings) about what contemporary religion is and does (truth), especially as they intervene in contemporary debates about the *appropriate* position of religion vis-à-vis society and politics. They are, quite simply, driven by plot and purpose. In this essay, I am focused on a particular subset of documentary films made for movie screens (not television), produced or filmed in the United States, and primarily engaged with U.S. Christian and Jewish congregations.[23] Religion documentaries such as *Trembling Before G-d* (Dubowski, 2001), *Searching for the Wrong-Eyed Jesus* (Douglas, 2003), *Jesus Camp* (2006), *For the Bible Tells Me So* (2007), *8: The Mormon Proposition* (2010), and *God Loves Uganda* (Williams, 2013),[24] all tell stories for quite specific and contemporary reasons. They function as art more than as journalism, and they are clear weapons in the arsenal of the current culture wars. I want to examine the *effectiveness* of these documentaries in light of the relative intensity of their binding of truth and meaning.[25] What is the relation of the overt rhetoric (their truth-claims) of these films to the *formal* elements that structure the protagonists' emotional displays and the audience's affective responses?

## Religion, Film Form, Affect

The subtle force of film form has been a persistent interest of mine. Most research on religion and film attends to narrative and dialogue, that is, to specific assertions made about God, redemption, or grace, or to character names and relationships that seem to mirror or evoke familiar religious figures. The most powerfully *religious* films, however, are so through the film's structural/formal properties. In earlier work I have examined how directors convey religiosity through cinematic devices that evoke religion nostalgically, that is, as something beautiful and true that belongs to a past and better time. In these films, notions such as religious transcendence or religious truth are signaled less through the purported existence of a god, paradise, or nirvana beyond human space and time and more through sets of ethico-religious ideals and practices that stand as forgotten but still available tools for shaping human dispositions and relationships, and hence might still be used to transform the lived textures of our world. Films like the Coens' *The Man Who Wasn't There* (2001) or Kiarostami's *Taste of Cherry* (1997), in my view, finagle nostalgia into an elusive but active desire for personal and social transformation precisely through careful manipulation of film form—for example, through devices such as flashbacks, high-contrast lighting, and oblique camera angles.[26] Another, more broadly applicable technique for examining religion through a film's structure is to attend to oblique religious sensibilities or dispositions that are evoked through less cognitively received filmic elements, such as patterns and interruptions of music, color, and mise-en-scène. By this approach a film's use of and references to religion are not perceived so much as *felt* through film form.[27]

ENTER IN THE POWER OF AFFECT THEORY

At its most general level, affect is the capacity to influence and be influenced, to stir and be stirred, to move or be moved. Over the last decade, however, the proliferation of affect theory has introduced a confused complexity to the term's meanings and use. Under the banner of affect theory, scholars have attended to a range of key words—including impulse, emotion, affect, and feeling—and conflated their psychological and physiological distinctions. Affect theorists have also relied on a range of methodologies that have variously emphasized the epistemological, ontological, psychological, phenomenological, sociological, or political stakes of analysis. Some affect theory situates itself in the psychoanalytical approaches of Freud and Lacan, which dwell on affects that consolidate pathologies and sustain human unhappiness. Eve Sedgwick's work, on the other hand, relies on the psychologies of Melanie Klein and Sylvan Tomkins to reconsider affect as potentially reparative, that is, as something that can generate healing and creative engagements with the world. Raymond Williams stands at the crossroads of a sociological approach to affect with his notion of "structure of feeling," a tool, he says, for studying emergent cultural formations that are *felt* as personal and idiosyncratic even when they are actually social and structural. The Public Feelings Group—including Lauren Berlant, Ann Cvetkovich, José Muñoz, and Kathleen Stewart—conjoins Williams's Marxian analysis of feeling with queer theory and gender politics to analyze what Stewart has called "the private life of public culture." Theirs is a wide-ranging approach that looks at socially striated affects not as emergent but rather as what generates social obstacles and makes oppression so difficult to overcome. Gilles Deleuze's corpus, and Deleuzian scholars such as Brian Massumi and John Protevi, weave a counterlineage of philosophers from Spinoza and Nietzsche to Bergson to examine affect ontologically, as the flowing intensities that create the ground for both rational subjectivity and social cohesion.

Sara Ahmed threads a sociological and ontological approach in her notion of "affective economies" that track the circulation of affect as it "sticks" to certain bodies and concepts, and through this stickiness forms and deforms the boundaries of social groups and social (dis)approbation. Michael Hardt and the Italian autonomist economists Maurizio Lazzarato and Christian Marazzi, as well as a number of social anthropologists, analyze what they term "affective labor" as a conscious and pressured dimension of social relation, either what is expected and rewarded in the workforce (Hardt, Lazzarato) or what the state apparatus galvanizes in un- or underemployed persons as a means of generating volunteer labor to weave the social safety net for civil society (Muehlebach). Finally, politically bent literary theorists such as Fredric Jameson, Sianne Ngai, and Eugenie Brinkema attend to affect through close readings of texts; affect is here a category of literary form, aesthetics, or style that both captures and circulates political possibilities.[28]

For my work in film, I find it most useful to examine affects as denominating physiological and social matrices by which humans (and other mammals) feel and respond to their worlds and situations. This feeling and response are related to but not determined by language and memory, a relationship I denominate with the neologism *affecognitive*. I do distinguish *affects* from emotions, even though both necessarily occur together at any but the most abstract ontological levels. Where emotions have cognitive tags and psychological profiles and are possessed by conscious subjects, affects are paralinguistic, pheromonal, and mammalian sensorial impulses that have intensity and duration but no clear name. I am drawn to Raymond Williams's *structure of feeling* because it enables me to consider affects as both emergent and elusive but also as related to clear social and embodied structures. In film theory, this conversational puddle of affect theory connects with the 1990s development of phenomenological film analysis (Vivian Sobchak, Laura Marks, Jennifer Barker) in terms of its focus on bodies and sensations, the way the screen generates haptic visuality and flows of feeling.[29] Another important intellectual source for my theorizing affect comes from Deleuze's use of Peirce in his *Cinema* books, precisely because Peirce embeds affect (Firstness) and reaction (Secondness) within thought or habit (Thirdness), and because the strength or *intensity* of affect, for Deleuze, lies in its flows or circulations.[30]

Film plunges viewers into worlds drenched with noise, color, landscape, and texture; worlds riven by the sound effects of doors, feet, punches, and sex, and attentive to the grain and emotional resonance of voice. This sensuousness of film actually can *heighten* the challenge of representing emotion, because it is so easy to fall into cliché: for example, the slow tracking-in on a character's face to convey the dawning of awareness, or the sudden rainstorm to signal sadness and loss. These clichés posit emotion as internal mood: my anger is mine; her sadness is hers. I am interested in emotional displays of documentaries, but I am even more interested in the circuits of *affects* generated by the disturbance of emotion. Affect is like the atmosphere or musical *key* of a film, and affect is also its dynamics, its aesthetic *volume* and stylistics of execution. As I suggested above, cinematographers set this kind of circulating affective structure in motion, by manipulating aspects of a film that viewers attend to less consciously, such as color, pacing, framing, and music.

In seeking religion in film, I typically look for how film form works on viewers affectively, using camera movements, pacing, montage, mise-en-scène, music, sound effects, and color to render the cultural connotations of religion as *felt* and not *thought*. Let me pause here, however, and restate the question I brought to religion in documentary films. If documentaries are not representations of reality (truth) but instead arguments internal to high-stakes cultural debates (meanings), how helpful and how sufficient for understanding the religious and cultural work of these films are the *felt* dimensions of these arguments as articulated by affect theory? Certain forms of affect theory are highly useful for analyzing what I take to be religious dimensions of narrative cinema, precisely because the *avoidance* of discursive statement creates a really useful channel for presenting and sensing contemporary connotations of religion that remain paratactic to ideological divides that are familiarly sustained by identity, doctrine, and geopolitical stereotype. Attending to affects works well in these analyses because, instead of *talking* religion, it *shows* the hopes and potentialities that are carried through cultural connotations of religion. But if identity, doctrine, and geopolitics are precisely what are central to the social purpose of contemporary religion documentaries, how useful are the nondiscursive dimensions of affect theory for this wordy kind of film and these articulated kinds of religious expressions?

My answer returns me to the Syracuse faculty meeting I discussed at the outset. The affects work in documentary film as transpersonal movements that pass between screen and audience, and among audience members, and yet they also are decidedly *structured* through discursive, relational, and cinematic forms. Like Williams's "structure of feeling," affects lean on dominant cultural formations (such as the propriety of faculty meetings, or the set expectations of religious ways of life) and yet they flow as physiological and transpersonal responses to both the *performance* and the *disturbance* of that dominant formation. Affect theory thus tracks the satisfying stability, and also the limits, cracks, or failures of the norms or rules of public culture. Affect theory locates the physico-social site of enactments of and challenges to acceptable or legal behavior at their most incipient and most fragile stage. It attends to the purr and hum of community ritual in the very enactment of community life, norm, and boundary, and also marks the tension and alertness of disturbance. This function of affects to confirm but also potentially to remap community boundaries makes its analysis in religion documentaries both useful and interesting.

## The Films

Sandi Dubowski's film *Trembling Before G-d* (2001) engages the public culture of Orthodox Judaism, and highlights its constitutive teachings about sexuality and family life. The film opens with a title citing Leviticus 20:13, a scriptural passage that prohibits intimate relations between men. A second title presents words from the Sulchan Aruch Even HaEzer 20:2 prohibiting intimate contact between women. The words from both texts float on a black screen and are accompanied by an earthy klezmer music that pervades this film. Because the conversations about Jewish homosexuality are framed in terms of *halachah* and ritual expectation, these two opening passages seem to stand in for halachah generally and for the specific religious public culture woven through its steady enactment. The proper structure of this religious culture is both reinforced and disturbed by the emotional displays of self-denominated gay, lesbian, and queer Jews who, importantly, wish to remain devout even though they are no longer accepted by the Orthodox community. During the *personal testimony* interviews of David, Mark, Michelle, and Israel—as well as through the partially obscured interviews with Leah and Malkah—the camera cuts from the expected close-ups to record the subjects' Jewish dress, prayer, and Shabbos preparations (bread, wine, prayer), and often pans away from the speakers to show Jewish art and ritual objects as insistent markers of their commitment to devout life. Viewers hear Jewish persons declare their desire for a vital relation with HaShem, even though their sexual expression renders them suspect within Orthodox Judaism. The filmic repetition of this discrepancy functions to highlight an important boundary that separates Orthodoxy from *secular culture*, namely, the refusal of *gay rights*.[31] On the inside of this boundary, the ritual devotions to family and community establish and sustain affective intimacy; on the outside, the contested availability of *gay rights* breaks and resists these affective bonds and these practices of religious propriety. The film generates affective circuits in the space given to the expression of this loss: gays and lesbians are dead to their community but also are viscerally repulsed by a gay rights movement devoid of Jewish commitments to purity, devotion, prayer, and study. They stand on the boundary of the community . . . and cry.[32]

Is there is a way for the Orthodox community to acknowledge Orthodox Jews who express gay and lesbian sexuality *as* Orthodox? This is the essential question of the film and it inevitably leads to tears. Consider the subject, David. He is shown walking his dog in the rain just at the moment when his narrative describes his coming out to his father. The camera cuts back to a large, oblique image of his face as he wipes a threatening tear from his eye. Later in the film David tears up when he returns to the rabbi who counseled him, twenty years earlier, to eat figs and pray the psalms as a way to recover from being homosexual. And later still, David cries as he reads out loud a prayer to HaShem that he wrote for his visit to the Wailing Wall. His voice cracks and his face contorts as he asks God to accept him as he is and allow him happiness. At the Wailing Wall itself, the soundtrack of David's heaving sobs overwhelm the visual image of the bustling crowd.

Like the grief shown by the Syracuse University history chair, David's emotional despair highlights the normative boundaries of Orthodoxy by disturbing them. Also like the chair's welling tears, witnesses register David's tears as equally understandable and inappropriate. As the man, Israel, declaims with exasperation, "Whoever heard of a queer Orthodox Jew? No one. It's not possible!" Another subject, Michelle, echoes this impossibility: "There is no such thing as an Orthodox lesbian, so you just keep it bottled up inside." To cry over something impossible is just as inappropriate as to cry about a death at a faculty meeting. The very impropriety of emotional display sets off affective circuits in the film and between the screen and the audience, highlighting and questioning the impossible situation. Just as the history chair was surrounded by the academic authority and expectations of the dean and gathered faculty, so the film surrounds David's emotional displays with the *expert testimony* of rabbinic and psychological authorities. The former speak with utmost respect and love for men like David, and yet continue to uphold the boundary of impossibility: an Orthodox man simply cannot be actively homosexual and also in good standing with the Jewish community. The psychological authorities do not speak directly to the emotions poured out by the film's subjects, but instead throw that emotion into relief against the textured fabric of Jewish life, Jewish scripture, and Jewish understandings about who God is and what God requires. In short, the film does a lovely job of presenting a sense of the religious public culture of Orthodox Judaism, its discursive and relational norms, and its disturbance by homosexuality. The community seems clearly to say, *abide by halachah or relinquish your sense of belonging*, and the disturbing emotional displays come from those who refuse that stark choice. In the interviews with Mark, David, and Devorah, despair arises from their inability to inhabit Orthodoxy properly and their equal inability to leave Orthodoxy. This despair, plus the associated psychological commentary on the damage done to gays and lesbians by their impossible situation, added to the rabbis' reaffirmations of Orthodox life together generate skittering affective circuits between persons in the film, and between the film and its viewers.

Despite its clear attempt to shift the contours of Orthodox culture, *Trembling Before G-d* keeps an interval between truth and meaning, just as Trinh would advise. The film draws on two techniques that corral the pattering of affective response and allow it either to dissipate back into hegemonic meaning or ripple into new understandings about sexuality and Jewishness. These techniques are the silhouette sequences and the cutaway shots of sunsets, sky, animals, grass, and long-shot urban landscapes. The silhouettes literally frame the film, appearing at its very beginning, middle, and end. For Jewish viewers, the images and music of these sequences register viscerally as the aesthesis of Jewish family life. They wordlessly convey the life that is loved and desired by the gay and lesbian subjects of the film, and yet is foreclosed to them. The silhouettes are the affective equivalent of the film's constellated arguments from the rabbis, the gay and lesbian Orthodox, and the psychologists. The cutaway shots are each about twenty seconds long. The first—a series of five shots of sunsets—occurs directly after the film's first narrative segment that records a queue of very loud and bitter Hasidic Jews protesting against homosexuality. The second—a sequence moving from a tree branch to a long shot of a hillside, then burros, dewy grass, and sky—occurs after the psychotherapist, Schlomo Ashkinazy, tells an anecdote in which an Orthodox rabbi comes to call sexual behavior a *taive*, an inclination that has no rhyme or reason to it. Other sequences function similarly; in each case, the slide from intense narrative argument and emotional display to these visual and narrative breaks allows the unsettling affective disturbance to dissipate or to resolve into some kind of felt position toward the arguments in the film. The emotional displays and psychological advocacy index the boundaries of Orthodox public culture in the moment of their disturbance. The film's personal and expert testimonies pit halachah against sexual orientation and rapidly build up layer upon layer of affects in viewers like the piling up of thunderclouds. Though the reasons attached to this affective disturbance can differ quite a bit from viewer to viewer, the cuts to silhouettes or environment allow time to feel and then to think the *interval* between truth and meaning.

I want to contrast this use of pauses in *Trembling Before G-d* with another documentary film about religion and homosexuality, Daniel Karslake's production *For the Bible Tells Me So* (2007). This film also centers on the felt contradiction between doctrine and lived practice, this time between fundamentalist Christian doctrine (in particular the virulent homophobia of Jim Dobson's Focus on the Family) and the social reality of practicing Christians who are gay and lesbian. But where *Trembling Before G-d* attunes itself to the *problem* of devout homosexuals, *For the Bible* foregrounds the *error* of conservative Christians. The difference is made clear from the outset. The film begins in the middle of a press conference held in 1977 with Christian conservative Anita Bryant, shot in close-up and already in midsentence about her ministry's mission.[33] The context of her words is unclear, but it hardly matters because Bryant's message is not the point of showing this scene. While viewers are still absorbing her words and trying to find some kind of narrative anchor, a hand reaches in from screen left and shoves a cream-topped pie into her face. The shock is intense. Film viewers jump back a bit, and we hear gasps and guttural response from the unseen pressroom audience. Someone calls for security, but the man sitting next to Anita Bryant tells the crowd to let the pie-thrower stay. The television camera swings to the perpetrator, now standing with his hands up, and we hear the man sitting next to Bryant ask her to pray for him, "right now." And so Bryant prays, bending her pie-globbed face toward her lap. She says, "Father, we want to thank you for the opportunity of coming to Des Moines, and Father I want to ask that you forgive him and . . . [the man with her interjects, 'that we love him'] that we love him, and that we're praying for him to be delivered from his deviant lifestyle, Father." The shock of the assault and the ludicrous sight of a woman praying with pie all over her face make it difficult to focus on her words. As Bryant gets to the phrase, "to be delivered," her voice cracks and she begins to cry. Whether she is crying for the pie-thrower's redemption, or out of shame that her face is covered in pie, or in frustration that she's been assaulted, or on account of all the so-called deviants in the United States is unclear and, again, beside the point. The film opens this way in order to perform the affective and emotional divide between proponents of gay rights and proponents of Christian conservatism, a felt divide that *forms and deforms* rational commitments as much as it is formed and deformed by them.

*Trembling Before G-d* opens with a sensorial presentation of the warm, communal aesthetic of Jewish family life, but *For the Bible* opens with assault, the physical assault on Bryant and the sensory assault on film viewers. From the outset, *For the Bible* maps U.S. Christian debate about homosexuality along the lines of a dire choice: either embrace gay rights or eradicate deviance. The choice is carried forward *as violent* by the film's rhetorical attention to hate language, gay bashing, murder, spiritual violence, LGBQ teen homelessness, and the suicide of one subject's daughter. But the choice also is carried forward as violent by the film's suffocating form—and I write this as someone who agrees with the film's arguments. *Trembling Before G-d* possesses an equally strong desire to persuade its viewers, but it orchestrates its argument along the lines of problem, question, and compassion, not choice. *Trembling* works to build up the affective disturbance of contradiction and then gives space for that build up to be dissipated or settled. *For the Bible*, on the other hand, slams viewers into the breach of choice and forces them to opt for one corner or the other. It bundles technologies of reality such as the *personal testimony* of Christian families with gay and lesbian children (including Dick Gephardt's family), *expert testimony* from ministers, rabbis, and religion scholars, decontextualized and unexplained interviews with *plain folks* on the street, and an almost endless flood of home-movie clips, photographs, and newsreel footage. It even includes a segment from Aaron Sorkin's TV show *The West Wing*. The film revs up affective circuits to fever pitch and never lets up.

Ironically, although the film is structured to pressure choice, and although it nearly suffocates the viewer with data saturation, its discursive argument is that Christian conservatives should *loosen* interpretation, particularly scriptural interpretation but also strongly held cultural stereotypes. To address scripture, the film gathers expert testimony from rapidly sequenced biblical scholars and theologians from various institutional locations, including, of course, Gene Robinson (the first gay bishop of the Episcopal Church), Desmond Tutu (Anglican archbishop and Nobel Peace Prize laureate), and members of religious activist groups such as SoulForce and Faith in America. Cultural stereotypes about homosexuality are addressed through an animated short embedded inside the film. Taking aim at the conservative denunciation of homosexuality as a *lifestyle choice*, the cartoon uses a deep male voice to present "what science tells us" about "genes, hormones, and birth order," concluding (of course) that homosexuality *in fact* is not a choice at all. Though the film lambasts dogmatic beliefs and literal interpretation, it also wages battle precisely around the truth of sex, the truth of science, and the truth of scripture. *For the Bible* elicits and concentrates powerful affects but it channels them into a Manichaean aesthetic that allows only one side to breathe: truth and meaning belong to gay rights, untruth and unmeaning belong to homophobia. Again, I agree with embracing LGBTIQ rights and doing whatever is possible to lessen social and physical violence against LGBTIQ persons. But I find it telling that American Christianity does not—perhaps cannot—present the question as a problematic that feels out the textured contours of community boundaries instead of dictating truth and righteousness.

*For the Bible* has only two cutaways. These are short sequences tracking a car and then a truck driving along a road, which function as establishing shots for the interviews with the parents of Gene Robinson and Jake Reitan, respectively. The rest of the film, however, remains airtight, performing a collapse of truth and meaning that corroborates Trinh's critique of hegemonic documentaries and shows the suffocating effect of not giving the audience space to reflect. Like Roland Barthes's words in the epigraph to this essay, the meaning of *For the Bible* is imposed like the authoritarian doctrines it opposes, and it saturates the audience with its truth. As a result, the film's overt messages about love and hermeneutical looseness are inverted (if not undone completely) by the film's *structural* commitment to coercion and dogmatic truth. As I ponder the formal difference between this film and *Trembling Before G-d*, I find most telling and important the unexplained *plain folks* testimony. Throughout *For the Bible*, the camera shows short snippets of commentary from people who are apparently caught by an interviewer on the street as they are walking to work or grabbing a latte. The interviewer's questions are not filmed, and the *plain folks* are not allowed very many sentences before the film segues to the next personal or expert testimony. The function of these rapid and scattershot *plain folks* interviews seems to me to register something like American national common sense. It conveys the general sensibility of a poll.

Rethinking the film through this lens of national common sense, it seems to me that the real public culture assumed and addressed by the film is less Christianity writ large and more the specific and battling Christianities within U.S. public culture. Put even more precisely, the public culture addressed by *For the Bible* is that constituted by the assumed *equation* of the American population as (still) a (primarily) Christian population.[34] Such a national address explains why the proprieties and improprieties of emotional displays are so tightly imbricated in the film with cable news media and human rights discourse. The linkage of truth and meaning here has everything to do with the imagined community of American democracy as also a *Christian* community and Christian democracy, and the film's affective circuits match the necessary intensity of any battle for cultural hegemony.

Let me briefly build on this discussion with reference to Heidi Ewing and Rachel Grady's production *Jesus Camp* (2006) and Andrew Douglas's production *Searching for the Wrong-Eyed Jesus* (2003). Like *For the Bible*, *Jesus Camp* also assumes that the public culture of Christianity intercalates with the dominant public culture of the United States. The film circulates liberal anxiety over the growing power of U.S. Christian evangelicalism, in particular how the stridency of evangelical beliefs shapes children's lives in ways that become imminently political as they grow up. Much of the film contains personal testimony from children, especially Levi, Rachael, and Tory, all of whom attend Rev. Becky Fischer's "Kids on Fire" summer camp for evangelical children in Devil's Lake, North Dakota. If their words can sometimes be dismissed as thin echoes of their parents' beliefs, their emotion-laden and passionate participation in camp programming is not only convincing but also affectively disturbing to the expected boundaries of our putatively secular public culture.

I find particularly noteworthy the manner in which the film's competing messages about liberal and conservative Christianity are mediated through technology and images of American consumerism. Radio programs are played in cars and over the soundtrack, accompanied by images of telephone wires, radio station technology, video screens, microphones, and audiovisual tech rooms, interspersed with pans across sweeping images of strip malls, fast-food restaurants, and the cityscape of Washington, D.C. Through these images of civilizational success, the liberal Christian voice (represented primarily by Mike Papantonio, radio host of *Ring of Fire*) does not underscore the *error* of evangelicals but rather their *extremism*. Pointing especially to the evangelical tendency to *indoctrinate* children and their desire to *erode* the separation of church and state, Papantonio's critiques caress the norms of public culture and feel out the hegemonic boundary between polity and belief that is as structured by public education and the presumptions of secularity as the Orthodox halachah is structured by heteronormativity. Papantonio challenges Becky Fischer's targeting of children, attempts to draw a solid line between indoctrination and education, and claims that the separation of church and state is what "has made this country special, [it is] what's always set this country apart."

*Jesus Camp* thus foregrounds the emotional intensity of Pentecostal evangelical Christians as a disturbance to the boundary and propriety of democratic polity. Two scenes display this boundary between democracy and theocracy particularly well. The first is when the director films Ted Haggart's megachurch in Colorado Springs. In an interview with the minister after the service, shot Ozu-like at eye level as Haggart sits on the stage of his megachurch, the minister notes that, "there's a new mega-church like this every two days in America. It's got enough growth to essentially sway every election. If the evangelicals vote, they determine the election." Throwing his arms wide and smiling he adds, "It's a fabulous life!" Here is another affective punch, since Haggart's glee seems to reside in evangelicals using the mechanics of democracy to reward their own *extremism*. The glee bounces against secular assumptions laid into democratic liberalism and shows them up as disturbingly contingent. Toward the end of the film another scene shows Mike Papantonio in his radio studio, now himself interviewing Becky Fischer who has been so central to this film. He concedes that it is every family's right to raise their children in their own religious beliefs, but he urges against letting those beliefs *bleed over* into politics. That threatens democracy, he says, but Becky responds: "You know democracy is the greatest political system on earth, but that's just it—it's only *on earth*, and it's ultimately designed to destroy itself because we have to give everyone equal freedom and ultimately that's going to destroy us." As we hear Fischer's voice the camera pans around the mostly shadowed radio studio and cuts in to blinking red lights and oblique, partial images of Papantonio's face (lips, eyes, occluded profile). These two scenes—added to the extraordinary emotional displays shown by the children—generate affective circuits in liberal viewers that skip through the structure of American *secular* (Christian) culture as indices of unexpected disturbance. *Wake up*, Papantonio urges liberal Christians. On the inside of this bounded public culture is something like the felt sanity of the democratic process; on the outside is something like the felt threat of an emotion-driven frenzy—the radical Christian hordes at the gate who fight against climate change, abortion rights, evolutionary theory, and public schools, and who want to catapult their religious values to federal law.

Interestingly, for all its circulating liberal anxiety, *Jesus Camp* actually creates the space to call into question the obviousness of liberal secularism. The film contains a number of image-laden but voiceless sequences that, to me, constellate the impulses of ideology, consumerism, and political enfranchisement in ways that tie the workings of democracy clearly to issues of access and purchasing power, rather than the clean line between church and state. Though it remains strongly weighted toward the viewpoints of liberal Christianity, the film shatters the solid equations between education and rationality, and between education and the separation of church and state. Using the disturbance of evangelical emotional impropriety (*extremism*), the film shows that *all* values are nested in theories that are taught to very young children, and thus the separation of church and state wobbles into something like an ideal conceit instead of a confirmed *specialness*. Civil society, this film demonstrates, is made up of citizens with beliefs of all kinds, and they take these beliefs to the voting booth. The camp for Jesus is not the only American Christian camp, and not always the most extreme.

Andrew Douglas's film turns the *Jesus Camp* relationship of education, consumerism, and political enfranchisement inside out. Built around the premise that southern folk music evokes a world that barely exists anywhere anymore, the film is an odd, self-indulgent work that walks the knife's edge of romanticizing poverty. It also remains wrongly, even shockingly, focused on the poor white population of the U.S. South though everyone knows that to say anything legitimately about the South requires attunement to race relations, particularly the legacy of slavery and the more recent economic slavery of Latino/a undocumented workers. That said, to watch this film alongside *Jesus Camp* is to understand what Lauren Berlant calls the "juxtapolitical"; *Searching* feels out the contours of a subculture where people cannot yet articulate their beliefs as political projects because they barely hold their lives together enough to think of themselves as citizens. If *Jesus Camp* wields emotional impropriety as a threat to democratic polity, *Searching* catapults us to the wastelands beyond the border of American public culture, where the emotional displays of religion are not threaded into moral righteousness but rather into sheer survival strategies. Lacking something like halachah, the Christians in *Searching* are not a bounded community like the Orthodox Jews in *Trembling*, nor are they as articulate and motivated as the Christians in *For the Bible* or *Jesus Camp*. Indeed, the randomness and isolation of suffering generates tremors of affect in viewers in response to the ugliness of poverty, the suffocating normativity of small towns, and the haunting beauty of religious expressions that attempt to salve and stave off human desperation. Viewed in isolation, *Searching* can enable these affective disturbances around poverty and religion to remain self-enclosed and whitewashed (literally!) in a compelling aesthetics of music and hope. Only when viewed alongside these other twenty-first-century religion documentaries do its indices of unexpected disturbance open into a political-economic critique of a hegemonic public culture that is complacent with rural Christian poverty. Quite the opposite of *For the Bible*, I find that *Searching* presents a relation between truth and meaning that is *too* open, wallowing in the sentiment of meaning and skirting the hard truths of the rural South.

*Conclusion*

I have tried to show the usefulness of affect as a tool for analyzing recent religion documentaries. I have shown how these films denominate a particular public culture and articulate emotional propriety and impropriety through specific religious dispositions and practices. The emotional proprieties are familiar and known, and so they do not generate affective circuits, but emotional improprieties are indices of unexpected disturbance *through* the matrix of expected public norm and, as such, these improprieties do generate affective patter in the audience. Affect is at once personal and social, textual and physiological. Affect registers an embodied, sensory reaction to the world. I have focused on moments when affect is unsettling or disturbing because

I am interested in the liminality of these moments, the possibility that they can throw into relief the contours of expectation and also the desire to change those contours. Using Trinh T. Minh-ha's 1990 essay on documentary film, I have discussed the successfulness of religion documentaries in light of her call to keep open the interval between truth and meaning in film, and I have tried to show how this interval needs to be present in film form or structure, and not only in the intentions of plot.

NOTES

*Epigraph:* Roland Barthes, *Empire of Signs* (New York: Hill and Wang, 1982), 70.

1. The anecdote draws to mind the oft-cited opening of Teresa Brennan's *Transmission of Affect* (Ithaca, NY: Cornell University Press, 2004), 1: "Is there anyone who has not, at least once, walked into a room and 'felt the atmosphere'?" The difference between Brennan's account and that of this essay is Brennan's focus on psychoanalysis and physiology as general categories of explication for the transmission of affect, whereas I am less interested in the corporeal explanation than the sociocultural effects of this transmission in forming, disturbing, and/or reinforcing group boundaries.

2. See Ben Anderson, *Encountering Affect: Capacities, Apparatuses, Conditions* (Burlington, VT: Ashgate, 2014), 13. Please note that I use the term *boundary* to indicate a lived and practical sensibility of what is accepted or expected, and what is not. This boundary is not visible and not solid, which is precisely why affect studies opens important avenues for examining its constitution and mutability.

3. In her work on depression and on lesbian archives, Ann Cvetkovich draws attention to the fact that disturbances that seem *out of place* are actually most important for clarifying and archiving that public culture as something real and worthy of attention. See *Depression: A Public Feeling* (Durham, NC: Duke University Press, 2012), and *An Archive of Feelings: Trauma, Sexuality, and Lesbian Public Cultures* (Durham, NC: Duke University Press, 2003). As I wish to stress in this chapter, affects are constitutive of public culture by bodily indexing the contours of expectation and surprise. These contours then form *practically* the lived boundaries of that public culture. As indicated in note 2, these boundaries are fluid and negotiated *precisely through affective response* more than through rational—that is, linguistic, conscious, and intentional—argumentation.

4. By *pattering of affect* I simply indicate the ways that a felt intensity—or bodily acknowledgment of unexpected disturbance circulates paraconsciously and transversally through a gathered crowd or audience. (This patter might also occur through a bodily acknowledgment of an expected accomplishment, such as when a pastor states, "I pronounce you married," or when a dean states, "*This* is the graduated class of 2016!")

5. Ben Anderson defines his use of *mediation* as "a general term for relational processes of relation that involve translation and change and from which affects as bodily capacities emerge as temporary stabilisations [*sic*]." See *Encountering Affect*, 13.

6. Eugenie Brinkema, *The Forms of the Affect* (Durham, NC: Duke University Press, 2014), xi. With her typical brilliance and wit, Brinkema both legitimates and questions

the turn to affect by denominating this turn as an *episteme*. The latter term is deployed by Foucault in his archaeological works (e.g., *Birth of the Clinic* and *The Order of Things*) and then dropped precisely for connoting too much of a sense of knowledge (epistemology, *savoir*) and of *conscious* discursive structures, instead of (also) emphasizing bodily and institutional habits of power and practice that are more implicit.

7. Tiziana Terranova, *Network Culture: Politics for the Information Age* (Ann Arbor, MI: Pluto Press, 2004), 1.

8. Steven Shaviro, *Post Cinematic Affect* (Hants, UK: o-Books, John Hunt, 2010), 2–3.

9. Adi Kuntsman and A. Karatzogianni, eds., *Digital Cultures and the Politics of Emotion: Feelings, Affect, and Technological Change* (New York: Palgrave, 2012), 1.

10. Zizi Papacharissi, *Affective Publics: Sentiment, Technology, and Politics* (New York: Oxford University Press, 2014), 4.

11. I cite the media theorists in this paragraph since, like film scholars, their research is focused on particular technologies of media culture (e.g., film, television, radio, social media, and weblogs) and they aptly examine the ways that the quantitatively increasing density of global media has led to a qualitative shift in what counts as *public*, how publics are formed, and the central role of affects in the rapid formations and equally rapid dissolutions of global public cultures. See also Patricia Ticineto Clough and Jean Halley, eds., *The Affective Turn: Theorizing the Social* (Durham, NC: Duke University Press, 2007); Alex Galloway, *The Interface Effect* (New York: Polity Press, 2012).

12. The essays collected in Brian Winston, ed., *The Documentary Film Book* (London: Palgrave Macmillan on behalf of the British Film Institute, 2013), demonstrate a general agreement that documentary films' "claim on the real" (Winston, cited by John Corner, 111) lies as much in audience reception as in the processes of production and editing. In Carl Platinga's contribution to this collection, "I'll Believe It When I Trust the Source: Documentary Images and Visual Evidence," the philosopher writes about the video of the Rodney King beating in 1992, deftly showing how photographic evidence, which is assumed to be *obvious* because it is indexical (that is, technologically produced without human, subjective bias), also necessarily remains silent on the intentionality of the police officers and about events that occurred before and after the video. The *obvious* culpability of the officers was thus successfully challenged by the defense attorneys. See *Documentary Film Book*, 42–45.

13. Patricia Aufderheide, *Documentary: A Very Short Introduction* (Oxford: Oxford University Press, 2007), 2.

14. John Grierson, "The First Principles of Documentary," in *Grierson on Documentary*, ed. Forsythe Hardy (1932; repr. London: Faber and Faber, 1966), 147.

15. Cf. John Izod and Richard Kilborn, "The Documentary," in *The Oxford Guide to Film Studies*, ed. John Hill and Pamela Church Gibson (Oxford: Oxford University Press, 1998), 426–27.

16. Trinh T. Minh-ha, "Documentary Is/Not a Name," *October* 52 (spring 1990): 76.

17. Trinh, "Documentary Is/Not a Name," 76.

18. Bill Nichols provides a correlative and equally influential description of documentary as that which "operates in the crease between life as lived and life as narrativized." Cited in Brian Winston, introduction to *The Documentary Film Book*, 4.

19. Following Foucault's delineation of technologies of production, technologies of sign systems, technologies of power, and technologies of self. See his essay, "Technologies of the Self," in *Technologies of the Self: A Seminar with Michel Foucault*, ed. Luther H. Martin, Huck Gutman, and Patrick H. Hutton (Amherst: University of Massachusetts Press, 1988), 18.

20. Trinh, "Documentary Is/Not a Name," 88. These technologies become visible through parody in the series *Documentary Now!* that began in August 2015; accessed May 3, 2016, http://www.ifc.com/shows/documentary-now.

21. Trinh, "Documentary Is/Not a Name," 88. Trinh is quoting from John Mercer, *An Introduction to Cinematography* (Champaign, IL: Stipes, 1968), 159.

22. Documentary film form has developed beyond the poststructuralist dispositions of Trinh, but primarily by absorbing their lessons and grounding new film techniques in them. For instance, in our digital age we know that photographs can lie, but this simply puts more pressure on audience reception. Winston ends his introduction to *The Documentary Film Book* by shifting from Grierson's "creative treatment of actuality" to "the narrativised [*sic*] recorded aspects of witnessed observation received as being a story about the world" (24). Winston provides a helpful chart gridding the differences in preproduction aesthetics, production, and postproduction documentary techniques and decisions from the 1920s through the 1990s (25).

23. As of this writing, no film has been made *about* American Muslims. The closest three are Zarqa Nawaz's Canadian production *Me and the Mosque* (2005); Parvez Shama's production *Jihad for Love* (2007), which looks at global repression of Muslim homosexuals but does not focus on its U.S. instantiations; and the PBS television production *Muhammad: Legacy of a Prophet* (2011), which does include *snippets* of American Muslim families but is primarily a historical biopic of the Prophet.

24. I decided not to include films like *The God Who Wasn't There* (2005) and *Fall from Grace* (2007), which are independent productions instead of feature-length films made with the film festival circuit in mind. I also did not include films like *Baraka* and *Samsara* that do not specifically chronicle an aspect of religion. And I did not include films like *Happiness* or *Reconvergence* that insert religious voices into a larger set of questions about the meaning of human existence. These exclusions are relatively arbitrary.

25. This essay focuses on contrasting *Trembling Before G-d* with *For the Bible Tells Me So*, and ends with a few general comments about *Jesus Camp* and *Searching for the Wrong-Eyed Jesus*.

26. M. Gail Hamner, *Imaging Religion in Film: The Politics of Nostalgia* (New York: Palgrave, 2011).

27. M. Gail Hamner, "Religion and Film: A Pedagogical Rubric," *JAAR* 81, no. 4 (2013): 1139–50.

28. Here is an abbreviated list of salient texts on affect: Sara Ahmed, *The Cultural Politics of Emotion* (New York: Routledge, 2004), and *The Promise of Happiness* (Durham, NC: Duke University Press, 2010); Lauren Berlant, *Intimacy* (Chicago: University of Chicago Press, 2000), *Compassion: The Culture and Politics of an Emotion* (New York: Routledge, 2004), and *Cruel Optimism* (Durham, NC: Duke University Press, 2011); Teresa Brennan, *The Transmission of Affect* (Ithaca, NY: Cornell University Press, 2004); Eug-

enie Brinkema, *The Forms of the Affects* (Durham, NC: Duke University Press, 2014); Ann Cvetkovich, *An Archive of Feelings: Trauma, Sexuality, and Lesbian Public Cultures* (Durham, NC: Duke University Press, 2003), and *Depression: A Public Feeling* (Durham, NC: Duke University Press, 2012); André Green, *The Fabric of Affect in the Psychoanalytic Discourse*, trans. Alan Sheridan (New York: Routledge, 1999); Melissa Gregg and Gregory J. Seigworth, *The Affect Theory Reader* (Durham, NC: Duke University Press, 2010); Michael Hardt, "Affective Labor," *boundary 2* 26, no. 2 (1999): 89–100; Fredric Jameson, *The Antinomies of Realism* (Durham, NC: Duke University Press, 2015); Maurizio Lazzarato, *The Making of the Indebted Man* (Los Angeles: Semiotext(e), 2012); Erin Manning, *Politics of Touch: Sense, Movement, Sovereignty* (Durham, NC: Duke University Press, 2006); Christian Marazzi, *Capital and Affects: The Politics of the Language Economy* (Los Angeles: Semiotext(e), 2011); Brian Massumi, *Parables for the Virtual: Movement, Affect, Sensation* (Durham, NC: Duke University Press, 2002); Andrea Muehlebach, *The Moral Neoliberal: Welfare and Citizenship in Italy* (Chicago: University of Chicago Press, 2012); José Esteban Muñoz, *Disidentifications: Queers of Color and the Performance of Politics* (Minneapolis: University of Minnesota Press, 1999), and *Cruising Utopia: The Then and There of Queer Futurity* (New York: New York University Press, 2009); Sianne Ngai, *Ugly Feelings* (Cambridge, MA: Harvard University Press, 2007), and *Our Aesthetic Categories: Zany, Cute, Interesting* (Cambridge, MA: Harvard University Press, 2015); Elizabeth Povinelli, *The Empire of Love: Toward a Theory of Intimacy, Genealogy, and Carnality* (Durham, NC: Duke University Press, 2006), and *Economies of Abandonment: Social Belonging and Endurance in Late Liberalism* (Durham, NC: Duke University Press, 2011); John Protevi, *Political Affect: Connecting the Social and the Somatic* (Minneapolis: University of Minnesota Press, 2009); Jasbir Puar, *Terrorist Assemblages: Homonationalism in Queer Times* (Durham, NC: Duke University Press, 2007); Eve Kosofsky Sedgwick, *Touching Feeling: Affect, Pedagogy, Performativity* (Durham, NC: Duke University Press, 2003); Eve Kosofsky Sedgwick and Adam Frank, eds., *Shame and Its Sisters: A Silvan Tomkins Reader* (Durham, NC: Duke University Press, 1995); Kathleen Stewart, *Ordinary Affects* (Durham, NC: Duke University Press, 2007); and Raymond Williams, *Marxism and Literature* (Oxford: Oxford University Press, 1977).

29. See Jennifer Barker, *The Tactile Eye: Touch and the Cinematic Experience* (Los Angeles: University of California Press, 2009); Laura U. Marks, *The Skin of the Film: Intercultural Cinema, Embodiment, and the Senses* (Durham, NC: Duke University Press, 2000), and *Touch: Sensuous Theory and Multisensory Media* (Durham, NC: Duke University Press, 2002); and Vivian Sobchak, *Carnal Thoughts: Embodiment and Moving Image Culture* (Los Angeles: University of California Press, 2004).

30. Gilles Deleuze, *Cinema 1: The Movement Image*, trans. Hugh Tomlinson and Barbara Habberjam (Minneapolis: University of Minnesota Press, 1986), and *Cinema 2: The Time Image*, trans. Hugh Tomlinson and Robert Galeta (Minneapolis: University of Minnesota Press, 1989).

31. The woman named Devorah in the film uses this stark division to describe the situation, but it seems to apply to the film as a whole, a supposition borne out by the segment's position as the midpoint of the film, and the only in-film *personal testimony* that is intercut with the silhouette sequences.

32. Standing on the boundary is literalized in a scene with Michele when she takes the camera crew for a walk through her childhood Hasidic neighborhood where she is no longer welcome. Standing on the threshold of an amusement park, hugging a chain-link fence, she giggles and says she would love to walk through it if she knew there was an exit on the other side. Well, she is *not* sure, but she walks into the park anyhow. She stands literally on the boundary, and feels her exclusion acutely.

33. "Anita Bryant Gets a Pie in the Face! Prays Thrower Is Delivered from Deviant Lifestyle," accessed May 27, 2016, https://www.youtube.com/watch?v=H-A2Q181WTY.

34. The Pew Foundation's "Religious Landscape" survey, published in fall 2015, still pegs Christian-affiliation at 71 percent of the overall U.S. population, despite the fact that the percentage of "nones" (those citizens with no particular religious affiliation) grew faster than any other demographic group between 2009 and 2014. "Complete Report," 11, accessed June 2, 2016, http://www.pewforum.org/2015/11/03/u-s-public-becoming -less-religious/#trends-in-religious-beliefs-and-practices.

## 5. DARK DEVOTION

*Religious Emotion in Shakta and Shi'ah Traditions*

Religious emotion can be studied in many ways. Much modern analysis has emphasized knowledge at a distance, with emotion interpreted as a brain function or a cognitive event, a biochemical process or a philosophical category. This chapter will use a different approach. Instead, it will emphasize what our informants understand religious emotion to be, and the ways they experience it. This approach is more anthropological and phenomenological, giving value to the understandings of other cultures, and examining their concepts of body, mind, and spirit.

Why is this important? Other cultures construct the self and its feelings and ideas in very different ways from Western psychologists and philosophers do, and their understandings have an impact on their values and behavior. Religious emotion is often the basis of cultural identity, and this identity shapes the ideals for which cultures strive. Understanding cultural ideals may shed light on behavior that seems otherwise irrational. As an example from this chapter, we cannot understand the acceptance of child martyrs, and the value of misery and death to its practitioners, until we understand the meaning of suffering in Shi'ah Islam. In this tradition, suffering brings kinship with the family of Muhammad—it is a good and valuable thing. Mourning together brings deep unity to people. Even world destruction follows the pain and passion of Muhammad's family, and the tortured deaths of Hassan and Hussein have influenced a politics that not only tolerates but also exalts and glorifies suffering. Having people torture themselves until they bleed in the streets is considered a holy act. If we wish to avoid war with Iran today, diplomatic claims that peace will make people richer and more self-satisfied are not compelling arguments against this background.

Privileging the analyst's position does not give us insight into the norms and values of other cultures. Stripping away culture makes us lose much that is important in the study of religion. An important aspect of the study of religious emotion is gaining insight into the feelings of believers and ritual specialists, in order to communicate with them. Imposing our own theories does not necessarily help in such communication, and may well alienate us from the groups that we wish to understand.

I chose the two traditions for this chapter because they both value the darker religious emotions: pain, grief, anger, and fear. These are emotions that are not emphasized in the study of religious emotion today. In the West, we have some studies of these areas, especially in the fields of psychology and philosophy. However, such passions are often relegated to madmen and fanatics, and not taken seriously—mainstream religions and theologies prefer to emphasize love, service, and adaptation to mainstream values. But the darker emotions inform our attitudes toward both life and death, and neglecting them does not mean that they disappear. Indeed, they often return to disturb people in less-direct ways.

Older Western religious traditions would emphasize the role of pain in certain situations—in dealing with anti-Semitism in Judaism, with the people of Israel taking on humanity's suffering, and Christ's agony on the cross as atonement for sin, with imitation of that suffering through ascetic practices. However, ascetic practices have fallen out of favor in the modern world, seen as a psychological problem rather than a religious act. But having a popular culture that emphasizes the Jamesian notion of "healthy-mindedness" has not gotten rid of the "sick souls." A variety of recent studies have shown high levels of use of mood-altering drugs in the modern USA, with one in five people using such drugs "almost every day."[1] Feelings of depression and unhappiness are widespread, and avoiding the darker emotions does not necessarily mean that people will be happier. Both of the cultures in this chapter incorporate suffering as important parts of life, bringing meaning to pain, and an understanding of death that is positive.

Non-Western cultures incorporate emotions in a variety of ways. While in most forms of Western philosophy, we assume one body and perhaps at most one soul, in the schools of Indian philosophy, there are many bodies and multiple souls. In the Hinduism of West Bengal, religious emotion is not a brain event but rather a substance out of which souls are developed and shaped. Emotion is like a liquid, which can be boiled and condensed and sculpted. It flows in through the ear, when the person hears religious music and poetry, and goes down into the heart, where it can be used for strength and creativity, and to create inner bodies. The *bhava* or state of religious emotion can be affected by the *rasa* or emotional essence that the person encounters, and the religious tradition that gives detailed meditations to control such transformations of religious emotion is called devotional Hinduism or *bhakti*.[2] In Vaisnava bhakti, death is overcome by building immortal bodies. In Shakti bhakti, it is the goddess who guides the soul, and death can be welcomed rather than feared.

In the Shi'ah religion of Iran, emotion can also be understood through the metaphor of substance. It is the bond that unites families and tribes, an identifier that stretches over time and space, linking together the past and present. It organizes kinship, a major factor in how the person lives in the world, and determines clan ties and family obligations. Sorrow is a more powerful bond and unifier than joy. The concept of the *shahid* or martyr includes such religious emotions as loyalty, dedication, and passion for the good, and is associated with nobility and kingship. The person overcome by emotion, the *mast*, is a madman, but still full of the love of God and kindness to others. Mediocre emotion is for average people, but passionate emotion is for great ones.

In the religious context, both for Shakta bhaktas in West Bengal and Shi'ah Muslims in Iran, the passions bring salvation. Religious emotion is central to both traditions—especially the dark emotions. These must be studied through literature and the arts—simply looking at current events is insufficient. These ideas have been building over the centuries, and many of the most relevant documents have not been translated into English. This chapter will include some of the important sources for these concepts.


*Religious Emotion in Bengali Shaktism*

In the Bengali bhakti tradition, religious passion is the path to the divine. Religious emotion in India is most well known through the Vaishnava tradition, which has a long literature in which religious states are analyzed. In Bengali or Gaudiya Vaishnavism, the worshipper may love the god Krishna through basic religious roles or *bhavas*, as a lover, a friend, an infant, a master, and an aspect of self. These roles have been elaborated in the Bengali Vaishnava literature, with a great focus on *shringara rasa* or erotic passion.

However, the major emotions and roles of the Bengali Shakta tradition have never been organized in this way. In the poetry to Kali, we see a different selection of religious emotions emphasized: there is wonder at her compassion, terror at her power, sorrow at the state of the worshipper's life, and anger and complaint at human suffering, as well as love of her beauty. A goddess who is universal can express and appreciate all these emotions. The primary role of the worshipper is beloved child, rather than erotic lover, and the roles of both admirer and victim are also found. In this chapter, we will examine these major emotional essences or *rasas* in the poetry of two major Bengali Shakta poets, Ramprasad Sen and Kazi Nazrul Islam. Rather than emphasizing union with the deity through vividly imagining an ideal, transcendent world of love and play, the Shakta poetry finds the goddess immanent in the physical world of sorrow and suffering. Poetic beauty recognizes her presence in the lowest as well as the highest, in terror and pain as well as flirtation and happiness. Thus, we see a distinction between the rasa of the ideal and the rasa of the real, a major distinction in the mystical paths of Bengali bhakti.

These theories of religious emotion are based on the philosophy of art and beauty in the *Natyasastra* of Bharata. The writer Bharata lived somewhere between the second century BCE and the second century CE (his exact dates are disputed by scholars). He is most well known for his long and detailed work, the *Natyasastra*, an encyclopedic work on the arts. It includes drama, dance, poetry, music, and painting, and gives details on how these should be created and appreciated. For Bharata, the central purpose of art is the experience of rasa or aesthetic emotion. The ultimate aim of the arts is to provide delight, which is communicated through emotional essences that are suggested by the work of art. Appreciation of these artistic and emotional essences gives not only happiness, but a glimpse of spiritual bliss (or *ananda*).

Each work of art creates a world of emotion and beauty (called *bhava-jagat*). The spectator enters into this artistic world, and leaves the ordinary, material world behind. He or she becomes the *rasika*, the person who is able to appreciate the art, because he is able to perceive the rasa within it.

The term *rasa* literally means sap or juice, and was originally used in the *Rig Veda* to refer to the juice of the soma plant, used in ritual. Bharata used it to refer to an emotional or artistic essence, a flavor or *sap* that is beyond the world of the senses. It is an abstract, emotional essence, which is supernatural (*alaukika*), yet capable of being evoked by the natural world. While its ancient use was to understand mantras and hymns, its later focus came to be works of art. Dictionary definitions of the term *rasa* include sap, juice, water, liquor, milk, nectar, poison, mercury, taste, savor, essence, flavor, relish, love, desire, beauty. Early meanings include the soma used in the Vedic soma sacrifice, and the Vedanta understanding of *brahman*.

In his *Natyasastra*, Bharata described eight basic emotional essences (later writers have added on a ninth rasa, the peaceful or *santa rasa*). The rasas have corresponding bhavas, moods that they evoke in people. The eight rasas are the loving or erotic, the comic, the tragic or pathetic, the furious, the heroic, the terrible, the disgusting, and the marvelous. They evoke moods of love, humor, sorrow or compassion, anger, courage, terror, loathing, and amazement. The value of a work of art can be seen in its ability to evoke these basic emotions or moods in observers. Bharata also included a variety of *sanchari bhavas* or temporary emotional states, *vibhavas* or ways of evoking these responses, and *anubhavas* or subtle types of emotional states.

The work of art becomes a channel for the rasa, and it delivers it to the observer, who responds by entering into a special type of bhava. The transmission is both individual and universal, for a single work of art can inspire audiences in many places. When the emotion of the actor or poet becomes the emotion of all observers, this is *sadharanikarana*, the universalizing of a particular state, a transfusion of emotion into the world. Bharata's understanding of artistic experience became the major Indian aesthetic theory. It was important in both Hindu and Muslim courts, and a major source for scholarship on the dramatic arts, both secular and religious.

Later writers followed Bharata's ideas on rasa. The ninth-century writer Anandavardhana developed a theory of rasa based on the *Natyashastra*. He emphasized the role of suggestion or *dhvani*. This is sometimes described as perceiving the echoes or resonances of dramatic moods. In the experience of *rasadhvani*, the emphasis is on emotion rather than ideas. A description of a place or a situation can evoke longing, sadness, homesickness, or hope. The emotion is not directly stated, but people feel it as a result of the situation expressed in the writing.

Anandavardhana states that words have two meanings, the obvious or expressed meaning and the suggested or subtle meaning. In the aesthetic state of consciousness, the observer focuses on the aspect of suggestion. It is impersonal, appreciated in a detached, contemplative mood, a paradox of experience and nonattachment. The ideal observer shares a common, latent experience (*vasana*) with the writer, which is evoked by the writing. We might say that the experience of rasa here triggers an unconscious memory that allows the person to respond emotionally. It is this common experience or shared cultural background that makes the observer appreciate the beauty of the writing. This is also why people without a common background of experience often miss the subtleties within works of art.[3]

The ideal viewer is the *sahridya*, who has polished his heart like a mirror, through training in literature and the understanding of rasas. Such a viewer can experience delight through the arts, or through religious visions, or even through food. A person who is sensitized in this way can experience depths that others cannot perceive. This is why training in the arts is important.

The writer Abhinavagupta later described a more detailed psychological understanding or rasa. In his commentary on the *Natyasastra*, he noted that "*Rasa* arises in a poem if we see things as if they were happening before our very eyes."[4] He elaborated on many details of aesthetic emotion. He stated that the permanent emotions (*sthayibhavas*) are like kings, for the other bhavas depend on them.[5] They are primary and stable, while the secondary emotions or *vyabhicaribhavas* are the signs that accompany them. Thus, with fear, we might have symptoms of paralysis, sweating, stuttering, and trembling, while with love, we might have flirtatious movements, frowning, side glances, and soft speech. In the tragic rasa we might have longing, panic, confusion, and tears, while wonder is shown with wide eyes, hair standing on end, and tears of joy. The ideal observer, the *rasika* or *sahridya*, has a heart like a polished mirror, so these symptoms are reflected, and the rasa is realized.[6] Rasa itself is supernatural, alaukika, and the experience of the poet and spectator are shared in a timeless immersion in which ordinary experience is intensified.

In the Shakta poetry, we can see five major rasas, thus following classical rasa theory. *Rati* or *shringara rasa* is the essence of love, the erotic and sensual essence, which is later found in the bhakti tradition and is transformed into love of the gods. In Shaktism, it is primarily the love of a child for its mother, a form of *vatsalya bhava*, which was briefly mentioned by Bharata (and later elaborated by Visvanath Kaviraj). *Karuna rasa* is the tragic essence, which evokes pity, sorrow, and compassion, and develops altruism in the audience. The *adbhuta rasa* brings forth wonder, amazement, and surprise at the marvelous. We see this in literature that expresses intensity and enthusiasm. *Raudra rasa* expresses the anger over human misery that is part of life, and calls the goddess to task over her neglect of her children. The terrible or *bhayanika rasa* shows the frightening aspect of the goddess in her association with death, and it makes the worshipper into the *vira* or hero to confront her. All these rasas represent ways that the goddess interacts with her devotees. They can be seen clearly in two of the most famous poets of Bengali Shaktism, Ramprasad Sen and Kazi Nazrul Islam.

The eighteenth-century poet Ramprasad Sen is most well known for his songs to the goddess Kali. He has been called the founder of the Sakta bhakti movement, the first Sakta poet to sing of the goddess Kali as a loving mother or as a little girl. His poetry is still popular in West Bengal today, as a major part of *Sakta padabali* or poetry dedicated to the goddess. He is often called the most beloved of Bengali poets, and its greatest religious practitioner or *sadhaka*. There are stories of the goddess's miraculous interventions in Ramprasad's life, which are sometimes called supernatural stories (*alaukika katha*). He is said to have died of love on Kali Puja, as the Kali statue was being immersed in the Ganges River, with the vision of the goddess before his eyes.

Ramprasad's poetry and songs (called *syama sangit* or songs to the dark goddess) focus on a single great goddess, who is most frequently called Kali, though sometimes she is called Durga, Bhairavi, Sita, Uma, or Kalika. The poems of Ramprasad are often called *Ramprasadi*, a genre named after him. Ramprasad was frequently called love-mad (insane due to his love of the goddess) by his friends and family, but, for Ramprasad, their opinions were not important. Here, he describes his ecstatic experience of wonder, as bhava, an abbreviation for *mahabhava* or highest state:

> O Ma Kali, wearing a garland of skulls
> What an experience (*bhava*) you have shown me!
> You taught me how to call you
> And at the moment I chanted "Ma"
> You drove me to ecstasy!
> Ma Tara, please tell me the source (of your sweetness).
> Where did you get this name full of nectar?
> When worldly people look at me
> They call me mad from love.
> The members of my family
> Hurl curses and insults at me.
> But whatever people say, dark mother
> My faith will not waver.
> Let people say what they want
> I will chant the name of Kali forever.
> If you get rid of this illusory world
> Insults and pride are unimportant.
> I have made your red feet my goal.
> I am no longer concerned with worldly opinions.[7]

He marvels that she can save people from sorrow:

> My mother is pure joy, a fountain of laughter . . .
> This is eternal wonder.

He who reaches out to her
Is not turned away.[8]

We see the rasa of the wondrous and marvelous in his hopes of her vision:

Mother, I long to see the day
When my eyes will be full of tears,
Crying at the thought of you!
The clouds that fill my soul will break
And my eyes will see your light.
I shall enter a new world
Where I shall sing praises
And my soul will soar to heights
Where sorrow cannot reach! . . .
Vedantists say my Mother is formless
But I see into the heart of things.
My Mother is everywhere.
Her smile lights the universe.[9]

For Ramprasad, she is a compassionate mother:

You who are born of the Divine Mother
Need not fear death.
She will be at your side, and will keep you safe.
Fear death no more, for
The Lord of Death worships her . . .
She is your loving mother, who softens
When she hears you sob.
She will take you up in her arms
If you cry.[10]

While Kali is beautiful and mysterious, she does not always answer her worshippers' prayers, and many songs involve complaining about the goddess's neglect and ill treatment. The bhava of anger and complaint is a popular mood for Sakta poetry. Ramprasad shows anger toward the goddess, as in this poem:

I'm not calling you Mother anymore.
You've given me such agony,
and you keep giving me more.
I used to be a happy householder.
You've made me into a crazy ascetic.

What else can you do to me, Wild-Haired One?
I'd rather go from house to house and beg my food,
rather than call you Mother, or come to your arms,
or sit in your lap again.
I kept calling "Mother, Mother,"
but Mother, your eyes didn't see
and your ears didn't hear.
How can any other misfortune compare
when a son suffers like an orphan
while his mother is still there?[11]

Sometimes we have the bhava of sorrow mixed with anger, as in this poem:

Human rebirth offers high hopes,
but my coming into the world
was just coming, and came to nothing in the end.
A bee imagines a painting to be the real lotus
and stubbornly hovers near.
Mother, you tricked me with words
and fed me bitter neem leaves
saying they were sugar.
My mouth watered for sweetness
but tasted only bitterness.
You have cheated me my whole life long.
You put me on earth saying
"It's time for us to play,"
but the game you played
only disappointed me.
Ramprasad says this outcome
of the game of existence
was always meant to be.
Now night falls, Mother, come and take
your tired child home.[12]

Sometimes anger is shown in a struggle:

Earth has seldom seen such a trial of strength between
A mother and her son.
I will show you my strength
As I cross swords with you right now!

You are mistaken if you think that you will win this fight.
I will struggle until I take your crown.
I will not give in.[13]

She is a goddess of compassion toward her worshippers, but she is described also by the terrible or frightening rasa. We see imagery of death; a partial version of this next poem was popularized in a recent film about the Thuggee sect, *The Deceivers*:

Because you love the burning ground
I have made a burning ground of my heart
So that you, dark goddess, can dance there forever.
I have no other desire left, O Mother.
A funeral pyre is blazing in my heart.
Ashes from corpses are all around me, my Mother
In case you decide to come.
Prasad prays, "O Mother, at the hour of death
Keep your devotee at your feet.
Please come dancing with rhythmic steps
Let me see you when my eyes are closed."[14]

The most popular songs by Ramprasad show a goddess who is beyond human concerns of good and evil, sorrow and joy. The devotee must accept the experiences that the goddess gives him, in order to perceive her true nature. In sorrow and terror, his limited scope revealed, his karma is purged, and he is able to see beyond the finite world. Death is the embrace of the Mother, so it can be valued, and not feared.

The twentieth-century writer Kazi Nazrul Islam has been named the national poet of Bangladesh, and he is a Muslim writer who uses Hindu imagery. He shows the same mixture of devotion and anger toward the goddess. He was a controversial writer, and he was very prolific. He wrote twenty-one books of poems, nine plays, six novels, and worked on ten movies, as well as writing over three thousand songs, short stories, and essays. He wrote love songs, ghazals (which came to be known as Nazrul sangit, named after Tagore's Rabindra sangit), comic songs, religious songs, children's songs, and hymns.[15] He wrote in Sanskrit, Bengali, Arabic, Persian, and Urdu. In his writing he uses a variety of moods. These include love, sorrow, fear, and heroism.

Nazrul writes of religious separation in his poem "The More You Escape Me." His writing of divine love in separation, the mood of *vipralambha*, is expressed in similar ways in both his religious and secular poetry. While this approach is most often found in Hindu bhakti, it may also be found in Sufi poetry.

> The more you escape me, my God
> The more that I weep for you.
> When you hide yourself away
> Then I search for you madly.
> How many forms and colors are part of your *maya*?
> I seek you beyond your veils.
> I do not know why, but still
> My restless mind pursues you.
> Why did you offer so much love
> If I receive only tears?
> When will your game of hide and seek end, Lord?
> These endless comings and goings make me suffer, my God.
> Life after life, I follow this path.
> I have wept so much, that my tears are gone.[16]

He writes songs of both union and separation from the loved one. One example of Kali devotion, or Shakta bhakti, is the poem "Shyama's Name":

> Shyama's name has lit the incense of my body.
> The more it burns, the further the fragrance spreads.
> My love is like incense, rising ceaselessly
> To touch Mother's lovely feet in Shiva's temple.
> With that holy fragrance my soul is blessed.
> Oh, Mother's smiling face floats in my mind
> Like the moon in the blue sky.
> When will everything of mine be burnt, and turned to ashes forever?
> I'll adorn Mother's forehead with those glorious ashes.[17]

He is able to see her as beautiful.[18] But one of his most powerful moods is that of the tragic or *karuna rasa*. A poem that expresses this rasa is "The Pain of the Poor." It condemns the wealthy, and questions the Mother who allows her children to suffer:

> These children are suffering, they lack a mother's care.
> They are ragged and covered with dirt
> Their faces are hollow from starvation
> With skin rashes and fevers.
> They work all day, but they can barely eat.

O wealthy people, how can you ignore them
And feast on rich desserts?
When they see you eat
They beg silently with sad eyes
Shame on you! How can you gorge yourselves
When just a small portion of the rice you have stored
Could feed them all!
You have all sorts of clothing
These children barely have a rag
With which you would polish your shoes.
You have trunkloads of clothes
These children freeze to death . . .
When they have fevers, none offer them water
Reduced to skeletons
They die in their mother's arms.[19]

Nazrul has also written about religious themes involving the tragic and sorrow-ful mood—one example is his poem on the death of Muhammad, which shows how the death affects nature itself:

Mother earth clasps the corpse of her son to her breast
Her whole body shakes with deep signs
The jinn mourn in the caves of hell
Why did Solomon die a second death?
The doe does not care today for her young ones,
They go without their mother's milk
The birds, too, have forgotten to sing.
All the leaves and flowers fall off the trees
And a cold north wind blows over the land . . .
Even the Kaaba trembles violently
The whole creation seems to be suffering . . .
Tears roll down Abu Bakr's cheeks
And Ayesha's cry frightens even the stars.
Maddened with grief, Omar grasps his sword and cries,
"I shall not spare even God, I shall kill Him!"
Madly the hero rants, "Who says that the prophet is dead?
Who wants to take his body to the grave?
Let him come near, and I'll chop off his head!" . . .
Fatima sobs in heart-breaking grief,
"Where has father gone?" she cries,

And she runs around madly, with her hair wild . . .
The world looks somber and dark
And the people cry tears of blood.
The seven seas churn and foam,
It seems they will drown the heavens![20]

Nazrul is perhaps most famous for the terrible rasa, in which he expresses both passion and patriotism. The Mother is the Motherland who is hungry and ragged, who cries from door to door for her sons, angry and violent. He states:

Open the doors, not for the goddess of pity, but for the goddess of terror.
She is fierce, belligerent, serpent-toothed
For the motherland, hold high your flags.[21]

He identifies with the strength and power of the destructive deities:

I am both Joy and Grief
I am the demonic power
Which will overwhelm all on Earth's last day.
I am the violence of the typhoon
The impulse of the Ocean
Resplendent in the sea's raging waves . . .
I am the deluge which brings wealth and devastation
In the rainy season . . .
I am Durga, the goddess of terror
And like her, I dance in joy
In the midst of the flames.[22]

He sees such destruction as a part of the pains of birth:

There comes the Terrible One
Like a fierce executioner of eternal time
Across the dark well of death
Through smoldering smoke
Lighting the torch of thunder . . .
Oh, have no fear!
The deluge will soon overtake the universe.
The final hour is fast drawing near
The old and rotten will be wiped out . . .
Why should the sight of destruction frighten you?
All of this upheaval is but the birth pains
Of a new creation.[23]

Nazrul also writes on tragedy. When he writes on "The Nobility of Sorrow" in his *Jiban Vigyan*, he shows the ways that universal sorrow can help mankind, and make people more sensitive and aware: "To feel the pain of others is to realize the nobility of sorrow. It has no selfish motivation. Such pain is felt through the memory of one's own pain. The soul is amazing in its ability to share the feeling of others. Such sharing can give a deep sense of joy. . . . It is the same kind of sorrow which the prophets felt, sharing the pain of humanity. Words cannot express it. It is this realization which elevates human beings towards divinity."[24] Nazrul is concerned with sorrow in both Hinduism and Islam. This focus on sorrow is found particularly in Shi'ah Islam, where it has led to a different outcome—a legacy of war and ritual mourning.

*Religious Emotion and Shi'ah Islam*

The emotions of anger and sorrow are found throughout world mysticism. Sorrow over the death of Jesus, and following his path of the cross, have been understood to bring union throughout the history of Christianity, and the painful "imitation of Christ" is a well-known practice. What is less well known is the role of the emotion of sorrow in Shi'ah Islam, which shares with the Shakti rasas a mood of pathos that leads one toward divinity. The heart is important in Islamic tradition, and may be influenced in many ways. As the Muslim theologian and mystic Shaikh Shahābu-d-Dīn 'Umar ibn Muḥammad-i-Sahrawardī phrases it in his thirteenth-century *A Dervish Textbook* ('*Awārif al-ma'ārif*), ecstasy or *wajd* is an event that comes from God, and turns the heart to "great grief, or to great joy."[25] The Shi'ah tradition has emphasized grief.

Shi'ah Ashura observances are commemorations of the martyrdom of Imam Husayn, the son of Ali and grandson of the Prophet Muhammad. He was killed by the caliph Yazid in the desert of Karbala in 680 CE, and his family and followers were also tortured and killed. During rituals held at the time of Ashura, the tenth of the month of Muharram, Shi'ah participants may re-enact the narrative of the events at Karbala in *ta'ziyah* plays, passion dramas of mourning, which include the bloody massacre of Husayn's forces by the Umayyad army. Other observances of Shi'ah Ashura include public displays of mass mourning, showing humanity's struggle against injustice. Shi'ah followers seek to heighten their spiritual awareness to reach the purity and generosity of Husayn, who fought evil in a righteous struggle in the desert while he was on pilgrimage to Mecca. Karbala became such a sacred site that, even today, clay and soil from the ground is compressed into pieces and exported around the world for Shi'ah followers to use in rituals, and they press their foreheads against it while bowing in prayer.[26] Karbala has often been invoked in the historical wars between Sunni and Shi'ah Islam.

Love, in Shi'ah doctrine, includes three categories: love for God, love for the Prophet and his Household, and love for the faithful. In a famous hadith, Muhammad is reported as questioning his followers concerning the "firmest handhold of faith" (*awthaq 'urwat al-iman*). When they cannot reply, he declares: "The firmest handhold of faith is to love for the sake of God and to hate for the sake of God, to befriend God's friends and to renounce His enemies."[27] Love and hatred are thus related to each other, and both are considered to be basic to faith.

In Shi'ah tradition, there is a great focus on Muhammad's household, especially the family of his grandson Husayn. (They are sometimes called the household of Prophethood: Muhammad, his daughter Fatimah, her husband Ali, and her sons; Muhammad's wives are not included.) Mourning with the family of Muhammad makes one a part of the family—a form of salvation by association. Those who grieve together are the deepest form of family.

The Hadith al-Kisa, the Tradition of the Cloak, is a particularly important hadith in Shi'ah belief, and is understood to be narrated by Fatimah, Muhammad's daughter. It quotes Muhammad, who has spread his Yemeni cloak or mantle over his family:

O Allah, these are the people of my Household (Ahlul-Bayt).
They are my confidants and my supporters.
Their flesh is my flesh and their blood is my blood.
Whoever hurts them, hurts me too.
Whoever displeases them, displeased me too.
I am at war with those at war with them.
I am at peace with those at peace with them.
I am the enemies of their enemies and
I am the friend of their friends.
They are from me and I am from them.
O Allah! Bestow Your Blessings, Benevolence, Forgiveness and Your
   pleasure upon me and upon them. And remove impurity from them
   and keep them thoroughly pure.
Then the Lord, Almighty Allah said: "O My angels! O Residents of
   My Heavens, verily, I have not created the erected Sky, the stretched
   earth, the illuminated moon, the bright sun, the rotating planets, the
   flowing seas and the sailing ships, but for the love of these Five lying
   underneath the cloak."[28]

This hadith is particularly important to remember because it is associated with special blessings to all Muslims by Muhammad.[29]

The worshipper has been instructed to love Muhammad's family, because they are the highest exemplars of obedience to the commands of God, they have exalted stations in the eyes of God, and they are pure, without any traces of polytheism, sin, or anything that deprives Muslims of divine mercy. The Shi'ah follower loves Muhammad's family, but is distressed at their plight in Karbala, and feels hatred toward the false caliph who has betrayed the ideals of Islam. He or she becomes close to the family by sharing their emotions. As the "Excellences of the Ahl al Bayt" states, "The mantle is a symbol of divine mercy and blessing covering the Prophet and his holy family. It is, moreover, a source or haven of consolation and serenity in the face of the great sufferings and martyrdom which the Prophet's family had to endure after him. In this infinite source of divine mercy, the pious also share in times of sufferings and afflictions."[30]

In the Islam of the Shi'ah Ali or the followers of Ali and his household (commonly known as *al-shi'a*), the most intense ecstatic state is not joy, but rather grief. It occurs at the yearly commemoration of the torture and death of Husayn, the grandson of Muhammad. This event, which happened on Ashura day during the month of Muharram, was of cosmic significance. The death of the rightful heir to the caliphate represented the death of innocence, and the life in the House of Sorrows, which will call forth the coming savior, or Mahdi.

This event is understood both historically and theologically. Historically, there was much infighting over leadership in early Islam in the days after Muhammad's death, and most of Muhammad's early descendants, the *imam*s who claimed the right of leadership, were killed. In the year 680, Muhammad's grandson Husayn, son of his daughter Fatimah and his cousin Ali, was killed in the desert of Karbala. The troops of the Umayyad ruler Yazid attacked Husayn and his family while they were on pilgrimage. Husayn and his family were dying of thirst in the desert, and eventually the soldiers killed them in brutal fashion. This came to aggravate Shi'ite hatred of the Umayyads, and caused a long chain of wars and bloodshed.

Theologically, Husayn was understood to be the innocent sacrifice who would save the world, whose death transforms the universe. There are many parallels between the death of Husayn for the Shi'ah, and the death of Christ for the early Christians. As Mahmoud Ayoub states: "The martyrdom of Imam Husayn has been regarded by the Shi'i community as a cosmic event around which the entire history of the world, prior as well as subsequent to it, revolves.... Husayn's death may be regarded as a redemptive act ... through the participation of the faithful in the sorrows of the Imam and his beloved family. It will be seen, moreover, that not only mankind, but all creation as well, is called upon to participate in this tragic event."[31] By his death, which was understood to be voluntary, Husayn transformed suffering itself from a negative and evil power to a road to salvation. This was due to human faith and divine mercy.[32]

Muhammad's family, the *ahl al-bayt*, underwent poverty and sorrow and murder, but in death they went to paradise, and now they can save those who suffered on earth. As Ja'far al-Sadiq stated, "Truly affliction is nearer to the pious man of faith than is the fallen rain to earth."[33]

Through sorrow, the soul is in contact with God, and during Husayn's death, which was the peak of human suffering, all persons and creatures of the past, present, and future suffer together with the martyrs of Karbala. Human history revolves around Husayn, whose martyrdom was predestined, and who gained control over all human destiny by this event. (He was associated with the tablet, the record of human destiny, and the pen, which writes out the divine decrees of fate.)[34]

Those who have been saved by mourning for the blood of Husayn will be raised on the Day of Judgment with the prophets, and taken with them and the angels to sing praises before Allah's throne. They will be counted among those martyred with Husayn at Karbala, and as members of the family of Muhammad.

The goal of the Ashura rituals, which commemorate the death of Husayn, is ecstatic sorrow. This is grief that ceases to be individual, and is understood to be a cosmic emotion. The entire universe mourns for Husayn, humans and animals and nature itself. The prophets knew that Husayn must die, and Adam and Noah and Ibrahim and the other prophets mourned long before Husayn was born. It is said that Adam and Hawa (Eve) mourned their son Habeel (Abel) so long that their tears formed a stream.[35] Mourning was described in the lives of other prophets, including Noah and Abraham, and it showed God's grace in their lives.[36] As it is said from the Shi'ah perspective, "Crying is the Sunnah of the prophets."[37] Shi'ah poetry describes how the sky shed tears of blood for Husayn for forty days, and even wild beasts roamed in anxiety in the jungles and forests. Lions and other beasts paced around the body of Husayn to protect it, and *jinns* recited elegies. The sun darkened at noon, and stars collided with each other. Blood gushed from the ground, for sky and earth shared the Muslim faith.

Nature mourned Husayn in the past, and continues to mourn him. As Ameed said in his book *The Importance of Weeping and Wailing*: "Man expresses his grief by shedding tears, while other creatures express their grief in their own different ways. A river or a sea expresses its grief by a stormy rush of water or violent surging of waves. A fish expresses its grief by coming to the surface of [the] water and running in agitation to and fro. The air expresses its grief by flowing in the form of a stormy yellow or red or black wind. The earth expresses her grief by violent pouring of water or dust. The sun expresses its grief by turning pale."[38]

All the visible and invisible creatures of Allah mourned for Husayn, the jinns and men and angels. Seventy thousand angels will continue to weep for him until the Day of Judgment. The lower angels had to cool the burning fire of their sorrow with their wings, to prevent the heat from creating floods. As the sixth imam stated, "The heavens wept for forty days with blood; the earth wept for forty days as it was covered in black [literally, in mourning]; the sun similarly wept for forty days with eclipses and redness. The mountains were torn asunder and scattered, and the seas burst."[39]

Such events are still going on for those who mourn. As the sixteenth-century treatise *The Garden of Martyrs* states in a Muharram lamentation poem:

Earth and heaven weep at the death of Husain;
from the Throne on high to the dirt far below, all beings weep.
Fish in the ocean depths, birds in the sky's upper heights:
all weep in mourning for the King of Karbala.[40]

Such mourning brings unity with mankind and nature on earth, and salvation in the afterlife. It is shared emotion that determines one's locale in paradise. Such emotion is always possible because, as Imam Riza phrases it, heaven is eternally Ashura day, when Imam Husayn was killed.[41] Ali and Fatimah are eternally clad in black robes, sorrowing and weeping in paradise, until the end-times.

Ecstatic sorrow is total immersion in cosmic grief, and the person joins "the universal chorus of mourners." Eternal tragedy is happening now, and every Muharram becomes the month of death, and every Ashura is the day of Husayn's martyrdom.[42] Those who participate in this mourning are marked by Husayn's blood, and considered to be a part of his family. At the final resurrection, they will go to the area of paradise meant for the *ahl al-bayt*, and will be considered to be members of Muhammad's family.

For those who mourn on earth, the Day of Judgment will be joyous. Tears evaporate sins, and they create a barrier between heaven and hell, so that the soul will not be tempted toward hell. The mourner will witness the presence of his fathers at death, and this mourning is considered to be *tasbeeh* (glorification of Allah) and *jihad* in the path of Allah.[43] According to the Shi'ah hadith Bihar al Anwaar, Muhammad says to Fatimah, "Whosoever weeps and cries for Husayn, we shall take them by their hand and lead them into the Garden of Paradise."[44]

This entry into heaven brings a final purification from sin and temptation, and eternal focus on both mourning and love, which erases sin. Events on earth give insight into events in heaven, and emotion shared between the worlds connects the Shi'ah worshipper with Muhammad, and with God.

Why the dark emotions? How do the dark emotions work in these religions? Why does the literature emphasize pain instead of joy?

For Shaktism, the focus on these emotions shows a recognition of the complexity of the goddess, who has power over all experience, and shows herself through all rasas. She is present on earth as well as in heaven, in both creative and destructive aspects, in pain as well as in joy. The heroic devotee is one who can perceive her through the *maya* of human experience. Anyone can love a god of blessing and happiness. But, as in the case of the biblical Job, it is harder to love a God who brings suffering. In Shaktism, one is devoted in the face of challenges. The *vira* or hero, who in tantra is unmoved in the midst of forbidden rituals of sexuality and death, becomes in Shakta bhakti the devotee who can see beyond pain. But in this case, such far vision does not bring brahman, the goddess's formless aspect. Instead, it brings a devotional love that includes the goddess and the world. This approach presupposes multiple lives, with many forms of experience. As day and night alternate, the emotions fluctuate in response to the variations through lives.

There is a different dynamic in the Shi'ah tradition. It assumes only one life, created by a single God in a single heaven. The focus is not on complexity, but on simplicity. The earth is a place of mourning, because heaven itself is a place of mourning, and the earth reflects heaven. Sorrow is the basis of life and death, and recognition of that universal sorrow unites human and divine worlds. The grief of Muhammad's family continues in heaven, where even those blessed by God wear black robes and mourn. To share this mourning makes one part of Muhammad's family, able to enter his special area in heaven. Sorrow gives insight into the universal, allowing the person to transcend individual concerns. Sharing the mourning for Husayn shares the grief of the world, and the heavens.

Life begins in sorrow—the newborn baby's response to the world is crying and wailing. This echoes the weeping of Adam, the first prophet, when he was sent from heaven to earth.[45] Lamentation is also a major act of believers, showing their humility before God. Muhammad deeply mourned his uncle Hamza, and his support for mourning is stated in many Shi'ah hadiths or traditions.

We see today that the Shi'ah focus on death and lamentation has been adopted for political ends by Sunni groups. The Palestinian Authority, which is primarily Sunni Arab, has come to emphasize the ideal of martyrdom. Palestinian television periodically plays this song:

Yasser Arafat: "Millions of Martyrs are marching to Jerusalem!
Oh Lord, let me become a Martyr among the Martyrs of Jerusalem."
Singer: "Massive armies are advancing on Jerusalem.
They do not fear the attackers.
May our convoy die as Martyrs to redeem the forlorn Al-Aqsa . . .
Jerusalem is shouting 'O Homeland.'
It needs a mausoleum
Until your heart comes to rest in Jerusalem,
the land of Ribat [religious conflict/war over land claimed to be Islamic]."[46]

We see this perspective in the well-known statement of the Hamas Al Qassam Brigades: "We love death more than you love life!" This passion for death is involved with martyrdom as a pathway to heaven and a sign of bravery and honor. It is dark devotion on the political front. When dark devotion is mixed with politics, as it often is in the fundamentalist strains of religion, it may bring destruction to friends and enemies alike.

We can also see the destructive aspect of dark devotion in religious nationalism, especially in India. The goddess is Bharat Mata, Mother of the Land of India, and it is the obligation of her sons to protect her. This obligation has been taken up by groups like the Bhartiya Janata Party (BJP) and the Rashtriya Seva Sangh (RSS), who try to emphasize the Hindu identity of India in opposition to both Christianity and Islam. The sorrow over what has been done to Mother India has resulted in riots, bombings, and destruction of life and property.

However, dark devotion is not always destructive. Sorrow is significant in many world religions. In Buddhism, insight into the universality of suffering and sorrow are basic doctrines, part of the four noble truths shared by all sects of the religion. It motivates compassionate action and the vows of the bodhisattva. In Christianity, Jesus's suffering on the cross represents the broken and sinful situation of humanity, and it is realization of the significance of his suffering that brings salvation. In Judaism, contemplation of suffering over history has brought the Kabbalistic understanding of the soul's exile, and the questions of divine mystery and power seen in the Book of Job. In these religions, sharing in the dark emotions brings the person to the light.

*Discussion*

In Bengali bhakti, religious emotion is dramatically expressed. People scream, laugh, weep, and roll in the dust, both at ritual kirtans and spontaneously, when they are overwhelmed by the love of a god during daily life. The highest deity, according to Bengali Vaishnava informants, is not the god Krishna, but rather his beloved Radha. She is the personification of all forms of religious emotion occurring simultaneously (in the state of mahabhava). Thus, they can say, "We are the true Shaktas, for we worship Radha." Among the Vaishnavas, even hatred of God can lead to heaven, as one's heart is focused on the deity. Bengali Shaktas love, fear, and yearn for the Mother. Scholars study the ways that such religious emotion expresses tension and conflict, brings affiliation and a sense of safety and security, and keeps the society moral and hierarchical through fear and creative through love. For many scholars, the interpretation of the emotional event is more important than the event itself. This perspective has led to the constructivist position.

In the popular study of mysticism today, the constructivist approach is popular. It states that raw emotion is irrelevant, and perhaps even nonexistent, and what should be studied is cultural and theological interpretation. Certainly these are easier for an observer to analyze. But they are not necessarily what is most important to practitioners. For Bengali bhaktas, the most highly valued emotions are those that occur spontaneously, outside of cultural control. Such states are not evoked by ritual, though ritual may be used to limit them (this was the theme of my first book).[47] Spontaneous emotional extremes can look to observers like insanity, and people who experience them have been rejected as mad in many world cultures and religions. But these experiences are also understood by religions to show new paths to the gods, hacked with metaphorical machetes through the underbrush rather than following the paved roads of religious ritual. It is often the religious founders who have spontaneous emotions, and the followers who imitate them through ritual. In West Bengal, spontaneous emotion was considered to be very valuable by informants. Divine passion is good if you spend your life praying for it, as many bhaktas do, but it is great if the god gives it to you as grace, or if it comes even before belief in the religion does.

In the two religions described in this chapter, Bengali Shaktism and Shi'ah Islam, we have both ritualized and spontaneous religious emotion. In the Bengali tradition, drama evokes the various rasas or archetypal dramatic moods, which trigger individual bhavas or emotional states. Contemplation of the dramatic actions and adventures of the gods is a traditional ritual for evoking religious emotion. However, there are many saints and *siddhas* whose lives are filled with spontaneous emotion, and that emotion (and the ability to spread it to others) is itself the criterion for sainthood.

In Shi'ah Islam, there are ritualized ways of evoking religious emotion as well. There are annual dramatic reenactments of the martyrdom of Husayn at Karbala, and the tragedies of Muhammad's family. People weep and mourn at the *taziyahs*, and some express their sorrow by self-flagellation on Ashura. Yet there are also imams and saints whose intense sorrow comes over them suddenly, outside of the ritual context. Such emotion is not just a memory of a historical event, but a cosmic passion that changes the universe. Should scholars study such emotions as solely social constructions?

Emotions in both religions are understood by practitioners as bringing a connection with the gods and prophets. Tragedy shows the finitude of personal life, and places it in a larger context. While most academic studies of religious emotion emphasize its impact on culture, practitioners are more interested in its transcendent aspects. When such emotion gains a mystical dimension it becomes existential, allowing practitioners to experience the basis of the universe. History and culture become secondary concerns for them.

While some modern scholars have condemned such mystical experiences as not open to all, and thus undemocratic and elitist,[48] there are many experiences that are not open to all. People have different skills; photographic memory and perfect pitch are not open to all, yet they are not condemned as elitist in the way that religious and mystical experiences are. Skills do not need to be equally distributed to exist.

In the religions described in this chapter, the great question is how to respond to suffering. Should one turn the dark emotions against the perceived sources of evil, which may help particular situations, but may also lead to fanaticism and terrorism? Should one try to help the suffering, seeing God in the oppressed, like Gandhi, Ambedkar, and Mother Teresa? Or should suffering be acceptable, as in Calvin's glorification of the elect and rejection of the sinful, and Ayn Rand's glorification of the powerful and rejection of the weak? For some people, suffering is how things get done in the world—you need to break eggs to make omelets. Destructive emotion brings change, for Stalin and revolution, and for the robber barons and the growth of capital. Dark devotion can make a person the sword arm of a God who kills, or the heart of a God who helps those who suffer. The worshipper is placed with Job in the whirlwind, trying to understand the mystery of a God who both cares and causes suffering.

In Bengali Shaktism and Shi'ah Islam, the heart is not a field of conflicts, but rather a doorway. Sorrow over experience, past and present, is the key that opens it. Religious sorrow lessens the person's desire for the current world, so he or she can have a good death, and peacefully enter the next one.

NOTES

1. Maintaining emotional balance in the West is not an easy process, and we see the use of antidepressants as a way of dealing with emotion rather than illness. According to a 2014 Gallup "State of the States" poll, almost one in five Americans takes a mood-altering substance; nationally, 18.9 percent take drugs to relax "almost every day" (accessed June 2015, http://www.gallup.com/poll/182192/mood-altering-drug-highest-west-virginia-lowest-alaska.aspx). A 2015 study published in the *Journal of Clinical Psychiatry* reports some 69 percent of people taking selective serotonin reuptake inhibitors (SSRIs), the primary type of antidepressant, have never suffered from major depressive disorder (MDD), and 38 percent have never in their lifetime met the criteria for MDD, obsessive compulsive disorder, panic disorder, social phobia, or generalized anxiety disorder, yet still take the pills that accompany them. See Yoichiro Takayanagi et al., "Antidepressant Use and Lifetime History of Mental Disorders in a Community Sample: Results from the Baltimore Epidemiologic Catchment Area Study," *Journal of Clinical Psychiatry* 76, no. 1 (2015): 40–44, doi: 10.4088/JCP.13m08824.

2. The Sanskrit and Bengali term *bhava* has literally hundreds of referents and equivalent terms. For the purposes of this paper, I will define it as emotional/religious experience.

3. Anandavardhana, *The "Dhvanyaloka" of Anandavardhana with the "Locana" of Abhinavagupta*, ed. and trans. Daniel H. H. Ingalls Sr., trans. Jeffrey Moussaiff Masson and M. V. Patwardhan (Cambridge, MA: Harvard University Press, 1990), locana 70.

4. P. Patnaik, *Rasa in Aesthetics* (New Delhi: D. K. Printworld, 1997), 8.

5. Patnaik, *Rasa in Aesthetics*, 27.

6. Patnaik, *Rasa in Aesthetics*, 50.

7. Ramprasad Sen, *Ramprasadi Sangit* (Calcutta: Rajendra Library, n.d.), 47.

8. Pramathanath Chaudhuri, *Ramprasad and Western Man* (Calcutta: Gautam Mallick, 1976), 42, song #10, slightly rephrased.

9. Chaudhuri, *Ramprasad and Western Man*, 85, song #91.

10. Chaudhuri, *Ramprasad and Western Man*, 38, song #3, slightly rephrased.

11. Dhrubakumar Mukhopadhyay, ed., *Sakta Padavali* (Calcutta: Ratnavali, 1996), 271.

12. Ramprasad, in *Shashibhushan Dasgupta, Bharater Shakti Sadhana o Shakti Sahitya* (Calcutta: Samsad, 1993), 222.

13. Chaudhuri, *Ramprasad and Western Man*, 42, song #10, rephrased.

14. Sen, *Ramprasadi Sangit*, 46.

15. Rafiqul Islam, *Kazi Nazrul Islam: A New Anthology* (Dhaka: Bangla Academy, 1990), 150.

16. Mohammad Nurul Huda, ed., *The Poetry of Kazi Nazrul Islam in English Translation* (Dhaka: Nazrul Institute, 2000), 694, translated from Bengali.

17. Amarendranath Raya, ed., *Sakta padabali* (Calcutta: Calcutta University Press, 1989), 191.

18. Huda, *Poetry of Kazi Nazrul Islam*, 580.

19. Huda, *Poetry of Kazi Nazrul Islam*, 562, adapted from a translation by Sajed Kamal.

20. Huda, *Poetry of Kazi Nazrul Islam*, 176–77, adapted from a translation by Kabir Chowdhury.

21. Islam, *Kazi Nazrul Islam*, 165, slightly rephrased.

22. Islam, *Kazi Nazrul Islam*, 22, slightly rephrased.

23. Islam, *Kazi Nazrul Islam*, 48–49, slightly rephrased.

24. *Kazi Nazrul Islam: Selected Works*, trans. Sajed Kamal (Dhaka: Nazrul Institute, 1999), 185.

25. Shaikh Shahābu-d-Dīn 'Umar ibn Muḥammad-i-Sahrawardī, *A Dervish Textbook from the 'Awārif al-ma'ārif: Written in the Thirteenth Century*, trans. H. Wilberforce Clarke (London: Octagon Press, 1980), 82.

26. See Yasin T. al-Jibouri, "Why Prostrate on Karbala's Turba," accessed June 2015, http://www.al-islam.org/beliefs/practices/turba.html.

27. Al-Kulayni, *Usul al-Kafi*, "itab al-iman wa al-kufr," bab al-hubb fi Allah wa ai-bughd fi Allah," hadith 6 (Tehran: Dar al-Kutub al-Islamiyyah), ii, p. 126. Cited in Sayyid Muhammad Rida Hijaz, "*The Concept of Love in the Shi'i Creed*," accessed June 2015, http://www.al-islam.org/al-tawhid/conceptoflove.htm.

28. See Hadith-i-Kisa, "The Tradition of the Cloak," accessed June 2015, http://www.duas.org/hadis-e-kisa.htm.

29. 'Ali then said to my father, "O Allah's Messenger! Please tell me; what is the value of this gathering of us under this cloak in the sight of Allah?"

The Prophet, peace be upon him and his Household, said, "I swear this by Him Who has sent me with the truth as Prophet and chosen me, as holding communion, to convey the Message; whenever the tale of this gathering of us is mentioned in an assembly of the people of the earth in which a group of our adherents and lover are present, the (divine) mercy shall certainly be poured down on them and the angels shall certainly surround them, asking forgiveness for them until they depart."

'Ali, peace be upon him, commented, "Then, by Allah I swear it; we have won. So have our adherents. I swear it by the Lord of the Ka'bah."

"O 'Ali!" my father Allah's Messenger, peace be upon him and his Household, added, "I swear this by Him Who has sent me with the truth as Prophet and chosen me, as holding communion, to convey the Message; whenever the tale of this gathering of us is mentioned in an assembly of the people of the earth in which a group of our adherents and lover are present and among them there is a distressed one, Almighty Allah shall certainly release him from distress, or there is among them an aggrieved one, Almighty Allah shall certainly relieve him from grief, or there is among them one who needs a request to be granted, Almighty Allah shall certainly grant him his request."

'Ali, peace be upon him, said, "Then, we have won and attained pleasure. I swear it by Allah. So have our adherents; they have won and attained pleasure in this world and in the Hereafter. I swear it by the Lord of the Ka'bah." Hadith-i-Kisa, "Tradition of the Cloak."

30. See M. Ayoub, accessed June 2015, http://www.duas.org/Misc/excellences_of_the_ahl_al_bayt.htm.

31. Mahmoud Ayoub, *Redemptive Suffering in Islam: A Study of the Devotional Aspects of 'Ashura' in Twelver Shi'ism* (The Hague: Mouton, 1978), 141.

32. Ayoub, *Redemptive Suffering in Islam*, 24.

33. Ayoub, *Redemptive Suffering in Islam*, 26.

34. Ayoub, *Redemptive Suffering in Islam*, 29.

35. Ta'rikh Ya'qubi, vol. 1, 3, Islamic history book, cited online at http://www.ziyaraat
.net/books/AzadariMourningForImamHussain.pdf.

36. "Mourning for Imam Husayn," 29, accessed June 2015, http://www.ziyaraat.net
/books/AzadariMourningForImamHussain.pdf.

37. "Mourning for Imam Husayn," 39.

38. Syed Mohammed Ameed, *The Importance of Weeping and Wailing* (Karachi:
Peermahomed Ebrahim Trust, 1974), 7.

39. Ayoub, *Redemptive Suffering in Islam*, 145.

40. David Pinault, *Horse of Karbala: Muslim Devotional Life in India* (New York: Palgrave, 2001), 164.

41. Ayoub, *Redemptive Suffering in Islam*, 56.

42. Ayoub, *Redemptive Suffering in Islam*, 149.

43. See "Mourning for Imam Husayn," 101–2.

44. "Mourning for Imam Husayn," 125.

45. "Mourning for Imam Husayn, 29.

46. Palestinian Authority TV, November 9, 2014.

47. See my *The Madness of the Saints: Ecstatic Religion in Bengal* (Chicago: University
of Chicago Press, 1989).

48. See, for example, Ann Taves, *Religious Experience Reconsidered: A Building-Block
Approach to the Study of Religion and Other Special Things* (Princeton, NJ: Princeton University Press, 2009).

SARAH M. ROSS

## 6. SOUND AND SENTIMENT IN JUDAISM

*Toward the Production, Perception, and Representation*
*of Emotion in Jewish Ritual Music*

It is generally acknowledged that music is a central part of Jewish rituals that
are performed inside as well as outside the context of synagogue services in all
streams of Judaism (Ultra- and Modern-Orthodox, Conservative and Reform
Judaism, as well as the Jewish Renewal and Reconstructionist Movement). In
this regard, and according to musicologist Amit Klein and religious scholar
Frank B. Brown, it is recognized that music's importance to Jewish worship
has much to do with its *expressive aspects* (such as the combination of pitches,
rhythms, timbres, durations, and dynamics, etc.), which generate emotive excitement, and with its *direct effect and impact* on the inexpressible realm of
human emotion.[1] Thus, as will be shown in this chapter, the act of prayer in
Judaism is mainly a process of singing and chanting, an act in which, not only
every text, but also every time, has its own specific melody and mood.

Within the context of the synagogue service, we find diverse forms and
genres of music that accompany different kinds of liturgical drama, such as
*K'riat HaTorah* (the reading from the Torah; biblical cantillation), *Nusach*
(chants that are based on prayer modes used for recitative passages), *Piyyutim*
(liturgical poems or hymns designated to be sung, chanted, or recited during
synagogue service but also in communal contexts outside the synagogue), and
*Pizmonim* (extraliturgical Jewish songs that are mostly sung throughout religious rituals and festivities connected to life cycle events) as well as *Z'mirot*

(table songs). Depending on the religious orientation of a Jewish community and its openness toward musical innovation, Jewish ritual music is performed in various ways: a cappella or with instrumental accompaniment; as choral music; solo or congregational singing, combined with or without words and ritual action; as ecstatic or meditative music. Consequently, the different dimensions of Jewish ritual music induce, engage, and reflect varied levels of emotional excitement and religious experience. These levels of experience are filtered by the worshippers (listeners) and are shaped by different categories of identity and belonging such as cultural background, age, gender, and degree of religiousness.[2]

Thus, there is an assumed congruence between the different ritual aspects and spiritual levels instigated by the music in a religious setting and emotion, and many will argue that the two are not one and the same. That is why a short related discussion on what an emotion is considered to be within the context of this chapter is required.

Emotions are complex, and there is no scientific consensus on what an emotion actually is.[3] The usage of the term emotion in academic discourses, however, is different from the same in everyday speech, in which it is mainly understood as state of feeling. For the purpose of this chapter, a multicomponential description of emotion is used that involves at the same time physiological and cultural factors as well as expressive body actions and the appraisal of situations and contexts, such as Peggy Thoits suggests it:[4] "Emotions involve: (a) appraisals of a situational stimulus or context, (b) changes in physiological or bodily sensations, (c) the free or inhibited display of expressive gestures, and (d) a cultural label applied to specific constellations of one or more of the first three components. All four components need not be present simultaneously for an emotion to be experienced or to be recognized by others."[5] Within the context of studies on music and emotion in particular,[6] which are mainly located in the field of music psychology, the understanding of the psychological relationship between music and human emotion is paramount. In this regard, it has to be differentiated between the conveyance and elicitation (the perception and production) of emotion through music. Regarding music's ability to convey emotion, particularly the question of which structural factors in music are relevant for the different ways of experiencing emotional expressions is of high interest. This question is approached from two different perspectives: (1) cognitivists argue that music only represents an emotion, but does not take into account the individual perception of emotion in the listener; (2) on the other hand, so-called emotivists claim that music does indeed elicit emotional responses in the listener.[7]

It has been argued that the emotion perceived from a piece of music is a multiplicative function of the following features that influence expressed emotion at different magnitudes, and their effects are compounded by one another: *structural features* (such as tempo, mode, loudness, melody, rhythm), *performance features* (refers to both the musical skills of a performer and the way he or she executes a piece of music as well as to his or her appearance, stage presence, and motivation, etc.), *listener features* (that is, the individual and social identity of the listener, but it also refers, for example, to the listener's knowledge of music), and *contextual features* of the piece (refers to certain aspects of the performance, such as time, location, occasion, etc.).[8]

Emotion is also produced within the listener, which is of course hard to measure. But to do so, Juslin and Västfjäll developed a model of six ways that music can elicit emotion, called the BRECVEM model, which consists of the following factors: brain stem reflex, rhythmic entrainment, evaluative conditioning, emotional contagion, visual imagery, and episodic memory.[9] Nevertheless, there are debates on whether emotion can be elicited through music.[10] In this regard, studies focusing first of all on structural features of music as well as on listeners' features have shown evidence for elicited emotions through music, which may be an expansion of previous emotional events or entirely new feelings. In this context, aspects such as the familiarity of the tune, musical expectations, or associated memories with the music, like social events or religious ceremonies, are highly relevant for the elicitation of emotion through music.[11] Within the context of the following discussion on emotion and Jewish ritual music, both the cognitivist and emotivist perspectives are considered to be relevant. Beyond that, the perception of emotion in music is also subject to cultural influences, as William Forde Thompson and Laura-Lee Balkwill discuss with regard to the so-called *cue-redundancy model*, which allows us to "account for cross-cultural similarities and differences in the expression and recognition of emotion in music."[12]

Against the background of scholarly discourses on the production and perception of musical emotion just outlined, my keen interest in the experiential and emotive dynamics of Jewish ritual music grew out of my own experience. In 2011, I attended a concert of the HaOman Hai Ensemble in London[13] entitled "Raza D'Shabbat" (Secrets of the Sabbath).[14] The music performed at this concert was newly composed popular music based on ancient Hassidic *nigmunim* (wordless melodies through which the worshipper is drawn to a higher sphere).[15] The music at the concert was meant to evoke the experience of strolling through the streets of Jerusalem on the evening of the Sabbath.

The HaOman Hai Ensemble was directed by the Israeli composer, teacher, and researcher Professor Andre Hajdu. The group is made up of multitalented musicians,[16] all composers, players, and performers who are active in Israel and abroad. The ensemble is known for its rearrangements of traditional (mostly Hassidic) songs in the spirit of these young musicians, for whom the ancient world of niggunim initially represented a completely new soundscape that lay outside their musical experience. Thus, the secret of the ensemble's work does not lie in the attempt to make a pastiche of the musical tradition of the Hassidim (or any other Jewish group), but in its attitude: they rearrange traditional Jewish ritual music in the style of Béla Bartók, Maurice Ravel, or George Gershwin, where the original is faithfully preserved alongside additions offered by each composer. In this process, each new contribution embodies the spirit of the composer's generation, consciousness, and personality.[17]

"Raza D'Shabbat" has thus to be understood as a musical journey through time (between the beginning and end of Sabbath) and space (the streets of Jerusalem), while passing through the sacred texts of Judaism, such as the *Zohar* (the foundational work of Jewish mysticism), as well as traditional prayer texts and other liturgy (e.g., Piyyutim). During the one-hour performance, the concert attendees experienced a synthesis of the essence of Sabbath, namely, the transition from the profane time to the sacred time and back to the profane time of the week. Hassidic traditions of songs, as well as contemporary Israeli musics, are used as the main medium for conveying the emotional ebb and flow characterizing the Jewish day of rest. Indeed, Amira Ehrlich of "Tipecha: Jewish Arts and Education" makes this point about "Raza D'Shabbat" on her webpage: "Time flows on through waves of desire and longing. We punctuate our passion of existence in drifting moments of sacred time: Sabbath and holy days, and we sing: Can we give our inner passion eyes to experience and contemplate experience at the same time? Can we give time eyes to see? Give eyes to the voices we create? May we behold all this just as a man raises his sacred wine reciting his blessing with a smile on his lips."[18] With regard to the production, perception, and representation of emotion in Jewish ritual music, it was particularly the reaction and the comments of the (largely Jewish) audience that attracted my attention. In conversations with mostly Ashkenazi Jewish concert attendees during the break and after the concert, it turned out that most of them could indeed relate and connect to the spirit and particular atmosphere of the different stages of the Sabbath liturgy that were represented by the tunes played by the ensemble.[19] At the same time, some of the concert-goers reported that they also experienced a continuous process of attachment and detachment in their emotional involvement in this musical journey. On my inquiry to explain why they think this had happened, they answered that the constant change of musical style during the performance—ranging from Western and Eastern Ashkenazi, to Moroccan, Sephardi to Indian, and modern

Israeli tunes—had a rather irritating effect. As such, their (musical) expectations were not always met. For the primarily Ashkenazi respondents, the liturgical texts correlated with those they knew from services at their synagogues at home. However, the rearranged Hassidic, Moroccan, Sephardi, or Indian tunes differed from the musical tradition in which they were raised.

The participants' reactions revealed how particularly complex the issue on the perception of emotions in Jewish ritual music actually is, how informed these emotions are by the social-musical environments in which the respondents were raised, and that most musicological works on emotions in Jewish (ritual) music only focus on the conveyance (rather than elicitation) of sentiment in music: that is, on the "musical mechanisms employed by composers, performers and others."[20] The few works that touch on the subject of Jewish music and emotion, such as the contributions in Jonathan Friedmann's anthology *Emotion in Jewish Music*,[21] tend to focus on the performative aspects of synagogue music rather than on analyzing the actual emotions of real people. That is why I started to further question how far, in worship settings, music brings "intimate understanding to often distant or abstract religious concerns, [and how songs can effectively] heighten one's attentiveness during prayer, [and infuse] sacred text with its necessary emotional qualities."[22]

On the one hand, much can be said about the way emotions are knowingly induced and represented in Jewish music, particularly the musically designed emotions. On the other hand, until today, only little can be said about how these emotions are perceived by the individual worshipper as well as the community. How is it possible that we know hardly anything about the different shades of emotional perception within the context of synagogue service, in which music plays a central role?

Although Jewish scriptures have shown a positive interest in human emotions, which are portrayed and discussed in the Hebrew Bible, the Talmud, in medieval Jewish philosophical works, as well as in the writings of Jewish mysticism and Hassidism, little has been written about how the actual performance of Jewish ritual elicits emotions in the worshipping community. Nevertheless, these scriptures are still the main resources informing contemporary studies on emotions in Jewish thought and tradition.[23] Similar scripture-based approaches inform contemporary studies on Jewish music and emotion, although in a less comprehensive way. These studies also tend to lack empirical and experimental approaches to the research topic.[24] The reasons for this are that the study of Jewish music in general is only situated at the fringes of different fields of research, such as historical musicology, ethnomusicology, Jewish studies, and cultural studies, as well as research carried out at theological institutions (rabbinical seminaries and cantorial schools).[25] Each of these disciplines follows its own interests, politics, theories, and methods, which inform their corresponding engagement with and studies of Jewish music. Moreover, general empirical research on music and emotion is mainly carried out within the fields of music cognition and music psychology, which are both fields of research that rarely intersect with those of the study of Jewish music. In recent years, research has been undertaken in the field of cognitive ethnomusicology that recognizes cross-cultural differences in the study of music and emotion.[26] Nevertheless, Jewish ritual music—as an object of research—has not been acknowledged here either. Indeed, Moisala argues that cognitive studies in music have paid insufficient attention to the role of cultural particularity in negotiating musical perception: "Since the bulk of cognitive studies of music has been conducted either as computer simulations of musical material or according to the experimental procedures of cognitive psychology, attention has not been paid to contextual and cultural factors. Most of these studies have focused on musical perception within western music [that per se excludes Jewish ritual music] and have thus been ethnocentric in nature."[27]

Thus, we not only know little about the emotional effects of Jewish ritual music, but most of the writings, which are often shaped by ideological, theological, sometimes even romanticized views on synagogue music, neither include the actual circumstances that arouse emotion through Jewish ritual music nor the individual differences in the perception of music in synagogue worship.[28]

In the following, I will set out some thoughts for debate by discussing the present methodological limits in the study of emotions in Jewish ritual music. To give the reader a better understanding of emotions in Jewish ritual music, I will first outline the traditional way of producing emotions in synagogue music through the use of so-called Nusach (the Jewish prayer modes). In this context, the sensitive listener and connoisseur of the traditional Jewish prayer modes is encouraged by music to experience the Jewish ritual more deeply. The chapter closes with a discussion on the problem of studying and analyzing the actual perception of emotion by Jewish worshippers, in a way that goes beyond relying on identitarian conceptions of self.

*Musical Timescapes: Creating and Experiencing Sacred Time through Emotional Effects in Jewish Ritual Music*

The singing and chanting of prayers, blessings, psalms, and sacred texts throughout synagogue services makes up the core of liturgical practice in Judaism. The music is characterized by a large variety of local traditions and styles that have been (mostly orally) transmitted; some forms of Jewish liturgical music are newly invented traditions.[29] One form of synagogue music is that of so-called Nusach haTefilah, the improvisational, nonmetric chanting of Jewish prayer texts based on musical modes and a certain set of melodic motives. Throughout the performance of Jewish ritual, Nusach is used as the main musical and emotional tool, and will thus be discussed in order to demonstrate the *traditional* way of setting the pace and spiritual atmosphere of the service.

The (musical as well as cultural) concept of Nusach haTefilah[30] includes the basic musical content of the Jewish prayer modes, such as scales, intervals, and motifs. It not only describes how the liturgy has to be intoned, but also how an appropriate mood, atmosphere, and sentiment is created through the "dialectical interplay between simple traditional patterns of synagogue chant."[31] Like Indian *Raga* or Arabic *Maqam*, Nusach identifies and situates a particular religious and musical moment, creating a musical-emotional correspondence to the season, time of the day, or a particular holiday.[32] In addition, the Jewish prayer chants are characterized by the worshipper's inspiration in response to the words of the prayer that he or she expresses through the music. That is why Nusach always "comes from someone's musical imagination [that] was applied to text."[33] Besides the actual use of the Jewish prayer modes throughout synagogue services, a lot of judgmental discussions and associations are connected with the common understanding of the importance of Nusach haTefilah as a central tradition of synagogue music. Cantor Mark S. Goodman aptly describes the unifying function of the traditional Nusach: "Nusach is the means to tell the story and translate the experience of the Jewish people moving towards redemption. It conveys that story with an emotional intensity deeper than intellect, strengthened and bolstered by generations of musical meaning and associations."[34] Or as the American ethnomusicologist Mark Slobin summarizes it: "[Nusach] is involved in everything from hiring through youth relations, viewed as anything from a discipline gratefully accepted to a hindrance proudly rejected. Nusach is so basic as to be a job requirement [of the cantor], but not in every denomination; it is simultaneously musical and political, [tangible and ineffable, and somewhat mystical]. The only point of agreement is that nusach is the emblem of tradition and it somehow specifies, stipulates, or situates a musical moment, perhaps in a particular locale."[35] As discussed by the Israeli musicologist Amit Klein in his article "Singing Their Heart Out," as well as by comparative historian of religion Gabriel Levy and me in our article on "Emotional and Cognitive Rhythms in Jewish Music,"[36] the importance of Nusach—with regard to the representation of emotions—lies in the dramatization of the service; that is, in how the dramatic tension of the service is moved to its climax through the use of certain musical mechanisms and techniques employed by the cantor or prayer leader. This process of dramatization—and thus of creating emotional excitement through the musical representation of certain sentiments—can be analyzed on a macro level, for example, of the whole twenty-four-hour cycle of the Sabbath liturgy, as well as on a micro level, that is, in the actual way a single prayer is chanted by the cantor.

In the following discussion on the interrelationship between Jewish ritual and liturgical music, I understand the different spiritual levels that will be described and that are stimulated by the Nusach, as different levels of *emotion*. So, on a general level, the emotional development throughout the Sabbath day is basically induced by a constant change between the two modes *Adonai Malach* ("God reigns"; similar to a major scale but using a flat seventh and a flat tenth; the regal nature of this mode is used to praise God) and *Magen Avot* ("Shield of our fathers"; Aeolian minor mode with a tender and lyrical strain), which convey best the particular spirit of Sabbath.[37] Only during the Sabbath morning service (*Shaharit*) does the cantor switch into the so-called *Ahavah Rabbah* mode ("Great Love"; Phrygian minor mode, characterized through the popular augmented second, denoting an intimate connection to God).[38] The emotional effect that is created by the constant oscillation between major and minor modes is closely connected to the characteristics and associations that are traditionally ascribed to each Nusach as well as in how each mode is tied to a particular part in the Sabbath liturgy. Thus, the musical changes indicate not only the different liturgical stages of the twenty-four-hour Sabbath cycle and its rituals, but also different stages in the atmosphere of the same.[39] In this regard, Levy and I adopted an image, called "Talk to the Universe," as a hermeneutic tool,[40] which we received from one of our interview partners. We used this tool to illustrate the emotional development and musical flow throughout the twenty-four-hour Sabbath cycle. We included the parts of the service where the cantor switched between the different prayer modes (see figure 6.1).

The image illustrates the Jewish day of rest as one continuous time flow, starting on Friday night with the *Kabbalat Shabbat* ("Receiving of the Sabbath") service that marks the transition from secular into sacred time. Musically, this transition period is marked by the use of the Adonai Malach mode. Because of its major tonality that conveys a majestic feel and grand atmosphere, the Adonai Malach mode is commonly used to distinguish the festival days (such as the Sabbath) from other days. The mode is used "for praising and thanksgiving prayers" as well as for signifying exaltation.[41] By singing the liturgy of the Kabbalat Shabbat service in this mode, which "[echoes] the aspiration of the

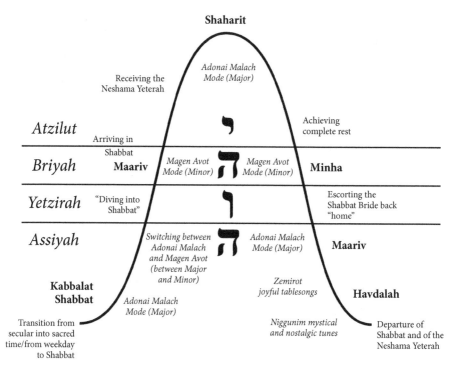

FIGURE 6.1. Adopted image of "Talk to the Universe." Credit: Diagram by Sarah
Ross and Gabriel Levy. Source of picture: Levy and Ross, "Emotional and Cognitive
Rhythms," 114.

Jewish people for connection to God," the cantor sets the sweet *peace and rest*
attitude of the Sabbath day and helps the worshipping community enter
the Sabbath and leave the weekdays behind.[42] The intersection between
Kabbalat Shabbat and the *Maariv* service on Friday night is characterized
by the interplay between major and minor modes, between Adonai Malach
and the Magen Avot (which is the so-called Friday evening minor mode
that dominates the evening service, the Maariv). This intersection marks a
phase in the liturgy in which the worshippers "dive into Shabbat."[43]

The Magen Avot mode is similar to the natural minor Western scale, and
usually transmits the impression of melancholy.[44] However, as the feeling of
sadness is forbidden on the Sabbath day, the Magen Avot mode is commonly
said to convey serenity and calmness, and to create a spirit of rest. Thus, the cantor musically creates a pleasant atmosphere in which the community gets the
chance to reconnect to God, its Jewish heritage and roots, and where it arrives
to the sacred time of Sabbath. The Friday night service closes with a return to

the Adonai Malach mode, which is the same mode that opens the *Shaharit* service on the next morning.[45]

The Shaharit service on Saturday morning is the heart and highlight of the twenty-four-hour Sabbath cycle; it is an unhurried time that is carried—again—by the majestic feeling of the Adonai Malach mode. By employing this major mode, the cantor little by little builds up an ecstatic experience, which culminates in the Torah service—the most important ritual part of the Sabbath day. When the Torah scrolls are taken out of the ark, the cantor switches for the first (and last) time into the Ahavah Rabbah mode that is known for its distinct Middle-Eastern, and oriental sound. The modal (minor) tonality of Ahavah Rabbah is what identifies the day as Sabbath and draws the musically sensitive congregant into the prayer experience. By the use of this mode, the cantor also expresses his deep devotion and unwavering faith in God.[46] As soon as the public reading from the Torah and the study of the weekly Torah portion begins, the cantor switches back into major mode, and thus into the known Adonai Malach mode, as this is the most exciting and solemn moment of the Sabbath service that, once again, requires a grand atmosphere. The cantor stays in this mode throughout the *Musaf* (the additional prayer).[47]

Only at the *Shabbat Minha* prayer (the afternoon service), does the mode change again from major to minor. The community now enters a time of complete rest and relaxation, of calm and conciliation. In order to convey this sentiment musically, the cantor uses a special version of the Magen Avot mode that has a very relaxed character. Thus, the liturgical chants sung to this mode not only reflect the particular peaceful atmosphere of the Sabbath afternoon, but also set the pace for the departure of Sabbath. Throughout the "Third Meal" (the *Seudat Shlishit*) following the Minha service, joyful songs—that in part are based on the major Adonai Malach mode—are sung, in order to honor the day of rest. The following *Maariv Motzai Shabbat* (the conclusion of Sabbath) that later concludes with the *Havdalah* (separation) ritual, is marked by the singing of nostalgic niggunim and slow songs that are meant to prolong the transition back into secular time.[48] It can thus be summarized that "according to the tradition, these *Nusachot* [Adonai Malach, Magen Avot, and Ahavah Rabah] are not only meant to create a general mood of peace and rest, but also to relax the mind, to raise the worshipper to a higher spiritual level and to lead her toward a deeper concentration in devotion."[49]

Levy and I have demonstrated that, through the constant change between major and minor modes, the cantor directs the attention and concentration of the worshipping community toward the most important parts of the Sabbath liturgy, such as the Torah service. This could be observed in ethnographic fieldwork where we measured the level of participation (increasing or decreasing) of each worshipper in communal singing, as well as in the sound intensity and richness of the cantor's solo (crescendo and piano; use of more or less musical flourishes). This observation corresponds to the aspect of *brain stem reflex* in Juslin and Västfjäll's B R E C V E M model (mentioned earlier), which "refers to a process whereby an emotion is induced by music because one or more fundamental acoustical characteristics of the music are taken by the brain stem to signal a potentially important and urgent event."[50]

Beyond that, the use of the Jewish prayer modes on a macro level functions as an "external oscillator entraining [the worshippers'] internal oscillator, in order to affect [their] sense of time," and thus their "sentimental connection to the different phases of the Shabbat day."[51] Two main mechanisms are applied in this context through which music can induce certain sentiments, that is, *musical expectancy*, which refers to the induction of emotion on the basis of specific features in the music that confirm, violate, or delay the listener's expectation about the continuation of the music, and *episodic memory*, which refers to a process of emotion induction whereby the music evokes a personal memory in the listener.[52]

On the micro level, when singing a cantorial recitative, the cantor employs different musical mechanisms in order to generate the appropriate emotional state that should accompany the prayer, as Klein has demonstrated.[53] As in every other religion, the Jewish liturgy encompasses different kinds of texts expressing various emotional moods, such as supplication or thanksgiving. These moods are further transmitted by the cantor's solo recitative through the use of ornate virtuosic ornamentations.[54] In describing this mode of virtuosic solo performance, Klein considers that this process often blurs the line between the cantor as a prayer-leader and the cantor as a performer. According to Klein, in this process the cantor often seeks to impress the listener rather than inspire the worshipper.[55]

It is particularly the notion of supplication that dominates a large part of the Jewish prayer texts due to its emotional significance and central placement within synagogue services. Indeed, supplication characterizes most of the cantorial solo singing—at least within the Eastern European tradition. Within this context, supplication is communicated musically by evoking the image of a crying person. To form this image, the cantor musically imitates the weeping and crying of a person pleading to God by using, for example, a steep and abrupt melismatic rise in the melody, adding appoggiatura and repeating the prayer text and musical motives many times. The culmination of these elements results in the creation of a sorrowful mood through music and gesture. What is important in this regard is that the music itself does not express these emotions, but the cantor—as a sentient independent agent—puts his emotions into the music.[56]

Another musical technique employed by the cantor to arouse emotional excitement, which Klein terms an "intensification process," is the dramaturgical application of the musical crescendo. Here, the cantor systematically and gradually increases the volume of the sound, as well as the pitch height and density over the range of the entire piece, which generates an emotionally charged atmosphere.[57] Thus, "[the] aroused atmosphere, together with the supplicatory mood of the music gives the [cantorial] recitative its unique character and generates the appropriate emotional state in the listeners."[58] The "Ya'aleh" prayer ("May he rise") as sung by cantor Yossele Rosenblatt illustrates these musical techniques and mechanisms quite well.[59] The "Ya'aleh" is the additional prayer recited on *Rosh Chodesh* (the new moon) as well as at festivals, during the evening, morning, and afternoon *Amidah* (the standing prayer), and also during the Grace after Meals. On *Yom Kippur* (the Day of Atonement), the prayer introduces the *S'lichot* (penitential) section of the evening service. The "Ya'aleh" is about asking God for mercy and about expressing one's faith in his eternal grace.

ENGLISH TRANSLATION OF THE "YA'ALEH" PRAYER

May our supplications ascend at evening, Our pleas arrive before You in the morning, And our songs of joy descend at dusk.

May our voice ascend at evening, Our righteousness arrive before You at morning, And our redemption descend with the dusk.

May our affliction ascend at evening, Our forgiveness be granted by You at morning, And our cries echo down at dusk.

May our faith ascend at evening, Arrive for Your sake at morning, And our atonement come down at dusk.

May our salvation ascend at evening, Our purification come to You at morning, And Your graciousness to us descend at dusk.

May our merits remembered ascend at evening, Our assembly be perceived by You at morning, And Your glory descend to us at dusk.

May our petition ascend at evening, Our grateful gladness reach You at dawn, And the granting of our request ascend at dusk.

May our cries ascend at evening, Reach You with the dawn, And echo down to us with the dusk.[60]

The Eastern European version sung by Yossele Rosenblatt unmistakably evokes a mood of supplication and creates a rather sorrowful atmosphere. In contrast to this, the Western European version of the "Ya'aleh" (see figure 6.2), composed by the German cantor Samuel Naumbourg (1817–1880), reflects the grand atmosphere of Yom Kippur. Today, Naumbourg's composition is still an integral part of the Jewish musical tradition in the German-speaking parts of Switzerland, and reflects the cultural (and musical) differences that exist between the different Jewish ethnic groups (between Eastern and Western Ashkenazi Jews). Comparing Rosenblatt's interpretation of the prayer and Naumbourg's composition reveals the different sociocultural norms that define what mood and sentiment are appropriate when singing one and the same prayer. This piece of the Western European tradition of synagogue music contrasts with the Eastern European version. The former is characterized by a preference for a Western major tonality, a strict rhythmical structure, and the abdication of free recitatives and excessive use of melodic ornamentation.

As shown above, with regard to Nusach haTefilah, there are basically two ways of producing emotions in Jewish ritual music, which might lead to a different spiritual perception of the same. First, that occurs by synchronizing the worshipping community through a constant oscillation between major and minor modes, between the feelings of majesty and calmness respectively. In doing so, the cantor calls to the worshippers' musical expectancy and episodic memory, for the emotions conjured by Nusach are largely dependent on associations.[61] Second, music can evoke emotions in the listener/worshipper through representation, that is, through the musical imitation of sounds and sentiments.[62] However, the music's emotional impact is always personally and culturally specific and the reactions it evokes stem largely from previous knowledge and experience.[63] Thus, the Nusach patterns of the Jewish worship service are an essential element of the foundation on which the service is built. The Jewish prayer modes primarily serve to connect the knowledgeable and sensitive congregant to the emotion of the ritual:[64] "[Knowledgeable] congregations should seek the combination of piety and a mastering of traditional *nusach* which is part of the spiritual fabric of *tefillah* . . . the absence of these hallowed *niggunim* during the davening [the recitation of the Jewish prayers] would be unthinkable to any worshipper who has an inbred affinity for the feelings and stirrings of the heart, rendered by the proper *nusach*."[65]

Dov Schwartz emphasizes the importance of the inclusion of specific niggunim to prompt appropriate emotional responses in the "informed" worshipper. This statement prompts reflection on what the emotional experience of an unknowledgeable or nonsensitive listener might be. Moreover, such an approach does not take into account the fact that worshippers may not have been raised in a traditional environment and may well not be trained in the complex art of Nusach haTefilah.

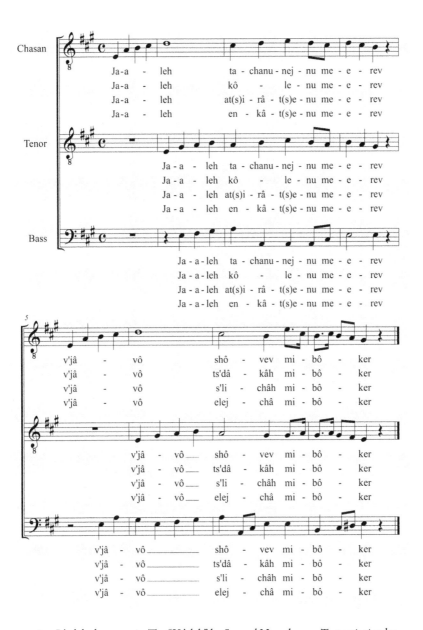

FIG. 6.2. Ja'a-leh sheet music. The "Ya'aleh" by Samuel Naumbourg. Transcription by Sarah Ross. The sheet music of the "Ya'aleh" has been provided by the synagogue choir of the Jewish community of Basel, Switzerland.

As outlined above, within traditional synagogue music, the focus is on the cantor—the main actor in the performance of Jewish ritual music—and how he (in Reform and progressive communities also she) consciously instigates emotional excitement or calmness. However, other forms of Jewish religious worship have developed in which the cantor is no longer the central agent of musical design. Around the mid-twentieth century, young Jews (among them Jewish feminists),[66] who felt alienated by the traditional Jewish melodies, started to invent a new contemporary form of synagogue music. So-called New Jewish Music essentially grew out of the contemporary Jewish Reform tradition in North America, and focuses on engaging the whole congregation, men and women alike, to pray as *one people*. Singing as a full congregation, that is, communal singing, "expresses the sweetness of Judaism" and "transmits the joy of prayer," as singer-songwriter Rabbi Hanna Tiferet stated.[67] These young people employed different ways of songwriting in which the traditionally unmetered Nusach became (a) harmonized (according to Western musical standards), (b) rhythmicized (replacement of the nonmetrical cantorial chant by simple metric melodies), or (c) even replaced by *non-Jewish* musical traditions set to the traditional Jewish prayer texts. The aim was, and still is, to achieve a sense of groove while singing with the congregation. This was done by employing instances of responsorial singing throughout synagogue services.[68] In contradiction to the Eastern European a cappella art song of the cantor, which primarily creates a sorrowful atmosphere, the focus of this new form of liturgical song is to create a joyful, happy, and participatory atmosphere.[69] As with the other examples described herein, in the context of liberal and progressive synagogue services, where this form of Jewish ritual music is practiced, conclusions about the actual perception of emotion on the part of the worshipping community are still very limited. Perhaps some underlying reasons for this lack of academic focus have to do with the challenge of constructing appropriate and sufficient methodological approaches and the challenge of effectively representing the worshippers' emotions in studies on Jewish ritual music.

### Methodological Challenges in the Study and Representation of Emotion in Jewish Ritual Music Studies

Jewish musical emotions occur just like any "musical emotions . . . in complex interactions between the listener, the music, and the situation."[70] Thus, it could be fair to say that, within the field of ethnomusicology, in which most of the studies on Jewish music take place, the method of fieldwork is appropriate and sufficient enough to study these interactions, and thus to represent the emotional effects of Jewish ritual music. By leaving their familiar environment and submerging themselves in an unknown world of the studied group, ethnomusicologists produce musical knowledge by collecting data, observing and interviewing people, as well as by experiencing and finally understanding music. This process is how fieldwork should optimally occur. The study on the "Emotional and Cognitive Rhythms in Jewish Music" that Levy and I conducted, as well as the years of fieldwork experience among Jewish communities in the USA and Switzerland,[71] have shown that standard methods of fieldwork (participant observation and conducting interviews) are not sufficient for getting a deeper understanding of how emotions that are elicited through Jewish ritual music are actually perceived on an individual level.

Within the discipline of ethnomusicology different scholars and schools of thought have influenced the production of musical knowledge through fieldwork. Allan Merriam, for example, proposed in his book *The Anthropology of Music* a tripartite model for the study of ethnomusicology, centering on the study of "music in culture" (later *as* culture). His model focuses on the study of music on three analytic levels, namely, the conceptualization about music, behavior in relation to music, and the sound of music. For Merriam and others, ethnomusicology was about data, and thus about explaining and "sciencing about music,"[72] while the actual personal experience of the research partner and the ethnomusicologist, including the relations with each other in the field that affected and constituted the meaningfulness of data, were absent.[73] In comparison to that, Ki Mantle Hood held a different view on ethnomusicology. His concept of "bi-musicality" puts the emphasis of the study on people making and experiencing music.[74] For him, ethnomusicology was about understanding, rather than explaining music. However, Hood also put the focus on the student (the future ethnomusicologist), who is required to learn to play the music he or she is going to study. While Hood's approach of bi-musicality thus enables the researcher to learn more about the *inside* of a musical practice and culture, it does not necessarily enable him or her to study and analyze the relationship between music and emotion comprehensively.

Nevertheless, the importance of traditional fieldwork methods in ethnomusicological research has been revised within the last decades. In his article "Knowing Fieldwork," Jeff T. Titon challenged the idea that one can really acquire genuine scholarly knowledge about the musical experience, through fieldwork or otherwise. Since the *writing culture debate* in anthropology,[75] scholars have discussed the need for the ethnographer to attempt to understand concepts from the inside. It was recognized that the knowledge of the actor's view of music is very much influenced by the dialogical relationship between the researcher and the research partner. As a result of these discussions, a second set of ethnomusicological literature emerged that deals with the transformative impact of fieldwork/of the ethnomusicologist on those we study.[76] Within this context, a third set of discussions has to be mentioned, which emphasizes the role and importance of interpersonal relationships emerging out of field contacts.[77] Particularly the notion of friendship as a fieldwork epistemology is implied in some applications of so-called *reflexive* ethnography.[78] The so-called *friendship-model of fieldwork*, as illustrated, for example, by Jeff Titon,[79] is very much influenced by feminist theory, and offers the possibility of achieving subjectivity between individuals while maintaining a balance between separateness and appropriate interdependence. This perspective on fieldwork relationships does not seek to break up the self-other dichotomy but to advance knowing and understanding in a world of difference. Titon labeled this path toward such understanding a "musical being-in-the-world,"[80] a process by which the individual seeks to gain a shared understanding of music through knowing people by means of collective music making.[81] In short, the ideal way of producing musical knowledge within ethnomusicology is not only to experience the music itself, but also to experience, and reflect critically on, fieldwork.

As much as I share Titon's thoughts outlined above, I still miss one crucial aspect in his (and other authors') explanations. This *missing* element is a critical approach to the analysis and representation of the interactions between the listener, the music, and the situation we observe within the context of fieldwork, while acknowledging the fact that these interactions are also based on the cognitive perception of music and additional factors contributing to the emotional reactions to music.[82] Discourses on ethnomusicological fieldwork (in comparison to anthropological discourses) seldom discuss how emotions in general are involved in ethnomusicological research and writing, and thus in our anticipation of the field.[83] Moreover, academic music research has yet to systematically explore the particular challenges researchers face when working in Jewish contexts.[84] In this regard, Marcy Brink-Danan states that anthropologists of Jews not only "regularly enter into dialogue about how the study of Jews calls into question accepted disciplinary boundaries, methods, and practices," but also take on "the issue of how Jewishness itself is defined, contested, negotiated, transmitted, and transformed."[85]

In order to set out a discussion on how to cope with the problem of studying and representing the individual's emotions in ethnomusicological research on Jewish ritual music, I would like to link back to the 2013 study that I undertook with Gabriel Levy on the emotional and cognitive function of synagogue music. The focus of our study was on the modal and melodic patterns and variations of Jewish liturgical music (Nusach) and how they stimulate communal emotions and religious feelings and, furthermore, synchronize the emotions of the worshippers. In the process of collecting the ethnographic data for our study, the quest for integrating the interviewees' (but also the researcher's) emotions first emerged, and at the same time, also exposed the methodological challenges in doing so.

Although the most critical method for gaining insight into music perception and cognition is perhaps the experimental method, ethnomusicologists still need to develop "research strategies and methods, which examine musical cognition in the framework of mental models of culture in real-life situations."[86] In this regard, the most important challenge that researchers of Jewish music and emotion have to face is how to study emotions and musical perception in Jewish ritual contexts, without violating Jewish religious law (e.g., the prohibition to work and to use any kind of electronic device on Sabbath) or intruding on the worshippers' privacy, such as by approaching the study of emotion in Jewish ritual music through the use of music psychological experiments that require electronic devices to measure emotional responses, which would probably change the emotional response. Also, it is not possible to replicate the musical-ritual experience in a laboratory outside of the *holy time*. Here, Levy and I were very limited in our research method, as, for example, audio and video recordings during synagogue services on Sabbath were prohibited, and even our taking notes was not very welcomed. Thus, it is obvious that computer-based experiments and simulations do not fit very well into the field of Jewish ritual music studies.

Furthermore, within the context of controlled experiments, which either eliminate cultural and contextual influences or do not problematize the interaction between culture and music, participants are usually not informed of the researcher's hypothesis, nor sometimes even of the feature(s) of interest. However, adopting this approach would be highly problematic in the context of ethnographic fieldwork due to the ethical conventions researchers must follow when collecting ethnographic data. The building of mutual trust is one of the most important aspects during fieldwork; not disclosing the goals of the field encounter could easily be perceived by participants as violating this trust. Indeed, Pirkko Moisala demands that experiments, which are conducted within the context of ethnomusicology, should not only be meaningful to the researcher but to the people whose music we study. With regard to synagogue music, which is mostly perceived as an unchangeable and untouchable (sacred) tradition, considerations like these are very important. Consequently, our research partners (informants) should be able to decide what kind of music material used in a music psychological experiment is culturally relevant.[87] Moving forward, for future research on Jewish ritual music and emotion, it might be useful to take a multidisciplinary approach and to combine the fieldwork process with methodological approaches from the field of music psychology.

## REAPPROACHING THE QUANTITATIVE AND QUALITATIVE ELEMENTS OF NUSACH

Simon Liljeström, Patrik N. Juslin, and Daniel Västfjäll state that "music may arouse intense emotions in listeners, but little is known about the circumstances that contribute to such reactions."[88] Motivated by this lack of academic scholarship, Liljeström, Juslin, and Västfjäll set up a listening experiment through which they investigated the roles of selected musical, situational, and individual factors in emotional relations to music.[89] The study of Liljeström, Juslin, and Västfjäll on "Experimental Evidence of the Roles of Music Choice, Social Context, and Listener Personality in Emotional Reactions to Music" but also Mandi M. Miller and Kenneth T. Strongman's study on "The Emotional Effects of Music on Religious Experience"[90] both draw on a combination of data collected in laboratory experiments (psychophysiological responses to music, such as heart rate or skin conductance) as well as field studies consisting of interviews and questionnaires. Field studies enable the researcher "to capture listeners' response to music in their natural environment," but do not "enable [them] to draw definite conclusions regarding causal relationships" between music and the arousal of emotion.[91] Applying these approaches to the study of the Jewish prayer modes discussed above would mean closely scrutinizing the so-called quantitative and qualitative elements of Nusach, that is, the musical, situational, and individual factors.[92]

According to Sholom Kalib, the quantitative elements of the prayer modes, such as scales and motifs, can be presented in musical notation, while the qualitative elements, such as mood, atmosphere, and emotionally engendered nuances, cannot.[93] The quantitative elements (musical features) are consciously employed by the cantors (as discussed earlier) to arouse emotions in the worshipper. But at the same time, they are the less-understood features: there is a difference between what the cantor and worshippers think has influenced their own emotional reactions, and what has really aroused their emotions. Overall, it is difficult to find simple links between musical characteristics and aroused emotions.[94] Moreover, the literal meaning, religious message, and significance of sacred texts are related to a particular religious occasion that determines the qualitative elements of the Nusach. The qualitative elements are thus further influenced by the social, cultural, economic, political and historical circumstances of the Jewish community.[95] In this regard, the listener's musical preferences, which to a large extent are shaped by these qualitative elements of the prayer modes, also influence both the perception of the musical features of the Nusach (the quantitative elements) and the emotions experienced in response to them. This makes it difficult to predict (in fieldwork settings) how a worshipper will respond to singing and chanting throughout a synagogue service.[96]

Against the background of the situational features (place, time, social interaction, etc.),[97] the interrelationship of qualitative and quantitative elements of Jewish prayer music is relevant with regard to the experience of emotion within Jewish worship. This is particularly obvious within the context of Reform and progressive Jewish communities, where the focus lies (in comparison to traditional and Orthodox Judaism) on the active participation of all worshippers in communal singing, and thus on the performance of a liturgical musical repertoire that represents the contemporary musical language of those communities.[98] Here, the social interaction encouraged through the group singing of modern synagogue music produces positive individual and group effects, such as happiness and emotional well-being.[99] In this context, the personality traits (the individual features) of the worshippers also come into play, such as their openness to experience—for example, new sounds of synagogue music. However, according to Liljeström, Juslin, and Västfjäll, only very few studies exist that analyze the individual differences in musical emotions.[100]

BEING YOUR OWN INFORMANT

Emotion is a notoriously difficult variable to *measure*. As Haucke Egerman et al. explain, different approaches were developed to measure the subjective feeling component of emotion. It would be beyond the scope of this chapter to give a detailed report on research methods used in this context. Nonetheless, it is noteworthy that, as well as adjective lists and categorical emotion models, dimensional emotion models have been used for emotion research.[101] According to Klaus Scherer,[102] emotions are typically defined to consist of three components, namely, a subjective feeling component, a physiological response, and a behavioral or motor response. The result of this complexity is that, for every single component of emotions, several methodological approaches exist.[103] Thus, the scholarly focus has emphasized the importance of the subjective feeling component of emotions.

Although there are many theories about musical emotions, they have yet to adequately account for the intensity of musical experience felt throughout synagogue services.[104] Besides that, my research project revealed the challenge of limited data collection, an accumulation that was confined to data gathered through introspection and ethnographic investigation.[105] When subsequently discussing these research problems with a colleague who works in the field of music psychology and systematic musicology, he suggested that the researcher should become his/her own informant. This means considering the researcher's own religious, musical, and emotional experiences as a source of data, which can be compared to interviews with other worshippers conducted after services. While my colleague's suggestion was logical and helpful, its application could be viewed as challenging.

The first argument in favor of this suggestion is that the researcher might have a personal relationship to Judaism, too, and regularly attends synagogue services. In this context, it might be considered that "cognition and emotion are closely linked in music," as Carol L. Krumhansl states,[106] and that the experience of musical pattern recognition, like other experience, is linked to emotional responses, whose understanding is essential for the understanding of music's essence.[107] Thus, in cases where informants and researcher share the same set of beliefs and at least a similar religious knowledge about the appropriate form of performing Jewish rituals, it can be assumed that their emotional response to and experiences of Nusach, to Jewish ritual music in particular, are similar. This argument is supported by other research results on music, cognition, and emotion, which state that, although music is often connected to significant personal memories, emotional responses to music do not vary greatly from individual to individual depending on their unique past experiences.[108] Nevertheless, it is important to note that there is a difference between perceived and felt emotions in music: "Music is able to express a certain emotional expression, but this expression is not always induced in every listener automatically."[109]

Second, the syntax of music is subject to cognitive constraints and interactions with other aspects of culture. Therefore, the perception of music within a given culture is inextricably linked to the historical development of the syntax and semantics of a musical language in that culture.[110] This is also true regarding the musical conventions within Jewish liturgy that are also determined and influenced by the social, cultural, political, and historical circumstances of the community. However, these conventions in turn influence how people perceive music, how they react emotionally to it, and what meaning and value they ascribe to the music they hear.[111] Conducting fieldwork within one's own Jewish community (or within Jewish communities that are not the *home* Jewish community) means that the interview partners and the researcher share at least some cultural background. Scherer and Zentner discuss this phenomenon under the category of "listener features," which are relevant in the production of emotion in music listeners. The authors state that "listener features are based on the individual and sociocultural identity of the listener and on the symbolic coding convention prevalent in a particular culture or subculture. They can consist of interpretation rules (e.g. musical systems) that are shared in a group or culture [such as the different traditions of Nusach], or of inference dispositions based on personality, prior experiences, and musical talent."[112] Scherer and Zentner further summarize these factors as "musical expertise" (referring to cultural expectations about musical meaning), "stable dispositions" that are not related to music (e.g., personality or perceptual habits), and "associative coding," referring to musical and nonmusical aspects of a performance that can be "associated with emotional content in an individual's memory due to learned associations and conditioning."[113]

Finally, conducting fieldwork within one's own religion means that, on some level, researcher and research partners do have religious assumptions and traditions in common. This common ground can be viewed as beneficial in determining the role of religious and musical expectations, and knowledge. Within the context of the study Levy and I conducted, it became evident that within a Jewish religious context (which might be separated from a Jewish cultural context), a certain amount of religious and musical expectations and knowledge is required in order to be able to tune in and respond to the stimuli of Jewish ritual music, and thus to synchronize the individual with the group. As psychologist Carol Krumhansl explains, "expectations play the central psychological role in musical emotions,"[114] as the interplay between expectations and the sounded event are relevant for the creation of musical, and in this case also to the spiritual tensions and relaxation. That is why musical emotions change over time in intensity and quality.

SELF-REPORT OF FEELINGS

In terms of methodology, the question still is how to integrate the researcher's, and, of course, our fieldwork collaborators,' emotional experiences into the ethnomusicological account. Among the methods used to study emotion induced through music, the *self-report of feelings* has been the most widely used one. The self-report of feelings would not be limited to accessing the subjective emotional experiences of the research partners, but could also be applied to the researcher's own subjective experiences. Scherer and Zentner discuss how the self-report of feelings is often used in so-called mood induction studies that seek to investigate the "effects of different affect states, moods, and emotions on cognitive and evaluative processes, memory, behaviour, and physiology."[115] Scherer and Zentner's focus corresponds to the aim of research on the qualitative elements of the Jewish prayer modes in relation to the cognition and experience of emotion in Jewish ritual music. Within the field of psychology, a wide range of self-report methods and instruments have been developed, which are normally derived from different theories and models of emotion. These methods are meant to access and assess subjectively experienced states with some reliability.[116] Marcel Zentner and Tuomas Eerola discuss several types of self-report instruments and methods that have been used and tested in different studies on music and emotion. Against the background of the practical problems related to the study of emotions in Jewish ritual music, which prohibits the collection of data in live performance situations, two tools of self-report mentioned by Zentner and Eerola can easily be integrated into ethnomusicological research: the diary study and the free report (also known as phenomenological narrative). While the former consists of a "daily report of the central emotional episodes and their causes and effects," the latter contains descriptions of personal experiences, whereby the actual format and focus can be defined individually, according to the particular research question.[117] Besides the obstacles mentioned above that complicate the investigation of the qualitative elements of Nusach and their effect on the worshippers' sense and experience of religious emotions, there are further problems that have to be considered.

First, constantly evaluating one's emotional experience throughout a synagogue service might overstrain the worshipper and his/her attention and perceptive capacities. Second, within a diverse and multicultural Jewish setting, the researcher has to be aware that vocabularies for emotions may vary across cultures, even though certain emotion concepts can be found in most cultures. Third, different cultural traditions or habits might affect the self-report as well. And finally, "another demarcation line in the self-rating methodology is whether the ratings are collected post-performance or continuously." In this regard, and as Zentner and Eerola explain, "music unfolds in time, and affective experiences also change as the music progress." In order to catch and measure the "moment-by-moment fluctuations" in the emotional experience of music, but also with regard to the first two problems mentioned here, it is even more worthwhile to integrate and use the research's self-report of feelings as a distinct set of data within ethnomusicological research.[118]

Despite its potential methodological usefulness, "the use of self-report measures as evidence for emotion production has both advantages and disadvantages," as Scherer and Zentner explain: "It remains the only method that allows access to the subjective emotional experience. . . . However, the data collected in this way are sensitive to the following potential biases and artefacts that need to be carefully considered before conclusions are drawn. Firstly, demand characteristics can be responsible for the mood effects found. Secondly, listeners [the researcher included] may confuse the emotions expressed in the music with what they actually feel unless they are specifically requested to distinguish between the two emotion modalities."[119]

Notwithstanding the possible shortcomings of the method, the self-report of feelings in the form of free descriptions of emotion-like reactions to music, in diary entries, does not differ much from field notes taken by the ethnomusicologist. The only difference here might be that these *field notes* are taken with the intention of using them as equivalent data, next to data collected by means of narrative interviews, participant observation, and so forth. Particularly in fieldwork situations, in which *live* recordings are forbidden and in which interviews only can occur after the musical event in question, the researcher's self-report of emotion can be a fruitful methodological addition to ethnographic research. It allows the researcher to synchronize his/her report of feelings with the ongoing musical event, and thus to link observations of his/her own affective responses to significant parts of the performance/the ritual. Furthermore, he/she can compare his/her own experiences with that of his/her informants. As Scherer and Zentner also suggest, the self-report of feelings might serve as a so-called manipulation check.[120]

In the process of using the self-report method, it is important to recognize that, next to structural features of music, the individual and sociocultural identity of the listener (the researcher included), the symbolic coding conventions prevalent in a particular culture, as well as the listener's musical expertise, including cultural expectations, and perceptual habits are relevant with regard to the emotional experience of music. Equally important are contextual features such as certain aspects of the performance and listening situation. However, encounters between individuals also influence the emotional dimension, as G. Hubbard et al. state: "Emotions are inescapable because how we make sense of the world and our interactions with others is an emotional relation. Researchers investigating sensitive topics [such as music] are aware that the interview [as well as the broader context of fieldwork] will be an emotional experience."[121] Evaluating the impact of these encounters, not only as applied to the research partner but also to the researcher him-/herself, might help unveil the range of emotional responses to music, and, thus, the worshippers' experience of emotion as elicited through ritual music.

Last but not least, the self-report of feelings—as a text—can further be analyzed against the background of cultural theories, such as Sara Ahmed's idea on the cultural practice of emotions (in contradiction to the view of emotion as psychological state), which she discussed in *The Cultural Politics of Emotions*.[122]


## Conclusion

In this chapter, I have demonstrated different ways that emotions are conveyed through Jewish ritual music and have further discussed the methodological challenges in studying, analyzing, and representing them in ethnomusicological writing, particularly with regard to the elicitation of emotion through music. For future studies on emotions and Jewish ritual music, I suggested taking a multidisciplinary approach that combines ethnomusicological fieldwork with methods and approaches from the field of music psychology, which—to some degree—already happens within the studies of cognitive ethnomusicology.[123]

Overall, in order to bring the study of emotion in Jewish ritual music into a new, more encompassing and comprehensive direction, it is first of all necessary to widen the view on emotion within Jewish music studies. Emotions are not only "universal facts of nature," or abstract phenomena differently formulated and represented in Jewish scriptures or compositions of synagogue music. Emotions are also bodily reactions to the outer world, and thus individually felt experiences that—to some extent—are also learned as well as situationally deployed.[124] However, most studies of emotion and (Jewish) music, while firmly in the tradition of cultural theory, still regard music as text, as a sonic object that needs to be decoded. But even in the expanded sense, in which the term text is nowadays used, researchers run the risk of turning their focus away from people's diverse musical experiences and falling "back into that limiting approach of locating emotion in the work and its exposition by experts."[125] Admittedly, this approach is much easier for scholars to capture, particularly for those who want to keep with the academic tradition of studying ideas. But for the study of emotions and music within the context of ritual experience, "this is definitely not the whole story . . . experiences of 'the same' text are not necessarily uniform."[126] To maintain analytical rigor in the study of music and emotion, music can thus not be detached from its context.

Although synagogue music is commonly said to connect the Jewish people over time and space, future study of emotion in Jewish ritual music should acknowledge (1) that music itself, as well as the process of producing, performing, and listening to it, is—according to John Blacking—a "result of a synthesis of cognitive processes, which are present in culture and in the human body,"[127] and (2) that cognition therefore evolves as much from culture as it does from biology. In order to comprehend the production and perception of emotion in and through (Jewish) music, it is therefore necessary to elucidate the ways that cognitive processes of musical experience function in different (Jewish) cultures around the world.[128]

Furthermore, and as Udo Will elaborates, the rapprochement of the cognitive sciences and ethnomusicology (in the 1980s and 1990s) not only challenged concepts of cognition at the time,[129] but also of culture. According to these developments, culture could no longer be conceptualized solely as an autonomous and symbolic system, but as one that is also dependent on biological conditions.[130] Consequently, the concept of *cultural construction* also needs to be revisited. It was helpful indeed for questioning generalized concepts of emotions as primeval internal impulses; but the pendulum can also swing too far. Substituting cultural for biological determinism is surely shortsighted, as culture cannot only be explained through biology, and vice versa: the one cannot be understood without the other.[131]

With regard to the suggested multidisciplinary approach to Jewish ritual music and emotion, Udo Will makes an important objection by asking for a reconsideration of the so-called *emic* assessment (viewpoints obtained from within the social group; from the perspective of the interview partner) and *etic* perspective in music research (viewpoints obtained from outside; from the perspective of the researcher).[132] It is particularly the emic/insider's approach that investigates how the people perceive and give meaning to music, which is of high priority within ethnomusicological research, as it is considered to be the only appropriate one for the understanding of human behavior.[133] But against the background of the insights gained from cognitive sciences, ethnosemantics,[134] and because of their fixation with verbal behavior, insiders are not in the position to identify the meaning of nonverbal behavior.[135] In this regard, Udo Will concludes: "emic rules of verbal behavior are not reliable indicators of significant etic regularities in sociocultural systems."[136]

Therefore, for a better understanding of the perception of emotion in Jewish ritual music, relevant investigations could be conducted when no corresponding (emic) verbal information is available. The etic examination (e.g., in the form of real-time physiological and psychological measurements and experiments) can serve as a supplement, and possibly even as an important corrective, to the emic interpretation. Without doubt, "thoughts can influence action, but it is of considerable concern when verbal expressions of actors are taken as causal explanations of their actions because these expressions are posthoc explanations, justifications, or rationalizations of behavior rather than causal explanations."[137] Thus, etic—which means cognitive ethnomusicological—studies can produce important evidence that an emic interpretation can support or even contradict.[138] However, within the context of real-time ritual settings, a range of methodological problems have to be solved. Tackling these problems would require the invention of noninvasive research methods that are flexible enough with regard to religious laws and emotionalism, simultaneously recognize aspects of biological inheritance, and are sensitive to cross-cultural similarities and differences in the production and perception of Jewish ritual music as well as to aspects of enculturation.

For obvious reasons, the future study of religion, ritual music, and emotion needs collaborations between different fields of expertise such as Jewish music studies, cognitive ethnomusicology, religious studies/cognitive studies of religion, and music psychology. At this point, perhaps it is worthwhile to ask why we need to know how emotions are actually perceived by worshippers. Is it too private a matter? The answer might be that if carried out carefully and tactfully, with particular consideration of the cultural context(s), such studies will help form a more complete picture of how human beings negotiate emotion, religion, and music.

NOTES

1. Frank Burch Brown, "Musical Ways of Being Religious," in *The Oxford Handbook of Religion and the Arts*, ed. Frank Burch Brown (Oxford: Oxford University Press, 2014), 110–11; Amit Klein, "Singing Their Heart Out: Emotional Excitement in Cantorial Recitatives and Carlebach Nusach," in *Judaism and Emotion: Texts, Performance, Experience*, ed. Sarah Ross, Gabriel Levy, and Soham Al-Suadi (New York: Peter Lang, 2013), 68.

2. Brown, "Musical Ways," 110–11.

3. See Michael Lewis, Jeannette M. Haviland-Jones, and Lisa Feldman Barrett, eds., *Handbook of Emotions*, 3rd ed. (New York: Guilford Press, 2008); Paul R. Kleinginna Jr. and Anne M. Kleinginna, "A Categorized List of Emotion Definitions, with Suggestions for a Consensual Definition," *Motivation and Emotion* 5, no. 4 (1981): 345–79.

4. Peggy A. Thoits, "The Sociology of Emotions," *Annual Review of Sociology* 15 (1989): 318.

5. Thoits, "The Sociology of Emotions."

6. For further discussion, see also P. N. Johnson-Laird and Keith Oatley, "Emotions, Music, and Literature," in *Handbook of Emotions*, ed. Michael Lewis, Jeannette M. Haviland-Jones, and Lisa Feldman Barrett (New York: Guilford Press, 2010), 102–13.

7. See Klaus R. Scherer and Marcel R. Zentner, "Emotional Effects of Music: Production Rules," in *Music and Emotion: Theory and Research*, ed. Patrik N. Juslin and John A. Sloboda (Oxford: Oxford University Press, 2001), 361.

8. Scherer and Zentner, "Emotional Effects," 362–65.

9. Patrik N. Juslin and Daniel Västfjäll, "Emotional Responses to Music: The Need to Consider Underlying Mechanisms," *Behavioral and Brain Sciences* 31, no. 5 (2008): 563–68.

10. Juslin and Västfjäll, "Emotional Responses," 561–63.

11. See W. J. Dowling, "The Development of Music Perception and Cognition," in *Foundations of Cognitive Psychology: Core Readings*, ed. Daniel J. Levitin (Cambridge, MA: MIT Press, 2002), 481–502; Scherer and Zentner, "Emotional Effects"; John A. Sloboda and Patrik N. Juslin, "Psychological Perspectives on Music and Emotion," in *Music and Emotion: Theory and Research*, ed. Patrik N. Juslin and John A. Sloboda (Oxford: Oxford University Press, 2001), 79–96.

12. William Forde Thompson and Laura-Lee Balkwill, "Cross-Cultural Similarities and Differences," in *Oxford Handbook of Music and Emotion: Theory, Research, Applications*, ed. Patrik N. Juslin and John A. Sloboda (Oxford: Oxford University Press, 2010), 756.

13. The concert was part of the Jewish Music Institute Conference "Art Musics of Israel" and took place at Brunei Gallery Theatre at SOAS University of London on March 29, 2011.

14. To see the whole performance of "Raza D'Shabbat," accessed February 2, 2015, please visit https://www.youtube.com/watch?v=EYGoATXFXhg.

15. For a more detailed discussion on Hassidic music, see Shmuel Barzilai, *Chassidic Ecstasy in Music* (Frankfurt am Main: Peter Lang, 2009).

16. Next to Andre Hajdu (music director, piano, and vocals), the ensemble consists of Baruch Brenner (artistic director, vocals, and narration), Yair Harel (percussion, tar, and vocals), Nori Jacoby (viola and vocals), Jonathan Niv (cello and vocals), Matti Kovler (piano and vocals) and Eitan Kirsch (double bass guitar, vocals, and recordings).

17. See Andre Hajdu, *Kulmus HaNefesh: A Musical Journey into the Hassidic Niggun*, CD booklet, CJM 0901 (Jerusalem: Jewish Music Research Center—Hebrew University of Jerusalem, 2009).

18. See "HaOman Hai Ensemble," Tipeha: Jewish Arts and Education, accessed August 13, 2016, https://tipehamusic.wordpress.com/haoman-hai-ensemble/raza-dshabbat/.

19. Such as the well-known Piyyutim "Yedid Nefesh" ("Friend of the Soul") that marks the beginning of Sabbath on Friday night; "Lecha Dodi" ("Come my friend towards the bride"), a song of deep devotion that is sung during the *Kabbalat Shabbat* service (the welcoming and receiving of the day of rest); "El Adon" ("God, Master of All"), which is known from the *Shacharith*, the Saturday morning service; or "Omar LaEl mahasi" ("I say to God my shield"), which marks the end of the Sabbath during the so-called *Havdalah* ritual (farewell to the Sabbath).

20. Klein, "Singing Their Heart Out," 70.

21. Jonathan L. Friedmann, ed., *Emotions in Jewish Music: Personal and Scholarly Reflections* (Lanham, MD: University Press of America, 2012).

22. Jonathan L. Friedmann, "Emotions and Devotion in Synagogue Song," *Jewish Magazine*, March 2009, accessed August 13, 2016, www.jewishmag.com/131mag/prayer_music/prayer_music.htm.

23. These have been discussed at length elsewhere; see Joel Gereboff, "Judaism," in *The Oxford Handbook of Religion and Emotion*, ed. John Corrigan (New York: Oxford University Press, 2008), 95–110.

24. See Friedmann, *Emotions in Jewish Music*.

25. For a detailed discussion on the study of Jewish music in different fields of research, see Judah M. Cohen, "Wither Jewish Music?: Jewish Studies, Music Scholarship, and the Tilt between Seminary and University," *AJS Review* 32, no. 1 (2008): 29–48; and Philip V. Bohmlan, "Introduction: Jewish Music in Dialogue with Jewish Studies," in *The Oxford Handbook of Jewish Studies*, ed. Martin Goodman, Jeremy Cohen, and David Sorkin (Oxford: Oxford University Press, 2002), 852–69.

26. See Pirkko Moisala, "Cognitive Study of Music as Culture: Basic Premises for Cognitive Ethnomusicology," *Journal of New Music Research* 24 (1995): 8–20; Carol L. Krumhansl et al., "Cross-Cultural Music Cognition: Cognitive Methodology Applied to North Sami Yoiks," *Cognition* 76, no. 1 (2000): 13–58; Udo Will, "Perspectives of a Reorientation in Cognitive Ethnomusicology," *ResearchGate*, December 2013, accessed August 13, 2016, www.researchgate.net/publication/259451150_Reorientation_in_Cognitive_Ethnomusicology_(English_Version); William Forde Thompson and Laura-Lee Balkwill, "Cross-Cultural Similarities and Differences," in *Handbook of Music and Emotion: Theory, Research, Applications*, ed. Patrik N. Juslin and John A. Sloboda (Oxford: Oxford University Press, 2010), 755–88.

27. Moisala, "Cognitive Study of Music," 8.

28. Simon Liljeström, Patrik N. Juslin, and Daniel Västfjäll, "Experimental Evidence of the Roles of Music Choice, Social Context, and Listener Personality in Emotional Reactions to Music," *Psychology of Music* 41, no. 5 (2012): 581–82; Mandi M. Miller and Kenneth T. Strongman, "The Emotional Effects of Music on Religious Experience: A Study of the Pentecostal-Charismatic Style of Music and Worship," *Psychology of Music* 30, no. 1 (April 2002): 8–27.

29. See Mark Kligman, "Judaism and Music," in *The Oxford Handbook of Religion and the Arts*, ed. Frank Burch Brown (Oxford: Oxford University Press, 2014), 263–67.

30. For a detailed discussion on the musical, cultural, and religious meaning of Nusach, see Mark Slobin, *Chosen Voices: The Story of the American Cantorate* (Urbana: University of Illinois Press, 2002), 256–80; Mark Goodman, "Why *Nusach* Still Matters," in *Emotions in Jewish Music: Personal and Scholarly Reflections*, ed. Jonathan L. Friedmann (Lanham, MD: University Press of America, 2012), 30–44; and Gabriel Levy and Sarah Ross, "Emotional and Cognitive Rhythms in Jewish Ritual Music," in *Judaism and Emotion: Texts, Performance, Experience*, ed. Sarah M. Ross, Gabriel Levy, and Soham Al-Suadi (New York: Peter Lang, 2013), 104–7.

31. Klein, "Singing Their Heart Out," 73; Levy and Ross, "Emotional and Cognitive Rhythms," 104–5.

32. Kligman, "Judaism and Music," 264.

33. Kessler, as quoted in Levy and Ross, "Emotional and Cognitive Rhythms," 105.

34. Goodman, "Why *Nusach* Still Matters," 37.

35. Slobin, *Chosen Voices*, 260. The bracketed words in the quotation are supplementary words added by the author.

36. Gabriel Levy and Sarah Ross, "Emotional and Cognitive Rhythms in Jewish Ritual Music," in *Judaism and Emotion: Texts, Performance, Experience*, ed. Sarah Ross, Gabriel Levy, and Soham Al-Suadi (New York: Peter Lang, 2013), 99–120.

37. See Kligman, "Judaism and Music," 264–65; Goodman, "Why *Nusach* Still Matters," 41–42.

38. Kligman, "Judaism and Music," 264–65.

39. Levy and Ross, "Emotional and Cognitive Rhythms," 106.

40. The image was originally designed and published by Marcia Prager; see Levy and Ross, "Emotional and Cognitive Rhythms," 117n16. The reason we adopted this image is because this figure derives from Kabbalistic tradition that seeks to incorporate the body into cognition, and which focuses on the dynamic and interpersonal space of emotion we discussed in our article (113).

41. Goodman, "Why *Nusach* Still Matters," 40–41.

42. Levy and Ross, "Emotional and Cognitive Rhythms," 108.

43. Levy and Ross, "Emotional and Cognitive Rhythms," 108.

44. Goodman, "Why *Nusach* Still Matters," 41–42.

45. Levy and Ross, "Emotional and Cognitive Rhythms," 109–10.

46. Goodman, "Why *Nusach* Still Matters," 39–40.

47. Levy and Ross, "Emotional and Cognitive Rhythms," 109–11.

48. Levy and Ross, "Emotional and Cognitive Rhythms," 108–13.

49. Levy and Ross, "Emotional and Cognitive Rhythms," 112.

50. Juslin and Västfjäll, "Emotional Responses," 564.

51. Levy and Ross, "Emotional and Cognitive Rhythms," 116.

52. Juslin and Västfjäll, "Emotional Responses," 567–68; Levy and Ross, "Emotional and Cognitive Rhythms," 115–16.

53. Levy and Ross, "Emotional and Cognitive Rhythms," 73–81.

54. This technique is an extension of the simple traditional prayer chant (Nusach) sung by the community. For a detailed discussion of this topic, see Klein, "Singing Their Heart Out."

55. Klein, "Singing Their Heart Out," 73.

56. Klein, "Singing Their Heart Out," 74–76.

57. Klein, "Singing Their Heart Out," 76–81.

58. Klein, "Singing Their Heart Out," 80–81.

59. This musical example can be found on YouTube, accessed January 5, 2015, https://www.youtube.com/watch?v=rZylIJBCWHQ.

60. English translation of the prayer text, accessed January 5, 2015, http://www.mrwinikoffmusic.com/choral/yaaleh-yomkippur-jewishchoir.html.

61. Levy and Ross, "Emotional and Cognitive Rhythms," 115.

62. Klein, "Singing Their Heart Out," 76.

63. Friedmann, *Emotions in Jewish Music*, 2.

64. Goodman, "Why *Nusach* Still Matters," 30.

65. Gedalia Dov Schwartz, as quoted by Goodman, "Why *Nusach* Still Matters," 37.

66. See Sarah M. Ross, *A Season of Singing: Creating Feminist-Jewish Music in the United States* (Waltham, MA: Brandeis University Press, 2016).

67. Rabbi Tiferet, telephone interview by author, February 2007.

68. See also Ross, *Season of Singing*, 180–84.

69. These new liturgical songs relied on upbeat and accentuated rhythms, simple melodies with catchy and symmetric phrases, as well as on basic tonic-dominant harmonies.

70. Liljeström, Juslin, and Västfjäll, "Experimental Evidence," 580.

71. See Ross, *Season of Singing*; Sarah M. Ross, "Sense or Absence of Nationalism: Searching for a Swiss-Jewish Musical Identity," in *Music and Minorities from around the World: Research, Documentation and Interdisciplinary Study*, ed. Ursula Hemetek, Essica Marks, and Adelaida Reyes (Newcastle upon Tyne: Cambridge Scholars Press, 2014), 115–41.

72. Alan P. Merriam, *Anthropology of Music* (Evanston, IL: Northwestern University Press, 1964), 25.

73. Jeff Todd Titon, "Knowing Fieldwork," in *Shadows in the Field: New Perspectives for Fieldwork in Ethnomusicology*, ed. Gregory F. Barz and Timothy J. Cooley (New York: Oxford University Press, 1997), 91.

74. Mantle Ki Hood, "The Challenge of Bi-Musicality," *Ethnomusicology* 4 (1960): 55–59; Titon, "Knowing Fieldwork," 92; and Jeff Todd Titon, "Bi-Musicality as Metaphor," *Journal of American Folklore* 108, no. 429 (1995): 288.

75. James Clifford and George E. Marcus, eds., *Writing Cultures: The Poetics and Politics of Ethnography* (Berkeley: University of California Press, 1986).

76. See Kay Kaufman Shelemay's article in which she outlined her own inclusion into the transmission of musical practices among Syrian Jews living in Brooklyn, New York: Kay Kaufman Shelemay, "The Ethnomusicologist and the Transmission of Tradition," *Journal of Musicology* 14, no. 1 (1996): 35–51.

77. Examples are too numerous to itemize here but include the following works: Liz Bondi, "The Place of Emotions in Research: From Partitioning Emotion and Reason to the Emotional Dynamics of Research Relationships," in *Emotional Geographies*, ed. Joyce Davidson, Liz Bondi, and Mick Smith (Aldershot, UK: Ashgate, 2005), 231–46; James Clifford and George E. Marcus, eds., *Writing Cultures: The Poetics and Politics of Ethnography* (Berkeley: University of California Press, 1986); Timothy J. Cooley, "Theorizing Fieldwork Impact: Malinowski, Peasant-Love and Friendship," *British Journal of Ethnomusicology* 12, no. 1 (2003): 1–17; G. Hubbard, K. Backett-Milburn, and D. Kemmer, "Working with Emotion: Issues for the Researcher in Fieldwork and Teamwork," *International Journal of Social Research Methodology* 4, no. 2 (2001): 119–37; and Sherryl Kleinman, "Field-Workers' Feelings: What We Feel, Who We Are, How We Analyze," in *Experiencing Fieldwork: An Inside View of Qualitative Research*, ed. William B. Shaffir and Robert A. Stebbins (Newbury Park, CA: Sage, 1991), 184–95.

78. See Cooley, "Theorizing Fieldwork," 11.

79. Jeff Todd Titon, "Music, the Public Interest, and the Practice of Ethnomusicology." *Ethnomusicology* 36, no. 3 (1992): 315–22.

80. Titon, "Bi-Musicality," 295.

81. See Cooley, "Theorizing Filedwork," 11.

82. See Liljeström, Juslin, and Västfjäll, "Experimental Evidence," 580–82.

83. Bondi, "Place of Emotions in Research"; Barbara Laslett, "Unfeeling Knowledge: Emotion and Objectivity in the History of Sociology," *Sociological Forum* 5, no. 3 (1990): 413–33; and Rebekah Widdowfield, "The Place of Emotions in Academic Research," *Area* 32, no. 2 (2000): 199–208.

84. One exemption that has to be mentioned here is the book edited by Fran Markovitz, *Ethnographic Encounters in Israel: Poetics and Ethics of Fieldwork* (Bloomington: Indiana University Press, 2013).

85. Marcy Brink-Danan, "Anthropological Perspectives on Judaism," *Religion Compass* 2, no. 4 (July 2008): 674–88, and "Anthropology of the Jews," accessed August 3, 2016, *Oxford Bibliographies Online Datasets* (2012), doi: http://dx.doi.org/10.1093/obo/9780199840731-0070.

86. Moisala, "Cognitive Study of Music," 17.

87. Moisala, Cognitive Study of Music," 12.

88. Liljeström, Juslin, and Västfjäll, "Experimental Evidence," 579.

89. Liljeström, Juslin, and Västfjäll, "Experimental Evidence," 579.

90. Miller and Strongman, "Emotional Effects."

91. Liljeström, Juslin, and Västfjäll, "Experimental Evidence," 582.

92. Liljeström, Juslin, and Västfjäll, "Experimental Evidence," 580–82.

93. Sholom Kalib, *The Musical Tradition of the Eastern European Synagogue* (Syracuse, NY: Syracuse University Press, 2002), 1:92–101.

94. Liljeström, Juslin, and Västfjäll, "Experimental Evidence," 580.

95. Kalib, *Musical Tradition*, 1:92–101.

96. Liljeström, Juslin, and Västfjäll, "Experimental Evidence," 580.

97. The situational features are taken into consideration by Liljeström, Juslin, and Västfjäll, "Experimental Evidence," 58, as well as Miller and Strongman, "Emotional Effects," 9.

98. Ross, *Season of Singing*, 171–79.

99. See Miller and Strongman, "Emotional Effects," 9–10.

100. Liljeström, Juslin, and Västfjäll, "Experimental Evidence," 582.

101. Hauke Egerman, Frederik Nagel, Eckart Altenmüller, and Reinhard Kopiez, "Continuous Measurement of Musically-Induced Emotion: A Web Experiment," *International Journal of Internet Science* 4, no. 1 (2009): 5.

102. Klaus R. Scherer, "Which Emotions Can Be Induced by Music? What Are the Underlying Mechanisms? And How Can We Measure Them?," *Journal of New Music Research* 33 (2004): 239–51.

103. Egerman et al., "Continuous Measurement," 4.

104. Richard Parncutt, "Perception of Musical Patterns: Ambiguity, Emotion, Culture," *Nova Acta Leopoldina* 92, no. 341 (2005): 41.

105. Levy and Ross, "Emotional and Cognitive Rhythms."

106. Carol L. Krumhansl, "Music: A Link between Cognition and Emotion," *Current Directions in Psychological Science* 11, no. 2 (2002): 45.

107. Parncutt, "Perception of Musical Patterns," 34.

108. Krumhansl, "Music," 45–46.

109. Egerman, "Continuous Measurement," 5.

110. Parncutt, "Perception of Musical Patterns," 45.

111. Parncutt, "Perception of Musical Patterns," 45.

112. Scherer and Zentner, "Emotional Effects," 364.

113. Scherer and Zentner, "Emotional Effects," 364.

114. Krumhansl, "Music," 46.

115. Scherer and Zentner, "Emotional Effects," 379.

116. Marcel Zentner and Tuomas Eerola, "Self-Report Measures and Models," in *Handbook of Music and Emotion: Theory, Research, Applications*, ed. Patrik N. Juslin and John A. Sloboda (Oxford: Oxford University Press, 2010), 187.

117. Zentner and Eerola, "Self-Report Measures and Models," 189.

118. Zentner and Eerola, "Self-Report Measures and Models," 192–94.

119. Scherer and Zentner, "Emotional Effects," 379.

120. Scherer and Zentner, "Emotional Effects," 379.

121. G. Hubbard et al., "Working with Emotion," 127.

122. Sara Ahmed, *The Cultural Politics of Emotion* (New York: Routledge, 2004).

123. See Moisala, "Cognitive Study of Music."

124. Ruth Finnegan, "Music, Experience, and the Anthropology of Emotion," in *The Cultural Study of Music: A Critical Introduction*, ed. Martin Clayton, Trevor Herbert, and Richard Middleton (New York: Routledge, 2003), 183.

125. Finnegan, "Music, Experience, and the Anthropology of Emotion," 189.

126. Finnegan, "Music, Experience, and the Anthropology of Emotion," 189.

127. John Blacking, *How Musical Is Man?* (Seattle: University of Washington Press, 1973), 89.

128. See Moisala, "Cognitive Study of Music," 10.

129. Concepts of cognition were no longer understood as merely rational, abstract activity, but as based on behavior and body.

130. Will, "Perspectives of Reorientation," 5, 12.

131. Will, "Perspectives of Reorientation," 19; Finnegan, "Music, Experience, and the Anthropology of Emotion," 189–90.

132. See Conrad Phillip Kottak, *Mirror for Humanity: A Concise History of Cultural Anthropology*, 5th ed. (Boston: McGraw-Hill Higher Education, 2007).

133. Will, "Perspectives of Reorientation," 12.

134. The term *ethnosemantics* describes the study of how the members of a culture use language to describe certain fundamental and universal classifications (e.g., color, kinship, emotions, weather, plants, and animals, etc.).

135. Will, "Perspectives of Reorientation," 12.

136. Will, "Perspectives of Reorientation," 13.

137. Will, "Perspectives of Reorientation," 15.

138. Will, "Perspectives of Reorientation," 15.

ANNA M. GADE

# 7. BEYOND "HOPE"

*Religion and Environmental Sentiment in the USA and Indonesia*

An expectation is widespread across the study of religion and ecology, namely, that the world's religions provide materials to foster environmental care, concern, hope, and so forth—or the reverse, that they have served as obstacles to environmentally friendly feelings and attitudes. To observe this is also to recognize that a latent theory of affect rests at the nexus of global scholarly fields of religious and environmental studies. This theory and practice is a legacy of nature-writing and other strains in Anglo-American tradition, and it is also a matter of global outreach as well. For example, in 2003 James D. Wolfensohn, then-president of the World Bank, championed a religious sentiment of globalized hope in the foreword of the influential book *Faith in Conservation* (part of the World Bank's series on Development):

> The World Bank is committed to the struggle to overcome poverty. At the same time we must protect the biodiversity of the planet. This is an enormous task and one for which the Bank needs as many allies as possible.... This is why the World Bank cooperates with the major faiths as partners.... The reason is simple.... These are serious stakeholders in development. They are also the oldest institutions in the world and *possess wisdom about how to live and how to keep hope alive, which we need to hear and respect* ... [This book opens] up ideas and possibilities that may

well be new to many in the world of development and economics, but which, as I know from personal experience, do work.[1]

A projection of environmental sentiment to *keep hope alive* in a mainstream form (i.e., as what *we* need to hear) draws on an unspoken Christian heritage,[2] even as it reaches out energetically to non-Christian societies.

This chapter compares two patterns of sentiment in environmental tradition and outreach that are grounded in religious tradition. First, it considers celebrated American environmental feeling-types, such as uplifting experiences of nature and wilderness, as one case study. Second, contemporary Islamic environmentalism in the world's most populous Muslim-majority nation, Indonesia, is the other case. The affective systems, Christian/Anglo-American and Islamic/Southeast Asian, actually resemble one another in terms of the kinds of emotions they seek to evoke and cultivate in regard to the environment. However, with respect to understandings of environmental disaster, extinction, and the end of the world, they differ significantly.

The key difference between messages of environmental emotion across these religious and ethical systems lies in whether feeling is constructed for environmental ends on the one hand, or for religious ends on the other. Religious practices and exercises for the sake of the environment in the Islamic cases, as studied here, demonstrate less determinacy in terms of the formal types of religious environmental affect they express. This is despite their rather formalized ritual frames of dedication and devotion for environmental performance. In contrast, instrumentalized affect in pluralistic environmental religious traditions, as in the quote from the World Bank leader just mentioned, is patterned on moral sentiments that correspond closely to more specific narratives and ideologies of fear and hope.

MAINSTREAM ENVIRONMENTAL EMOTION:
*NATURE* AND *THE SACRED*

Sentiment is commonly construed as a resource to extract from the world's religious systems, one's own or another's, in order to further environmental goals. For example, available academic materials as well as learners' goals in the field of religion and environment tend to conform to an expectation that a collective project is to recognize in religious systems essential techniques or practices for fostering moral sentiments. These take the form of named feelings of environmental care, such as concern, perceptive awareness—or hope that simultaneously counters and contrasts with despair.[3]

This comes in no small measure from the half-century legacy of an essay by the historian Lynn White Jr., titled "The Historical Roots of Our Ecologic Crisis."[4] It remains the most-reprinted article of all time from the journal *Science* and is still cited in practically every English-language academic overview of religious thought and the environment. Like Aldo Leopold's *Sand County Almanac* and Rachel Carson's *Silent Spring*, each to be discussed below, in 1967 White's article captured both the tone and the message of an emerging approach in humanistic environmental studies, especially with respect to religion. It illustrates more generally the degree to which religious theory is foundational to modern environmentalism. Coincidentally, both religious and environmental studies were fairly new fields that developed in English-language universities in the 1970s, alongside the activism of the environmental movement itself.

Along with (European) medieval technological change, White named a (European) Christian religious worldview as the root of the global environmental crisis. Religion had estranged Europeans from nature ideologically, and had supported mechanized technologies of exploitation, he writes in the article. White claims this originates in the ideological implications of the doctrine of dominion in the Bible's Book of Genesis. While much of White's article explains changes in agricultural methods of cultivation, and the author's academic discipline is the history of science, the critique is hardly materialist. White writes in the conclusion to his article: "Since the roots of our trouble are so largely religious, the remedy must also be essentially religious, whether we call it that or not. *We must rethink and refeel* our nature and destiny."[5]

Religion, here and throughout White's article, is placed within a problem/solution binary with respect to the biosphere's sustainability. While religious ideas are seen as largely negative (sanctioning exploitation), the sentimental dimensions of religion are nevertheless largely positive (as in, a "remedy" for "nature and destiny").

The resolution that White proposed to "our ecologic crisis" is a religious model that depends on affect to undermine anthropocentrism. White proposes a "patron saint for ecologists" at the end of the article, whom he heralds as "the greatest radical in Christian history since Christ." This is Saint Francis of Assisi. White explains, "The key to an understanding of Francis is his belief in the virtue of humility—not merely for the individual but for man as a species." White's rationale for the selection of St. Francis as the model environmentalist, however, goes beyond the celebration of a type of virtue ethics grounded in moral sentiment. Besides "a unique sort of pan-psychism of all things animate and inanimate" purportedly espoused by St. Francis, and along with representing the "religious remedy" to religious/environmental "trouble,"

White selects Francis for an affective connection with all species, and with nature itself. Like the formative hagiographer of St. Francis in the thirteenth century, Bonaventure, White invents a uniquely sentimental characterization of the figure of St. Francis. White zeroes in on Francis's acts of experiential glorification as the model for environmental ethics, religious and secular, Christian and non-Christian.[6]

White here follows well-established academic approaches to religion that cast normatively, and arbitrarily, experience and feeling, and nature-feeling sublimely above all, as the meaningful (if not definitional) aspect of religion.[7] This also follows formulas that are prevalent both in the folk-theory and romantic strains in the study of religion; these are well known and widely studied in courses on theory and method in the field. Usually first presented to students in this capacity is Rudolf Otto, for his numinous sensorium of wholly other "mysterium tremendum et fascinans"; that Otto celebrates nature for invoking his ideal of primordial religious feeling is also relevant here.[8] Today, the view is different in the academic study of religion. Most would agree, just as we stand comfortably with William James on the point that there is no single feeling-type that constitutes religious emotion, neither is there a unique phenomenon of environmental emotion, phenomenologically speaking.[9] Coming out of the same experiential tradition as James, however, certain affective modes nevertheless come to be cast as normative environmental emotion in Anglo-American tradition.

Moreover, when environmentalists turn to religion, what they often seek out is ethics and affect. Well into the twentieth century, other forebearers in religious studies were positioning affect as definitional to religion, as much as did Protestant theologians like Otto. Émile Durkheim's effervescent totemic response, outlined in *Elementary Forms of the Religious Life*, is a key sociological example. Clifford Geertz, whose definition of religion coming out of fieldwork on Java has been so long-lasting, powerful, and pervasive, frames religion in terms of its "moods and motivations" that constitute the symbolic systems of world-making, largely through ritual. Assumptions that religion should be affective at its core transfer smoothly into American white-settler concepts of nature and wilderness,[10] which systems scholars would wish to call environmental, especially if the landscape is somehow to be experienced as sacred.

That the environment, a relatively recent concept historically speaking, seems cognate to older notions of *nature* from comparative theory of religion from nineteenth-century Europe assures the continuity, if not critique, of such a heritage for the treatment of sentiment and environment. The canonical tradition of American nature-writing, such as that of Ralph Waldo Emerson,

Henry David Thoreau, and John Muir, represents an affective tradition around nature and wilderness respectively, with characteristic feeling-types such as restorative remedy. For example, consider the following words from Thoreau's *Walden*, the chapter on solitude:

> The indescribable innocence and beneficence of Nature,—of sun and wind and rain, of summer and winter,—such health, such cheer, they afford forever! and such sympathy have they ever with our race, that all Nature would be affected, and the sun's brightness fade, and the winds would sigh humanely, and the clouds rain tears, and the woods shed their leaves and put on mourning in midsummer, if any man should ever for a just cause grieve. Shall I not have intelligence with the earth? Am I not partly leaves and vegetable mould myself?[11]

And, on nature, from a journal of John Muir:

> Nature is always lovely, invincible, glad, whatever is done and suffered by her creatures. All scars she heals, whether in rocks or water or sky or hearts.[12]

Romantic notions that construct nature,[13] which is then recast with respect to imaginaries of environmentalism such as wilderness (a term also developed by Muir), connect to an experiential tradition found prominently also in American revival Protestantism of the nineteenth century.[14]

Protestant ideas about the sacred come to underlie these environmental attitudes, even when they are self-identified as "spiritual—not religious." In his landmark essay "The Trouble with Wilderness," environmental historian William Cronon documents these shifts in American environmentalism. He explains, at the time that European settlers came to North America in the eighteenth century, "many of the word's [wilderness] strongest associations then were biblical, for it is used over and over again in the King James Version [of the Bible] to refer to places on the margins of civilization where it is also all too easy to lose oneself in moral confusion and despair."[15] Writing of the changes in affective and religious dimensions of the concept wilderness, in the late nineteenth and early twentieth century (such as with John Muir's legacy), Cronon states, "To gain such a remarkable influence the concept of wilderness had to become loaded with some of the deepest core values of the culture that created and idealized it: it had to become sacred." Cronon continues, wilderness was no longer a place of "spiritual danger and temptation," but a place where one might "meet God."[16] Taking a part of this story further into the twentieth century, Bron Taylor documents more contemporary trends in the approach to *nature as sacred* across landscapes of American environmentalism (what he calls "dark green religion") through Wittgensteinian family resemblances of commitments that may or may not be normatively religious.[17]

In his books on comparative global environmentalisms, Ramachandra Guha gives a typology that contextualizes an American tradition of wilderness thinking (which he also calls primitivism) in terms of other dominant *environmental utopias*, like agrarian utopianism (as with Gandhi's thought), technological management (for which he also uses the expression, "scientific industrialism"), and so forth.[18] These ideologies, which construct environmental affect as it is promoted globally, now in postcolonial programs such as with the World Bank's initiatives, mix wilderness thinking and other strains of environmental affect that emerged in the late twentieth century, the period of Lynn White Jr.'s article. These may be illustrated by way of the foundational literature of the environmental movement, represented by the discovery of the writings of two American figures, Rachel Carson and Aldo Leopold. Through their underlying ethics, these authors developed norms for environmental feeling, such as that of experiencing the sacred, into the specifically modern moral sentiments of global environmentalism.

## WONDER, LOSS/FEAR, AND HOPE
## AS MORAL SENTIMENT

Celebrated canonical writing of the environmental movement of the 1950s and 1960s, popularized widely by the 1970s, conveys key patterns of environmental affect, including standard feeling-types like wonder and hope. This is the period during which the term *the environment* was coined as it is used today in global English. Key emotional textures of environmentalism were developed in the book that many say was the touchstone for the environmental movement, Rachel Carson's *Silent Spring* (1962).

Scholar Lisa Sideris sums up a sense of overwhelming wonder and awe at nature as being a dominant theme of Carson's writings,[19] starting with her earliest books on the ocean. In Carson's work, Sideris shows, wonder relates to science as much as experience. Sideris summarizes the approach to nature and affect that Carson established early in her career when she published on oceans, writing, "The belief that knowledge of nature engenders humility and reverence was, for Carson, an article of faith, with roots in the religion of her childhood and the nature religion she loved."[20] Sideris recognizes a continuous religious theme throughout Carson's work, and she explains, "Perhaps nowhere in Carson's writing is the association of mystery and magic with the unveiling of elemental and essential realities more pronounced than in *The Edge of the Sea*. . . .

Here too we encounter her conviction that mystery continually outstrips scientific knowledge."[21] Carson's famous phrase, "the real world around us," which may at times be taken to mean science, was constantly coupled with what Sideris calls the mystery and wonder of her affective, environmental ethics.[22]

Similar tendencies toward wonder/science take the form of a call to a vocation of redemptive restoration in the work of another American, Aldo Leopold, who had also been discovered as a voice of American environmentalism by the later 1960s. His collection of naturalist essays, *A Sand County Almanac* (originally written in 1949), was elevated to become another foundational text of the movement.[23] Leopold's *A Sand County Almanac* is read aloud communally like an annual spring liturgy in the arboretum of the University of Wisconsin–Madison, his academic home.[24]

Common affective themes are found in the texts and the reception of the work of both Carson and Leopold, the writings of each that became so influential only posthumously, in the USA as well as internationally. For example, Sideris explains, Carson came to understand the mystery of nature in terms of a famous metaphor in *Silent Spring*, a "magic forest," which was potentially threatened and threatening in a transformed state as a toxic, "poisoned forest." Along with wonder at naturalism and science as expressed in their books, both Carson and Leopold articulated patterns of sadness/fear and related love/hope that came to constitute moral sentiment and are still promoted as forms of mainstream American environmentalism.

Being a martyr to cancer shaped Carson's legacy. Leopold passed away tragically and selflessly while fighting a neighbor's fire. His commemoration remains bound to sentiments of redemptive hope that were symbolized in his life by his family's project to restore ravaged land along the Wisconsin River to pine forest and native prairie around his weekend recreation retreat, a chicken coop fondly called "The Shack." In addition, in the writings of both authors, the sadness of mourning also connects to fearful realization or anticipation of extinction. Leopold's famous "Land Ethic," for example, is based in theory and practice on an affective love of the land that is an extension of belonging in community.[25] He often expresses this in *A Sand County Almanac* through narrative, as a melancholy that connects love through loss to a moralized sentiment of remediation, restoration, and redemption. In Carson's *Silent Spring* and her other work in the same period, realization of potential annihilation relates more directly to a moral mission to save the earth.

The recognition of an ethical and emotional connection to other species, all as members of community, is an extension of feelings of loss throughout *A Sand County Almanac*. This is encapsulated in Leopold's story in his essay,

"Thinking Like a Mountain," in which he watches the "green fire" die out gradually in the eyes of a wolf he had just shot on a hunt. Leopold opens another of the book's essays, "On a Monument to the Pigeon" (the plaque is located on a hill overlooking the confluence of the Wisconsin and Mississippi Rivers), with the following emotional words of eulogy for the extinction of Wisconsin's native bird, the passenger pigeon: "We have erected a monument to commemorate the funeral of a species. It symbolizes our sorrow. We grieve because no living man will see again the onrushing phalanx of victorious birds, sweeping a path for spring across the March skies, chasing the defeated winter from all the woods and prairies of Wisconsin."[26] Part of the call to mourn is for the passing of the very feeling of bereavement itself, as in the next sentence: "Men still live who, in their youth, remember pigeons. Trees still live who, in their youth, were shaken by a living wind. But a decade hence only the oldest oaks will remember, and at long last only the hills will know."[27]

In his essay "The Good Oak," a meditation on splitting apart an ancient tree ("We mourned the loss of the old tree, but knew that a dozen of its progeny standing straight and stalwart on the sands had already taken over its job of wood-making"),[28] he shows the utilitarian function of melancholy to engender awareness of time and of the land itself. The essay documents the cuts through the tree's rings along with a catalog of memory, describing each fall of the axe while concurrently listing events that progressively recede across decades of Wisconsin's history.

In the conclusion to "On a Monument to the Pigeon," Leopold connects great melancholy to a sentiment, love, which is the foundation of the Land Ethic. Here are his words at the end of the essay, which link pigeon love, human love, and the ability to have an affective relationship to the land and its history:

> The pigeon loved his land: he lived by the intensity of his desire for clustered grape and bursting beechnut, and by his contempt of miles and seasons. Whatever Wisconsin did not offer him gratis today, he sought and found tomorrow in Michigan, or Labrador, or Tennessee. His love was for present things, and these things were present somewhere; to find them required only the free sky, and the will to ply his wings.
>
> To love what *was* is a new thing under the sun, unknown to most people and to all pigeons.[29]

With "Land Ethic" and related writing, Leopold presents a historicized confrontation with environmental loss and degradation that, in his presentation, may always potentially be transformed into redemptive moral sentiments like love and hope.

Carson, like Leopold, also confronts environmental loss and ethical disso-
ciation in modernity in registers of affect in *Silent Spring*. In the book, Carson
presents environmental crisis (the impacts of pesticides) in terms of the oblivion
of species extinction, the key trope of *Silent Spring*. The opening story of *Silent
Spring* establishes a moving parable, depicting even the emotions people have
as they realize, "puzzled and disturbed," that the birds had inexplicably dis-
appeared: "There was a strange stillness. The birds, for example—where had they
gone? Many people spoke of them, puzzled and disturbed. The feeding stations
in the backyards were deserted. The few birds seen anywhere were moribund;
they trembled violently and could not fly. It was a spring without voices."[30]

The opening story of *Silent Spring* is not just critique, nor is the point of the
rest of the book merely the scientific exposition that it offers in detail; it is a
dire warning. To read Carson's words is also to recognize the strain of apocalypticism that has become an enduring and dominant aspect of modern environmentalism, present also in climate change and antinuclear activism.

The fear of future oblivion that Carson engenders in *Silent Spring*, in its
opening legend, Lisa Sideris explains, represents a call to action, a campaign
even Carson herself called a crusade. Elsewhere in Carson's later career, her
voice took on something of the tone of her Calvinist background in writing
about the moral challenge of modernity, as Sideris quotes Carson: "The modern world . . . worships the gods of speed and quantity, and of the quick and
easy profit, and out of this idolatry monstrous evils have arisen."[31]

To Carson, it had become clear that humans are not insignificant in the
face of natural forces, but rather now have the capacity to bring ultimate devastation to the biosphere itself. Carson was greatly influenced by the ethics of
Albert Schweitzer at this time, and increasingly linked moral critique to scientific facts, which, to Carson, would still connect to experiential knowledge and
even mystery. According to Sideris, in a speech delivered around the time of the
publication of *Silent Spring*, Carson addressed the problem of man's "intoxica-
tion with power," and claimed that the antidote is what Sideris calls Carson's
abiding sense of the "inseparable wonder and reality of our world."[32]

Feeling-types of mainstream environmentalism continue to circulate as they
were established in work such as that of Carson and Leopold. These are emotions of wonder/love, fear/hope, and individualized moral obligation to save
an entire earth in peril, inspired by affects like concern and awareness. The overall approach, one which has typified the mainstream approach to religion and
the environment, tends to accent the positive in the affective spectrum. Writings like *Silent Spring* helped set up this dialectic of *hope* that pervades so much
contemporary rhetoric of environmentalism, whether religious, postreligious,

or neoreligious, and represents a key theme of much contemporary academic ecocriticism.

When environmentalism or environmental studies turns to religion as an extractive industry, it has tended to essentialize world religions along the lines of uplifting moral sentiments. Courses on religion and environment typically expand such normative sentiments out across the array of world religions, presented in terms of their respective demonstrations of equivalent care for the environment.[33] In some academic study of religion and the environment, dominant assumptions about affect derive transparently from religious faith commitments, even as they seek to embrace all world religions. Influences flowing from Thomas Berry and the Roman Catholic teleology of Teilhard de Chardin have infused parts of the field of religion and ecology with a confident and persistent theological undercurrent, for example, and in *The Sacred Universe*, Thomas Berry posits an evolutionary consciousness as an uplifting and inspirational feeling-type. A recent film *Journey of the Universe* and related publications by scholars of religion and ecology who are influenced by Berry develop this tendency as well.[34]

Generalizing environmental sentiment across an invented structure, world religions,[35] furthers it as rationalized, global ethics to be discovered, enhanced, and preached in any postcolonial context. When propagating normative environmentalist messages, world-religions pluralism promotes cognate sentiments apparently universally, while also supporting a global mission to *save* the Earth. Nonreligious actors, nonacademics, deploy these commitments and sentiments instrumentally. For example, NGOs such as the World Wildlife Fund for Nature (WWF) seek to identify and then train religious leaders to spread messages such as conservation, expressed in a confessional vocabulary of doctrine and ritual. A widely known example from Southeast Asia is the WWF's initiation of the movement of Thai Buddhist monks to ordain trees for the purpose of environmental protection and conservation.[36] While the WWF and World Bank are secular organizations, they nevertheless may operate under the assumption that religious outreach is more salient, meaningful, and effective than compatible, or duplicate, secular approaches.[37]

Religious authorities who are appointed to represent faith traditions by such organizations subsequently may perform in public pageants of pluralism, such as occurred with the influential Assisi Declaration on Nature (1986, with leaders of five religions convened by the president of the w w f ).[38] One effect of these events is to sanction and universalize a particular environmentalist stance. For example, a follow-up statement to the Assisi Declaration, sponsored by the World Bank in 1996, explains the rationale for developing and promoting religious doctrine for the sake of the environment among the world's religions:

> Ultimately, the environmental crisis is a crisis of the mind. And likewise, appropriate development is ultimately an appropriate development of the mind. We see, do, and are what we think, and what we think is shaped by our cultures, faiths, and beliefs. This is why one of the more extraordinary movements of the past few decades began to take shape. For if the information of the environmentalists needed a framework of values and beliefs to make it useful, then where better to turn for allies than to the original multinationals, the largest international groupings and networks of people? Why not turn to the major religions of the world?[39]

Consistent with Anglo-American tradition, the actual statements of faith leaders in the Assisi Declaration and subsequent documents focus on inspirational, affective messages.

For example, here is the opening of the statement representing Buddhism in the Declaration, by Venerable Lungrig Namgyal Rinpoche, Abbot of Gyuto Tantric University. It emphasizes emotional capacities with keywords such as happiness, compassion, loving-kindness, and so forth:

> Therefore, a human undertaking motivated by a healthy and positive attitude constitutes one of the most important causes of happiness, while undertakings generated through ignorance and negative attitude bring about suffering and misery. And this positive human attitude is, in the final analysis, rooted in genuine and unselfish compassion and loving kindness that seeks to bring about light and happiness for all sentient beings. Hence Buddhism is a religion of love, understanding and compassion and committed towards the ideal of non-violence. As such, it also attaches great importance to wildlife and the protection of the environment on which every being in this world depends for survival.[40]

In the same document, the Hindu perspective (as given by Karan Singh, president of Hindu Virat Samaj) is also emotional (featuring reverence), while also affirming the authority of sacred texts: "Not only in the Vedas, but also in later scriptures such as the Upanishads, the Puranas and subsequent texts, the Hindu viewpoint on nature has been clearly enunciated. It is permeated by a reverence for life and an awareness that the great forces of nature—the earth, the sky, the air, the water and fire—as well as various orders of life including plants and trees, forests and animals, are all bound to each other within the great rhythms of nature."[41]

As in an orientalist imaginary, no actual persons or communities are referenced. Furthermore, as the religious-environmental commitment of the Assisi Declaration and those that followed it, framed in terms of named traditions, does leave out most of the people of the world, it also implies that all global citizens ought to feel the same way. The colonial heritage of world religions, which was once also propagated through categories like the primitive, still naturalizes indigeneity (here, without any declarative voice), while also failing to unsettle long-standing romantic projections onto native systems.

This universalization, compatible with long-standing assumptions in academic fields of religious studies, may take the form of a concrete strategy for environmental action, or it may merely mask vaguer modern anxieties. The obverse of such instrumentality for the sake of environmental goals is how people deploy environmental affect to further *religious* goals. My field research in Muslim Indonesia suggests that, even when subject to similar constructions like world religions and the environmental crisis, the emotional landscape differs. The feeling-types are rather similar to those just expressed, but what is prescribed is not the same as instrumental affect, like hope. Instead, the entire notion of the environment itself becomes instrumentalized.

## ISLAMIC ENVIRONMENTAL SENTIMENTS IN INDONESIA

Complementing the application of religious sentiment for environmental goals is an alternative question: How do religious people foster emotion with respect to the environment for the sake of their own religion? While the feelings may be the same, what structures sentiment is not. Below, I consider material from original research in the world's most populous Muslim-majority nation, Indonesia. Sentiments of the pious, practically by definition, connect to greater systems of cause and effect, the unseen, and related ontologies—the types of ethical correspondences that environmentalists also seek to cultivate. However, fieldwork shows that feelings promoted by religious-environmental scholars and activists in Qur'anic frames differ from moral sentiments as described earlier, by virtue of being explicitly religious.

Religious sentiments of religion and the environment, self-consciously Qur'anic and Anglo-American, seem at the outset to be cognate in terms of expressing named feeling-types like *love* and *fear*, and perhaps even *hope*. However, they differ by virtue of the religious dimensions of environmental sentiment.

One aspect of this discrepancy is doctrinal. In mainstream environmentalist tradition, there is the expectation that humans will *save* the earth through an ethical awakening leading to action; to the degree that environmental crisis is cast as a moral crisis (as it usually is), religion is salient in this respect, even for secular perspectives. With the exception of some environmental justice movements, following the Protestant tradition, such action is often presented as if it is a matter left to individual conscience, with the added corollary that each individual would have the privilege to make a change, for the self as well as for others, near and far. Usually, the idea that life on earth would end represents affective despair, for which hope provides a necessary antidote. While current literature in environmental humanities on the anthropocene has a dystopian and existential flavor,[42] and typically questions human hope and agency with respect to climate disaster and other conditions, in contrast, normative Islamic worldviews are eschatologically apocalyptic in the fullest sense.

Following the Qur'an, Muslim religious environmentalists in Indonesia see the earth as inevitably to be destroyed. This is not a teaching that is usually recognized, or even mentioned, in world-religions environmentalism branded for Muslims, yet it is a core understanding of activists and preachers with whom I worked outside of the pluralism framework. Whether through remorse or mercy, affect is promoted in order that the consequences of actions in and toward the world are mercifully dispensed in the world to come. Thus, while the systems compared here, both American and Indonesian, each attempt instrumentally to awaken affect as a means to desired ends, and while affective registers do appear quite similar, the sentiment differs depending on the orientation toward change and human responsibility in this world and the next.

From a Qur'anic stance, humans, a part of God's creation, are responsible for the earth, Part of God's creation, in a contingent and even ambivalent sense. While world-religions pluralism focuses on Islamic notions of stewardship (*khilafah*) that are cognate to biblical norms, the Qur'an teaches that this earth does not need saving any more than it deserves exploitation; the Qur'an instructs humanity merely to walk humbly upon it (Qur'an 25:63). In the Qur'an, Earth actually speaks for herself when the time comes; the Qur'an documents Earth telling her own story of imposed burdens on Judgment Day (Qur'an S. 99). There is, in fact, much material to quote about the *earth* (*al-ard*) and its processes from the Qur'an, as well as citation of nature images like water (clouds and rain, oceans, reproductive fluid, rivers in heaven, and so forth) that emphasize humans' response to the world as participating creatures (*makhluq*) rather than as executive custodians. In addition, the Qur'an offers many statements about such elements in balance (*mizan*), related principles of measured conservation or even protection (*hijab*), and condemnation of states of degradation (*fasad*) and oppression (*dhulm*).

Interpreting the Qur'anic doctrine of *khalifah* or stewardship, a point on which world-religions environmentalism usually focuses, humans are responsible for the earth's care, whose dominion (*mulk*) and the judgment of this very care remains with Allah alone. The Qur'an expresses creation's own ambivalence about humans taking on this trust (*al-amanah*) with their innate foolishness even when mountains protested that this would be too much for them to uphold (Qur'an 33:72). And even angels, who practically never talk back to God, question Him disparagingly in Qur'an 2:30–31 about the decision to afford humanity this responsibility. Repeatedly, the Qur'an also evidences the nature of people to be forgetful, wasteful, complacent, ungrateful, hypocritical, and destructive even in the face of the presentation of the consequences of these dispositions; this includes depiction of direct confrontation with future generations impacted by their ancestors' harmful choices, as communities shout across the altered landscape of the life to come.

With respect to the processes of the divine creation, sustaining and eventual destruction and reconstitution of worlds, Qur'anic affect is a varied emotional landscape. The Qur'an is highly prescriptive about emotional response to the natural phenomena that it describes. God's creation is full of signs (*ayat*) that demand responses like *shukr* (thankfulness) and *taqwa* (pious apprehension). The verses (ayat) of the Qur'an are described in the holy book as themselves causing "hearts to soften" and making humans, including prophets, fall down and weep, even as its words are read. The Qur'an's portrayals of judgment, when all creation is transformed into a new state and "hearts leap into throats," are varied and intense.

About one-fifth of the Qur'an describes this moment of judgment, often in terms of the affective shock when humans realize that it is too late to alter a certain fate. With dramatic, dynamic, and dialogical rhetoric, humans engage in active and noisy dialogue across the apocalyptic space to confirm that God's promises and warnings are true. They interact, such as when those in the Fire beg for water from those above in the Garden, and when, looking down from heaven to see a friend below, a soul realizes that this was a fate s/he himself had only narrowly escaped. The Qur'an describes a rich diversity of responses to these inevitable events, from bickering and blaming even on the road to hell, to gratitude and satisfaction; the moral and affective dispositions of people in the life of this world, seemingly, naturally carry on into the next.

I have carried out fieldwork in Southeast Asia with global Muslims who attempt instrumentally to foster environmental sentiment, drawing on the Qur'an and other sources of tradition such as devotional religion. These Islamic leaders, some of whom have worked with the secular NGO industry, select and promote environmental feelings for themselves and others through practices like ritual devotion. Muslim religious activists working outside of interfaith environmental expectation tend to fill in a modern environmental frame with an affective Qur'anic paradigm, invoking the present moment at which one realizes that the created world is changing, anticipating the dread of the feeling that it may already be too late to alter choices in the past that now will result in a certain fate. This means facing the religious facts of a reconstituted world during and after its destruction. The understanding of moral and physical consequences with respect to the experiential world to come, as expressed vividly and viscerally in much of the Qur'an, shapes the sentimental program of the present for pious environmentalists.

Religious scholar-activists thus seek to develop relational extensions beyond the ontology of the phenomenal world, in the tradition of Al-Ghazali's final book of the *Ihya' Ulum Al-Din* (Revivification of the Religious Sciences), which cultivates positive sentiment in the present around recognition of the inevitable moment of death, and ensuing resurrection and judgment. When Muslim environmentalists turn to this apocalyptic paradigm to embrace care in this world, it is typically expressed with one of two poles of feeling-types. These correspond to Qur'anic promise and warning, respectively. The affective registers look like post-Christian environmental *hope*, *love*, and *fear* in some respects, but contrast with the global mainstream as moral sentiments for environmental thought and action. This is because of the role that environmentalism itself comes to play as a means to ultimate ends in the life to come.

An illustration is the lyrics of a *nashid* (religious song) composed by the well-known religious scholar and teacher K. H. Affandi at his ecological *madrasa* in West Java. The words emphasize a present intervention in the form of cautionary, projected sentiment:[43]

We will all regret
Suffer and weep
If/when this beautiful world
Becomes degraded and polluted
Come, let's all together
Care for and protect our world

Stop the destruction
And corruption of the earth
Humans will be buried
Their torment ever-greater

Such anticipation of future regret is characteristic of Muslim religious emotion as cultivated in Indonesia for the sake of the present world, as well as the next one.

Muslim religious scholars have promoted sentiments or feeling-types of care, compassion, and concern for other beings, not just as an environmental end, but as religious means. The most common expression of this type looks like loving nature, and may even be expressed by a term that is a direct translation of eco-friendliness (*ramah lingkungan*), but it is also different from American notions. A *hadith* (authoritative report of a saying of the Prophet Muhammad) prominently in circulation in Muslim discussions of the environment (but which I have never seen cited in NGO environmentalist literature for Muslims) points to the difference. The meaning of the hadith is, Allah has love/mercy for those who act mercifully toward His own creation. This is love for the sake of the life in a world *after* destruction, not this world. And the application must be in terms of care in *this* present world. This affective system thus may instrumentalize the environment as much as the sentiment love.

A highly respected *kiai* (religious scholar), K. H. Thonthawi Jauhari Musaddad, illustrates this teaching explicitly, although it is also widespread across Muslim Southeast Asia in unspoken form. K. H. Thonthawi of Pondok Pesantren "Al-Wasilah" in West Java is renowned for his Islamic religious knowledge as well as his environmental activism. For example, he helped develop Islamic law of the environment through key *fatwa*s (nonbinding legal opinions) under the authority of the national organization Nahdlatul Ulama. K. H. Thonthawi explained environmental ethics of moral sentiment in the following manner during conversations we had at his home in Garut, Indonesia, over a period of years.[44] K. H. Thonthawi expresses an Islamic worldview of Qur'anic promise as a call to environmental engagement, extending moral and material realities of this world into indeterminate states of the next.

The goal is to return to the original Garden, the landscape of Adam in heaven, he preaches. For this, good deeds can only get the pious so far. It is only through the mercy (*rahmat*) of God that one may have a chance at obtaining God's mercy, he says. And as indicated by the hadith just cited, the best way to obtain this mercy is to show mercy and care for God's creation, just as He does. K. H. Thonthawi therefore declares environmental activism to be the "ticket to paradise." In K. H. Thonthawi's teaching and praxis, this loving-kindness is rooted in environmental action such as reforestation, education, and social justice that are typical not only of Islamic systems but also of other religions of mainland and island Southeast Asia. If this is a kind of hope that leads to environmental care, it is also a heartfelt and moral calculation of cause and effect that is predicated on the ultimate end of this world.

K. H. Thonthawi claims that the quickest and most efficient way to heaven in the world to come is to undertake environmental action in this one. K. H. Thonthawi has here reversed the view from asking, "What can religion do for an environmentalist cause," to "What can environmental care do for religious reality?" Like Lynn White Jr., he sees environmental crisis to be a moral crisis at its heart, one with a religious solution. Instrumental religious affect, universalized in a Qur'anic frame, comes not out of hope to avoid disaster, but rather from feeling and accepting responsibility in the most profound way possible in this world for the sake of hope in the life to come.

When turning next to the promotion of these environmental religious feelings in Muslim Indonesia outside of NGO frameworks, there is a further contrast with the Anglo-American tradition as well. One might expect the scripturally based tradition in Asia to be quite formal in its articulation of emotional states. It is actually quite conservative in terms of the ritual forms adapted environmentally, as illustrated below. However, the religious nature of the activity and activism, like the Sufi theory and practice on which it draws,[45] shape the affective fields of environmental emotion expansively and in relation to an unseen world.

## DEVOTION AND DEDICATION: ISLAMIC RITUAL
## ENVIRONMENTAL AFFECT

Independent of patronage by the international NGOs that do sponsor religious initiatives like Islamic environmental law, K. H. Thontawi and others in Indonesia have developed Islamic practices that are meant to foster environmental sentiment. These draw largely on traditions of Muslim devotions in Arabic such as prayers venerating the Prophet Muhammad in a tradition known as *salawat al-nabi* (*salawat*). Such techniques inflect environmental emotion through alterations of individualized intent while preserving outward religious form. Apocalyptic and esoteric (Sufi) modes connect the environmental devotion to religious goals, thus rendering environmental-Qur'anic emotions like *love* and *fear* to be open-ended projects.

A trend I have seen developing in Indonesia for almost two decades has been for Muslims to recast Arabic devotional practices such as *salawat* and *dhikr* (repetitive devotional formulas) for specific intents and purposes.[46] Salawat, prayers of peace and blessings devoted to the Prophet Muhammad, represent a long-standing tradition with Qur'anic support that became increasingly popular in the Islamic revival since the 1990s. This has been somewhat surprising to some observers, given historical controversy around the practice. Dhikr is a performance associated with Sufi (mystical) practice as well as supererogatory piety meant to cultivate remembrance, and is usually Qur'anic in content. Indonesian devotions for the environment add a third term to the dialectic of God on the one hand and the worshipper/supplicant on the other: His creation. This is clear in an environmental prayer such as canonical prayers for rain (*salat al-istisqa'*), which are increasingly common across the Muslim world due to climate disturbance and popular in Indonesia in recent years as the only relief from the annual environmental catastrophe of uncontrolled peat forest fires and related transboundary smoke haze.

In Indonesia, Muslim religious environmental theory and practice commonly cite a tripartite division that introduces creation into the human-divine relationship. To notions of *hablun min al-nas* and *hablun min Allah* which are the horizontal and vertical connections among-humans and humans-to-God respectively (as supported by the Qur'an's verse, 3:112), there often is added a third Qur'anic concept, *rahmatan lil 'alamin* (alternatively expressed as a *hablun min al-'alamin*). This is cast as a connection to the *environment* among those who are so inclined. That the word *alam* means natural or wild in Indonesian, as well as world in Arabic (as in, "Lord of and sustainer of worlds" in the Qur'an's first chapter, called Al-Fatihah) makes for an easy extension of these concepts to explicitly environmental commitments. The word *rahmat*, meaning mercy, is also the basis for much environmental teaching in Southeast Asia that emphasizes compassion for God's creation, just as the Prophet Muhammad was known to practice it, in order to receive the mercy of God in this life and the next.

K. H. Thontawi himself has developed new forms of environmental religious devotion, "eco-*salawat*," that preserve traditional forms while supporting the teachings.[47] As he presents *salawat lingkungan*, the first verse is from standard Arabic salawat nabi, as have been recited worldwide by Muslims in this fashion for centuries. The second part, in the national language of Bahasa Indonesia, is for the sake of the environment (*lingkungan*). A new intent and affect has been created explicitly, while the ritual structure and authority remain the same.

In another example at an "eco-*pesantren*" (madrasa) across the island of Java, new forms of environmental religious observance have developed along similar lines: conservation of form with repurposed affective intent. Here, however, with theory and practice that is cognate with Sufi tradition, environmental purpose is internalized and left to individual choice within formal frameworks. "Eco-*dhikrs*" I attended in the period 2010–2014, at an institution called Pesan Trend Ilmu Giri in the area of Imo Giri located on the southern side of the city of Jogjakarta, corresponded with a calendrical observance traditional to Java, in which various forms of Muslim chant occur on certain nights of certain months. These had an opening dedication of the salawat for the sake of the environment, as well as to the Prophet Muhammad. The affect of these performances and the overall invocation of the environment itself was subordinate to a religious framework.

In July 2014, the eco-dhikr at Ilmu Giri fell on the night of Selasa Pon, in which the first chapter of the Qur'an, Al-Fatihah, is recited forty-one times according to local custom.[48] Since it was also Ramadan, the observance followed the prayers known as *tarawih* that come in the first part of the evening and feature the reading of the Qur'an. The introspective and participatory nature of the dhikr invited a dedicated intent of environmental well-being at this eco-pesantren, which itself is devoted in its mission to sustainability and environmental care. Notably, however, there was no specific mention of the environment during the ritual, nor was there any particular change in the sentimental texture from what would be expected from other observances.

Nevertheless, the officiant of this ceremony and the leader of the Ilmu Giri community, H. M. Nasruddin Ch. (who prefers to be called Gus Nas) succinctly introduced the ritual as an environmental, eco-dhikr on the night of its observance.[49] He framed the practice in terms of a regime of self-cultivation, along traditional Sufi lines. Among various terms derived from Sufi teaching, he used the word *batin*, which invokes an interiorized or esoteric perspective. He called the quality to be developed "khalifah" (Ar. *khalifah/khilafah*), or stewardship (a Qur'anic term that can also mean a form of leadership more generally, as in the caliphate). Nasruddin's words implied that affective alignment of internal order and cosmological order lead to environmental well-being, as he stated, "After this [ritual], it is not possible to destroy the environment" because the ritual has "humanized humanity, naturalized nature, and divinized the Divine."

The particular eco-feelings would be the same love, fear, and hope as expressed in the teachings from K. H. Affandi and K. H. Thonthawi. The nature of the observance, however, renders its focus more clearly to be a generalized religious affect that instrumentalizes the environment. The religious ritual frame of the dhikr shifts emotional emphasis subtly away from specific feeling-states as moral sentiments to cultivate purposefully for environmental ends. In turn, it incorporates feelings like environmental care into the very same cosmology that would support Muslim environmental emotions within fundamentally Qur'anic and religious terms.

## Conclusion

Observation shows us that religions cover a diverse sentimental landscape with respect to the subject matter of environmental study. There are bright prairie flowers of nature's conservation to love, uplifted by a regenerative healing ethic as hopeful as restoration itself. There are powerful and precarious one-day-at-a-time religious ethics and aesthetics of disaster preparedness. Even an embrace of apocalypticism, including mass extinction, does not inevitably lead to any particular experiential state with respect to environmental crisis. Nevertheless, while many religious systems manage power and protection only warily around unseen forces that are menacing, not benign, when global religion is said to generate feelings about the environment, academically and otherwise, they are often expected to be nice ones (like hope). This is despite the fact that forms of ritual and scripture in religious systems, named or unnamed, seem ambiguously inspirational at best with respect to a threatened biosphere. Reasons for this come from a particular emotional ideology in mainstream environmentalism, projected on the religions of the world even in secular paradigms like academic study and international development projects.

There is some productive irony here and throughout the secular tradition of environmental feeling, that while espousing alternatives to anthropocentric notions, these perspectives nevertheless promote the attitude that it is up to humanity (and humans alone?) to feel or perceive in the right way in order to prevent or reverse environmental harm. This point may be taken as a more general feature of environmental criticism in the age of the anthropocene, in which human actions dominate planetary conditions. This contrasts with trends in contemporary Islamic environmental thought, which represent a distinctive kind of deep ecology that highlights humans' participation *as* (not just *in*) creation.[50]

This chapter compared affective genealogies from the field of religion and ecology with material on Muslim environmentalist sentiment drawn from fieldwork in Asia. While there are no environmental emotions sui generis, distinctive feeling-types based in religious systems, such as white Protestant Christianities or the Qur'an, are privileged in each respective instance. In a modern environmentalist mode, particular feeling-types, constrained to formal modes like cheerful inspiration or ominous foreboding that are calculated to inspire action, become depicted in scenarios like a cosmic struggle for hope against modern-scale evils of moral/environmental corruption, and related human apathy and despair. In Indonesia, Qur'anic frameworks invoke many of the same registers of feeling (e.g., love and fear), yet nevertheless differ since the inevitable, and possibly immanent, destruction of the world is a basic religious fact. This leads to a heightened sense of responsibility, not despair, in a Qur'anic system.

Systems of mainstream environmental sentiment, as constructed in the writings of foundational figures in American environmentalism, from Thoreau and Muir to Carson and Leopold, have come to convey a particular ideology, as expressed in the article by Lynn White Jr. This is the notion that religion and especially religious experience, ethics, and emotion may be deployed instrumentally in order to elevate environmental concern or other moral sentiments globally. The wwf and other conservation and development agencies are active in Indonesia and globally in this regard, developing specific outreach to Muslim and other named faith communities. The promotion of environmental affect in Indonesia by Muslims working outside of the direct conservation-development influence, however, differs from programs like these. One reason for this difference is because they enroll the environment in light of religious goals, not the reverse. The teachings and practices of these communities, which emphasize the cultivation of sentiment in Islamic frames such as the Qur'an, structure religious environmental practice conservatively in terms of the formal aspects of ritual; at the same time, they also support fluidity of the experience and expression of emotion. The sentimental focus is the potentially emotionally redemptive response of the deity, His mercy, as a result of human affect. What is instrumentalized is therefore not the specific moral sentiments of modern environmentalism (although they are present as love, fear, and so forth). Rather, these Muslim systems go beyond *hope* to reshape even environmentalism itself in the context of irreversible conditions, and an ultimate ontological and ethical landscape of justice, in this world and the next.

*Acknowledgments*

Thanks to Amanda Baugh and John Corrigan for suggestions on an earlier draft of this chapter. I am grateful also for helpful comments from colleagues who attended the workshop at the National Humanities Center in North Carolina in 2015, whose work appears in this volume, and also for support and feedback from Anna Bigelow and Robert Beattie. Recent research in Indonesia was supported by the Wisconsin Alumni Research Foundation (warf) and the Graduate School of the University of Wisconsin–Madison (2010–14) as well as the Social Science Research Council (2014).

1. Martin Palmer and Victoria Finlay, *Faith in Conservation: New Approaches to Religion and the Environment* (Washington, DC: World Bank, 2003). Emphasis added.

2. See discussion and historical analysis, for example, in two important recent works: Evan Berry, *Devoted to Nature: The Religious Roots of American Environmentalism* (Berkeley: University of California Press, 2015); and Mark Stoll, *Inherit the Holy Mountain: Religion and the Rise of American Environmentalism* (New York: Oxford University Press, 2015).

3. For example, the first version of this article was written in response to an invitation by the editors of *Tikkun* magazine in 2014, to reflect from the position of a religious tradition (Islam) and to respond specifically to what was put as a question of "hope in an age of climate disaster." (The issue was published in spring 2015; see http://www.tikkun.org /nextgen/the-place-of-hope-in-an-age-of-climate-disaster.) This coincided roughly with the release of Naomi Klein's book, *This Changes Everything: Capitalism vs. the Climate* (New York: Simon and Schuster, 2015), and a widely publicized protest march on climate issues in New York City.

4. Lynn White Jr., "The Historical Roots of Our Ecologic Crisis," *Science* 155, no. 3767 (1967): 1203–7. See also contemporary reflections in Todd LeVasseur and Anna Peterson, eds., *Religion and the Ecological Crisis: The "Lynn White Thesis" at Fifty* (New York: Routledge, 2016), and other articles that have appeared around the time of the fiftieth anniversary of White's original publication.

5. White, "Historical Roots," 1207. Emphasis added.

6. White, "Historical Roots," 1206–7.

7. For recent work theorizing *religious experience* in religious studies, see Ann Taves, *Religious Experience Reconsidered: A Building-Block Approach to the Study of Religion and Other Special Things* (Princeton, NJ: Princeton University Press, 2009); see also Wayne Proudfoot, *Religious Experience* (Berkeley: University of California Press, 1987), which analyzes Otto closely and others in this tradition such as Schleiermacher.

8. Rudolf Otto, *The Idea of the Holy: An Inquiry into the Non-Rational Factor in the Idea of the Divine and Its Relation to the Rational*, trans. John W. Harvey (New York: Oxford University Press, 1973).

9. William James makes the point in *Varieties of Religious Experience: A Study in Human Nature* (New York: Penguin Books, 1911), and elsewhere.

10. For a critique of American systems of environmentalism with respect to structures of race and power, see Carolyn Finney, *Black Faces, White Spaces: Reimagining the Relationship of African Americans to the Great Outdoors* (Chapel Hill: University of North Carolina Press, 2014).

11. Henry David Thoreau, *Walden: A Fluid-Text Edition*, Digital Thoreau Project, Geneseo: State University of New York, accessed July 15, 2016, http://digitalthoreau.org /walden/fluid/text/05.html.

12. From *John of the Mountains: The Unpublished Journals of John Muir* (1938), 337, accessed July 15, 2016, http://vault.sierraclub.org/john_muir_exhibit/writings/favorite _quotations.aspx.

13. For discussion, see Neil Evernden, *The Social Construction of Nature* (Baltimore: Johns Hopkins University Press, 1992).

14. Roderick Frazier Nash, *Wilderness and the American Mind*, 5th ed. (New Haven, CT: Yale University Press, [1967] 2004).

15. William Cronon, "The Trouble with Wilderness: Or, Getting Back to the Wrong Nature," *Environmental History* 1, no. 1 (1996): 8.

16. Cronon, "Trouble with Wilderness," 10.

17. Bron Taylor, *Dark Green Religion: Nature Spirituality and the Planetary Future* (Berkeley: University of California Press, 2009).

18. Ramachandra Guha, *How Much Should a Person Consume?: Environmentalism in the United States and India* (Berkeley: University of California Press, 2006), and *Environmentalism: A Global History* (New York: Longman, 2000).

19. For a complete treatment of the notion, see Robert C. Fuller, *Wonder: From Emotion to Spirituality* (Chapel Hill: University of North Carolina Press, 2006).

20. Lisa H. Sideris, "The Secular and Religious Sources of Rachel Carson's Sense of Wonder," in *Rachel Carson: Legacy and Challenge*, ed. Lisa H. Sideris and Kathleen Dean Moore (Albany: SUNY Press, 2008), 241.

21. Lisa H. Sideris, "Fact and Fiction, Fear and Wonder: The Legacy of Rachel Carson," *Soundings: An Interdisciplinary Journal* 91, no. 3/4 (2008): 343.

22. Sideris, "Fact and Fiction," 335.

23. Aldo Leopold, *A Sand County Almanac and Sketches Here and There* (New York: Oxford University Press, [1948] 1968). See also Curt Meine, *Aldo Leopold: His Life and Work* (1988; repr., Madison: University of Wisconsin Press, 2010); and Susan L. Flader, *Thinking Like a Mountain: Aldo Leopold and the Evolution of an Ecological Attitude toward Deer, Wolves, and Forests* (1974; repr. Madison: University of Wisconsin Press, 1994).

24. Accessed July 15, 2016, https://arboretum.wisc.edu/visit/events/madison-reads-leopold/.

25. Leopold writes, "The land ethic simply enlarges the boundaries of the community to include soils, waters, plants, and animals, or collectively: the land," *Sand County Almanac*, 204. That, for humans, this biotic community constitutes affective relations is encapsulated in a concluding sentence, "The evolution of a land ethic is an intellectual as well as emotional process," *Sand County Almanac*, 225.

26. *Sand County Almanac*, 108–9.

27. *Sand County Almanac*, 109.

28. *Sand County Almanac*, 109.

29. *Sand County Almanac*, 111–12.

30. Rachel Carson, *Silent Spring* (Boston: Mariner Books, [1962] 2003), 2.

31. Sideris, "Secular and Religious," 244.

32. Sideris, "Secular and Religious," 243.

33. An example is Roger Gottlieb's anthology, *The Oxford Handbook of Religion and Ecology* (New York: Oxford University Press, 2010), in which named *world religions* are each presented in terms of scripture, ritual, and religious thought that fosters positive attitudes of environmental concern. This approach echoes *world religions* ideology, and

also the extractive tendencies of Lynn White Jr. See also the volume edited by Willis J. Jenkins and Mary Evelyn Tucker, eds., *The Routledge Handbook of Religion and Ecology* (New York: Routledge, 2016).

34. See Thomas Berry, *The Sacred Universe: Earth, Spirituality and Religion in the Twenty-First Century*, ed. Mary Evelyn Tucker (New York: Columbia University Press, 2009), and the more recent *Journey of the Universe*, by Brian Thomas Swimme and Mary Evelyn Tucker (New Haven, CT: Yale University Press, 2014).

35. Tomoko Masuzawa, *The Invention of World Religions: Or, How European Universalism Was Preserved in the Language of Pluralism* (Chicago: University of Chicago Press, 2005).

36. Susan Darlington, *The Ordination of a Tree* (Albany: SUNY Press, 2012).

37. For more discussion of this claim, see Anna M. Gade, "Indonesian Islamic Law of the Environment: *Fatwa* and *Da'wa*," *Worldviews: Global Religions, Culture, and Ecology* 19, no. 2 (2015): 161–83.

38. Alliance of Religions and Conservation with WWF, "The Assisi Declarations: Messages on Humanity and Nature from Buddhism, Christianity, Hinduism, Islam and Judaism," September 29, 1986, accessed July 15, 2016, http://www.arcworld.org /downloads/THE%20ASSISI%20DECLARATIONS.pdf.

39. Included in Palmer and Finlay, *Faith in Conservation*, xv, accessed July 15, 2016, http://tinyurl.com/3c13wf.

40. Palmer and Finlay, *Faith in Conservation*, xv.

41. Palmer and Finlay, *Faith in Conservation*, xv.

42. For an introduction, see Jeremy Davies, *The Birth of the Anthropocene* (Berkeley: University of California Press, 2016).

43. See and hear a recording of its performance in K. H. Affandi's home on the website Green Islam in Indonesia (www.vimeo.com/hijau), accessed July 15, 2016, https://vimeo .com/37345606. This example is presented and discussed in more detail in Anna M. Gade, "Tradition and Sentiment in Indonesian Environmental Islam," *Worldviews: Global Religions, Culture, and Ecology* 16, no. 3 (2012): 263–85.

44. "Green Islam in Indonesia," www.vimeo.com/hijau (accessed May 20, 2017; https://vimeo.com/album/1854899), has videos documenting his teachings as he gave them in these conversations.

45. See Anna M. Gade, "Islam," in *The Oxford Handbook of Religion and Emotion*, ed. John Corrigan (New York: Oxford University Press, 2008), 35–50.

46. Anna M. Gade, *Perfection Makes Practice: Learning, Emotion, and the Recited Qur'ān in Indonesia* (Honolulu: University of Hawai'i Press, 2004), describes changes in emotional systems of Qur'an reading and other Arabic recitation.

47. A short sound recording of part of his "eco-*salawat*" from 2011 (accessed July 15, 2016) can be found at http://vimeo.com/video/103290561.

48. The Fatihah is the *sura* (chapter) recited with each cycle of *salat*, making seventeen times in one day with five prayers. A video recording of the entire "Selasa Pon" ritual, edited down from its original length of about forty minutes to twenty minutes (accessed July 15, 2016) can be viewed at http://vimeo.com/video/102569428.

49. His words are from the following recorded interview (accessed July 15, 2016): http://vimeo.com/video/102382599, with English translation by the author.

50. For examples of emergent strains in contemporary global Islamic environmental theology, see the recent writing of Sara Tlili in English, *Animals in the Qur'an* (Cambridge: Cambridge University Press, 2012), and work in Arabic by the scholar Yusuf Al-Qaradawi, *Ra'ait al-bi'ah fi shari'at al-islam* (Cairo: Dar Al-Shuruq, 1421/2001), which has seen widespread influence among Muslims worldwide.

## 8. BODILY ENCOUNTERS
*Affect, Religion, and Ethnography*

Anthropologist Clifford Geertz defined religion as a "cultural system" wherein there is a direct correlation between sign and signification, symbol and meaningful communication.[1] In such a scheme, religion becomes the expression of belief rendered legible and rational such that worldview and identity map in a representational mode that the researcher can access, see, capture, and diagram. Ideologically grounded in cultural practices and artifacts, religion becomes curiously static and predictable—particularly so, according to Geertz, when considered in light of moods so pervasive they "vary only as to intensity: go nowhere. They spring from certain circumstances but they are responsive to no ends. Like fogs, they just settle and lift; like scents, suffuse and evaporate. When present, they are totalistic: if one is sad, everything seems sad and everyone dreary."[2] Investigating relationships between religion and emotion within the schema of a cultural system, the researcher is limited to observing and translating a relationship between sacred object and human subject as feeling hovers, lifeless and listless. Anthropologist Talal Asad has critiqued this definition of religion for its universalism.[3] He argues that as an essentialized category, religion becomes transcultural and transhistorical outside of its discursive formation, and therefore separated from any imbrication with power.

This chapter is shaped by both approaches to the study of the religion. Aligned with Asad, I consider religiously inflected forms of power as discursively and historically situated, even as they are transsubjective, entangling human and nonhuman bodies across time and space. I also rethink Geertz's use of metaphor to link mood to fog and scent as a gesture toward a bodily, sensory engagement with emotion worth exploring. In this examination, I take up anthropologist Kathleen Stewart's claim that "writing culture through emergent forms means stepping outside the cold comfort zone of recognizing only self-identical objects."[4] By approaching religion as an assemblage rather than a system, and emotion as economic rather than personal, variations in intensity matter.

In affect theory, the concept of assemblage is used to reframe language, representation, identity, and subject formation as the privileged modes through which to theorize power. Affect theorist Jasbir Puar describes the concept and its usefulness this way: "Assemblage is actually an awkward translation—the original term in Deleuze and Guattari's work is not the French word assemblage, but actually Agencement, a term which means design, layout, organization, arrangement, and relations—the focus being not on content but on relations, relations of patterns. . . . Assemblages do not privilege bodies as human, nor as residing within a human/animal binary. Along with a de-exceptionalizing of human bodies, multiple forms of matter can be bodies—bodies of water, cities, institutions, and so on. Matter is an actor."[5]

As an assemblage, religion becomes lively rather than lived, opening up the possibility for human and nonhuman agents to interact, phenomenologically doing religion and ontologically being religious outside of semiotic and representational frames. The space and medium of communication collapses, exposing circuits of resonance across disparate worldviews, physical distance, and temporal lag. Feminist affect theorist Sara Ahmed writes: "In such affective economies, emotions do things, and they align individuals with communities—or bodily space with social space—through the very intensity of their attachments. Rather than seeing emotions as psychological dispositions, we need to consider how they work, in concrete and particular ways, to mediate the relationship between the psychic and the social, and between the individual and the collective."[6]

As emotions circulate affective value, visceral processes of mediation trouble dichotomous relations of speaker/listener, spiritual/worldly, and human/nonhuman. In *History and Presence*, Robert Orsi investigates relations of spirit and matter as intersubjective, but he does not consider the agency of technology or emotion in these relationships.[7] By contrast, my analysis opens up the definition of religion such that objects and feelings are also social agents of spirit and matter. My empirical evidence shows that rather than passive, disembodied, or schematic, visual and digital culture is affective, material, and desirous.

In anthropological theory, affect has been described by William Mazzarella as carrying "tactile, sensuous, and perhaps even involuntary connotations," implying "a way of apprehending social life that does not start with the bounded, intentional subject while at the same time foregrounding embodiment and sensuous life."[8] Rather than an emotional state that can be named and is "always already semiotically mediated," according to this definition affect is precognitive, prelinguistic, and prepersonal.[9] As Mazzarella's formulation suggests, affect is difficult to examine by conventional discursive methods given that it is radically grounded in the body to the extent that it cannot be articulated or rendered immediately intelligible in language.

Therefore, in this analysis, I use two distinct scenes—one in which I am sitting at my laptop watching a video and another at the same laptop scanning headlines—whose affective and perceptual scripts involve human and non-human bodies that include media technologies and animate moods entangled in relations that are networked and contagious.[10] On the whole, this chapter explores how ethnography contributes to the analysis of religion as a collective yet embodied process akin to what cultural theorist Raymond Williams theorizes as "structures of feeling."[11] Rather than a finished product of human design rendered in the habitual past tense, which is where Geertz's definition of religion as a cultural system simultaneously begins and gets stuck, I examine religion as an assemblage that conscripts affective labor at once voluntary and nonintentional, of body and atmosphere.

In this chapter's opening ethnographic example, then, I respond to the question "How do we study religion and emotion?" by reflecting on the ways that fieldwork at a multisited evangelical megachurch troubled my positionality as a researcher and identity as a non-Christian. I use autoethnography to theorize coming under conviction as spastic and infectious—a generative bodily encounter beyond the regulatory jurisdiction of institutions, doctrine, or ideology. Historian Wendy Brown surmises that even under secular conditions, "being convicted" of an error or crime echoes its usage in relation to sin: "being pinned, trapped, unfree to act . . . an urgent, yet also paralyzing state."[12] Rather than an aggressive argument that renders individuals impotent and hinders social mobilization, I argue that the political power of conviction lies in its affective capacity to register as a belief that feels like one's own but may be steered toward circulating emotions such as fear, hate, love, and paranoia. In this sense, conviction entails contagions of belief, described by philosopher William Connolly as "spiritual dispositions to action that both flow below epistemic beliefs and well up into them . . . the tightening of the gut, coldness of the skin, contraction of the pupils, and hunching of the back that arise when an epistemic belief in which you are invested has been challenged."[13] I reassess conviction in terms of gut feeling that signals desires and passions simultaneously biological and social that can be suggested and manipulated—a porously open-ended process that troubles dichotomies of sinner and saved or profane and sacred.

From 1996 to 2014 Mars Hill Church of Seattle multiplied into fifteen facilities in five American states serving approximately thirteen thousand attendees as Pastor Mark Driscoll's preaching on "biblical oral sex" earned him international celebrity:[14] "Men, I am glad to report to you that oral sex is biblical. . . . Ladies, your husbands appreciate oral sex. They do. So, serve them, love them well."[15] In sermons such as "The Porn Path" and an e-book called *Porn Again Christian*, Driscoll stated in no uncertain terms that "free and frequent" sex between a husband and wife is necessary to assure fidelity within Christian marriages and secure masculine leadership within evangelical churches.[16] "Our world assaults men with images of beautiful women," he warned. "Male brains house an ever-growing repository of lustful snapshots always on random shuffle. . . . The temptation to sin by viewing porn and other visual lures is an everyday war."[17] As Driscoll claimed, "sometimes pornography is in an image, sometimes it is in your imagination";[18] his sexualized hermeneutic revealed women's body parts cloaked in biblical metaphor.[19] Meanwhile, question and answer sessions during services encouraged congregants to text queries that materialized as sound-bite confessions to sins and desires on large screens surrounding Mars Hill's sanctuary. The church's use of visual and digital media served to amplify Driscoll's sermonizing on sex by enlisting audience participation in animating a pornographic imaginary, legitimizing his spiritual authority through the bodily and virtual circulation of shame, fear, and paranoia as affective political and economic value.

As Mars Hill's facilities multiplied, imperatives to support the church's propagation were framed in violent terms of combat readiness and the embodiment of "visual generosity" and "sexual freedom" by Christian wives. The orchestration of this affective labor was articulated in terms of "air war" and "ground war," with the aim to "rally one thousand churches behind one pulpit."[20] In my ethnographic monograph *Biblical Porn: Affect, Labor, and Pastor Mark Driscoll's Evangelical Empire*,[21] I analyze how this strategy of biopolitical control infused Mars Hill's ministry, including sermon study in small group settings, social media forums, men's and women's training days, church leadership boot camps, and military missions that gifted *Porn Again Christian* to troops in Iraq and Afghanistan. Globalized logics of warfare constituted and intensified terrorist assemblages of religious, racialized, and sexualized Others—threats that included hypersexualized single women; wolves within the flock that challenged

Driscoll's authority; a crisis of masculinity within institutional Christianity; and the rising popularity of Islam among men in U.S. urban centers.[22] Mars Hill's facilities steadily replicated until 2014, when a deluge of evidence surfaced online supporting several accusations against Driscoll. These charges included the surreptitious use of a marketing ploy to cull the buyers lists necessary to achieve best-selling status for Driscoll's book *Real Marriage: The Truth About Sex, Friendship, and Life Together* (2012);[23] they also identified bullying, micromanagement, and shunning procedures as tactics of intimidation and social isolation used to suppress information and stifle dissent.[24]

From 2006 to 2008 I conducted participant-observation at Mars Hill's central facility in Seattle as it began multiplying into satellite campuses throughout the city and its suburbs, attending not only sermons but also gospel classes required for membership; seminars on how to embody biblical gender and sexuality; a women's training day called "Christian Womanhood in a Feminist Culture"; and Film and Theology Nights, when Hollywood movies were screened and discussed. From 2014 to 2016 I spoke with former leaders and members who worked for the church during the stages of its foundation, expansion, and dissolution, including interviews that suggest congregants remain haunted by feelings of betrayal and shame. This chapter's opening scene depicts how affective entanglements and labor during my initial years of fieldwork bodily recruited and disturbed me in unexpected ways, as well. While the second scene takes place two years later on the morning of the mass shooting at Pulse nightclub in Orlando in 2016, it also begins with me sitting alone at my computer. These seemingly disparate events are ethnographically interconnected by affective processes that queer space and time as well as distinctions between subject and object, signaling structures of feeling that are unruly and viral yet situated and historicized.

By narratively privileging "risk and uncertainty over researcher control and reflexivity," my analysis demonstrates the scholarly potential and ethical necessity of reflecting on what anthropologists Kevin Lewis O'Neill and Peter Benson call the "phenomenology of 'doing' fieldwork" wherein "ethnography's ethical possibilities are *actualized* when ethnographers change . . . not simply for the self and its interests, but rather for the sake of new kinds of collective affiliations across interpersonal and intercultural boundaries."[25] In this mode, the researcher is instrument rather than authority. Kathleen Stewart suggests that writing culture is "an attunement, a response, a vigilant protection of a worlding."[26] My examination illustrates how ethnographic engagement with affect elicits attunement to ecological and phenomenological worlding acutely generative for the study of religion and emotion.

*Coming Under Conviction Online*

By the summer of 2014, evidence had surfaced online supporting several allegations against Pastor Mark Driscoll of Mars Hill Church, including the use of the book-marketing firm Result Source to achieve best-selling author stature and profits; plagiarism; and well-documented abuses of authority.[27] After numerous former leaders posted confessions seeking repentance for sinning as—and being sinned against—church administration,[28] a protest was organized outside the main facility, which had shifted from Seattle to suburban Bellevue.

I watched the man I quickly became accustomed to calling Pastor Mark preach live at Mars Hill's former headquarters in a renovated hardware warehouse from a stage loaded with high-end sound equipment and beat-up guitars. Flat-screen TVs projecting his image flanked the pulpit and surrounded the amphitheater seating over one thousand. The church's cream-colored lobby bearing members' artwork, well-stocked bookshelves, and canisters of free coffee affected the contemplative ambience of a gallery in stark contrast to its black-box exterior and the buzz of the crowd before services. Young guys lingered in the parking lot at all hours beyond an entryway announcing "meaning, beauty, truth, community" within, while worship music thundering outside after gospel classes testified to the authenticity of this promise. Driving past the suburban facility where Driscoll now spent Sundays, in a mall complex sprawling with buildings so uniform it was easy to lose a sense of space entirely, I tried to imagine what sermons in the beige faux cathedral planted next to an equally looming yet nondistinct Barnes and Noble would feel like by comparison to those I had attended from 2006 to 2008.

While the issues cleverly summarized in colorful slogans on placards raised important questions, it was a thirty-minute video posted to the Mars Hill website that inspired ex-staff and congregants to mobilize behind the rally cry "We Are Not Anonymous." This performance began with Driscoll sitting down in a simple wooden chair in the imposing Bellevue sanctuary, his figure flanked by rows of empty seats rather than large screens, the pulpit lectern onstage out of focus behind his left shoulder. The camera angle was such that it felt as though Driscoll was facing me from where I sat with laptop open at my desk. His complexion was ruddy but grizzled with salt and pepper stubble. The only prop that appeared throughout his delivery was a leather-bound Bible, which he physically and verbally gestured with and to in the video's opening moments:

> Hi, Mars Hill, Pastor Mark here. I wanted to give you a bit of an update on the season that we have been in and continue to be in and I was

thinking about it and when I was seventeen years of age Jesus gave me this bible through a gal named Grace who is of course now my wife, and Jesus saved me when I was nineteen, in college as a freshman, reading this bible, and I started opening this bible when I was twenty-five and Grace and I were a young married couple in our rental home. We felt called to start Mars Hill Church and so we would have some people over for a bible study and there was not a lot of people so we didn't have a full service, instead I would sit in this chair and I would open this bible and just teach a handful of people, or a few handfuls of people that would show up in our living room, and that grew to be Mars Hill Church. Now that I'm 43 almost 44, looking back it's, it's overwhelming if I'm honest, it's shocking and amazing and staggering and wonderful. What Jesus has done has far exceeded even what I was praying for or hoping for or dreaming of.[29]

After this introduction littered with references to the Bible in his hands, a material manifestation of God's hand in Mars Hill's successful growth as well as his own spiritual authority, Driscoll explained that the purpose of this video was to communicate "in a way that is godly," by "directly" addressing congregants in a manner that was intended "as a means of loving you and informing you."[30] Within the first five minutes of this performance, publicly disseminated online yet purportedly broadcast for an audience of intimates, Driscoll made the statement that many I spoke with later attributed with triggering the protest:

> During this season as well, I have been rather silent and there are some reasons for that. First of all, we, including myself, needed to determine what exactly was happening. If I'm real honest with you, at first it was just a little overwhelming and a bit confusing. . . . As well, one of the things that has been complex is the fact that a lot of the people we are dealing with in this season remain anonymous. And so we don't know how to reconcile, or how to work things out with people because we're not entirely sure who they are, and so that has, that has made things a little more complex and difficult as well.[31]

Stunned, I looked at my browser, which was loaded with tabs open to websites with names such as Joyful Exiles, Repentant Pastor, Mars Hill Refuge, and We Love Mars Hill where multiple testimonies to spiritual, emotional, and financial exploitation were posted with the author's name clearly identified. My initial sense of betrayal seemed unreasonable given that I had no personal attachment to any of the people in these stories, had not seen Driscoll preach live for years, and had never considered him an authority figure since I did not and never have self-identified as a Christian. I was not the video's intended audience; there was no rationalization, let alone words, for how I felt. Such "affective space," suggests Kevin Lewis O'Neill, is "religiously managed and politically manipulated sensation [that] makes legible a series of spaces that are not necessarily territorial but that are nonetheless deeply political . . . for example, the felt distance that exists between *us* and *them*."[32]

I was not physically shaking as I watched Driscoll lie to my face through the computer screen, but my agitation was palpable and did not recede during the entirety of his message. Even more disconcertingly, I found myself not only hoping but also believing that he was going to change course and repent of his sin, as he had admonished audiences repeatedly and vehemently to do. I kept waiting for an acknowledgment of the specific charges of abuse, and the suffering they had caused to those who had the courage to openly testify to their prolonged spiritual and psychological toll. When that did not happen, instead of doubting Driscoll, I started wondering if I had misheard or misunderstood. In a sense, I kept the faith alive, until the final minutes of his message:

> Lastly, many of you have asked myself and other leaders, how can we be in prayer? I genuinely appreciate that, I would say, pray for your local leaders, they're dealing with things that, that I'm not dealing with . . . and, ah, there are some things in this season that are just, they're just, they're strange . . . ahh . . . unique. For example, at one of our churches, someone is folding up pornography and putting it in our pew Bibles. Just, all kinds of things in this strange season, so that when the lead pastor gets up and says, hey, if you're new or not a Christian, we've got some free Bibles in the pew, feel free to pick one up and go to page whatever for the sermon, and they open it up and they're exposed to pornography, and this can be adults or children, and so now there's a team having to go through our Bibles and take the pornography out to make sure their Bibles are clean on Sundays.[33]

The working title of my book on the church had been *Biblical Porn* for a couple of years. I was also writing a chapter on spiritual warfare, and never was my sense of it so keen as I unexpectedly burst out laughing at this story's end. It was a full-body laugh that erupted from my gut and lasted for a long time, but not because I found the act of vandalism described particularly funny. After all the lies I had listened to, I highly doubted the authenticity of this anecdote, but that did not make it any less affective. William Connolly describes laughter as "a manifestation of surplus affect," which can trigger "side perceptions at odds with the dominant drift of perception and interpretation" such that the flow of thought is interrupted to "open a window of creativity."[34] It was not what Mark said that made me laugh, but the sense that we were sharing an inside joke. This surplus affective value did not register in his rhetoric, reside in a commodity, or remain self-contained, but manifested as conviction so unfocused it emitted both within and without me. In this circulation of what Sara Ahmed posits as an "affective economy," "emotions play a crucial role in the 'surfacing' of individual and collective bodies through the way in which emotions circulate between bodies and signs."[35] After the video ended, I sought to interpret and identify what I was feeling in emotional terms and settled on paranoia, figuring this irrational response would quickly subside. After all, Mark's use of hyperbole and humor to excite and seduce audiences was renowned and considered to be among his gifts and strengths as a communicator. However, rather than fading, the intensity and unpredictability of sensations that were impossible to pin down kept me awake nights and indoors at my desk scanning the Internet for the unknown and unknowable. Information? Affirmation? Safety? And from whom or what, exactly?

At first, I rationalized my feelings in terms that I could understand and articulate as a feminist anthropologist—social justice. Put simply, I desired recognition for those whose suffering went unacknowledged. Despite its good intentions, such an explanation was no excuse for the disturbing and overpowering need I had to do something without knowing what that could be, other than endlessly tracking the explosion of media coverage surrounding Driscoll and the church. While Mark's opening posture and closing story provided the perfect tactile validation for my book's title, beyond anything I could ever dream or script, it was not until I asked permission to join the protest with former Mars Hill members via a public Facebook page entitled "We Are Not Anonymous" that its affective value became clearer. I had come under conviction, but not of my own sinful nature and need for salvation. I did not become born-again in Christian terms, but I had to confront the troubling reality that I had desired to believe in Pastor Mark. This was a desire that I did not feel I deserved, nor frankly wished to own, given that I had never sacrificed for the church nor ideologically seen eye to eye with Driscoll. That video haunted me with surplus affect, both possessed and inhabited, that was not truly mine.

Anthropologist Susan Harding notes that when social scientists have investigated why people convert to Christianity, they inevitably deduce that individuals have good reason to be "susceptible, vulnerable, and in need of something, so the question becomes 'Why? What's wrong? What's unsettling them?' Or, 'What's setting them up? How have they been predisposed to convert?'"[36] In turn, accounts of various ritual practices and psychological techniques that catalyze transformation from one worldview to another posit "conversion as a kind of brainwashing."[37] Harding describes her own experience of coming under conviction in terms of being "caught up in the Reverend Campbell's stories—I had 'caught' his language—enough to hear God speak to me when I almost collided with another car that afternoon. Indeed, the near-accident did not seem like an accident at all, for there is no such thing as a coincidence in born-again culture."[38]

By contrast, Driscoll was not witnessing to me personally in the video, nor was he using a biblical grammar that opened narrative gaps through which to insert myself as unbelieving listener. Rather than a sacred rite of passage, his concluding remarks conjured the folding of pornography into pew Bibles—a profane joke that complicated our subject positions of speaker/listener and believer/nonbeliever, given its ambiguity. I could not be certain whether the prank was *on* or *by* him. Semiotics was an unhelpful tool of analysis, as this affective process was unnecessarily dialogical and therefore porously open-ended; mediation occurred bodily without becoming meaningful. Harding describes coming under conviction as chronological and spatial—a crossing from the terrain of disbelief into a liminal space of suspension or limbo that precedes the (potential) conversion from non-Christian to born-again believer. Clearly defined, preordained subject positions of listener-lost and speaker-saved are acknowledged by individuals who choose to enter into a relationship situated through a specific language with a particular motive. Instead, I experienced conviction as irreducibly social sitting alone at my desk—compelling actions, events, and conversations I never imagined possible.

In the frantic days after watching the video, I found a link to the public Facebook group "We Are Not Anonymous." Without forethought or script, I woke up one morning and wrote to a former church leader that I had not met. That lengthy message is truncated here: "I'm writing for your thoughts on the question of whether my presence would be welcome at the protest this Sunday. . . . I have been reluctant to join anything that would make anyone uncomfortable, especially as I'm a non-Christian. . . . I'm in a strange limbo state where I'm not an 'insider' but not really an 'outsider' either, and it's hard for me to simply watch from the sidelines with all that's happened."

I never omitted that I was not a Christian or pretended to be anything but a feminist anthropologist. Openly informing those I spoke with of my identity was ethical according to my methodological training, yet positionality was inadequate to the task of explaining liminality and displacement through which I came to affectively, if not theologically, resonate with former church members. To claim any positionality in my case was feeble—a hollow gesture and ideological fiction in the face of sociality generated out of a dislocation and disaggregation of self.

When I described my experience of coming under conviction during the video to a former leader—how I trusted Mark would repent to the extent that I questioned myself—he emphatically gestured to my phone on the table as it was recording our conversation and exclaimed, "Put that down! Get that in!" At the wooden table where we sat, I was not the only one taking notes. I used pen and paper; he used a tablet. I had asked permission to record our time together, an interview that lasted nearly six hours, and whenever there needed to be a pause in the action, he would double-check to see if "we" were recording again.

Many of those I spoke with did not want to be recorded or have their names used. I understood. It was risky. I was asking people who had been socially isolated out of fear of being labeled gossips or divisive to discuss events that could be read as indictments of themselves and/or others. I asked people where they wanted to meet so that they could choose whether they would be more comfortable talking at home or in public. In one Seattle coffee shop in the vicinity of a Mars Hill facility before the church officially disbanded, a former pastor spent much of our thirty minutes together glancing around the premises, informing me when someone associated with the church walked in, eyes darting and brow lightly beaded with sweat. In one home, tears surfaced in the eyes of an ex-pastor as soon as we sat down; later during our conversation, tears welled up in mine. Many confessed they felt duped and betrayed as well as culpable. There was tension between what was attributable to human and divine will, individual agency and God's sovereignty. People were not looking to answer, but for answers themselves. None of my interviews with former church staff were a one-way affair. I played informant, too, describing the arguments of my book, experiences at Mars Hill, and fluctuating feelings in the aftermath of its dissolution.

As I watched the video I had no language for what I was experiencing, nor had I caught Pastor Mark's. I could not discern divine providence or impose self-will in explanations for what was bodily unfolding. I did not ask *why* I wanted to believe Mark would repent to the extent that I even doubted myself, as there were no religious or personal reasons for such an investment; instead, I kept asking *how*. While I could not have articulated it at the time or during the many months that I sought the fellowship of former Mars Hill members over longtime friends, the disjuncture I experienced was not a matter of worldview but the matter of worlding. This affective process of coming under conviction online was underway prior to 2014 and ongoing after the video's end, compelling my inquiry into distinctions between the human and nonhuman, materiality and discourse, as well as the boundaries constituted and policed by the categories *religious* and *secular*. Language was not the catalyst for a religious conversion; instead, there was a "conversion of the materiality of the body into an event."[39] An intensification of my body's relation to itself occurred in an event-encounter with other bodies—an assemblage of materialities that included Driscoll, his Bible, my laptop screen, tabs open to websites dedicated to former congregants' testimonies, the (supposed) prankster putting pornography into pew Bibles, paranoia, and Satan. All these bodies were affective conductors, rendering my positionality moot.[40]

Mark began blogging on the topic of spiritual warfare a few days after the anonymous video's release, a six-part series that ended the same week in late August when he preached what would be his last sermon from the Mars Hill pulpit. The first installment of that blog series began:

> In a day when, on the one hand, science often dismisses the supernatural
> altogether and, on the other, cultural pluralism tells us that all spiritual
> ity is equally desirable, it is hard to find anyone who believes in the reality
> of the spiritual world and evil. Anyone who opens the Bible with any in
> tegrity must admit that it is a book that consistently presents a worldview
> in which there is a very real war with the real God and his holy angels
> versus the fallen angel Satan and unholy demons. Sinners, including you
> and me, are taken as captives in this war.[41]

I was conscripted by the spiritual war that Driscoll promulgated through his ministry at Mars Hill. Too often accounts of evangelical cultural performances, even those that consider the politics of affect, only consider the aim of conversion.[42] In theorizing what he calls "structure of feeling," cultural studies scholar Raymond Williams offers an antidote for reducing cultural politics to the expression of ideology or projection of identity by foregrounding "the specificity of present being, the inalienably physical, within which we may indeed discern and acknowledge institutions, formations, positions, but not always as fixed products, defining products."[43] Structure of feeling offers a means for rethinking the social as "processes [that] occur not only between but within the relationship and the related."[44] In this modulation, political transformation does not register in "changed institutions, formations, and beliefs" but "changes of presence" that do not have to be cognitively understood "before they exert palpable pressures and set effective limits on experience and on action."[45] This concept is useful to think through in relation to ethnographic fieldwork insofar as it speaks to and offers insight concerning "structures of *experience*" that are "emergent or pre-emergent" which are not self-contained or the property of a given individual but rather a matter of "impulse, restraint, and tone; specifically affective elements of consciousness and relationships: not feeling against thought, but thought as felt and feeling as thought: practical consciousness of a present kind, in a living and inter-relating continuity."[46] Arguably, ethnographic research requires not only attunement to nuances in mood and milieu that speak to the affective elements of "a social experience that is still *in process*,"[47] but a willingness to acknowledge our vulnerability and lack of control as fieldwork involves us in unpredictable social experiences through unruly bodily encounters.

Ethical action is set in motion when ethnographers are open to risk that lies beyond the purview of their positionality or liberalist conceptions of self-empowerment. When the scholarly value of such possibility is foreclosed, the study of religion and emotion becomes trapped within a given cultural system. For example, cultural studies scholar Ann Pellegrini has taken up Williams's theorizing on structure of feeling to examine performances that bridge religious and secular publics or evangelical and popular tropes. However, the limitations of investigating culture-war conflicts in terms that reiterate hierarchical dichotomies between the saved and the sinner are apparent when the only potential outcome is the conversion of non-Christians into born-again believers, whereby affect becomes a by-product abstracted from the bodily experience of cultural politics as social and in process. Pellegrini analyzes Hell House performances in terms of "structures of religious feeling" whose strategic intent refutes the possibility of any social actors who are unidentifiable beyond the binary terms of believer or non-believer.[48] In turn, there is no affective space outside of the performances themselves, or political impact beyond cultural conflict that is only reconcilable through the personal transformation of a *lost* subject into one who is *saved*. In Pelligrini's examination, the analytic usage of structure of feeling to investigate how such cultural performances use affect to political effect is not grounded in the phenomenology of doing fieldwork but rather the empirical data collected by an outsider who remains adamantly so.

Pellegrini confesses toward the end of her investigation, "as a queer scholar of performance (not to mention an atheist) I find my own pleasures—and challenges—in thinking seriously about Hell House, what it does, what it fails to accomplish."[49] By signaling this failure in accomplishment in terms of the performances' inability to incite her own conversion, and relegating Hell House's ultimate political aim to such a *religious* transformation, Pellegrini limits the relationships of the cultural, social, and political to the domain of us and them: "Hell House speaks for much larger political and cultural currents, and represents a politics of division."[50] Additionally, she relegates her analysis of Hell House performances to observing others, such as "a low hum from the crowd," or descriptive statements that index her positionality as an unchangeable critic in command of any emotional response that may arise: "In comparison to the pyrotechnics of hell," she writes, "heaven was a let-down."[51]

By strictly policing her stance in relation to the Hell House performances in the name of academic objectivity and researcher reflexivity, Pelligrini indexes the ethical and political shortcomings of such an approach. Rather than investigating the politics of affect, she approaches religion as a cultural system to the detriment of her analysis. Despite her useful discussion of structure of feeling as a concept, her reading of the performance under examination curiously omits, ignores, and/or disavows affect as it bodily registered through her, rendering the relationship between religion and emotion as lifeless as the pervasive mood conjured then dismissed in Geertz's discussion. This cultural studies approach claims authority before it embarks on inquiry, whereas, as anthropologist James Clifford notes, "Ethnography is actively situated *between* powerful systems of meaning. It poses its questions at the boundaries . . . it describes processes of innovation and structuration, and is itself part of these processes."[52] While Pelligrini uses the primary method used by ethnographers in her study of religion and emotion—the clumsy hyphenate "participant-observation"— she wields it as a tool rather than an opportunity. As Clifford describes it, "The predominant metaphors in anthropological research have been participant-observation, data collection, and cultural description, all of which presuppose a standpoint outside—looking at, objectifying, or, somewhat closer, 'reading,' a given reality."[53] However, Clifford adds that participant-observation also enacts "a delicate balance of subjectivity and objectivity," whereby empathy becomes central.[54] My empirical evidence suggests that, more so than empathy, the ethnographic study of religion and emotion produces surplus affect that is unintentionally, even problematically, transformative. Longitudinal fieldwork forces the ethnographer to face the limits of scholarly control, whether they admit to it in writing or not.

*Economies of Love-Hate*

It was an emotional Sunday morning on June 12, 2016. I was scanning updates about the mass shooting in Orlando. The first news report I saw of the attack on Pulse nightclub announced that there was a possible terror link. This assumption was soon amplified by Senator Marco Rubio of Florida, who said that if "this is something inspired by radical ideology, then I think common sense tells you that he targeted the gay community because of the views that exist in the radical Islamic community about the gay community."[55] He continued,

"We have seen the way radical Islamists have treated gays and lesbians in other countries. We've seen that it's punishable by death. We've seen some horrible things that they have done."[56] Conjecture concerning the psychology of the shooter has been debated, but Rubio's statements have remained unchallenged. His common sense was bolstered by pundits such as the *New York Times* op-ed columnist Frank Bruni, who stated that the attack was against "freedom itself," given that the United States "integrate[s] and celebrate[s] diverse points of view, diverse systems of belief, diverse ways to love."[57]

In their responses, Rubio and Bruni construct a nationalist imaginary that posits the United States as exceptional in embracing diversity, freedom, and love. Notwithstanding the fact that the gunman was an American, both soundly rest blame for Omar Mateen's rampage on an amorphous elsewhere while framing the emotional narrative of the largest mass shooting in U.S. history in binary terms of us/them. Specifically, Rubio conjures a battle between two seemingly homogenous communities—*Islamic radicals* outside of the United States and *the gay community* within. He erases details such as the predominantly Latino patronage at Pulse that night while ignoring others such as Mateen's U.S. citizenship. His common sense resounds with the hubris of empire that circulates hate in the name of love.

Although President Obama is not ideologically aligned on paper with Rubio about policies such as gay marriage and transgender rights, his language in the massacre's aftermath resonated: "No act of hate or terror will ever change who we are, or the values that make us American."[58] Another quote from his speech read, "In the face of hate and violence, we will love one another. We will not give in to fear or turn against each other. Instead, we will stand united as Americans to protect our people and defend our nation, and to take action against those who threaten us."[59]

> Once again, a tragedy turned into an opportunity to proclaim *America* on the side of love and unity and *other countries* on the side of hate and radicalness. A possible terror link is a foregone conclusion based on ideological oppositions of good/evil, the very Manichaean logic that legitimized Operation Iraqi Freedom, a preemptive war fought over imaginary weapons of mass destruction. When President George W. Bush proclaimed an "axis of evil, arming to threaten the peace of the world" after the attacks on 9/11,[60] he set the emotional tone for U.S. foreign policy at the beginning of the twenty-first century using the rhetoric of crusade.[61] We can affectively examine this discourse through a lens offered by Sara Ahmed: "The reading of others as hateful aligns the imagined

subject with rights and the imagined nation with ground. This alignment is affected by the representation of both the rights of the subject and the grounds of the nation as already under threat. It is the emotional reading of hate that works to bind the imagined white subject and nation together. . . . The ordinary white subject is a fantasy that comes into being through the mobilization of hate, as a passionate attachment tied closely to love."[62]

Rubio referred to Mateen as "an animal" and warned, "It is a reminder that the war on terror has evolved into something we have never had to face before: individuals capable of carrying out attacks like these, with these numbers, in places you have not seen before."[63] As love and hate circulate in support of national defense, they prime an atmosphere of fear in which menace potential becomes increasingly banal and easier to spot.

As I scanned for further news on the shooting, directly below the Rubio update the *New York Times* reported, "Washington Plans Extra Security for Pride Festival." Underneath this announcement was a photo taken during the pride parade in Washington, DC, the previous day.

The picture was quickly removed within a few minutes of its posting, but rather than attribute it to a mere mistake and honor second guesses, I prefer to observe the initial impulse, which illustrates all too well what Ahmed describes in economic terms of hate:

FIGURE 8.1. Photograph of crowd at Washington, DC, parade. Credit: James Lawler Duggan/Reuters.

Hate cannot be found in one figure, but works to create the very outline of different figures or objects of hate, a creation that crucially aligns the figures together and constitutes them as a "common" threat. Importantly, then, hate does not reside in a given subject or object. Hate is economic; it circulates between signifiers in relationships of difference and displacement. . . . emotions work by sticking figures together (adherence), a sticking that creates the very effect of a collective (coherence). . . . My economic model of emotions suggests that while emotions do not positively reside in a subject or figure, they still work to bind subjects together. Indeed, to put it more strongly, the nonresidence of emotions is what makes them "binding."[64]

The woman in this photograph is not of the pride parade. According to the caption, she is a passerby wearing a hijab. Her image magnifies and augments the announcement that security has been amped up as protection against potential menace. In this image, a possible terror link is seen, captured, and identified. Hate circulates. Out of love, Americans bear arms, bolster security, and constitute a common threat that has no particular face but can be represented as different through displacement and certain signifiers—in this case, a woman wearing a hijab waiting to cross the street at the gay pride parade in Washington, DC. Love, not just hate, can lead to the careless and commonsensical depiction of future threat in the nebulous shape of racialized, radicalized, religious *Others*. Jasbir Puar contends that queer subjects in the United States are afforded benevolence in liberal discourses of diversity in lieu of "evernarrowing parameters of white racial privilege" and "a reintensification of racialization through queerness."[65] The woman wearing a hijab is depicted as uncomfortably out of place amid the freedom, love, and gay pride on open, colorful display.

In the following weeks, terrorist attacks hit cities in predominantly Muslim countries. Less than a month after 49 people were killed in Orlando, jihadists murdered 41 people in Istanbul, 22 in Bangladesh, and over 300 in Baghdad. However, the victims in these attacks gleaned far less global attention than those who were shot at Pulse. While the rainbow flag signifying gay pride was widely flown or posted in solidarity within and outside of the United States, the flags of Turkey, Bangladesh, and Iraq were not. This apparent lack of empathy and overt indifference led some to ask, "In a supposedly globalized world, do nonwhites, non-Christians, and non-Westerners count as fully human?"[66]

Mateen may have pledged allegiance to ISIS in a 911 call, but ISIS's subsequent praise of him did not make his connection to the terrorist group any clearer. He also used a gay dating app and frequented Pulse before the night of the shooting, but questions regarding his sexuality remain unanswered. The construction of his psychological profile to determine motive and label the killing a hate crime, act of terrorism, or both, stoked uncertainty rather than abating it. President Obama's speech only temporarily countered the empiric histrionics of the 2016 Republican Presidential nominee that soon became President-Elect Donald Trump, who proposed a ban on migrants from any part of the world with a "proven history of terrorism" against the United States.[67] When Americans declare love as *our* value, an object possessed and wielded as a shield in supposed unity for the sake of national security, such discourse is no defense against hate. Economically, emotion is not partisan, self-contained, or *good* or *bad* in moral terms. Love is not any better or worse, on the side of right or wrong, than hate is—insofar as affective value is concerned.

As I revise this chapter for publication two weeks after the 2016 Presidential Election, accounts of hijabs being wrenched from women's heads circulate on the Internet, and exit polls indicate roughly 80 percent of white evangelicals voted for Donald Trump. "Love Trumps Hate" may have been a well-intentioned campaign slogan, but in this election cycle it could not best "Make America Great Again." Affect theorist Lauren Berlant writes, "all attachments are optimistic . . . cruel optimism is the condition of maintaining an attachment to a significantly problematic object."[68] Belief is an intensely problematic object of desire that enlists affective attachment; its examination requires attunement to social transformation as a process of becoming that unnecessarily signals progress.

*Conclusion*

As an assemblage, religion is neither rational nor irrational but relational.[69] This analytic shift affords the opportunity to examine invisible demons, collective moods, and media technologies as agents rather than fictions, fogs, and tools. By examining emotion as economic, my aim was to emphasize how it mobilizes affect, transmitting value that is unnecessarily moral or monetary. To study religion and emotion in relation is to register what lies beyond language, signification, and normative regulation. Rather than postulate definitions of worlding and attunement, I have offered empirical examples to argue for ethnography's unique capacity to signal situations of bodily encounter. As with any methodology, what it means to practice ethnography shifts, is challenged, appropriated, and repurposed. However, at its most analytically evocative and ethically insightful, ethnography is ontological and phenomenological, a worlding in motion and an attunement in writing.

1. Clifford Geertz, *The Interpretation of Cultures: Selected Essays* (New York: Fontina Press, 1993).

2. Geertz, *Interpretation of Cultures*, 97.

3. Talal Asad, *Genealogies of Religion: Discipline and Reasons of Power in Christianity and Islam* (Baltimore: Johns Hopkins University Press), 1993.

4. Kathleen Stewart, "Precarity's Forms," *Cultural Anthropology* 27, no. (2012): 518.

5. Jasbir Puar, " 'I would rather be a cyborg than a goddess': Intersectionality, Assemblage, and Affective Politics," *European Institute for Progressive Politics*, 2001, accessed February 3, 2016, http://eipcp.net/transversal/0811/puar/en.

6. Sara Ahmed, "Affective Economies," *Social Text* 79, 22 2 (summer 2004): 119.

7. Robert A. Orsi, *History and Presence* (Cambridge, MA: Belknap Press of Harvard University Press, 2016).

8. William Mazzarella, "Affect: What Is It Good For?," in *Enchantments of Modernity: Empire, Nation, Globalization*, ed. Saurabh Dube (New York: Routledge, 2009), 91.

9. Mazzarella, "Affect," 93.

10. In using *scripts*, I refer to the term as used by Silvan Tomkins and discussed by Eve Kosofsky Sedgwick and Adam Frank in "Shame in the Cybernetic Fold: Reading Silvan Tomkins": "At least as often as paragraphs permit reader and writer to do—here to enjoy, but in other textual places to anger, or become excited or ashamed, or to enter scenes and perform scripts which call upon affective as well as perceptual and memory capacities— they permit one to *not do*." *Critical Inquiry* 21, no. 2 (1995): 496–522, 500. Emphasis in original.

11. Raymond Williams, *Marxism and Literature* (New York: Oxford University Press, 1977), 128.

12. Wendy Brown, *Politics out of History* (Princeton, NJ: Princeton University Press, 2001), 92.

13. William Connolly, *Capitalism and Christianity: American Style* (Durham, NC: Duke University Press, 2008), 85.

14. https://www.youtube.com/watch?v=J8sNVDyW-ws; Molly Worthington, "Who Would Jesus Smack Down?," *New York Times*, January 11, 2009, accessed January 12, 2009, http://www.nytimes.com/2009/01/11/magazine/11punk-t.html.

15. Don Hinkle, "Bott Radio Blocks Driscoll, Replaces Segment Mid-Show," *Baptist Press*, June 17, 2009, accessed June 20, 2009, http://www.bpnews.net/bpnews.asp?id =30700.

16. Mark Driscoll, "The Porn Path," *Real Marriage*, 2012, accessed February 10, 2013, https://www.youtube.com/watch?v=mEDG46NO-I4; Mark Driscoll, *Porn Again Christian*, 2008, accessed May 14, 2009, http://campusministryunited.com/Documents/Porn _Again_Christian.pdf.

17. Mark Driscoll, "Dance of Manahaim," *The Peasant Princess*, 2008, watched live, accessed May 7, 2015, https://www.youtube.com/watch?v=zO6ck9dDTw.

18. Driscoll, "Porn Path."

19. Driscoll, "Dance of Manahaim."

20. Mike Anderson, "Hello, My Name Is Mike, and I'm a Recovering True Believer," 2013, accessed January 5, 2014, http://mikeyanderson.com/hello-name-mike-im-recovering -true-believer.

21. Jessica Johnson, *Biblical Porn: Affect, Labor, and Pastor Mark Driscoll's Evangelical Empire* (Durham, NC: Duke University Press, 2018).

22. Mark Driscoll makes this connection between the threat of Islam gaining popularity in U.S. cities and a crisis of masculinity within institutional Christianity in a lecture titled "The Ox," presented in 2008 to an audience of potential church planters at an Acts 29 training boot camp.

23. Warren Cole Smith, "Unreal Sales for Driscoll's Real Marriage," *World Magazine*, March 5, 2014, accessed March 6, 2014, http://www.worldmag.com/2014/03/unreal_sales _for_driscoll_s_real_marriage.

24. Accessed September 2, 2014, http://wp.production.patheos.com/blogs/warren throckmorton/files/2014/08/FormalCharges-Driscoll-814.pdf.

25. Peter Benson and Kevin Lewis O'Neill, "Facing Risk: Levians, Ethnography, Ethics," *Anthropology of Consciousness* 18, no. 2 (2007): 29–31.

26. Stewart, "Precarity's Forms," 518.

27. Accessed September 2, 2014, http://wp.production.patheos.com/blogs/warren throckmorton/files/2014/08/FormalCharges-Driscoll-814.pdf.

28. Accessed June 11, 2014, http://repentantpastor.com/.

29. Mark Driscoll, "Anonymous Video," 2014. This transcription was done when the video was available on the now defunct Mars Hill Church website in July 2014. While evidence of this video in its entirety has been scrubbed from the Internet, there is record of its distribution and content. For example: http://www.christianpost .com/news/mark-driscoll-admits-he-should-have-acted-with-more-love-and-pastoral -affection-during-leadership-changes-at-mars-hill-123712/ or https://www.youtube.com /watch?v=dsGDCd1iLls.

30. Driscoll, "Anonymous Video," 2014.

31. Driscoll, "Anonymous Video," 2014.

32. Kevin Lewis O'Neill, "Beyond Broken: Affective Spaces and the Study of American Religion," *JAAR* 81, no. 4 (2013): 1095.

33. Driscoll, "Anonymous Video," 2014.

34. William Connolly, *Neuropolitics* (Minneapolis: University of Minnesota Press, 2002), 8.

35. Ahmed, "Affective Economies," 117.

36. Susan Harding, *The Book of Jerry Falwell: Fundamentalist Language and Politics* (Princeton, NJ: Princeton University Press, 2000), 35.

37. Harding, *Falwell*, 35.

38. Harding, *Falwell*, 59.

39. Puar, "I would rather be a cyborg."

40. Jane Bennett, *Vibrant Matter: A Political Ecology of Things* (Durham, NC: Duke University Press, 2010), 18.

41. Mark Driscoll, "Spiritual Warfare: Who, What and Why," 2014, accessed July 25, 2014, http://marshill.com/2014/07/24/spiritual-warfare-who-what-and-why.

42. Ann Pellegrini, "Signaling through the Flames: Hell House Performance and Religious Structure of Feeling," *American Quarterly* 59 (2007): 911–35.

43. Williams, *Marxism and Literature*, 128.

44. Williams, *Marxism and Literature*, 130.

45. Williams, *Marxism and Literature*, 128–29.

46. Williams, *Marxism and Literature*, 132.

47. Williams, *Marxism and Literature*, 132.

48. Pelligrini, "Hell House."

49. Pelligrini, "Hell House," 932.

50. Pelligrini, "Hell House," 932.

51. Pelligrini, "Hell House," 924.

52. James Clifford, "Introduction: Partial Truths," in *Writing Culture: The Poetics and Politics of Ethnography* (Berkeley: University of California Press, 1986), 2.

53. Clifford, "Introduction," 11.

54. Clifford, "Introduction," 13.

55. Nicholas Fandos, "Marco Rubio Suggests Gunman Targeted Gay Community," *New York Times*, June 12, 2016, accessed June 12, 2016, http://www.nytimes.com/live/orlando-nightclub-shooting-live-updates/marco-rubio-gunman-targeted-gay-community/.

56. Fandos, "Marco Rubio Suggests."

57. Frank Bruni, "The Scope of the Orlando Carnage," *New York Times*, June 13, 2016, accessed June 13, 2016, http://www.nytimes.com/2016/06/13/opinion/the-scope-of-the-orlando-carnage.html.

58. "President Obama: Values That Make Us American," *New York Times*, June 12, 2016, accessed June 12, 2016, http://www.nytimes.com/live/orlando-nightclub-shooting-live-updates/president-obama-2/.

59. "President Obama: We Will Love One Another," *New York Times*, June 12, 2016, accessed June 12, 2016, http://www.nytimes.com/live/orlando-nightclub-shooting-live-updates/president-obama-3/.

60. "Bush State of the Union address," CNN, January 29, 2002, accessed July 20, 2016, http://edition.cnn.com/2002/ALLPOLITICS/01/29/bush.speech.txt/.

61. Peter Ford, "Europe Cringes at 'Crusade' against Terrorists," *Christian Science Monitor*, January 19, 2001, accessed July 20, 2016, http://www.csmonitor.com/2001/0919/p12s2-woeu.html.

62. Ahmed, "Affective Economies," 118.

63. Fandos, "Marco Rubio Suggests."

64. Ahmed, "Affective Economies," 119.

65. Jasbir Puar, *Terrorist Assemblages: Homonationalism in Queer Times* (Durham, NC: Duke University Press, 2007), xii.

66. Anne Barnard, "Muslims Stung by Indifference to Their Losses in Terrorist Attacks," *New York Times*, July 5, 2016, accessed July 6, 2016, http://www.nytimes.com/2016/07/06/world/europe/muslims-baghdad-dhaka-istanbul-terror.html?hp&action=click&pgtype=Homepage&clickSource=story-heading&module=first-column-region&region=top-news&WT.nav=top-news.

67. Jonathan Martin and Alexander Burns, "Blaming Muslims after Attack, Donald Trump Tosses Pluralism Aside," *New York Times*, June 14, 2016, accessed June 15, 2016, http://www.nytimes.com/2016/06/14/us/politics/donald-trump-hillary-clinton-speeches.html.

68. Lauren Berlant, *Cruel Optimism* (Durham, NC: Duke University Press, 2011), 23–24.

69. Robert Orsi's *Between Heaven and Earth: The Religious Worlds People Make and the Scholars Who Study Them* (Princeton, NJ: Princeton University Press, 2006) also explores how scholars of religion inhabit an interstitial space between belief and analysis, if from a different methodological standpoint.

DAVID MORGAN

## 9. EMOTION AND IMAGINATION IN THE RITUAL ENTANGLEMENT OF RELIGION, SPORT, AND NATIONALISM

I would like to describe religion, sport, and nationhood as ritual activities in a way that neither isolates them from one another nor collapses them into a single identity. They share feeling and certain features of ritual structure, and they are integrated, as we will see, into patterns of behavior that sometimes support one another. I am less interested in a theoretical intervention than I am in working out a compelling description of what happens in the intermingled experience of sport, national piety, and religion, and in offering some interpretive work on why their entanglement happens. My thesis is that activities in these three domains of human behavior tend to overlap because they can do very similar work, constructing and maintaining social cohesion. They are not, as Émile Durkheim suggested of primordial society, the very basis of social organization or social order hypostatized as the divine face. But they are powerful forms of experiencing sociality or relatedness, group belonging. And they often work together, borrowing iconography from chants to signs and images to forms of gathering and ritual practice—not because one is collapsed into another or human beings are *Homo religiosus*. An account of the entanglement of religion, politics, and sport is able to preserve their peculiar properties, avoiding reductionism of one sort or another, and to recognize the importance of their interrelationship. By asserting that the common element is ritual experience, I want simply to describe the characteristic features of human interaction and social behavior that move through each of these three domains. Ritual is no more religious than it is political or a feature of sport. It is all of these because ritual is a fundamental way in which human beings interact with one another in order to assert collective effort toward a particular end. Like many higher mammals, human beings are wired to work together in any number of ways for the many benefits such behavior affords.

These three forms of ritual experience will be the focus of this chapter because I am especially interested in how their borrowing from one another urges us to consider that none is a pure essence as a public cultus, but each operates on the shared capital of a ritual kinship. In particular, I want to understand better how emotion is a *contagion*, a fluid medium that flows from one to another in the way that Durkheim described the sacred as something difficult but necessary to contain. My contention will *not* be that sport or national piety is the new religion of modern society, but rather that there is no need for the social or cultural analyst to erect a strong distinction among the three. They are not fully discrete any more than they are merely interchangeable. They are entangled, and we need to learn better how to describe and interpret them in just this way.[1] I suspect that the entangled nature of religion is what makes scrutinizing the place of emotion in religious experience useful since emotion is the effervescence that moves from one activity to another as a medium conveying value. More on that later.

### Emotion, Ritual, Sacralization

Scholars of media, material culture, and religious practice have made much of Benedict Anderson's thesis that nationhood is a largely imagined reality, something that citizens never actually see or experience in one large group face to face.[2] Instead, they envision their collective national identity in the shared practices of reading mass media and in their social formation in educational systems.[3] According to Anderson, print and photography, the modern, mechanical means of reproduction, were fundamental instruments for the imagination of the nation.[4] Media, in other words, contributed powerfully to the idea and experience of nationhood. A distinction that comes to mind regarding mediated constructions of nation and the role of ritual in modern social life is emotion versus intellection. The difference may be expressed by the power of feeling oneself to be a member of a nation through the emotions roused by participation in ritual, on the one hand, and on the other, the influence of epistemological structures absorbed by the taxonomies of museum installations, the visual orientation and sensibility of cartography, and the logic of quantification as the basis for gauging the concentration of peoples within national boundaries of time and space. One of the functions that religions in the modern era perform is to provide important tools for installing and maintaining a sense of national belonging, and they do so by reinforcing the cognitive operation of imagination with the emotional energies of ritual performance.

Émile Durkheim's sociology of religion is the source of both insights and problems with which we still toil today. His approach is responsible for promoting the idea of a primary function, a simple beginning that he argued was the basis for defining religion. At the same time, his useful analysis of ritual practice helpfully stressed emotion, even while overemphasizing frenzy. British sociologist Nick Couldry has pointed out that both the affective and the cognitive can be found at work in Durkheim's sociology. Where the production of social order is at a premium, the group relies on the medium or contagion of feeling conveyed in ritual as a collective effervescence to achieve cohesion.[5]

But there is also the Durkheim who insisted that science could not finally supplant religion. Although he believed that science was the offspring of religion and tended to supersede it "in everything that involves the cognitive and intellectual functions," Durkheim also concluded that religion could not ultimately be replaced by science or anything else since its purpose was "to reach, fortify, and discipline consciousnesses."[6] "Religion," he wrote, "is not only a system of practices but also a system of ideas whose object is to express the world."[7] This expression is not scientific representation, however, but epistemological conceptions of a moral nature. The purpose of religion is to act on moral life, to shape and regulate human relations. This is accomplished by the integration of ritual experience and symbolic structures in the devices or media that operate as the means of organizing relations.

Durkheim recognized that the two operations of religion—the modulation of emotion and the production of symbolic means—belonged together. He treated symbol and emotion as interwoven. Collective effervescence was *stored* in the symbol, the media, that is, the material medium that hosted the power of the collective rite.[8] Thought was the projection of each mind. Emotion was not mindless, but the accompaniment of apperception. As I have suggested elsewhere, we need a robust aesthetic account to do justice to this relationship lest we succumb to a familiar dualism that pulls emotion and thinking apart.[9] In fact, the two work together.

William Reddy pointed out that the distinction between emotion and cognition has been called into question by many researchers who urge that emotion is integral to cognitive processes.[10] A purely rational version of thought lacks the intensity that emotion provides any judgment. By this account, emotion is a nonsemantic system of signaling and affecting thought toward particular ends. Emotions code objects, people, or actions for their relevance to a particular aim or threat, serving to highlight what might matter more than other features of an environment. In other words, emotion is a form of valuation that enhances or at least facilitates cognition. Separating reason and emotion denigrates the embodied nature of cognition, resorts to an ancient dualism of mind and body, and erects a hierarchy of thought, feeling, and body that skews the explanation of human behavior as properly rational. The resulting dualism is strongly disposed to regard emotion as suspect for its inherent tendency to move one independent of reason. This becomes especially significant in political matters, where one's sympathy for the state or opposition to authority is the result of feeling, not rational reflection. The bonds of affection that hold together a nation rely on emotionally charged ritual practice to generate a broadly shared coherence since reason alone lacks the ability to produce group loyalty. The experience of belonging that is stoked by parades, sports events, national holidays, patriotic observances, and collective rites of remembrance is very useful for the feeling of collective or shared coherence that they impart. As Anderson urges, these practices *imagine* a nation in which one is a part since no citizens actually perceive the nation as a singular thing. Emotional thinking allows human beings to sense, anticipate, or intuit a larger presence without fully grasping it.

## Sports: Fandom, Nationhood, Sacralization

I have remarked so far on religion and nationhood, and would now like to turn to the third pervasive ritual activity in modern life, sport, in order to think about their entanglement and its relevance for the study of emotion and religion. To continue thinking about Durkheim's reflections on cognition and emotion, I would like to begin by suggesting that the experience of sport is not only mindless fans slobbering drunkenly over victory or scrapping angrily in defeat. Certainly they have a good time, fueled by large amounts of alcohol. But this frenzy should not be allowed to dominate our understanding of the experience of sport. Most people in the stadium are not screaming wildly, half-nude and colorfully painted. These sorts stand out as the exception and are disproportionately represented by photojournalists. If you google *sports fans*, you will see what I mean. Rather than boring images of large blocks of spectators absorbed in the game, you will get amusing photographs of ludicrously dressed, drunken men and scantily clad women. They are picturesque, but not the norm. The emotions that people experience in the stadium or at home watching television are usually far less flamboyant, erupting episodically, perhaps, but intermixed with mundane conversation and companionship. Moreover, many fans are actively engaged in summoning up robust archives of memory about each player's history of performance, scrutinizing intricate strategies at work on the field of play, or fondly recounting classic scenarios of the past. Their experience is intellectual as well as felt, so it is important to learn to recognize the discursive as well as the wide-ranging affective characteristics of fandom.

Sports fandom can soften class, ethnic, and racial distinctions, thereby invigorating a sense of shared identity. Fandom temporarily gathers a broad variety of people into a more or less homogeneous social mass, or at least a sprawling association in which traditional markers of difference are mitigated. This calls to mind Durkheim's description of collective effervescence. In many forms of professional sport, national identification is an important feature, particularly in the Olympics and World Cup football (soccer), but also in other sports that enjoy international tournaments, such as hockey, tennis, golf, gymnastics, and cricket. Americans are fond of imagining that baseball's *World Series* has any more than national scope. It is a kind of hyperbole that attends a national sense of international importance. But the impulse to celebrate the nation through athletic contest is widely shared. In modern nations people often look to professional sport for national pride, observing World Cup victories draped in their nations' flags, singing national anthems, parading in the streets, proud to be Brazilian, Ghanaian, Argentinian, or German.

It is also important to acknowledge the relevance of professional sports for nation building. One thinks of Nelson Mandela's use of rugby in postapartheid South Africa as a way of pulling racially and politically divided groups together. And because of its popularity, sport has powerful propaganda value.[11] In 1970 in Brazil, the military government used soccer as a way of mobilizing public support for its regime by declaring a national holiday in recognition of Brazil's victory in the World Cup, hosting the victorious team in nationally broadcast parades. In one image, flag-waving Brazilian children sit atop military vehicles in the parade. In another famous photograph, General Emilio Medici appears beside Carlos Alberto, captain of the champion Brazilian soccer team.[12] In the United States collegiate and professional sports events begin with the performance of the national anthem. Clearly, sport and religion have each played important roles in the construction of national identity, whether co-opted by authoritarian regimes or promoted by democratic governments in search of votes.[13] Often politics, for its part, can look very much like competitive team sports. Political factions take to the streets, waving their banners, marching as a horde, chanting slogans, singing party anthems, wearing the colors or iconography of the social body. They demonize their opposition, burn their leaders in effigy, stage massive rallies that seethe with charisma and pathos. The heat of battle and the intense longing for victory can invert conventional ethics to the end justifying the means. Just as cheating on the sports field by one's own team can be justified by bad referees or the other team's cheating or the importance of victory, so corruption and backroom politicking can come to be justified by political devotees since the opposition must be defeated at all costs. The same occurs in religions that undertake the persecution of nonbelievers for the sake of national redemption or simply for their own good. Triumph in politics, sport, and religion is easily characterized as *good*, that is, as inherently desirable. And if it is good, then how one brings victory about is often justified by its achievement.

I will say little more about the politics of sport, allowing the images of children riding tanks and a military dictator clasping a trophy with a soccer team captain to register the sober realization that sport and state power are knottily intertwined. Suffice it to recall George Orwell urging us to recognize the grim side of the state's involvement in entertainment. "Football, beer, and above all gambling, filled up the horizon of their minds," as he put it in *1984*. "To keep them in control was not difficult."[14]

The power of these forms of activity is the fervor of fandom, the euphoria of drunkenness, and the delusion of gambling. Addictive, one and all. But it is more subtle than that. When fans say that football is a religion, as they did, for instance, in a piece by comedian John Oliver,[15] and as many scholars and cultural commentators have over the years,[16] some may indeed have in mind the replacement of traditional religion by devotion to their sport. But quite often I think they are better interpreted to mean that they feel their adoration for the game is shared by everyone in their nation, or their conception of what the nation is or ought to be. In this way of thinking, religion is what *my people* do, what *we* do with gusto and dedication, and what sets *us* apart for doing so. Success in the World Cup therefore means national pride. The common joy of my community is the basis of my and our enduring identity.

But is this religion? It sounds much more like nationalism. Perhaps this only begs the question, "Is nationalism a religion?" To be sure, it is hardly difficult to imagine nationalists who consider their nation to be favored by destiny, deity, or ancestors, and worthy of devotion unto death. But one can also embrace one's nation as worthy of loyalty without regarding it as divinely elect or as the highest good in human life. Likewise, one can experience an intense sense of belonging, practiced quite ritually in sports fandom, that is not metaphysically oriented, if that is how we wish to define religion. In that instance, the expression that soccer is religion is a metaphor, not a straightforward description. A more apt designation would be *sacred*, or *special*, as Ann Taves has urged in lieu of the more loaded term sacred.[17] Religion, in other words, is not identical to the sacred. *Sacralization* is a procedure at work in any number of cultural activities, including but not limited to religion. Thus, when fans say *soccer is my religion*, they may be understood to say something like *soccer is how my people and I feel our common identity*. They might say the very same of their nation and their religion. Sacredness in this case means an object or activity of great esteem, something to which one is devoted with passion and ritually practiced adherence shared with and co-defined by others.

Recent studies of sacrality, or specialness, indebted to the Durkheimian tradition for their recognition of the utility of setting off or apart, have nevertheless departed from Durkheim by resisting the identification of the sacred and religion since the latter is a more complex composite, a historical formation of conditions, beliefs, and practices.[18] This is certainly prudent and it serves very well to help recognize what distinguishes such social phenomena as sport, nationalism, and religion from one another at the same time that we discern their common features and interrelatedness. All of them, I will argue, exhibit processes of sacralization, and therefore intermingle more readily, but should not be reduced to religion.

The literature on sport and religion is large.[19] Within it, a major strain of thought over the last few decades has argued for the identity of sports and religion. In the words of an outspoken advocate of this view, religious studies scholar Charles S. Prebish: "For me, it is not just a parallel that is emerging between religion and sport, but rather a *complete identity. Sport is religion* for growing numbers of Americans."[20] Prebish asks if the two are converging or if they are the same. According to him, sport is the new American religion and it is replacing the older versions. He goes on to provide the measure for his claim: "Sport is a religion only insofar as it brings its adherents to an experience of ultimate reality, radically alters their lives as a result of the experience of ultimacy, and then channels their gains back into society in a generally viable and useful fashion." In other words, religion is a good thing for what it does for social well-being, and sport satisfies this criterion. Prebish intends the identity quite literally, spurning any metaphorical sense to the comparison: "For sport to be considered a religion, it must quite self-consciously attempt to be just that. It must present all the rituals . . . that all traditional religions provide."[21] In his view, secularization accounts for this turn. With the decline of traditional religions, room is made for a new version. Sport was once, therefore, not religion, but became viable as one once its predecessor waned.

But there are serious problems with this approach. As Scholes and Sassower have pointed out, one problem is that traditional religions have not in fact waned in the United States.[22] It is not surprising therefore that many people who are avid sports fans happily remain committed Christians, Muslims, or Jews. Another problem is the mystification of sport that this approach induces. One writer in the tradition of European phenomenology included in the book Prebish edited describes sport as a cultural form that, like art as Hegel treated it, is an embodiment of Spirit, the Absolute, or ultimate reality.[23] That is what allows sport to enable the "experience of ultimacy" that Prebish claims dramatically alters or transforms the lives of practitioners. Sport is religion when it does this—religion in the sense of a mystic's union with the godhead or direct perception of ultimate reality. This use of the extraordinary experience of mystics as the basis for defining religion draws on William James's widely influential discussion of religious experience and on Rudolf Otto's definition of the sacred as the "mysterium tremendum." And it relies heavily on Mircea Eliade's notion of hierophany, or the eruption of sacrality as a kind of substance into the world.[24] Like Eliade, advocates of sport-as-religion are fond of regarding sport as *modern man's* recovery of the spiritual. Sport reestablishes contact with ultimate reality, and is therefore the return of religion to a secular world. The idea, taken from Eliade, is that *Homo sapiens* is better described as *Homo religious*. Thus, the perennial need for ritual drives humans to find it wherever they can, because humanity is by nature a religious being. The failure of religion as a formal institution simply means that humans will avail themselves of its ritual essence in another form.[25]

But if we do not insist on the extraordinary as the norm for understanding religions and if they are not so much about existential transformation as the social web to which they contribute (for better or worse, as the case may be), and if we are less interested in the few *mystics* than in the large numbers of *laity*, the hierophanic, mystical, and ineffable experience of the spiritual genius will be replaced by the far more prosaic, everyday, historically grounded, and widely shared experience of individuals massing in vast groups. Fan culture becomes far more interesting in this regard than the cult of the professional athlete-idol.

A much more compelling approach than the phenomenology of the athlete-mystic has been proposed recently by Jeffrey Scholes and Raphael Sassower, who reject the identification of religion and sport, arguing instead that both belong to the same web of human cultural productivity.[26] Thus, sports can be religious and religion can indulge an athletic intensity, but they are not the same thing. Extending Clifford Geertz's metaphor of culture as a web, Scholes and Sassower suggest that religion and sports remain discrete strands in the same web. My approach is very sympathetic to this position, but I am more concerned than are Scholes and Sassower to pursue a sociological approach to sacralization as a process undertaken in any number of settings. To reiterate, sacralization is not synonymous with religion nor is it essentially religious, but is rather the pervasive social mechanism for making something, someone, or someplace special. It happens in sports, art, politics, commerce, the family, and religions. Focusing on aspects of the ritual structure of sport, religion, and nationalism will reveal something important about their mutual operation, but also about the importance of emotion and media for the circulation of feeling generated by sacralization.

## Imagination, Spectacle, Enchantment

We may approach the study of the emotional importance of sport in regard to nationalism and religion by describing the principal mode of experience among fans: watching the game. Sport intensifies emotion by creating contests that unfold entirely within focused or enclosed spatial and temporal fields, discrete events that hold the attention in a separate time. The clocks governing play set off the event from ambient time. Spectators do not participate directly in the play, but watch it from the distance of bleachers or sidelines, on television, radio, or Internet, where they are constrained from immediate participation. As representations, sports events focus consciousness on spectacles: dramatic, time-sensitive action that induces spectators to forget the world beyond the event. Studies of affect have stressed the importance of mimesis as what Anna Gibbs has called "corporeally based forms of imitation, both voluntary and involuntary."[27] Human beings communicate intentionally and unintentionally by virtue of visceral responses to one another registered in gesture, facial expression, and movement. We can see a powerful version of this at work in fan behavior at sports events. The spectator's form of vicarious participation in the event might be understood in terms of the mimetic production of affect.

Emotional response is intensified by the rivalry or contest of the two opposing teams. The menace of defeat, shame, and humiliation sharpens one's response and investment in the outcome. But fans must watch the event from the distance of the stands or medium. They are not able to join in the play. We might, therefore, think of spectator emotion as frustrated desire fulfilled or dashed by the course and the result of the contest. Watching stimulates the desire to effect or to complete action, inducing a frustration or denial that craves resolution. Fans look on, but can do nothing but sublimate their desire to directly affect events in the form of cheers, groans, angry gasps, cursing, swinging their arms, jumping to their feet, clapping, laughing, yelling, stomping, or sitting down in a huff. The frustration may be excruciating when one's team is losing, but it is exhilarating when the vicarious behaviors are performed in order to produce action at a distance, such that one's yelling and clapping urges the players to do the right thing, and serves to move the game in the right direction, perhaps by confusing or disparaging the opposing team on the field. The imagined connection, a kind of enchantment, is not unlike watching one's child ride a bicycle for the first time: as the child wobbles down the sidewalk atop the bicycle, the parent leans or bends vicariously to correct the child's impending imbalance or turns the bicycle at a distance with a corrective gesture. Gestures and utterances are symbolic action—we might imagine they are communicating our power, but it is more accurate to say that they are provoked by our powerlessness. Spectators perform in truncated action what they want the other to do because they are all too conscious of the distance that separates them from what they can only watch.

The game insists that spectators watch at a distance, sublimating desire in a variety of acceptable behaviors. In this way, the game urges spectators to *imagine* direct involvement by performing or expressing it. Frustration from denial of direct participation urges many of them to engage in magic to affect the performance of players and the game's outcome. Fans wear the same clothing for each game, rehearse the same preparatory rites, say prayers, utter mantras and formulaic cheers, and put themselves in a proper frame of mind to will victory. Players may do the same before the game, and when they score or win, they visibly thank heaven for the favor. None of these behaviors needs to be part of a full-fledged religious sensibility because they are more immediately explained as practices of enchantment that belong to the repertoire of sacralizing events and behaviors that is evident in all departments of human society. The overwhelmingly male character of professional sport (athletes and fans) suggests that a key feature of the fan's virtual participation is the performance of masculinity. And indeed, sport readily shares this with nationalism and religion. The idols of each, the focal points of their performance, are commonly men who are admired for their manliness and whose gestures, facial expression, shouts, and ritualized celebration at making a touchdown are almost autonomically reiterated by fans in waves of mimetic response. The production of masculinity is clearly visible among sports fans at football and soccer games. The vicarious participation of fans in action on the field is an emotional enchantment that shapes their sense of shared masculinity.

*Watching* is the critical condition for the fan's experience and it is the primary condition for enchantment. It occurs within a well-rehearsed visual field, which launches a mode of experience in which spectators join the extended boundary of the team in the bleachers. They *behold* the game, a verb that suggests the virtually tactile contact that vicarious participation in the action on the playing field produces. The fan's experience by no means consists of a passive or inactive state, but is much better understood as an emotionally charged participation at a distance. The spell or enchantment is the result of frustrated desire and identification with the team. Physical and temporal limits and taboos (rules) structure the field in which emotion is intensified into a medium that joins fans and team in a sense of shared venture. The sports event is set off from ordinary time by the physical structure of the stadium, by the clock governing play, by the referees enforcing rules (for players as well as spectators), and by positive encouragements at work: music, chanting, cheering, and the spectacle of the entire event surrounding and engulfing the audience. To participate is to join in the collective behavior. The world outside the stadium temporarily recedes while fans are immersed in the game.

In this way of thinking, ultimately indebted to Durkheim, though not identical with his understanding of the sacred, sacrality is not an ontological feature of a thing, but a shared or social experience. The visual field engulfing the fan is comparable to the temple or shrine space surrounding the devotee and the patriotic parade, cemetery, or crowd gathered to listen to a speech on a national holiday. The sacred is a construction of many features—place, script, ritual practice, cult object, totem, referees, priests, politicians, law enforcement officers, and audience. The enchantment conducted by the event focuses attention on the person of player, priest, or speaker and the material implements of their performance, investing them with a kind of fluid aura or charisma that lingers, but must be renewed through the management of sacralizing events and practices. Sacralization is an ongoing work. The well-being of the nation, the status of one's team, and the work of invoking and satisfying deities, saints, or ancestors are all continual processes since the lives of fans, citizens, and devotees continue to require the pleasure and hope of victory, support for and by the state, and the spiritual and material favors that divine beings can be induced to provide.

Yet religions, it is important to grasp, are different sorts of networks. They assemble a different range of actors, human and nonhuman, from what happens in the sport setting. They may certainly overlap, and often do. The sight of a player genuflecting, praying, or wearing some sort of religious artifact like a cross or saint's medal is a common example of the collaboration of sport and religion. And the same may be said of nationalism, as when American sporting events open with the national anthem and the ritual display of the flag. The nationalistic rite serves to set off the audience, teams, and stadium for a special moment. Game time begins when the ceremony marks its commencement. But whereas religious worship is about worshipping a deity, sports are about entertainment and enjoyment. The function of the flag ceremony at sporting events is not to worship the nation, but to proclaim the unity of the two teams competing and the two groups of fans assembled to watch them. The competitive nature of the event threatens to pit the two groups against one another, so the flag ritual demonstrates that they are equally American and belong to something larger than the individual teams. Nationalism then serves to counterbalance fandom, not to make the sport a religion. Religions connect their devotees to other kinds of actors in the network that constitutes them: saints, gods, heaven or hell, the sacred past, the holy people. Sports fans do not seek any of that in their adoration of the team and the performance of its stars. Some scholars have maintained that players are saints or gods, that loss is hell, victory heaven, that the team's record is a sacred past, and that the team and its fans comprise a sacred people.[28] But aligning sport and religion in this way is always vague, impressionistic, idiosyncratic, and tasked with collapsing the two into one another.

Yet the three domains of social activity described here are not strictly discrete. I want to consider how and why they are so often intertwined. It happens that nationhood is a primary medium for devotion to sport, which is the ritual generating the collective effervescence that pulls the society together as other forces are pulling it apart. That is why governments and advertisers furiously harness the occasion to their public image. But it is also important to see that what fans get from sport is a way of seeing themselves and their nation on the world stage. They know who they are, see themselves, and imagine themselves seen and known by others, in terms of the game. The collective nature of adoration as contest was evident to me in the summer of 2006 when I saw a display of national flags in Leipzig, Germany, on the square bordering the landmark medieval church of St. Nicholas, during the World Cup. In an array of small flags stretching across the several stories of a public building, the German flags flanked and surmounted the field of others. The arrangement of flags preceded the tournament and was therefore an expression of patriotic hope for the German team's performance on the soccer field, but it was also an opportunity to convey national pride in a nation where such expressions are suspect for strong historical reasons. Moreover, the flags underscore the international character of the tournament. Nations win and lose, not merely teams. The association of national pride with a sports team is a mild sort of enchantment since the team members are on the team for their skill and their nationality. The intensification of one individual's purely accidental place of birth to representative of an entire nation in an international arena of contest is surely a grossly overdetermined coincidence. But it is an enchantment we find irresistible in the modern world of nation-states.

The important role that media play as the means of intermingling religion, sport, and national piety recommends that we take them up for analysis. An unusually compelling video allows us to do that here. In the summer of 2014, ramping up to the World Cup, an advertisement for Solo headphones presented by Beats by Dr. Dre was widely viewed on the Internet.[29] The video, called "The Game before the Game," is a five-minute advertisement that disguised itself as a striking audiovisual essay that celebrated the ritual preparations of world soccer stars and their fans for the World Cup competition. It opens with an inspirational phone call from a father to his son, the Brazilian football star Neymar, whom the video follows through his tense preparation for the tournament. The gendered nature of this relationship reflects the masculine spectacle of male soccer players and their fans, both male and female. Beyond the local setting of Brazil, the video also features teams from around the world and their fans. The collage of momentary vignettes joins the central motif of Neymar to push the video into the genre of the docudrama. Indeed, the hybridity of the video's genre matches the heterogeneous intermixture of sport, religion, magic, nationalism, masculine hero worship, and mythology. The piece is studded with national flags and colors. And visual references to Catholicism, Candomblé, Pentecostalism, and a variety of indigenous practices are plentiful. A rapid montage of images propelled by the pelvic beat of the soundtrack takes viewers in and out of dozens of worlds, references previous football champions, showcases the devotion of myriad fans, and foregrounds the cult of soccer and its celebrated national and international heroes.

The video is exciting because it captures the edgy anxiety that besets athletes and fans before the game. Their disquiet and absorption reveals the real nature and task of what happens in the *game before the game*: the contest with chance. The video assembles a broad range of strategies intended to ensure or at least encourage victory. There is work to be done to accomplish the task and this must be done before the tournament begins. It is a nervous struggle to concentrate one's efforts and to diminish bad luck. The need for enchantment runs through fans and players around the world. People engage gods, saints, magic, sacrifice, prayer, pledge, and libation to affect the odds, to negotiate better circumstances, to vow devotion and gratitude for favorable influence. A roaring Spanish crowd copiously consumes beer in a bacchanalia of ritual celebration, painted and adorned in the colors of their national flag.

Neymar listens to the devoted encouragement of his father, scribbles the name of his son on his shin guard, and gazes quietly and alone in the locker room. The video ends with Neymar's father urging his son in Evangelical prayer: "Put God's army in front of you, wear God's armour, from the helmet to the sandals, go with God. God bless you. I love you." With that, the young man bows his head briefly, then faces the teeming millions waiting in the stadium and the nation and the world watching on television and the Internet. Yet throughout the video Neymar also listens to the pounding beat and reverberating lyrics of "Jungle," whose refrain is unrelenting: "Ain't no god on my streets in the heart of the jungle. Won't you follow me into the jungle."

It is a curious choice of lyrics for use in a video that foregrounds the invocation of divine aid and pins great hope on the efficacy of ritual work in the preparation for victory. The song's use in this video seems to invite the fan to join the athletes and the national communities of their fans in the compelling moment of self-searching and tribulation, the battle before the battle, when self-control in the midst of terror is a key to success. But in amassing all the teams into a rousing mosaic, something happens: sports fandom is displaced or at least muted by the enjoyment of art. There "ain't no god," there's just me in my Solo headphones, absorbed in the song, but joined by the commoditization of music and communications media to an imagined community of fans in my country and all over the world. The artifact of a music video changes how we apprehend the subject by introducing a distance between the subject matter (soccer fans and their religious practices) and what we see (a masterfully choreographed commercial for headphones).[30] The former is the vehicle for the latter, although ideally the consumer is not supposed to be particularly mindful of the difference. But the difference is real. Fandom and its religious nationalism are made the subject of a work of art such that we do not watch as fans of one national team, but as aesthetic observers of them all in the global media event called the World Cup. In this setting, there ain't no god, there's just the jungle of self-reliance and mass-mediated stardom. The imagery leaps from soccer stars on teams on different continents to the frenzied bustle of their fans. It all happens at once, a far-flung web of citizens, fans, believers, and athletes comprising not one nation, but many brought together in a single, sensational tournament. Everyone in the video moves to the beat of the same song. The music pulses through the participants, merging them into a single, international quilt of contestants marked off by the colors of their national flags on banners, painted faces, tattoos, and underwear.

As a commercial artistic product, the video transforms fandom into orchestrated spectacle. It wants to suggest that we may imbibe the excitement by using these headphones. But there remains more at work in the video for us to consider. Within the individual worlds that the video assembles, we are able to see something of the actual engagement of sport, nationhood, and religion soaked in the medium of tense feeling and excitement. The video does a compelling job of documenting that, even while its point is to sell Solo headphones. Although this is a scripted product aiming at a mass market, the video represents the lived experience of fans and players for whom the ritual work powerfully fuses sport, national fervor, and religion. The idea is that you cannot win at sport and enjoy the glory of nationhood without the efficacious performance of preparatory rites. Because the World Cup in 2014 took place in Brazil, that nation gets a privileged portrayal in the video. Across the dense urban sprawl of Rio de Janeiro, we glimpse Brazilians busily adjusting satellite dishes and gathering before televisions; we watch little boys in the street of a favela playing *bafo* for player cards, and fans painting their faces or shaving their heads, lighting candles, praying, pouring libations, presenting offerings at altars. One man scribbles "for the team" on a piece of paper, then dunks it in a glass of cachaça. Presumably he will drink it to complete the ritual, ingesting his vow so that it may mingle in his blood with the spirits of the liquor to accomplish the work of his fond hope.

Contest, whether military or athletic, generates chance and resolves it. The result is good fortune or ill. To undertake contest is to risk failure. The possibility of losing generates an emotional investment in winning. This voluntary production and ritualized dissipation of randomness calls on enchantment to manage the risk. Religious ritual, music, national pride, and magic can all function as a kind of technology of enchantment applied to the challenge of fortune. And we need to recognize the importance of chance in sports culture. It goes to the heart of the athlete's and the fan's experience. One reason that soccer appeals the way it does to millions around the world is that it thrives on chance, on the allure of chance. The importance of fortune in religions from ancient Rome to modern Japan has been highlighted by scholars.[31] The emotion we see at work in the video answers to the menacing anxiety of averting loss and humiliation. Pregame rites are important because the game of soccer is riddled with chance that goes for one's team or against it. Fans rely on the skill of players and the genius they show in split instants of prowess. But it is not just about pure talent. It is also about the hand of God, about the smile of Fortuna or her insidious frown, about good luck or bad. It is no mistake that many sports matches begin with a coin toss to determine offense and defense.

Framed by the reality of chance, sport invites the use of technologies of enchantment. One finds this at work among baseball players who cross themselves or kiss a cross or an amulet before batting or perform other ritualized action in order to prepare themselves for the kairos of an instant when things go suddenly good or bad. One way to deal with the overwhelming pressure of randomness is to invoke miraculous intervention, and when they do hit a home run or score a goal, it is not unusual to see athletes look or point to heaven in acknowledgment of the favor.[32] What fans often admire in the great athlete is not his or her mechanical certainty and consistency or pure form, but the individual's ability to make an opportunity from random events in the heat of the game. When another's error produces the occasion to change events, to seize on a random occurrence and turn it to the benefit of one's team, to shift the dynamics and rhythm, to redefine the contest: that is athletic genius. For the winners, there is something magical at work when chance is turned to an alternative purpose and everyone on the field has to accommodate the new order of play. For the losers, it is just bad luck. For the spectators, you have to be there to see the magic of sudden metamorphosis. If you leave the arena to go to the bathroom or get a beer, you will return to find a game that you do not recognize.

Managing chance does not mean eliminating it since there is nothing exciting about watching a mechanical operation. Chance is built, anticipated, and turned to one's advantage. And we can see the various ways it is managed in *the game before the game.* The ritual practitioners know they must respect it. Both player and fan urge higher forces to assist them, to make opportunities appear and to bless their attempts to exploit them. Players discipline themselves with efforts at concentration and they practice the skills they will need on the field. Fans draw together in anticipation or drink themselves into a collective state of pregame excitement. So even if the video is a scripted artistic product, it captures something very real about the experience of soccer today. Sport, religion, and nationalism are structurally integrated in its music and imagery and this corresponds to the extensive ritual work done as fans and players prepare themselves for the contest of fortune that will send them into ecstasy or plunge them into suffering. Emotion is built and managed by the religious practices that are brought to the game and it is work that is shared by those who imagine in it a larger sense of self, a national honor to be celebrated in contest.[33]

In many ways, Durkheim's account of the totem and the collective effervescence that is generated by its ritual experience describes what happens with sports. But I do not think sport should be regarded as the new religion or a modern expression of a primitive religious state. I have wanted to suggest instead that sport can include forms of sacralization and enchantment without any appeal to or use of institutional religions. But we also commonly find religion and sport happening at once and brought together in the fan's and the player's experience. Rather than treating religion as society masquerading as god, as Durkheim argued, we might approach religion not as the discrete set of beliefs or an irreducible essence confined to the private sphere, as the logic of secular modernity wants it to be. Instead, religions perform as strands that are intimately interwoven with several others, such as nationalism and sports, with which they share key features, such as visual fields and sacralization, in order to intensify experience, construct communal life, transfer value, and manage randomness. When the game is over, the strands unravel and return to separate careers and discrete functions.

The interlacing of the strands works well episodically. States, citizens, advertisers, and fans sacralize sport and nationhood because ritualized activities like religion, sport, and national fervor all produce charisma and symbolic capital that is fungible, that groups and institutions want to expend to their own benefit. Ritual amalgamation leavens or tinctures an event or a hero with the aura of an authority or institution in order to enhance its prestige and apply it to the benefit of the sponsoring organization—advertisers, professional organizations, politicians, religious institutions, or the state. The attention afforded the ritual event urges spectators to recognize in it a compelling medium for imagination and shared sensibility. The episodic nature of each—the sports game, the patriotic occasion, and religious worship in the modern age of privatized religion relegated to one day per week—fits the secular calendar of the work week. Durkheim's account of an ecstatic religion of collective enthusiasm that brings together the clan characterizes far better the modern, secular world than any so-called primitive one. But rather than call this *religion*, I think we get further by describing such modern experiences as sport, nationalism, and religion as ritual practices that generate powerful cultures of thought and feeling that enable moderns to imagine the bonds of affection that tell them who their group is and what matters to them.

NOTES

1. Useful work in the study of networks includes Ian Hodder, *Entangled: An Archaeology of the Relationships between Humans and Things* (Malden, MA: Wiley Blackwell, 2012); Bruno Latour, *Reassembling the Social: An Introduction to Actor-Network Theory* (Oxford: Oxford University Press, 2005); Bruno Latour, *We Have Never Been Modern*, trans. Catherine Porter (Cambridge, MA: Harvard University Press, 1993); and Wiebe E. Bijker and John Law, eds., *Shaping Technology/Building Society: Studies in Sociotechnical Change* (Cambridge, MA: MIT Press, 1992).

2. Benedict Anderson, *Imagined Communities: Reflections on the Origin and Spread of Nationalism*, rev. ed. (London: Verso, 1991), and many others have argued that nationalism is a modern social, cultural, and political phenomenon, probably originating in the seventeenth century in Western Europe, and globally disseminated both by European colonial domination of indigenous peoples and by their eventual reaction against the occupying force. Of course, the entanglement of religion, sport, and national identity is hardly limited to modernity. Yet modern sport as an incorporated business that is mass-mediated and situated within a global field of nationalistic competition is certainly unprecedented. Nevertheless, I am not making an argument that is limited to the mod-

ern era, though any articulation of it in another historical era would have to be carefully tailored to the historical setting.

3. Anderson, *Imagined Communities*. For discussion of Anderson's thesis in regard to the study of religious media, and consideration of its limits, see Birgit Meyer and Annelies Moors, introduction to *Religion, Media, and the Public Sphere*, ed. Birgit Meyer and Annelies Moors (Bloomington: Indiana University Press, 2006), 1–25.

4. Anderson, *Imagined Communities*, 182.

5. Nick Couldry, *Media Rituals: A Critical Approach* (London: Routledge, 2003), 8. For a clear and very instructive reflection on the legacy of Durkheim, correctives to it, and recognition of its enduring value for the sociology of religion and of the sacred, see Gordon Lynch, *The Sacred in the Modern World: A Cultural Sociological Approach* (Oxford: Oxford University Press, 2012), 20–29.

6. Émile Durkheim, *The Elementary Forms of Religious Life*, trans. Karen E. Fields (New York: Free Press, 1995), 431, 422.

7. Durkheim, *Elementary Forms of Religious Life*, 430.

8. Durkheim, *Elementary Forms of Religious Life*, 220–22.

9. David Morgan, "Religion and Media: A Critical Review of Recent Developments," *Critical Research on Religion* 1, no. 3 (2013): 347–56. In a series of recent publications, Birgit Meyer has undertaken this task. See, for instance, *Sensational Movies: Video, Vision, and Christianity in Ghana* (Berkeley: University of California Press, 2015).

10. William M. Reddy, *The Navigation of Feeling: A Framework for the History of Emotions* (Cambridge: Cambridge University Press, 2001), 14–15, 21–22.

11. For a brief discussion and bibliography, see Chris Shilling, *The Body in Culture, Technology and Society* (London: SAGE, 2005), 106–8.

12. The photographs and some discussion of their context are available online: accessed May 19, 2015, https://americasouthandnorth.wordpress.com/2013/02/03/get-to-know -a-brazilian-emilio-garrastazu-medici/ and http://www.portal2014.org.br/noticias/2067 /TODOS+JUNTOS+VAMOS+PRA+FRENTE+BRASIL.html.

13. The social, economic, and political uses of sport have been explored in a number of useful studies: Marion Keim, *Nation Building at Play: Sport as a Tool for Social Integration in Post-Apartheid South Africa* (Oxford: Meyer and Meyer Sport, 2003); Franklin Foer, *How Soccer Explains the World: An Unlikely Theory of Globalization* (New York: HarperCollins, 2004); and Gabriel Kuhn, *Soccer vs. the State: Tackling Football and Radical Politics* (Oakland, CA: PM Press, 2011).

14. George Orwell, *1984* (Boston: Houghton, Mifflin, Harcourt, 1977), 68.

15. *Last Week Tonight with John Oliver*: "FIFA and the World Cup" (HBO), accessed May 19, 2015, www.youtube.com/watch?v=DlJEt2KU33I.

16. This is the view conveyed by many contributors to (and others whom they cite) Charles S. Prebish, ed., *Religion and Sport: The Meeting of Sacred and Profane* (Westport, CT: Greenwood Press, 1993). See also various essays in Joseph L. Price, ed., *From Season to Season: Sports as American Religion* (Macon, GA: Mercer University Press, 2001). For an excellent overview of various positions on the relationship of sport and religion, see Jeffrey Scholes and Raphael Sassower, *Religion and Sports in American Culture* (New York: Routledge, 2014), 1–22; and Nick Watson and Andrew Parker, eds., *Sports and*

*Christianity: Historical and Contemporary Perspectives* (New York: Routledge, 2013)—see the opening essay by the editors, "Sports and Christianity: Mapping the Field," 9–88.

17. Ann Taves, *Religious Experience Reconsidered: A Building-Block Approach to the Study of Religion and Other Special Things* (Princeton, NJ: Princeton University Press, 2009), 26.

18. Taves, *Religious Experience Reconsidered*, 55; Lynch, *Sacred in the Modern World*, 22.

19. Bibliographies in Scholes and Sassower, *Religion and Sports in American Culture*, and Watson and Parker, eds., *Sports and Christianity*, are very helpful. Additional works to consult for their value as historical studies of the relationship between religion and sports (in the American context) are William J. Baker, *Playing with God: Religion and Modern Sport* (Cambridge, MA: Harvard University Press, 2007); Robert J. Higgs, *God in the Stadium: Sports and Religion in America* (Lexington: University of Kentucky Press, 1995); and Julie Byrne, *O God of Players: The Story of the Immaculata Mighty Macs* (New York: Columbia University Press, 2003). An entire series on Sports and Religion published by Mercer University Press includes a variety of useful titles, though written within a Christian perspective. One that takes strong exception to the idea of sport as religion is Robert J. Higgs and Michael C. Braswell, *An Unholy Alliance: The Sacred and Modern Sports* (Macon, GA: Mercer University Press, 2004). American scholarship has focused largely on the history of American sport and religion; for a study of sport and religion in ancient Greece, see Panos Valavanis, *Games and Sanctuaries in Ancient Greece: Olympia, Delphi, Isthmia, Nemea, Athens*, trans. David Hardy (Los Angeles: Getty Publications, 2004).

20. Charles S. Prebish, "Religion and Sport: Convergence or Identity?," in Prebish, *Religion and Sport*, 62. Emphasis in original.

21. Prebish, "Religion and Sport," 68.

22. Scholes and Sassower, *Religion and Sports in American Culture*, 7.

23. William J. Morgan, "An Existential Phenomenological Analysis of Sport as Religious Experience," reprinted in Prebish, *Religion and Sport*, 119–49.

24. Eliade is repeatedly invoked by Prebish: "Religion: Approaches and Assumptions," in Prebish, *Religion and Sport*, 5, 8, 11, 15–16, and "Religion and Sport: Convergence or Identity?," 73. For discussion of James and Otto, see Prebish, "Religion: Approaches and Assumptions," 8, 12. Eliade is also the major source for Joseph Price's treatment of the identity of sport and religion; see several of his contributions to the book he also edited, *From Season to Season*, and also, in the same volume, Bonnie Miller-McLemore, "Through the Eyes of Mircea Eliade: United States Football as a Religious Rite of Passage," 115–35. For a critical Protestant response, see Higgs and Braswell, "The Religion of Sports and That Old-Time Religion: In the Steps of Mircea Eliade," in Higgs and Braswell, *Unholy Alliance*, 153–78.

25. Another essay included by Prebish in his volume sympathetically applies Eliade's claim that humankind is properly understood as *homo religiosus*; see Howard Slusher, "Sport and the Religious," in Prebish, *Religion and Sport*, 181–82: "The evolution of man has demonstrated a constant and pervading *need* for ritual. Modern man's need for ritual continues. But to a greater degree than ever before, religion, and the associated rituals, play less of a role in man's life than at any other point in history. With the reduction of ritual in religion, it is not surprising that man turns to other 'rites' to again see some form of quasi-order to his life. For many, sport fulfills this function." Emphasis in original. Compare Mircea Eliade, *The Sacred and the Profane: The Nature of Religion*, trans. Willard R. Trask (San Diego, CA: Harcourt

Brace Jovanovich, 1959), 202: "Whatever the historical context in which he is placed, *homo religious* always believes that there is an absolute reality, the sacred, which transcends this world but manifests itself in this world, thereby sanctifying it and making it real."

26. Scholes and Sassower, *Religion and Sports in American Culture*, 22.

27. Anna Gibbs, "Sympathy, Synchrony, and Mimetic Communication," in *The Affect Theory Reader*, ed. Melissa Gregg and Gregory J. Seigsworth, 186 (Durham, NC: Duke University Press, 2010).

28. See, for example, Harry Edwards, *Sociology of Sport* (Homewood, IL: Dorsey Press, 1973), 261–66. Edwards's list is anything but systematic. It includes "high councils," "seekers of the kingdom," and "reliance on scribes," but not transcendent reality, totems, magic, mythology, revelation, or shamans. His account of religion is impressionistic at best: "Gods" in religion are equated to star players on the athletic field. "Beliefs" are the rules governing the game. Prebish organizes the list and enumerates it with explanations, but it remains impressionistic and highly selective; Prebish, "The Sports Arena: Some Basic Definitions," in Prebish, *Religion and Sport*, 27–29.

29. Beats by Dr. Dre is a division of Apple and was cofounded by the rapper and hip-hop producer, Dr. Dre. The soundtrack, "Jungle," is by Jamie N Commons and X Ambassadors. The advertising agency that created the video was the London- and Los Angeles–based firm R/GA. The video was directed by Nabil Elderkin. By November it had received 25 million hits and was selected by ADWEEK as one of the ten best ads of 2014. For production information, accessed May 19, 2015, http://www.adweek.com/agencyspy/rga-reveals-epic -world-cup-spot-for-beats/67681. For the video, accessed May 19, 2015, www.youtube.com /watch?v=v_i3Lcjli84.

30. Aesthetic distancing can become the basis in its own right for aesthetic understanding, as explored in a famous essay by Paul Ricoeur, "The Hermeneutical Function of Distanciation," *Philosophy Today* 17, no. 2 (summer 1973): 129–41.

31. See, for instance, Jacqueline Champeux, *Fortuna: Recherches sur le culte de la fortune à Rome et dans le monde romain des origines à la mort de César* (Rome: École française de Rome, 1982); and Inge Daniels, "Scooping, Raking, Beckoning Luck: Luck, Agency and the Interdependence between People and Things in Japan," *Journal of the Royal Anthropological Institute* 9, no. 4 (2003): 619–38.

32. In the 1986 World Cup match against England, Argentina's soccer star, Diego Maradona, committed a ball-handling foul that resulted in a goal. It should have been denied, but escaped penalty because no referee had seen the illegal contact with the ball. Instead, it scored one of the two goals by which Argentina defeated England. After the game, Maradona explained the goal was produced "a little with the head of Maradona and a little with the hand of God." In fact, it was not chance at all, but an illegal use of his hand as he headed the ball into the goal. But to Argentinians, at least, the explanation was plausible.

33. This is where magic becomes a noteworthy practice in sport. Defined as devices or practices that operate either separately or within conventional religions, magic is a way of managing chance. It has been studied in the context of sport: see D. Stanley Eitzen and George H. Sage, "Sport and Religion," in Prebish, *Religion and Sport*, 103–11; and Mari Rita Womack, "Sports Magic: Symbolic Manipulation among Professional Athletes" (PhD diss., University of California, Los Angeles, 1982).

ABBY KLUCHIN

## 10. AT THE LIMITS OF FEELING

*Religion, Psychoanalysis, and the Affective Subject*

*Framing Affect*

The term *affect* is a familiar one in psychology. Only lately, however, have scholars of religion taken it up. They have done so in order to theorize affect as a category that breaks down the boundary between subject and object, self and other, and to use it to analyze religious phenomena. What affect actually means in these contexts is harder to get a handle on. The word that I return to again and again when I try to speak about affect is *slippery*. In some sense and in certain formulations, the *point* of affect is that it is a thing, or *the* thing, that one cannot name; once you name it, bind it with words, it becomes emotion or feeling, quantifiable, addressable. In much the same way that Søren Kierkegaard insists, in *Fear and Trembling*, that Abraham cannot speak—that to be in the realm of the religious is to be structurally incapable of communication in the realm of the ethical and the universal—so, for some contemporary theorists of affect, it is the category that cannot be spoken. Of course, the question of how to represent that which is structurally unrepresentable is hardly a new one, as the example of Kierkegaard should illustrate. More recently, answers to this question appear in a variety of structuralist and poststructuralist texts, figured as a category or collapsed into a single term: as the trace, the Real, *différance*, the feminine, and so forth.[1] I understand affect as it appears in what has recently come to be known as *affect theory* as adding yet another item to that litany. At the same time, affect theorists are also engaged in what I consider to be an admirable attempt to return theoretical attention not only to material conditions but more specifically to the body and the intensities that traverse it.

However, some recent theories of affect and their use in religious studies have tended to ignore or to preclude how conceptions of affect are readily deployed in psychological contexts, especially in clinical settings.[2] Such theories belong to what Donovan O. Schaefer has recently termed the Deleuzian stream of affect theory rather than the phenomenological one.[3] In this chapter, I seek to remedy this omission by carrying out three primary tasks. First, I survey and clarify the strand of affect theory—exemplified in the work of Brian Massumi, particularly his touchstone essay "The Autonomy of Affect" (1995)—that has been influential in religious studies in recent years. Working through the example of Charles Hirschkind's use of Massumi in his analysis of Egyptian cassette sermon audition, I demonstrate how the category of affect allows religion scholars simultaneously to theorize the effects of affective visceral response at the level of the individual body and at the level of an entire community. Second, I offer a critique of Massumi and argue for a more capacious version of affect— and of an affective theory of the subject—than Massumi's work affords. Specifically, I ask what thinkers of affect, both within religious studies and beyond, might have to learn from psychology, and particularly from psychoanalysis, on this count. My contention is that much of what has come to be known as *affect theory* all too often conjures a version of affect that is so intent on exploding all sorts of boundaries that it forecloses the ways that affect is available to be known and contained and spoken about in any number of useful, everyday ways. In developing this position, I turn to a classic text by prominent post-Kleinian psychoanalyst Wilfred Bion, *Experiences in Groups*. Bion's description of the work of affective contagion in clinical encounters assists in a revision of Massumi's conception of affect that takes this contagion seriously, in order to generate a version of affect that is no respecter of boundaries, but nonetheless allows us to *postulate* such boundaries, whether in therapeutic treatment, in interpersonal relationships, in religious practice, or in political discourse. Yet, while this revised version of affective subjectivity also understands subjects as porous and traversable, it insists for both political and metaphysical reasons on the necessity of recuperating and reasserting the boundaries of individual selfhood in the wake of affective encounters. Finally, I examine the implications of this alternative conception of affect, with specific attention to its accompanying theory of affective subjectivity. In contrast to recent work on affect and religion—most notably Schaefer's *Religious Affects: Animality, Evolution, and Power*, which conceives affect as fundamentally *animal*, precognitive, and prelinguistic—a theory of affect that borrows from psychoanalytic thinking would traverse not only bodies, but also language. It would thus call scholarly attention back to human bodies, the bodies of speaking subjects.

## Genealogies of Affect

Religious studies as a discipline has been eager to adopt affect theory for a variety of reasons. Yet the expression *affect theory* sounds more monolithic than it is; it does not indicate a coherent field in which everybody agrees on the terms, any more than religious studies scholars endorse a single definition of religion. Crucial figures in this field include Sara Ahmed, Lauren Berlant, Teresa Brennan, Patricia Clough, Ann Cvetkovich, Brian Massumi, Eve Kosofsky Sedgwick, and Kathleen Stewart. Some affect theorists choose to emphasize a singular *affect*, while others examine *affects*, plural, often with specific attention to particular affects such as Berlant's "cruel optimism"; some, like Massumi, consider affect and emotion to be distinct, while others, like Cvetkovich,[4] do not; some, like Schaefer, are particularly interested in affect *qua* prelinguistic phenomenon, while others, like Sedgwick, are less wedded to this notion.[5] For present purposes, I will confine my account and subsequent critique to one version of affect that has been influential in religious studies, which originates with Massumi's "The Autonomy of Affect." I will also use the work of Teresa Brennan and Kathleen Stewart—distinctive affect theorists in their own right—to elucidate certain elements of this version of affect.

Massumi's key distinction is between affect and emotion. He writes, "An emotion is a subjective content, the sociolinguistic fixing of the quality of an experience which is from that point onward defined as personal. Emotion is qualified intensity.... It is intensity owned and recognized. It is crucial to theorize the difference between affect and emotion. If some have the impression that affect has waned, it is because affect is unqualified. As such, it is not ownable or recognizable and is thus resistant to critique."[6] That is to say: affects are things that we feel but for which we have no words. Emotions, on the contrary, are nameable and, as such, containable. They are subjective and personal but not, for all that, incommunicable. "Emotion is qualified intensity": this relation calls to mind (in family resemblance, at least) the Kierkegaardian/Heideggerian distinction between fear and anxiety, in which fear has an object, anxiety none. Affect escapes language in a way that emotion can be described by it. In fact, in Massumi's view, we notice affect only insofar as it always es-

*capes*: escapes capture, escapes assimilation, but, above all, escapes being bound in or by words. And its escape is not only *from* a particular body but also *to* other bodies, other sites. This is why it is helpful to conceive of affect in terms of intensities traversing the body, crossing from body to body, and circulating between bodies.

Teresa Brennan's emphasis on the *transmission* of affect is also useful here for envisioning how affects circulate among bodies. Brennan opens her book of that title with a disarming appeal to the everyday experience of walking into a room that is already "charged" in some way and feeling the atmosphere that precedes one's entrance. She does not take herself to be describing a purely subjective experience.[7] Rather, the atmosphere in this hypothetical room preexists the hypothetical reader's entrance and as she enters, the atmosphere actually makes its way *into* her in a meaningful sense. This transmission of affect involves an "energetic dimension," such that it can "enhance" or "deplete" the recipient.[8] Brennan also upholds a strong distinction (invoked a century earlier by Sigmund Freud)[9] between affects and thoughts. While I may walk into that room and find the anxiety or rage of one of its occupants to be contagious and begin to experience it myself, the transmission of the affect does not carry along with it a concomitant *copy* of the thoughts attaching to the transmitter's affect. In other words, to invoke another Freudian concept, the phenomenon of affective contagion should not be misread as a case of magical thinking, the infantile belief that a mere thought can materially influence the external world. "The point is that," Brennan writes, "even if I am picking up on your affect, the linguistic and visual content, meaning the thoughts I attach to that affect, remain my own: they remain the product of the particular historical conjunction of words and experiences I represent."[10] That is to say, two individuals walking into this affectively laden room, depending on their receptiveness, might experience a similar charge, but each would subsequently be referred to a wholly distinct set of thoughts, associations, and images.

Although Brennan does not put it in precisely these terms, the consciousness of the atmosphere in the affectively charged room is a vestigial experience, the remnants of a phenomenon that would once have been taken for granted. In her view, a robust adherence to the distinction between subjects and objects, which requires a severing of affective ties to an object in order to stake a claim to objectivity, has tended to obliterate the possibility of taking affect as a legitimate object of study. For, in order to do so, it would be necessary to conceive of the individual as porous and receptive rather than self-contained and autonomous, a view that runs wholly counter to the Cartesian subject and its many successors.

Kathleen Stewart also helps us make sense of Massumi in *Ordinary Affects* (2007), a short series of loosely connected vignettes and anecdotes that explicitly seeks to elicit affect from the reader. It is a provocative attempt at a deliberate performance of the *pull* of the text, as Stewart endeavors "to slow the quick jump to representational thinking and evaluative critique long enough to find ways of approaching the complex and uncertain objects that fascinate because they literally hit us or exert a pull on us."[11] Everything in the universe of ordinary affects is dynamic. Stewart's vocabulary, like Massumi's, is Deleuzian, full of circuits, flows, relays, intensities, energetics. This is not limited to the field of the individual, for Stewart, like Brennan, is also interested in affective contagion, and specifically in how a single event can transform the affect of a group, a room, or even a community. Stewart gets at this relative impersonality of affect by speaking of ordinary affects as "public feelings" that are "at once abstract and concrete."[12] Moreover, they are constantly in circulation, not bounded or contained neatly within individual bodies.

Describing the experience of an ordinary affect, Stewart writes that "a charge passes through the body and lingers for a little while as an irritation, confusion, judgment, thrill or musing. However it strikes us, its significance jumps. Its visceral force keys a search to make sense of it, to incorporate it into an order of meaning. *But it lives first as an actual charge immanent to acts and scenes* . . . a relay."[13] For many affect theorists, including Massumi, it is extraordinarily significant that this charge, this intensity, is phenomenologically prior to anything one can say about it. One can sense in such texts a deep fatigue toward poststructuralist language games, which can function to write out or efface the body. The word *autonomy* in the title of Massumi's essay is not a subject's capacity for agency or the Kantian autonomy of giving oneself the law, or even the autonomy of the floating signifier; it refers to the autonomic functions of the body that precede or function independently of thought. "The skin," Massumi says, "is faster than the word."[14] Stewart, likewise, brings affect into view most sharply as a visceral charge, something that hits out at you, passes through your body, impersonal or prepersonal, that one can only afterward name and speak about. The body comes to the forefront here, to the point that individual subjectivity almost entirely recedes. "The self is no match for all of this," Stewart writes.[15]

### Thinking Affect, Feeling Religion

Charles Hirschkind makes skillful use of Massumi's affect/emotion distinction in *The Ethical Soundscape: Cassette Sermons and Islamic Counterpublics* (2006), a study of the phenomenon of Islamic cassette sermon audition in Cairo. Writing about the effects of cassette sermon audition on what he calls the "Qurani-cally tuned body," Hirschkind appeals directly to Massumi's version of affect to talk about the level on which the effects of cassette sermon listening resonate within the body that is prepared for such audition, and how these effects on such bodies function to shape ethical practices. Hirschkind glosses Massumi for his own purposes as follows: "Affects are part of the presubjective inter-face of the body with the sensory world it inhabits, a linkage registered at the level of the visceral, the proprioceptive, and other sites where memory lodges itself in the body." He continues, performatively, and parenthetically, "(While I write these words at an outdoor café, a bird lands on the table in front of me. I casually watch the staccato motions it makes with its head. Each of these jerky movements rebounds off of my neck and upper body as a sort of shock wave. Now imagine a similar pulsation, though one carrying ethical potential, say the 'shock wave' that accompanies a reaction of moral disgust.)"[16]

For Hirschkind, thinking affect rather than thinking emotion works bril-liantly for a host of reasons. Above all, it allows him to theorize the effects of affective visceral response simultaneously at the level of an entire community *and* at the level of the individual body. In Ann Cvetkovich's vivid example, it al-lows questions like "How do I feel?" and "How does capitalism feel?" to nestle side by side.[17] In this sense, affect updates a familiar Hegelian maneuver, calling attention to a fundamental isomorphism between the singular individual bod-ies and social bodies, without eliding, however, the particularities of individual affective encounters and their moral consequences. For Hirschkind, deploying the category of affect also allows him to neatly anticipate and sidestep potential criticism along the lines that response to a sermon, or any auditory event, is merely individual, interior, and subjective, since affects do not, strictly speaking, *belong* to anyone. Rather, they are by their nature communal and public. They circulate as freely as cassette tapes, beyond the borders of discrete selves, while nonetheless impinging upon and meaningfully altering those selves. An em-phasis on affect works, here, too—and I suspect this may constitute its primary appeal for many religion scholars—to insist on the primacy of religious *feeling* without a naive return to a theory of universal religious feeling à la Schleier-macher or William James. It provides Hirschkind within another tool in his already impressive theoretical arsenal to zero in on what he calls the "sensory conditions" that create the condition of the possibility for shaping what he understands as a modern form of Islamic ethics.

The Hirschkind example brings into view the way that, at a very basic level, part of the purpose of thinking of affect as a category is to insist upon the entry of *that which is felt* into legitimate theoretical discourse. The insistence on the legitimacy of feelings as an object of study and of theoretical attention might appear both peculiar and unnecessary in the context either of any type of study of religion *on the ground,* or of any sort of psychoanalytic thinking. But it makes an enormous amount of sense when one traces the lineage of Massumi's writing back to the work of Gilles Deleuze and Félix Guattari and ultimately to how they understand Spinoza's *Ethics*, reading it as anomalous in the history of Western philosophy in its refusal of a Cartesian-style body/mind distinction and foregrounding the notion of how bodies affect and are affected by one another.

There is, of course, a very long history of excluding feeling, emotion, and bodily and visceral sensation from what counts as philosophical thinking. These have been coded, variously, as unreliable, interior, subjective, untrustworthy, irrational, feminine: one could give endless examples of this phenomenon from the history of philosophy, starting with Plato's rational and appetitive parts of the soul and the resulting struggle between reason and desire.[18] Affect theory gets, in part, to smuggle these things back in with an insistence that affect ought not to be identified with narrowly subjective, interior emotion. As theorists like Stewart have trenchantly observed, affects are in a certain sense impersonal; they are *public feelings*, intensities that traverse the body but do not belong to it or originate within it.[19] One doesn't *own* one's affects, at least not exclusively and perhaps not at all; they traverse borders of all kinds—of bodies, persons, rooms, communities, nations—crystallizing and even flaunting the limits of such boundaries.

### The Limits of Affect

To lay my own cards on the table, I am interested in what might be called an affective theory of the subject, and what affect theory can borrow from psychology, and particularly from psychoanalysis, in this regard. The Deleuzian strand of affect theory exemplified by Massumi's work has indeed been useful to scholars of religion. My concern, however, is that its investment in destabilizing boundaries and troubling distinctions and dismantling subjects can obscure the ways that affect is already available to be known and contained and treated in all kinds of eminently useful ways. While the phenomenological strand of affect theory, exemplified in the work of scholars like Eve Kosofsky Sedgwick and Ann Cvetkovich, sidesteps some of these concerns, it appears that there is something about the Deleuzian strand that is distinctively useful for religious studies, that allows affect to do the sort of work for which Hirschkind harnesses it. Hence the need, here, both to critique and attempt to alter or expand the Deleuzian strand rather than understanding it as adequately supplanted by the phenomenological version. My worry is that the emphasis on affect as something that circulates, that does not belong to any one individual, that traverses boundaries, and that is distinct from emotion, may preclude recourse to the eminently useful, long-standing language of affect drawn from psychology and specifically from psychoanalysis.

I turn to psychoanalysis for both its affinities with and its meaningful differences from Deleuzian affect theory. Since its inception, psychoanalysis has been preoccupied with contesting and troubling boundaries. As a body of knowledge, it straddles science and philosophy. It offers both sociological and philosophical insight, but no matter how high-flown or bewildering some of its theories may seem, psychoanalysis still remains grounded in physical spaces, in relationships, in human encounters. Psychoanalysis contests the distinction between rational and irrational; between the conscious and the unconscious; between self and other; between individuals and groups; between thoughts and feelings; and between language and biology. It insists upon overdetermination; meaning, motivation, and experience are plural, multivalent, unstable, brimming over with meanings both shared and idiosyncratic. The motor energy of psychoanalysis is the phenomenon of transference, the overdetermined relationship that develops in the here and now between analyst and analysand; it is the arena in which the latter's memories, archaic relationships, fears, desires, and fantasies express themselves and are enacted, providing material for ongoing interpretation and, ideally, psychic change. Transference attenuates the profound interchangeability of human relationships while simultaneously testifying to the capacity for genuine psychic dynamism, the ability not only to repeat and to remember, but also to *work through*. The twin phenomena of transference and countertransference are examples nonpareil of both the blurring and the reconstruction of precisely the sort of interpersonal boundaries that affect oversteps.

Before poststructuralism, before affect theory, Freud and his heirs radically decentered the self, showing it up as fragmented, inexhaustible, largely unknowable, fundamentally ambivalent, riddled with introjects, and haunted by the ghosts of previous encounters. But the subject of psychoanalysis is not wholly decentered. It is dethroned, but not erased, situated within the intersubjective milieu of the analytic setting and marked by an emphasis on intrapsychic processes. Further, the clinical setting of psychoanalysis acts as a sort of umbilical, tethering theory to practice, such that the reality of human selves and their idiosyncratic feelings and histories and families and problems can never wholly recede from view. This grounding in the quotidian realities of people who certainly feel and act as if they have selves, however porous those selves might be, provides a wealth of uses of the notion of affect that the Deleuzian version appears to ignore.

For instance, one might, in everyday language as well as in clinical discourse, describe an individual as having a warm affect, or a flat affect. That first hypothetical person, with the warm affect, would draw you in and make you feel comfortable, whereas the second would probably make you sense something a little bit off, and you would back away; or you might think they were sick, or tired, or depressed. The emphasis on the circulation of affects, their hectic Deleuzian traversals of bodies and boundaries, likewise seems to preclude the more readily accessible vocabulary of affective contagion *between* subjects, the way that other people's feelings sometimes seem to be *catching*. Think of a passenger in a car with an anxious driver, or a child walking into a room where her parents have been fighting. Think, too, of the daily effects of structural inequalities felt at the level of the body, the creeping sense of dread or fear or exhaustion from being in a toxic relationship, or living in a racist community, or working in a situation of precarious employment. All these examples highlight how what *seem* to be other people's emotions can nonetheless work on you, and can drain you, make you feel your energy either intensified or depleted, the daily ways that affective contagion cashes out in a daily setting in terms of its effects on a discrete individual. When selves nearly disappear into ebbs and flows of circuits and energies, it is also easy for the everyday effects of affective labor to recede from theoretical attention,[20] along with the reality that certain people are expected to bear much more of that burden than others (which has been well understood, often under the heading of emotional labor, in fields like sociology for decades).[21] When individual selves recede, so, too, does attention from the effort it takes to smile a thousand times a day, the often invisible work that it takes to make other people feel good, valued, meaningful, cared for. When individual selves recede, so, too, does attention from the labor of covering over one's own feelings to allow others to move smoothly, swiftly through their lives—not only concealing the unpleasant feelings that a person might be experiencing at a given moment, but also, in some cases, an overall structural situation of abjection and exploitation.

As such, without disputing that affects circulate, and without questioning the phenomenological experience of the visceral charge that Stewart and Hirschkind describe, I wish to push back against the necessity of conceiving affect as prelinguistic or nonlinguistic or precognitive or noncognitive, or as wholly impersonal. What is genuinely at stake in the category of affect, in my view, is a meaningful way to think about *intersubjectivity* without having to choose between foregrounding either language *or* bodies. To be quite clear about my own position: I *want* to be a subject, as well as a body—not merely a site that is traversed—and I am inclined to think that the ability to speak and signify is an indispensable part of that process. The status of *subject* is one that is still not equally awarded. If one takes a long view of the history of Western philosophy, for instance, women became subjects approximately five minutes ago, and I am disinclined to give that status away to be equal with dolphins and housecats and power tools, to flatten out the differences between all these entities and think of them first and foremost as bodies that affect and are affected by one another.[22] Metaphysical commitments notwithstanding, any approach to religious studies that wishes to engage seriously with questions of power and identity cannot afford to risk effacing either subjectivity or difference in this fashion.

Nonetheless, affect seems to me an excellent descriptor for a very common phenomenological and also specifically *cognitive* experience wherein the agential or autonomous self breaks down, where the distinction between where you start and I stop becomes porous and difficult to navigate. For we are not autonomous in the sense of being impermeable to the world or to other human beings. Others are inside us; we are haunted, inhabited by our parents and social mores and introjects. We are not contiguous with our earlier selves, nor are we wholly capable of predicting our future selves; we are susceptible to regret. Politically speaking, however, I find it crucial to insist on the meaningful and discernible difference between discrete bodies and individuals, *regardless of whether that distinction is fictive or not.* The types of agency and autonomy that such rigid policing of these boundaries yields is incredibly potent and absolutely necessary. These boundaries confer upon an individual the ability to say yes or no on her own behalf, to give or withhold consent. This would cash out, just to name a few instances, in terms of reproductive self-determination, in the ability to consent to or refuse a sexual encounter, to cast a vote—in other words, in the recognizable capacity to make an autonomous decision on one's own behalf.

Thus, in order to generate a version of affect that is no respecter of boundaries, but nonetheless allows us to *postulate* such boundaries at times for such reasons, I look toward psychoanalytic approaches. Specifically, I appeal to the work of Melanie Klein and her followers, particularly Wilfred Bion. Klein, of course, calls our attention to the pre-Oedipal, to the infantile, and to the overflowing, often raging, mass of affect that is all the child *is*, at first, before it is a self, an affective overflow that can either be contained as the self becomes consolidated or else become major features of a character disorder later in life.[23]

Here, I will confine myself to Bion, and I submit what I read as an exceptionally meaningful excerpt from his classic work *Experiences in Groups* (1961) as a synecdoche for what I believe psychoanalytic conceptions of affect have to offer. Bion adapts and extends Klein's concept of projective identification so as to suggest that one individual may project an affect such that another individual actually experiences himself as its recipient—*by experiencing it as his own.* Projective identification differs from projection in that the individual does not simply rid himself of troubling feelings or impulses by seeing them in others (who may or may not possess them). In projective identification, the individual projects (expels but remains connected to) part of the *self,* a bad self, into another individual or group of individuals, who wind up enacting the behaviors and experiencing the feelings that other person projects onto them. Teresa Brennan, who argues that Bion's work *should* be read as a theory of transmission of affect, puts the distinction succinctly: "A projection is what I disown in myself and see in you; a projective identification is what I succeed in having you experience in yourself, although it comes from me in the first place."[24] One of the most distinctive, and frequently the most distressing, features of projective identification, is the way that certain encounters with a particular individual can produce behavior that does not *feel* like one's own. In heated interpersonal encounters, one can find oneself doing or saying things that are completely out of character, but which—on reflection—uncannily resemble behaviors and actions of a significant figure in that other person's life or past.

Bion came to think about the way projective identification operates in terms of the analyst as a container for what the patient needed to be contained, and he also grew to believe that it was a major component of the analytic process, going so far as to claim that the patient's projective identifications actually make their way into the analyst. As psychoanalysts Stephen Mitchell and Juliet Black write:

> Klein describes the experience of the analyst in terms similar to Freud's. But Bion, by interpersonalizing the concept of projective identification, regards the analyst's affective experience as much more centrally involved in the patient's struggles. The analyst finds himself resonating with and containing intense anxieties and disturbing states of mind. . . .
>
> For Freud, psychoanalysis was an arena in which one person observes and interprets the affective experience of another from a measured distance. In the contemporary Kleinian perspective, psychoanalysis is an arena in which two persons struggle to organize and make meaningful the affective life of the patient *into which the analyst is inevitably and usefully drawn.*[25]

In the clinical context, the logical consequences of this theory require the analyst to pay very close attention to the affects that he experiences within the course of an analytic session. For the patient, or the group, may very well have *caused* him to experience them; the patient or the group has given these affects to the analyst in a very real way, and they are crucial data. This is a significant departure from a theory of transference and countertransference in which the former is a product of the patient's psyche and the latter of the analyst's, and the analyst is responsible for managing both, conscientiously attending to his own responses to the patient but never understanding them as the actual affect of the patient. In contrast, here is Bion leading a typical group: "The pauses are getting longer, comments more and more futile, when it occurs to me that the feelings which I am experiencing myself—in particular, oppression by the apathy of the group and an urge to say something useful and enlightening—are precisely those which the others present seem to have."[26]

Bion outlines a clinical manner and method that insists on the necessity of the analyst's taking his own affective response to the individual analysand or to the group as crucial to the work of analysis, well beyond the boundaries of other psychoanalytic conceptions of countertransference and its uses. While many of the post-Freudian psychoanalytic schools have theorized the phenomena of transference and countertransference differently from Freud, Bion's view is one of the most radical in this regard due to his use of the notion of projective identification *within* the clinical setting, as an interpersonal event that occurs in physical space.

Toward the end of *Experiences in Groups*, Bion formalizes what seems, here, to be a passing observation into a theory and tentatively hazards a mechanism by which the analyst can distinguish between the affects that are his own and those that are the result of projective identification:

> In group treatment many interpretations, and amongst them the most important, have to be made on the strength of the analyst's own emotional reactions. It is my belief that these reactions are dependent on the fact that the analyst in the group is on the receiving end of what Melanie Klein has called projective identification, and that this mechanism plays a very important role in groups. Now the experience of counter-transference appears to me to have quite a distinct quality that should enable the analyst to differentiate the occasion when he is the object of a projective identification from the occasion when he is not. The analyst feels he is being manipulated so as to be playing a part, no matter how difficult to recognize, in someone else's phantasy—or he would do if it were not for what in recollection I can only call a temporary loss of insight, a sense of experiencing strong feelings and at the same time a belief that their

existence is quite adequately justified by the objective situation without recourse to recondite explanation of their causation. From the analyst's point of view, the experience consists of two closely related phases: in the first there is a feeling that whatever else one has done, one has certainly not given a correct interpretation; in the second there is a sense of being a particular kind of person in a particular emotional situation. I believe ability to shake oneself out of the numbing feeling of reality that is a concomitant of this state is the prime requisite of the analyst in the group: if he can do this he is in a position to give what I believe is the correct interpretation, and thereby to see its connection with the previous interpretation, the validity of which he has been caused to doubt.[27]

In other words, the analyst must actually succumb not only to the experience of the affect but also to the earnest belief that it is his own. Only after he has thoroughly inhabited that position of identification can he begin to disentangle what is his own and what he has been given. The successful analysis will depend on the combination of the analyst's being sufficiently receptive actually to receive the affect of the other(s), yet possessing sufficient boundaries to eventually identify it as not-self and to bring it to the attention of the patient or the group. The lines between self and other are distinct, then blur, then separate again. This version of affect, and this conception of analysis, both create and demand not only a certain degree of porousness, but also an ability to reconstruct and demarcate boundaries between subjects. I use Bion as illustrative here because I think this example from the clinical setting vividly demonstrates a conception of affect that takes its contagion seriously and yet insists on recuperating and subsequently reasserting the boundaries of selfhood.

A theory of affect that would borrow freely from such psychoanalytic thinking—especially from material derived from theorizing clinical encounters—would traverse not only bodies, but also language, and it would thus call attention primarily to human bodies, the bodies of speaking subjects. Perhaps most crucially, it could begin to account for the way that *language itself traverses bodies*—not only in the analytic dyad or a therapeutic space, but also in political discourse, interpersonal relationships, religious ritual, or even scholarly activity—and to account for how language likewise moves us, to action as well as to feeling. What is more, it would account for the way that affect *can*, in fact, be contained and come to rest, ceasing its traversals, such that the distinctions between individual subjects can be reasserted. As such, we could preserve the crucial notion of affect as fundamentally impersonal, insofar as it is no respecter of the boundaries of bodies or subjects. Yet we could add much to this conception by insisting what psychology already knows: that affect or affects can—and, indeed, sometimes must—be *handled*, altered, amplified or lessened, whether through bodily action or linguistic intervention, which frequently means containing them or marshaling them in what is rightly understood as affective labor. In such circumstances, affect becomes unavoidably personal: one individual takes it upon herself to manage or contain her own or another's affects, and thus reinscribes the boundaries between self and other—a task that frequently proves necessary, if also, perhaps, impossible.

### Once More, with (Religious) Feeling

It is no coincidence that Massumi's original article takes political speeches and both individual and group reactions to them as a case study. Affect, after all, is the descriptor par excellence for what sweeps through bodies and crowds at political rallies and religious gatherings alike. More precise than Durkheimian collective effervescence in its ability to describe both discrete affects and a more general sense of being moved or being affected, it is what explains otherwise puzzling disjunctions between thought and feeling, between professed belief and visceral response. As Schaefer astutely notes, affect explains "how discourses attach to bodies and get them to move," and is not "baffled when bodies sincerely 'believe' one thing and do another."[28] It is not baffled when a convention speech moves the most cynical political observer to tears, though she long ago lost her faith in party politics; it is not baffled when atheists buy Christmas trees year after year; it is not baffled when otherwise kind and generous people disown their children when they come out as queer.

In particular, it is no coincidence that Massumi wrote about Ronald Reagan, the so-called "Great Communicator," whose success rested on his ability to transmit "an overweening feeling of confidence—that of the supposedly sovereign individual within a supposedly great nation at whose helm idiocy and incoherence reigned."[29] Massumi understood Reagan as congealing and foreshadowing in his person the entirety of the postmodern affective political regime—the primacy of feeling, distraction, sound bite, the mingling and ultimate collapsing-together of style and substance—within which we now exist.

The Massumi version of affect (to which Schaefer does not firmly adhere, but which, crucially, he affirms within his insistence in "thematizing power outside of language")[30] is more than adequate to our contemporary cultural and political moment, which is certainly characterized by fear, by the primacy of feeling. It is also more than adequate to theorize a vast range of current religious phenomena. It can speak to the persistent virulence of Islamophobia or anti-Semitism; it can even render the Westboro Baptist Church explicable. It can speak to the relationships within religious groups and the ties that bind their members together. It can explain the peculiar force of conviction itself, why belief *grips* you and does not easily let go, whether it is a belief in the shamefulness of premarital sex or in the sanctity of the Second Amendment. Affect can clarify the process of conversion or why people can abandon their religious upbringings but cannot always shed their attachment to the rituals and traditions of their childhood. It can explain why we persistently knock on wood or bless someone after they sneeze, or the discomfort with blasphemy that one sees among even the most thorough unbelievers, or why lapsed Catholics still cross themselves reflexively from time to time. Affect can help us make sense of the relationship between virtual and physical practices: What makes something go viral online? What is *catching* and why? How does hashtag activism turn into real bodies on the street, from the Arab Spring to #BlackLivesMatter? How can we theorize the response of a group of individuals to a sermon, to a political speech, to a ritual, and be licensed to speak about the visceral response of individual bodies and social bodies at once? For all of these and more, the Massumi version of affect—prelinguistic, unbounded—may suffice.

But the Deleuzian strand of affect theory that Massumi exemplifies is neither exhaustive nor definitive. In religious studies specifically, we need a more capacious and nuanced understanding of affect, and this is where psychoanalysis comes in. Using psychoanalytic frameworks of selfhood and subjectivity, we can still preserve the work that affect theory does for religion. That is to say, we can preserve what affect theory offers in terms of a return to conceiving of religion primarily in terms of feeling while also stressing that such feeling ought not to be understood only as singular, subjective, individual, personal, internal, or inaccessible—the insight that it is also public, circulating, belonging to everyone and no one at once, and primarily experienced in and through the body. Yet religious studies has along ago learned to beware the shortcomings of Jamesian talk of abstract "oneness," or the rhetoric of the "oceanic feeling" that Freud found insufficient nearly a hundred years ago. Against this backdrop, we can draw upon psychoanalysis to revise our definition of affect to insist that the phenomenological truth of the affective subject—that we are porous, that we lack control, that we are swept by energies largely outside of our control and often counter to our intellectual commitments—does not entail that we must succumb to those energies and be resigned to them. Our justifiable theoretical enthusiasm for the dizzying flows and peregrinations of affect need not come at the cost of eradicating essential boundaries. Such boundaries constitute the bedrock of subjectivity and social interaction, and have historically been hard-won—not only within the realm of the history of philosophy, but in terms of everyday life, particularly among marginalized subjects who are invariably called upon to give the most of themselves in affective labor and whose claims to personal autonomy are frequently the most tenuous. The affective subject is a site of intensities that exceed it—but it also exists at the nexus of social forces, historical processes, linguistic structures, and personal motivations, desires, and self-understandings.

Affect theory can grow up, as it were, when it ceases to merely describe the traversal of boundaries and the breakdown of selves and embraces, too, the distinctive affective work that comprises the containment of affects, the maintenance of boundaries, and the exercise of individual agency and volition, no matter how unfashionable the latter may be at present. This is a Freudian imperative: the unpleasant, impossible, but also necessary task that is *growing up*, acknowledging the reality principle alongside the pleasure principle, setting boundaries, and becoming a subject—all in the face of the truth that we can never wholly rid ourselves of the infantile experience of limitlessness nor ultimately disambiguate between self and other once and for all. Affect theory cannot afford to be so enchanted with itself—with its own bewitching linguistic formulations to capture the nonlinguistic—that it unwittingly re-enchants our thoroughly disenchanted world.

NOTES

1. See, for example, Jacques Derrida, "Différance," in *Of Grammatology*, trans. Gayatri Chakravorty Spivak (1967; Baltimore: Johns Hopkins University Press, 2016), *Writing and Difference*, trans. Alan Bass (1978; repr. London: Routledge and Kegan Paul, 2010), and *Margins of Philosophy*, trans. Alan Bass (1982; repr. Chicago: University of Chicago Press, 2009); Luce Irigaray, *Speculum of the Other Woman*, trans. Gilliam C. Gill (1985; repr. Ithaca, NY: Cornell University Press, 2010), and *This Sex Which Is Not One*, trans. Catherine Porter and Carolyn Burke (1985; repr. Ithaca, NY: Cornell University Press, 1996); and Jacques Lacan, *Écrits*, trans. Alan Sheridan (London: Routledge, 2001).

2. See, for example, the essays that make up Melissa Gregg and Gregory J. Seigworth, eds., *The Affect Theory Reader* (Durham, NC: Duke University Press, 2010).

3. See chapter 1 of Donovan O. Schaefer's *Religious Affects: Animality, Evolution, and Power* (Durham, NC: Duke University Press, 2015) for this helpful distinction, which Schaefer traces (accurately, in my view) from Massumi's essay on the one hand, and Eve Kosofsky Sedgwick and Adam Frank's edited volume *Shame and Its Sisters: A Silvan Tomkins Reader* (Durham, NC: Duke University Press, 1995), especially their opening essay "Shame in the Cybernetic Fold" on the other.

4. In *Depression: A Public Feeling* (Durham, NC: Duke University Press, 2012), Ann Cvetkovich deliberately plays fast and loose with some of this terminology, heralding

the Deleuzians as "intimates and fellow travelers of the Public Feelings interest in sensory experience and feeling," but noting that her own project has different roots. She talks about using affect "as a category that encompasses affect, emotion, and feeling, and that includes impulses, desires, and feelings that get historically constructed in a range of ways—but with a wary recognition that this is like trying to talk about sex before sexuality. I also like to use *feeling* as a generic term that does some of the same work: naming the undifferentiated "stuff" of feeling; spanning the distinctions between affect and emotion central to some of the theories; acknowledging the somatic or sensory nature of feelings as experiences that aren't just cognitive concepts or constructions." She continues, adding a third term, "I favor feeling in part because it is intentionally imprecise, retaining the ambiguity between feelings as embodied sensations and feelings as psychic or cognitive experiences" (4).

5. Eve Sedgwick, for example, stakes out a position that is much more moderate than Massumi's with respect to the question of the rigid exclusion of the linguistic from the affective. Sedgwick, in *Touching Feeling: Affect, Pedagogy, Performativity* (Durham, NC: Duke University Press, 2003), does profess a "disinclination ... to subsuming nonverbal aspects of reality firmly under the aegis of the linguistic," a tendency she attributes to thinkers like Jacques Derrida and Judith Butler. But Sedgwick's gesture is a refusal of the priority of the linguistic rather than of the linguistic itself: "I assume that the line between words and things or between linguistic and nonlinguistic phenomena is endlessly changing, permeable, and entirely unsusceptible to any definitive articulation" (6).

6. Brian Massumi, "The Autonomy of Affect," in *Parables for the Virtual: Movement, Affect, Sensation* (Durham, NC: Duke University Press, 2002), 26–27.

7. Teresa Brennan, *The Transmission of Affect* (Ithaca, NY: Cornell University Press, 2004), 1.

8. Brennan, *Transmission of Affect*, 6.

9. See, for example, the "Affects in Dreams" section of Sigmund Freud's *The Interpretation of Dreams* (1900). I used the James Strachey translation, which can be found in Volumes IV–V of the Standard Edition of the *Complete Psychological Works of Sigmund Freud* (London: Hogarth Press, 1958).

10. Brennan, *Transmission of Affect*, 7.

11. Kathleen Stewart, *Ordinary Affects* (Durham, NC: Duke University Press, 2007), 4.

12. Stewart, *Ordinary Affects*, 2–3.

13. Stewart, *Ordinary Affects*, 39, emphasis mine.

14. Massumi, "Autonomy of Affect," 25.

15. Stewart, *Ordinary Affects*, 58.

16. Charles Hirschkind, *The Ethical Soundscape: Cassette Sermons and Islamic Counterpublics* (New York: Columbia University Press, 2006), 82.

17. Ann Cvetkovich, *Depression: A Public Feeling* (Durham, NC: Duke University Press, 2012), 5.

18. For an excellent exposition of this phenomenon, see Elizabeth Grosz, *Volatile Bodies: Toward a Corporeal Feminism* (Bloomington: Indiana University Press, 1994).

19. This coinage belongs to the Public Feelings group, now Feel Tank Chicago, including Lauren Berlant, Ann Cvetkovich, and Kathleen Stewart.

20. See Sara Ahmed's groundbreaking book *The Promise of Happiness* (Durham, NC: Duke University Press, 2010).

21. See Arlie Russell Hochschild, *The Managed Heart: Commercialization of Human Feeling* (1983; Berkeley, CA: University of California Press, 2012).

22. Simone de Beauvoir's point in the introduction to *The Second Sex* regarding the essential incompatibility between "the situation of woman" and the ability to be an autonomous decision-making subject remains, unfortunately, deeply relevant today. See Simone de Beauvoir, *The Second Sex*, trans. Constance Borde and Sheila Malovany-Chevallier (1949) (New York: Vintage Books, 2009).

23. See Melanie Klein, *The Psycho-Analysis of Children* (1932), vol. 2 of *The Writings of Melanie Klein* (London: Hogarth Press and the Institute of Psychoanalysis, 1975).

24. Brennan, *Transmission of Affect*, 29.

25. Stephen A. Mitchell and Margaret J. Black, *Freud and Beyond: A History of Modern Psychoanalytic Thought* (New York: Basic Books, 1995), 106–7, emphasis mine. Bion's thought is integral to the "contemporary Kleinian perspective" that Mitchell and Black describe. Indeed, as they note, "In theorizing explicitly designated as 'Kleinian,' Klein's concepts have been extended and interpreted so fundamentally through the contributions of Wilfred Bion that contemporary Kleinian thought is more accurately designated Kleinian/Bionic" (102).

26. W. R. Bion, *Experiences in Groups and Other Papers* (London: Routledge, 2010), 48. This instance is characteristic of the confusion and apathy that Bion's groups often initially exhibit. In the sessions he narrates in *Experiences in Groups*, Bion subverts from the outset all the group members' expectations of his role. The experience of reading *Experiences in Groups* is a distinctive one. Bion keeps the reader continuously off balance in a way that is almost reminiscent of the deliberate disorientation provoked by Jacques Lacan's seminars, had Lacan been possessed of a dry British wit and a proclivity for short declarative statements. In a typical example, Bion writes: "When men meet together, for example in a committee, rules of procedure are established and there is usually an agenda; the formality with which work is done varying with the group. In the groups in which I am psychiatrist I am the most obvious person, by virtue of my position, in whom to vest a right to establish rules of procedure. I take advantage of this position to establish no rules of procedure and to put forward no agenda" (77). The stated purpose of the group, then—the "work group" in Bion's terminology—can be nothing other than to study the dynamics of the group itself as they unfold, revealing what he calls their "basic assumptions," which operate on a different level from the work group and may often run at cross-purposes to it.

27. Bion, *Experiences in Groups*, 149–50.

28. Donovan O. Schaefer, *Religious Affects: Animality, Evolution, and Power* (Durham, NC: Duke University Press, 2015), 35.

29. Massumi, "Autonomy of Affect," 42.

30. Schaefer, *Religious Affects*, 9.

Ahmed, Sara. "Affective Economies." *Social Text* 22, 2 79 (summer 2004): 117–39.
———. "Collective Feelings: Or, the Impressions Left by Others." *Theory, Culture and Society* 21, no. 2 (2004): 25–42.
———. *The Cultural Politics of Emotion*. New York: Routledge, 2004.
———. *The Promise of Happiness*. Durham, NC: Duke University Press, 2010.
———. *Queer Phenomenology: Orientations, Objects, Others*. Durham, NC: Duke University Press, 2006.
Al-Qaradawi, Yusuf. *Ra'ait al-bi'ah fi shari'at al-islam*. Cairo: Dar Al-Shuruq, 1421/2001.
Ameed, Syed Mohammed. *The Importance of Weeping and Wailing*. Karachi: Peerma-homed Ebrahim Trust, 1974.
Anandavardhana. *The "Dhvanyaloka" of Anandavardhana with the "Locana" of Abhi-navagupta*. Edited and translated by Daniel H. H. Ingalls Sr. Translated by Jeffrey Moussaiff Masson and M. V. Patwardhan. Cambridge, MA: Harvard University Press, 1990.
Anderson, Ben. *Encountering Affect: Capacities, Apparatuses, Conditions*. Burlington, VT: Ashgate, 2014.
Anderson, Benedict. *Imagined Communities: Reflections on the Origin and Spread of Nationalism*. Rev. ed. London: Verso, 1991.
Aquinas, Thomas. *De Veritate*. Translated by Robert W. Mulligan. Chicago: Henry Regnery, 1952. Accessed July 1, 2016. http://dhspriory.org/thomas/QDdeVer.htm.
———. *Summa Theologiae*. Translated by Fathers of the English Dominican Province. Benziger Brothers edition, 1947. Accessed July 1, 2016. http://dhspriory.org/thomas/summa/SS/SS025.html#SSQ250UTP1.
———. *Summa Theologiae*. Edited by Thomas Gilby. London: Eyre and Spottiswoode, 1964–74.
———. *Summa Theologiae. Latin/English edition of the Works of St. Thomas Aquinas*. Edited by John Mortensen and Enrique Alarcón. Translated by Laurence Shapcote. 8 vols. Lander, WY: Aquinas Institute for the Study of Sacred Doctrine, 2012.
Aristotle. *De Anima (On the Soul)*. Translated by J. A. Smith. In *The Basic Works of Aristotle*, ed. Richard McKeon, 534–603. New York: Random House, 1941.
———. *Ethica Nicomachea (Nicomachean Ethics)*. Translated by Terence Irwin. India-napolis: Hackett, 1985.

———. *Rhetorica* (*Rhetoric*). Translated by W. Rhys Roberts. In *The Basic Works of Aristotle*, ed. Richard McKeon, 1318–1451. New York: Random House, 1941.

Asad, Talal. *Genealogies of Religion: Discipline and Reasons of Power in Christianity and Islam*. Baltimore: Johns Hopkins University Press, 1993.

Aufderheide, Patricia. *Documentary: A Very Short Introduction*. Oxford: Oxford University Press, 2007.

Averill, James R. "A Constructivist View of Emotion." In *Emotion: Theory, Research and Experience*, vol. 1, *Theories of Emotion*, ed. Robert Plutchik and Henry Kellerman, 305–39. New York: Academic Press, 1980.

Ayoub, Mahmoud. *Redemptive Suffering in Islam: A Study of the Devotional Aspects of 'Ashura' in Twelver Shi'ism*. The Hague: Mouton, 1978.

Baker, William J. *Playing with God: Religion and Modern Sport*. Cambridge, MA: Harvard University Press, 2007.

Barker, Jennifer. *The Tactile Eye: Touch and the Cinematic Experience*. Los Angeles: University of California Press, 2009.

Barrett, Justin L. *Why Would Anyone Believe in God?* Walnut Creek, CA: AltaMira Press, 2004.

Barthes, Roland. *Empire of Signs*. New York: Hill and Wang, 1982.

Barzilai, Shmuel. *Chassidic Ecstasy in Music*. Frankfurt am Main: Peter Lang, 2009.

Beauvoir, Simone de. *The Second Sex*. Translated by Constance Borde and Sheila Malovany-Chevallier [1949]. New York: Vintage Books, 2009.

Bender, Courtney. *The New Metaphysicals: Spirituality and the American Religious Imagination*. Chicago: University of Chicago Press, 2010.

Bennett, Jane. *Vibrant Matter: A Political Ecology of Things*. Durham, NC: Duke University Press, 2010.

Benson, Peter, and Kevin Lewis O'Neill. "Facing Risk: Levians, Ethnography, Ethics." *Anthropology of Consciousness* 18, no. 2 (2007): 29–55.

Berlant, Lauren. *Compassion: The Culture and Politics of an Emotion*. New York: Routledge, 2004.

———. *Cruel Optimism*. Durham, NC: Duke University Press, 2011.

———. *Intimacy*. Chicago: University of Chicago Press, 2000.

Berry, Evan. *Devoted to Nature: The Religious Roots of American Environmentalism*. Berkeley: University of California Press, 2015.

Berry, Thomas. *The Sacred Universe: Earth, Spirituality, and Religion in the Twenty-First Century*. Edited by Mary Evelyn Tucker. New York: Columbia University Press, 2009.

Bijker, Wiebe E., and John Law, eds. *Shaping Technology/Building Society: Studies in Sociotechnical Change*. Cambridge, MA: MIT Press, 1992.

Bion, W. R. *Experiences in Groups and Other Papers*. London: Routledge, 2010.

Blacking, John. *How Musical Is Man?* Seattle: University of Washington Press, 1973.

Bohmlan, Philip V. "Introduction: Jewish Music in Dialogue with Jewish Studies." In *The Oxford Handbook of Jewish Studies*, ed. Martin Goodman, Jeremy Cohen, and David Sorkin, 852–69. New York: Oxford University Press, 2002.

Bondi, Liz. "The Place of Emotions in Research: From Partitioning Emotion and Reason to the Emotional Dynamics of Research Relationships." In *Emotional*

*Geographies*, ed. Joyce Davidson, Liz Bondi, and Mick Smith, 231–46. Aldershot, UK: Ashgate, 2005.

Boyer, Pascal. *The Naturalness of Religious Ideas: A Cognitive Theory of Religion*. Berkeley: University of California Press, 1994.

Brennan, Teresa. *The Transmission of Affect*. Ithaca, NY: Cornell University Press, 2004.

Brink-Danan, Marcy. "Anthropology of the Jews." Accessed August 3, 2016. *Oxford Bibliographies Online Datasets* (2012). doi: http://dx.doi.org/10.1093/obo /9780199840731-0070.

———. "Anthropological Perspectives on Judaism." *Religion Compass* 2, no. 4 (July 2008): 674–88.

Brinkema, Eugenie. *The Forms of the Affects*. Durham, NC: Duke University Press, 2014.

Broomhall, Susan, ed. *Gender and Emotions in Medieval and Early Modern Europe: Destroying Order, Structuring Disorder*. London: Routledge, 2016.

Brown, Frank Burch. "Musical Ways of Being Religious." In *The Oxford Handbook of Religion and the Arts*, ed. Frank Burch Brown, 109–29. Oxford: Oxford University Press, 2014.

Brown, Wendy. *Politics out of History*. Princeton, NJ: Princeton University Press, 2001.

Browne, Janet. *Charles Darwin: The Power of Place*. New York: Knopf, 2002.

Burke, Peter. *Popular Culture in Early Modern Europe*. New York: New York University Press, 1978.

Byrne, Julie. *O God of Players: The Story of the Immaculata Mighty Macs*. New York: Columbia University Press, 2003.

Callard, Felicity, and Des Fitzgerald. *Rethinking Interdisciplinarity across the Social Sciences and Neurosciences*. London: Palgrave Macmillan, 2015.

Cannon, Katie. *Black Womanist Ethics*. Atlanta: Scholars Press, 1988.

Carlson, Jennifer D., and Kathleen C. Stewart. "The Legibilities of Mood Work." *New Formations* 82 (2014): 114–33.

Carson, Rachel. *Silent Spring*. Boston: Mariner Books, 2002. First published 1962 by Oxford University Press.

Cates, Diana Fritz. *Aquinas on the Emotions: A Religious-Ethical Inquiry*. Washington, DC: Georgetown University Press, 2009.

———. *Choosing to Feel: Virtue, Friendship, and Compassion for Friends*. Notre Dame, IN: University of Notre Dame Press, 1997.

———. "Conceiving Emotions: Martha Nussbaum's *Upheavals of Thought*." *Journal of Religious Ethics* 31, no. 2 (2003): 325–43.

———. "Love: A Thomistic Analysis." In "Love," ed. David McCarthy and Joshua P. Hochschild. Special issue, *Journal of Moral Theology* 1, no. 2 (2012): 1–30.

Cave, David, and Rebecca Sachs Morris, eds. *Religion and the Body: Modern Science and the Construction of Religious Meaning*. Leiden: Brill, 2012.

Champeaux, Jacqueline. *Fortuna: Recherches sur le culte de la fortune à Rome et dans le monde romain des origines à la mort de César*. Rome: École française de Rome, 1982.

Chaudhuri, Pramathanath. *Ramprasad and Western Man*. Calcutta: Gautam Mallick, 1976.

Christian, William A., Jr. "Provoked Religious Weeping in Early Modern Spain." In *Religious Organization and Religious Experience*, ed. John Davis, 97–114. London: Academic Press, 1982.

Cicero. *Tusculan Disputations*. Translated by J. E. King. Loeb Classical Library. Cambridge, MA: Harvard University Press, 1945.

Clifford, James, and George E. Marcus, eds. *Writing Cultures: The Poetics and Politics of Ethnography*. Berkeley: University of California Press, 1986.

Clough, Patricia Ticineto. Introduction to *The Affective Turn: Theorizing the Social*, ed. Patricia Ticineto Clough and Jean Halley, 1–33. Durham, NC: Duke University Press, 2007.

Clough, Patricia Ticineto, and Jean Halley, eds. *The Affective Turn: Theorizing the Social*. Durham, NC: Duke University Press, 2007.

Code, Lorraine. "Taking Subjectivity into Account." In *Feminist Epistemologies*, ed. Linda Martín Alcoff and Elizabeth Potter, 15–48. New York: Routledge, 1993.

Cohen, Judah M. "Whither Jewish Music?: Jewish Studies, Music Scholarship, and the Tilt between Seminary and University." *AJS Review* 32, no. 1 (2008): 29–48.

Connolly, William E. *Capitalism and Christianity: American Style*. Durham, NC: Duke University Press, 2008.

———. *Neuropolitics: Thinking, Culture, Speed*. Minneapolis: University of Minnesota Press, 2002.

Cooley, Timothy J. "Theorizing Fieldwork Impact: Malinowski, Peasant-Love and Friendship." *British Journal of Ethnomusicology* 12, no. 1 (2003): 1–17.

Corrigan, John. *Business of the Heart: Religion and Emotion in the Nineteenth Century*. Berkeley: University of California Press, 2002.

———, ed. *The Oxford Handbook of Religion and Emotion*. New York: Oxford University Press, 2008.

Couldry, Nick. *Media Rituals: A Critical Approach*. London: Routledge, 2003.

Cronon, William. "The Trouble with Wilderness: Or, Getting Back to the Wrong Nature." *Environmental History* 1, no. 1 (1996): 7–28.

Cvetkovich, Ann. *An Archive of Feelings: Trauma, Sexuality, and Lesbian Public Cultures*. Durham, NC: Duke University Press, 2003.

———. *Depression: A Public Feeling*. Durham, NC: Duke University Press, 2012.

Damasio, Antonio R. *Descartes' Error: Emotion, Reason, and the Human Brain*. New York: Putnam, 1994.

———. *The Feeling of What Happens: Body and Emotion in the Making of Consciousness*. New York: Harcourt Brace, 1999.

———. *Looking for Spinoza: Joy, Sorrow, and the Feeling Brain*. Orlando, FL: Harcourt, 2003.

Daniels, Inge. "Scooping, Raking, Beckoning Luck: Luck, Agency and the Interdependence between People and Things in Japan." *Journal of the Royal Anthropological Institute* 9, no. 4 (2003): 619–38.

Darlington, Susan. *The Ordination of a Tree*. Albany: SUNY Press, 2012.

Darwin, Charles. *The Expression of the Emotions in Man and Animals*. New York: Penguin, 2009.

———. *The Life and Letters of Charles Darwin*. Edited by Francis Darwin. New York: Appleton, 1898.

Davies, Jeremy. *The Birth of the Anthropocene*. Berkeley: University of California Press, 2016.

Davis, Natalie Zemon. *Society and Culture in Early Modern France: Eight Essays*. Stanford, CA: Stanford University Press, 1975.

Dawkins, Richard. *The God Delusion*. New York: Mariner Books, 2006.

Dawkins, Richard, Daniel C. Dennett, Sam Harris, and Christopher Hitchens. *The Four Horsemen*. Digital video. Accessed July 20, 2016. Hour 1: http://www.youtube .com/watch?v=9DKhc1pcDFM. Hour 2: http://www.youtube.com/watch?v=TaeJf -Yia3A&feature=relmfu.

Deleuze, Gilles. *Cinema 1: The Movement Image*. Translated by Hugh Tomlinson and Barbara Habberjam. Minneapolis: University of Minnesota Press, 1986.

———. *Cinema 2: The Time Image*. Translated by Hugh Tomlinson and Robert Galeta. Minneapolis: University of Minnesota Press, 1989.

Dennett, Daniel C. *Breaking the Spell: Religion as a Natural Phenomenon*. New York: Penguin, 2006.

Derrida, Jacques. *Margins of Philosophy*. Translated by Alan Bass. [1982]. Chicago: University of Chicago Press, 2009.

———. *Of Grammatology*. Translated by Gayatri Chakravorty Spivak. [1967]. Baltimore: Johns Hopkins University Press, 2016.

———. *Writing and Difference*. Translated by Alan Bass. [1978]. London: Routledge and Kegan Paul, 2010.

Disraeli, B. *Church Policy: A Speech Delivered by the Right Hon. B. Disraeli, M.P. at a Meeting of the Oxford Diocesan Society for the Augmentation of Small Living in the Sheldonian Theatre, Oxford, November 25th, 1863*. London: Gilbert and Rivington, 1864.

Dixon, Thomas. "Emotion: The History of a Keyword in Crisis." *Emotion Review* 4, no. 4 (2012): 337–443.

Dowling, W. J. "The Development of Music Perception and Cognition." In *Foundations of Cognitive Psychology: Core Readings*, ed. Daniel J. Levitin, 481–502. Cambridge, MA: MIT Press, 2002.

Durkheim, Émile. *The Elementary Forms of Religious Life*. Translated by Karen E. Fields. New York: Free Press, 1995.

Eagleton, Terry. "Lunging, Flailing, Mispunching: Richard Dawkins." Review of *The God Delusion*, by Richard Dawkins. *London Review of Books*, October 19, 2006.

Edwards, Harry. *Sociology of Sport*. Homewood, IL: Dorsey Press, 1973.

Egerman, Hauke, Frederik Nagel, Eckart Altenmüller, and Reinhard Kopiez. "Continuous Measurement of Musically-Induced Emotion: A Web Experiment." *International Journal of Internet Science* 4, no. 1 (2009): 4–20.

Eitzen, D. Stanley, and George H. Sage. "Sport and Religion." In *Religion and Sport: The Meeting of Sacred and Profane*, ed. Charles S. Prebish, 103–11. Westport, CT: Greenwood Press, 1993.

Ekman, Paul. *Emotion in the Human Face*. Cambridge: Cambridge University Press, 1982.

Eliade, Mircea. *The Sacred and the Profane: The Nature of Religion.* Translated by Willard R. Trask. San Diego, CA: Harcourt Brace Jovanovich, 1959.

Elias, Norbert. *The Civilizing Process.* Translated by Edmund Jephcott. New York: Untzen, 1978.

Evans-Pritchard, E. E. *Theories of Primitive Religion.* Oxford: Clarendon Press, 1965.

Evernden, Neil. *The Social Construction of Nature.* Baltimore: Johns Hopkins University Press, 1992.

Finnegan, Ruth. "Music, Experience, and the Anthropology of Emotion." In *The Cultural Study of Music: A Critical Introduction,* ed. Martin Clayton, Trevor Herbert, and Richard Middleton, 181–92. New York: Routledge, 2003.

Finney, Carolyn. *Black Faces, White Spaces: Reimagining the Relationship of African Americans to the Great Outdoors.* Chapel Hill: University of North Carolina Press, 2014.

Flader, Susan L. *Thinking Like a Mountain: Aldo Leopold and the Evolution of an Ecological Attitude toward Deer, Wolves, and Forests.* [1974]. Madison: University of Wisconsin Press, 1994.

Foer, Franklin. *How Soccer Explains the World: An Unlikely Theory of Globalization.* New York: HarperCollins, 2004.

Foucault, Michel. *The History of Sexuality.* Translated by Robert Hurley. Vol. 1. New York: Vintage, 1990.

———. "Technologies of the Self." In *Technologies of the Self: A Seminar with Michel Foucault,* ed. Luther Martin, Huck Gutman, and Patrick H. Hutton, 16–49. Amherst: University of Massachusetts Press, 1988.

Freud, Sigmund S. *Civilization and Its Discontents.* Edited and translated by James Strachey. New York: W. W. Norton, 1989.

———. *The Interpretation of Dreams.* London: Hogarth Press, 1958.

———. *The Standard Edition of the Complete Psychological Works of Sigmund Freud.* Translated from the German under the General Editorship of James Strachey. 24 vols. London: Hogarth Press: 1956–1974.

Friedmann, Jonathan L. "Emotions and Devotion in Synagogue Song." *Jewish Magazine,* March 2009. Accessed January 28, 2015. http://www.jewishmag.com/131mag/prayer_music/prayer_music.htm.

———, ed. *Emotions in Jewish Music: Personal and Scholarly Reflections.* Lanham, MD: University Press of America, 2012.

Fuller, Robert C. *The Body of Faith: A Biological History of Religion in America.* Chicago: University of Chicago Press, 2013.

———. *Spirituality in the Flesh: Bodily Sources of Religious Experience.* Oxford: Oxford University Press, 2008.

———. *Wonder: From Emotion to Spirituality.* Chapel Hill: University of North Carolina Press, 2006.

Funk, Carolyn L., Kevin B. Smith, John R. Alford, Matthew V. Hibbing, Nicholas R. Eaton, Robert F. Krueger, Lindon J. Eaves, and John R. Hibbing. "Genetic and Environmental Transmission of Political Orientations." *Political Psychology* 34 (2013): 805–19.

Gade, Anna M. "Green Islam in Indonesia." 2012–15. Accessed May 20, 2017. www.vimeo.com/hijau.

———. "Indonesian Islamic Law of the Environment: *Fatwa* and *Da'wa*." *Worldviews: Global Religions, Culture, and Ecology* 19, no. 2 (2015): 161–83.

———. "Islam." In *The Oxford Handbook of Religion and Emotion*, ed. John Corrigan, 35–50. New York: Oxford University Press, 2008.

———. *Perfection Makes Practice: Learning, Emotion, and the Recited Qur'ān in Indonesia*. Honolulu: University of Hawai'i Press, 2004.

———. "Tradition and Sentiment in Indonesian Environmental Islam." *Worldviews: Global Religions, Culture, and Ecology* 16, no. 3 (2012): 263–85.

Galloway, Alex. *The Interface Effect*. New York: Polity, 2012.

Gartner, Corinne. "The Possibility of Psychic Conflict in Seneca's *De Ira*." *British Journal for the History of Philosophy* 23, no. 2 (2015): 213–33.

Geertz, Armin W. "How *Not* to Do the Cognitive Science of Religion Today." *Method and Theory in the Study of Religion* 20, no. 1 (2008): 7–21.

Geertz, Clifford. *The Interpretation of Cultures*. New York: Basic Books, 1973.

Gereboff, Joel. "Judaism." In *The Oxford Handbook of Religion and Emotion*, ed. John Corrigan, 95–110. New York: Oxford University Press, 2008.

Ginzburg, Carlo. *The Cheese and the Worms: The Cosmos of a Sixteenth-Century Miller*. Translated by John and Anne Tedeschi. New York: Penguin, 1982. First published 1980 by Johns Hopkins University Press.

Goodman, Mark. "Why *Nusach* Still Matters." In *Emotion in Jewish Music*, ed. Jonathan L. Friedmann, 30–44. Lanham, MD: University Press of America, 2012.

Gottlieb, Roger, ed. *The Oxford Handbook of Religion and Ecology*. New York: Oxford University Press, 2010.

Green, André. *The Fabric of Affect in the Psychoanalytic Discourse*. Translated by Alan Sheridan. New York: Routledge, 1999.

Green, J. Keith, Joel Gereboff, Diana Fritz Cates, and Maria Heim. "The Nature of the Beast: Hatred in Cross-Traditional Religious and Philosophical Perspective." *Journal of the Society of Christian Ethics* 29, no. 2 (2009): 175–205.

Gregg, Melissa, and Gregory J. Seigworth. *The Affect Theory Reader*. Durham, NC: Duke University Press, 2010.

Grierson, John. "The First Principles of Documentary." In *Grierson on Documentary*, ed. Forsythe Hardy, 144–56. [1932]. London: Faber and Faber, 1966.

Grosz, Elizabeth. *Volatile Bodies: Toward a Corporeal Feminism*. Bloomington: Indiana University Press, 1994.

Guha, Ramachandra. *Environmentalism: A Global History*. New York: Longman, 2000.

———. *How Much Should a Person Consume?: Environmentalism in the United States and India*. Berkeley: University of California Press, 2006.

Gunew, Sneja. "Subaltern Empathy: Beyond European Categories in Affect Theory." *Concentric: Literary and Cultural Studies* 35, no. 1 (2009): 11–30.

"Habit." Special issue. *Body and Society* 19 (2013): 3–281.

Hajdu, Andre. *Kulmus HaNefesh: A Musical Journey into the Hassidic Niggun*. CD booklet, CJM 0901. Jerusalem: Jewish Music Research Center—Hebrew University of Jerusalem, 2009.

Hamner, M. Gail. *Imaging Religion in Film: The Politics of Nostalgia*. New York: Palgrave, 2011.

———. "Religion and Film: A Pedagogical Rubric." *JAAR* 81, no. 4 (2013): 1139–50.

Harding, Susan. *The Book of Jerry Falwell: Fundamentalist Language and Politics.* Princeton, NJ: Princeton University Press, 2000.

Hardt, Michael. "Affective Labor." *boundary 2* 26, no. 2 (1999): 89–100.

Harpham, Geoffrey Galt. "Finding Ourselves: The Humanities as a Discipline." *American Literary History* 25, no. 3 (2013): 509–34. Accessed April 14, 2015. doi:10.1093/alh/ajt027.

Hedges, Chris. *I Don't Believe in Atheists*. New York: Free Press, 2008.

———. *War Is a Force That Gives Us Meaning*. New York: Anchor Books, 2003.

Hesketh, Ian. *Of Apes and Ancestors: Evolution, Christianity, and the Oxford Debate*. Toronto: University of Toronto Press, 2009.

Higgs, Robert J. *God in the Stadium: Sports and Religion in America*. Lexington: University of Kentucky Press, 1995.

Higgs, Robert J., and Michael C. Braswell. *An Unholy Alliance: The Sacred and Modern Sports*. Macon, GA: Mercer University Press, 2004.

Hirschkind, Charles. *The Ethical Soundscape: Cassette Sermons and Islamic Counterpublics*. New York: Columbia University Press, 2006.

Hochschild, Arlie R. *The Managed Heart: Commercialization of Human Feeling*. Berkeley: University of California Press, 1983.

Hodder, Ian. *Entangled: An Archaeology of the Relationships between Humans and Things*. Malden, MA: Wiley Blackwell, 2012.

Hood, Mantle Ki. "The Challenge of Bi-Musicality." *Ethnomusicology* 4 (1960): 55–59.

Hopkins, Peter E. "Women, Men, Positionalities, and Emotion: Doing Feminist Geographies of Religion." *ACME: An International E-Journal for Critical Geographies* 8, no. 1 (2009): 1–17.

Hubbard, G., K. Backett-Milburn, and D. Kemmer. "Working with Emotion: Issues for the Researcher in Fieldwork and Teamwork." *International Journal of Social Research Methodology* 4, no. 2 (2001): 119–37.

Huda, Mohammad Nurul, ed. *The Poetry of Kazi Nazrul Islam in English Translation*. Translated from Bengali. Dhaka: Nazrul Institute, 2000.

Huxley, T. H. "The Origin of Species." In *Collected Essays*, vol. 2, *Darwiniana*. London: MacMillan, 1896.

*Huxley Papers, The*. A Descriptive Catalogue of the Correspondence, Manuscripts and Miscellaneous Papers of the Rt. Hon. Thomas Henry Huxley. Preserved in the Imperial College of Science and Technology, London, by Warren R. Dawson.

Inglis, John. "Aquinas's Replication of the Acquired Moral Virtues: Rethinking the Standard Philosophical Interpretation of Moral Virtue in Aquinas." *Journal of Religious Ethics* 27, no. 1 (1999): 3–27.

Innes, John Brodie. "Recollections of J. Brodie Innes." *Darwin Online*. Accessed May 20, 2017. http://darwin-online.org.uk/content/frameset?pageseq=1&itemID=CUL-DAR112.B85-B92&viewtype=side.

Inwood, Brad. *Ethics and Human Action in Early Stoicism*. Oxford: Clarendon Press, 1985.

———. "Seneca and Psychological Dualism." In *Passions and Perceptions: Studies in Hellenistic Philosophy of Mind*, ed. Jacques Brunschwig and Martha C. Nussbaum, 150–83. Cambridge: Cambridge University Press, 1993.

———. "The Will in Seneca the Younger." *Classical Philology* 95, no. 1 (2000): 44–60.

Irigaray, Luce. *Speculum of the Other Woman*. Translated by Gilliam C. Gill. [1985]. Ithaca, NY: Cornell University Press, 2010.

———. *This Sex Which Is Not One*. Translated by Catherine Porter and Carolyn Burke. [1985]. Ithaca, NY: Cornell University Press, 1996.

Islam, Kazi Nasrul. *Kazi Nasrul Islam: Selected Works*. Translated by Sajed Kamal. Dhaka: Nazrul Institute, 1999.

Islam, Rafiqul. *Kazi Nazrul Islam: A New Anthology*. Dhaka: Bangla Academy, 1990.

Izod, John, and Richard Kilborn. "The Documentary." In *The Oxford Guide to Film Studies*, ed. John Hill and Pamela Church Gibson, 426–27. Oxford: Oxford University Press, 1998.

Jakobsen, Janet R., and Ann Pellegrini, eds. *Secularisms*. Durham, NC: Duke University Press, 2008.

James, William. *The Varieties of Religious Experience: A Study in Human Nature*. London: Longmans, Green, [1902] 1911.

———. *The Varieties of Religious Experience: A Study in Human Nature*. New York: Penguin Books, 1982.

Jameson, Fredric. *The Antinomies of Realism*. Durham, NC: Duke University Press, 2015.

Jenkins, Willis J., and Mary Evelyn Tucker, eds. *The Routledge Handbook of Religion and Ecology*. New York: Routledge, 2016.

Johnson, Jessica. *Biblical Porn: Affect, Labor, and Pastor Mark Driscoll's Evangelical Empire*. Durham, NC: Duke University Press, 2018 forthcoming.

Johnson-Laird, P. N., and Keith Oatley. "Emotions, Music, and Literature." In *Handbook of Emotions*, ed. Michael Lewis, Jeannette M. Haviland-Jones, and Lisa Feldman Barrett, 102–13. New York: Guilford Press, 2010.

Juslin, Patrik N., and Daniel Västfjäll. "Emotional Responses to Music: The Need to Consider Underlying Mechanisms." *Behavioral and Brain Sciences* 31, no. 5 (2008): 559–75.

Kalib, Sholom. *The Musical Tradition of the Eastern European Synagogue*. Vol. 1. Syracuse, NY: Syracuse University Press, 2002.

Karatzogianni, Athina, and Adi Kuntsman, eds. *Digital Cultures and the Politics of Emotion: Feelings, Affect, and Technological Change*. New York: Palgrave, 2012.

Keim, Marion. *Nation Building at Play: Sport as a Tool for Social Integration in Post-Apartheid South Africa*. Oxford: Meyer and Meyer Sport, 2003.

Klein, Amit. "Singing Their Heart Out: Emotional Excitement in Cantorial Recitatives and Carlebach Nusach." In *Judaism and Emotion: Texts, Performance, Experience*, ed. Sarah Ross, Gabriel Levy, and Soham Al-Suadi, 68–97. New York: Peter Lang, 2013.

Klein, Melanie. *The Psycho-Analysis of Children* [1932]. Vol. 2 of *The Writings of Melanie Klein*. London: Hogarth Press and the Institute of Psychoanalysis, 1975.

Klein, Naomi. *This Changes Everything: Capitalism vs. the Climate*. New York: Simon and Schuster, 2015.

Kleinginna, Paul R., Jr., and Anne M. Kleinginna. "A Categorized List of Emotion Definitions, with Suggestions for a Consensual Definition." *Motivation and Emotion* 5, no. 4 (1981): 345–79.

Kleinman, Sherryl. "Field-Workers' Feelings: What We Feel, Who We Are, How We Analyze." In *Experiencing Fieldwork: An Inside View of Qualitative Research*, ed. William B. Shaffir and Robert A. Stebbins, 184–95. Newbury Park, CA: SAGE, 1991.

Kligman, Mark. "Judaism and Music." In *The Oxford Handbook of Religion and the Arts*, ed. Frank Burch Brown, 263–69. Oxford: Oxford University Press, 2014.

Kosman, L. A. "Being Properly Affected: Virtues and Feelings in Aristotle's Ethics." *Essays on Aristotle's Ethics*, ed. Amélie Oksenberg Rorty, 103–16. Berkeley: University of California Press, 1980.

Kottak, Conrad Phillip. *Mirror for Humanity: A Concise History of Cultural Anthropology*. 5th ed. Boston: McGraw-Hill Higher Education, 2007.

Krumhansl, Carol L. "Music: A Link between Cognition and Emotion." *Current Directions in Psychological Science* 11, no. 2 (2002): 45–50.

Krumhansl, Carol L., Pekka Toivanen, Tuomas Eerola, Petri Toiviainen, Topi Järvinen, and Jukka Louhivuori. "Cross-Cultural Music Cognition: Cognitive Methodology Applied to North Sami Yoiks." *Cognition* 76, no. 1 (2000): 13–58.

Kuhn, Gabriel. *Soccer vs. the State: Tackling Football and Radical Politics*. Oakland, CA: PM Press, 2011.

Lacan, Jacques. *Écrits*. Translated by Alan Sheridan. London: Routledge, 2001.

LaMothe, Kimerer. "What Bodies Know about Religion and the Study of It." *JAAR* 76, no. 3 (2008): 573–601.

Laslett, Barbara. "Unfeeling Knowledge: Emotion and Objectivity in the History of Sociology." *Sociological Forum* 5, no. 3 (1990): 413–33.

Latour, Bruno. *Reassembling the Social: An Introduction to Actor-Network Theory*. Oxford: Oxford University Press, 2005.

———. *We Have Never Been Modern*. Translated by Catherine Porter. Cambridge, MA: Harvard University Press, 1993.

Lazzarato, Maurizio. *The Making of the Indebted Man*. Los Angeles: Semiotext(e), 2012.

Leopold, Aldo. *A Sand County Almanac and Sketches Here and There*. American Museum of Natural History Special Members Edition. [1949]. New York: Oxford University Press, 1968.

LeVasseur, Todd, and Anna Peterson, eds. *Religion and the Ecological Crisis: The "Lynn White Thesis" at Fifty*. New York: Routledge, 2016.

Levine, George. *Darwin Loves You: Natural Selection and the Reenchantment of the World*. Princeton, NJ: Princeton University Press, 2006.

Levy, Gabriel, and Sarah Ross. "Emotional and Cognitive Rhythms in Jewish Ritual Music." In *Judaism and Emotion: Texts, Performance, Experience*, ed. Sarah Ross, Gabriel Levy, and Soham Al-Suadi, 99–120. New York: Peter Lang, 2013.

Lewis, Michael, Jeannette M. Haviland-Jones, and Lisa Feldman Barrett. *Handbook of Emotions*. 3rd ed. New York: Guilford Press, 2008.

Leys, Ruth. "The Turn to Affect: A Critique." *Critical Inquiry* 37, no. 3 (spring 2011): 434–72.

Liljeström, Simon, Patrik N. Juslin, and Daniel Västfjäll. "Experimental Evidence of the Roles of Music Choice, Social Context, and Listener Personality in Emotional Reactions to Music." *Psychology of Music* 41, no. 5 (2012): 579–99.

Lutz, Catherine A. *Unnatural Emotions: Everyday Sentiments on a Micronesian Atoll and Their Challenge to Western Theory.* Chicago: University of Chicago Press, 1988.

Lynch, Gordon. *The Sacred in the Modern World: A Cultural Sociological Approach.* Oxford: Oxford University Press, 2012.

Mack, Phyllis. *Heart Religion in the British Enlightenment: Gender and Emotion in Early Methodism.* New York: Cambridge University Press, 2008.

Manning, Erin. *Politics of Touch: Sense, Movement, Sovereignty.* Durham, NC: Duke University Press, 2006.

Marazzi, Christian. *Capital and Affects: The Politics of the Language Economy.* Los Angeles: Semiotext(e), 2011.

Markovitz, Fran, ed. *Ethnographic Encounters in Israel: Poetics and Ethics of Fieldwork.* Bloomington: Indiana University Press, 2013.

Marks, Laura U. *The Skin of the Film: Intercultural Cinema, Embodiment, and the Senses.* Durham, NC: Duke University Press, 2000.

———. *Touch: Sensuous Theory and Multisensory Media.* Durham, NC: Duke University Press, 2002.

Martin, Luther H., Huck Gutman, and Patrick H. Hutton, eds. *Technologies of the Self: A Seminar with Michel Foucault.* Boston: University of Massachusetts Press, 1988.

Massumi, Brian. "The Autonomy of Affect." In "The Politics of Systems and Environments, Part II." Special issue, *Cultural Critique* 31 (autumn 1995): 83–109.

———. *Parables for the Virtual: Movement, Affect, Sensation.* Durham, NC: Duke University Press, 2002.

———. *What Animals Teach Us about Politics.* Durham, NC: Duke University Press, 2014.

Masuzawa, Tomoko. *The Invention of World Religions: Or, How European Universalism Was Preserved in the Language of Pluralism.* Chicago: University of Chicago Press, 2005.

Mattison, William. "Virtuous Anger? From Questions of *Vindicatio* to the Habituation of Emotion." *Journal of the Society of Christian Ethics* 24, no. 1 (2004): 159–79.

Mazzarella, William. "Affect: What Is It Good For?" In *Enchantments of Modernity: Empire, Nation, Globalization*, ed. Saurabh Dube. New York: Routledge, 2009.

McDaniel, June. *The Madness of the Saints: Ecstatic Religion in Bengal.* Chicago: University of Chicago Press, 1989.

Meine, Curt. *Aldo Leopold: His Life and Work.* [1988]. Madison: University of Wisconsin Press, 2010.

Mercer, John. *An Introduction to Cinematography.* Champaign, IL: Stipes, 1968.

Merriam, Alan P. *The Anthropology of Music.* Evanston, IL: Northwestern University Press, 1964.

Meyer, Birgit, and Annelies Moors, eds. *Religion, Media, and the Public Sphere.* Bloomington: Indiana University Press, 2006.

Meyer, Susan Suavé. "Fate, Fatalism, and Agency in Stoicism." *Social Philosophy and Policy* 16, no. 2 (1999): 250–73.

Milhaven, J. Giles. *Good Anger*. Kansas City, MO: Sheed and Ward, 1989.

Miller, Mandi M., and Kenneth T. Strongman. "The Emotional Effects of Music on Religious Experience: A Study of the Pentecostal-Charismatic Style of Music and Worship." *Psychology of Music* 30, no. 1 (2002): 8–27.

Miller-McLemore, Bonnie. "Through the Eyes of Mircea Eliade: United States Football as a Religious Rite of Passage." In *From Season to Season: Sports as American Religion*, ed. Joseph L. Price, 115–35. Macon, GA: Mercer University Press, 2001.

Mitchell, Stephen A., and Margaret J. Black. *Freud and Beyond: A History of Modern Psychoanalytic Thought*. New York: Basic Books, 1995.

Moisala, Pirkko. "Cognitive Study of Music as Culture: Basic Premises for Cognitive Ethnomusicology." *Journal of New Music Research* 24 (1995): 8–20.

Morgan, David. "Religion and Media: A Critical Review of Recent Developments." *Critical Research on Religion* 1, no. 3 (2013): 347–56.

Morgan, William J. "An Existential Phenomenological Analysis of Sport as Religious Experience." In *Religion and Sport: The Meeting of Sacred and Profane*, ed. Charles S. Prebish, 119–49. Westport, CT: Greenwood Press, 1993.

Muehlebach, Andrea. *The Moral Neoliberal: Welfare and Citizenship in Italy*. Chicago: University of Chicago Press, 2012.

Muir, John. *John of the Mountains: The Unpublished Journals of John Muir* (1938). Accessed July 15, 2016. http://vault.sierraclub.org/john_muir_exhibit/writings /favorite_quotations.aspx.

Mukhopadhyay, Dhrubakumar, ed. *Sakta Padavali*. Calcutta: Ratnavali, 1996.

Muñoz, José Esteban. *Cruising Utopia: The Then and There of Queer Futurity*. New York: New York University Press, 2009.

———. *Disidentifications: Queers of Color and the Performance of Politics*. Minneapolis: University of Minnesota Press, 1999.

Nash, Roderick Frazier. *Wilderness and the American Mind*. [1967]. 5th ed. New Haven, CT: Yale University Press, 2004.

Nathanson, Donald L. "Prologue: Affect Imagery Consciousness." In *Positive Aspects*, vol. 1 of *Affect Imagery Consciousness: The Complete Edition*, by Silvan S. Tomkins, with the editorial assistance of Bertram P. Karon, xi–xxvi. New York: Springer, 2008.

Ngai, Sianne. *Our Aesthetic Categories: Zany, Cute, Interesting*. Cambridge, MA: Harvard University Press, 2015.

———. *Ugly Feelings*. Cambridge, MA: Harvard University Press, 2007.

Nicolson, Paula. *Post-Natal Depression: Psychology, Science and the Transition to Mother-hood*. London: Routledge, 1998.

Nussbaum, Martha C. *The Fragility of Goodness: Luck and Ethics in Greek Tragedy and Philosophy*. Cambridge: Cambridge University Press, 1986.

———. *The Therapy of Desire: Theory and Practice in Hellenistic Ethics*. Princeton, NJ: Princeton University Press, 1994.

———. *Upheavals of Thought: The Intelligence of the Emotions*. Cambridge: Cambridge University Press, 2001.

O'Neill, Kevin Lewis. "Beyond Broken: Affective Spaces and the Study of American Religion." *JAAR* 81, no. 4 (2013): 1093–116.

Orsi, Robert. *Between Heaven and Earth: The Religious Worlds People Make and the Scholars Who Study Them*. Princeton, NJ: Princeton University Press, 2006.

———. *History and Presence*. Cambridge, MA: Belknap Press of Harvard University Press, 2016.

Otto, Rudolf. *The Idea of the Holy: An Inquiry into the Non-Rational Factor in the Idea of the Divine and Its Relation to the Rational*. Translated by John W. Harvey. Oxford: Oxford University Press, 1973.

Palmer, Martin, and Victoria Finlay. *Faith in Conservation: New Approaches to Religion and the Environment*. Washington, DC: World Bank, 2003.

Papacharissi, Zizi. *Affective Publics: Sentiment, Technology, and Politics*. New York: Oxford University Press, 2014.

Papoulias, Constantina, and Felicity Callard. "Biology's Gift: Interrogating the Turn to Affect." *Body and Society* 16, no. 1 (2010): 29–56.

Parncutt, Richard. "Perception of Musical Patterns: Ambiguity, Emotion, Culture." *Nova Acta Leopoldina* 92, no. 341 (2005): 33–47.

Patnaik, P. *Rasa in Aesthetics*. New Delhi: D. K. Printworld, 1997.

Pedwell, Carolyn. "Cultural Theory as Mood Work." *New Formations* 82 (2014): 47–63.

Pellegrini, Ann. "Signaling through the Flames: Hell House Performance and Religious Structure of Feeling." *American Quarterly* 59 (2007): 911–35.

Pinault, David. *Horse of Karbala: Muslim Devotional Life in India*. New York: Palgrave, 2001.

Porter Jean. "Desire for God: Ground of the Moral Life in Aquinas." *Theological Studies* 47, no. 1 (1986): 48–68.

———. "Mere History: The Place of Historical Studies in Theological Ethics." *Journal of Religious Ethics* 25, no. 3 (1998): 103–26.

Povinelli, Elizabeth. *Economies of Abandonment: Social Belonging and Endurance in Late Liberalism*. Durham, NC: Duke University Press, 2011.

———. *The Empire of Love: Toward a Theory of Intimacy, Genealogy, and Carnality*. Durham, NC: Duke University Press, 2006.

Prebish, Charles S., ed. *Religion and Sport: The Meeting of Sacred and Profane*. Westport, CT: Greenwood Press, 1993.

Price, Joseph L., ed. *From Season to Season: Sports as American Religion*. Macon, GA: Mercer University Press, 2001.

Protevi, John. *Political Affect: Connecting the Social and the Somatic*. Minneapolis: University of Minnesota Press, 2009.

Proudfoot, Wayne. *Religious Experience*. Berkeley: University of California Press, 1987.

Puar, Jasbir. " 'I would rather be a cyborg than a goddess': Intersectionality, Assemblage, and Affective Politics." *European Institute for Progressive Politics* (2001). Accessed February 3, 2016. http://eipcp.net/transversal/0811/puar/en.

———. *Terrorist Assemblages: Homonationalism in Queer Times*. Durham, NC: Duke University Press, 2007.

Raya, Amarendranath, ed. *Sakta padabali*. Calcutta: Calcutta University Press, 1989.

Reddy, William M. *The Navigation of Feeling: A Framework for the History of Emotions*. Cambridge: Cambridge University Press, 2001.

Ricoeur, Paul. "The Hermeneutical Function of Distanciation." *Philosophy Today* 17, no. 2 (summer 1973): 129–41.

Rorty, Amélie Oksenberg, ed. *Explaining Emotions*. Berkeley: University of California Press, 1980.

Rosaldo, Michelle Z. *Knowledge and Passion: Ilongot Notions of Self and Social Life*. New York: Cambridge University Press, 1980.

Ross, Sarah M. *A Season of Singing: Creating Feminist-Jewish Music in the United States*. Waltham, MA: Brandeis University Press, 2016.

———. "Sense or Absence of Nationalism: Searching for a Swiss-Jewish Musical Identity." In *Music and Minorities from around the World: Research, Documentation and Interdisciplinary Study*, ed. Ursula Hemetek, Essica Marks, and Adelaida Reyes, 115–41. Newcastle upon Tyne: Cambridge Scholars Press, 2014.

Ross, Sarah M., Gabriel Levy, and Soham Al-Suadi, eds. *Judaism and Emotion: Texts, Performance, Experience*. New York: Peter Lang, 2013.

Schaefer, Donovan O. *Religious Affects: Animality, Evolution, and Power*. Durham, NC: Duke University Press, 2015.

Schatzki, Theodore R. *Social Practices: A Wittgensteinian Approach to Human Activity and the Social*. Cambridge: Cambridge University Press, 1996.

Scherer, Klaus R. "Which Emotions Can Be Induced by Music? What Are the Underlying Mechanisms? And How Can We Measure Them?" *Journal of New Music Research* 33 (2004): 239–51.

Scherer, Klaus R., and Marcel R. Zentner. "Emotional Effects of Music: Production Rules." In *Music and Emotion: Theory and Research*, ed. Patrik N. Juslin and John A. Sloboda, 361–91. Oxford: Oxford University Press, 2001.

Schleiermacher, Friedrich. *The Christian Faith*. English translation of the second German edition. Edited by H. R. Mackintosh and J. S. Stewart. Edinburgh: T. and T. Clark, 1960.

———. *On Religion: Speeches to Its Cultured Despisers*. Edited and translated by Richard Crouter. Cambridge: Cambridge University Press, 1996.

Scholes, Jeffrey, and Raphael Sassower. *Religion and Sports in American Culture*. New York: Routledge, 2014.

Sedgwick, Eve Kosofsky. *Touching Feeling: Affect, Pedagogy, Performativity*. Durham, NC: Duke University Press, 2003.

Sedgwick, Eve Kosofsky, and Adam Frank. "Shame in the Cybernetic Fold: Reading Silvan Tomkins." *Critical Inquiry* 21, no. 2 (1995): 496–522.

Sedgwick, Eve Kosofsky, and Adam Frank, eds. *Shame and Its Sisters: A Silvan Tomkins Reader*. Durham, NC: Duke University Press, 1995.

Sen, Ramprasad. *Ramprasadi Sangit*. Calcutta: Rajendra Library, n.d.

———. *Shashibhushan Dasgupta, Bharater Shakti Sadhana o Shakti Sahitya*. Calcutta: Samsad, 1993.

Seneca. *De Beneficiis (On Benefits)*. Translated by Aubrey Stewart. London: George Bell and Sons, 1900.

———. *De Constantia Sapientis (On the Firmness of the Wise Man)*. In *Seneca: Moral Essays I*, translated by John W. Basore, ed. Jeffrey Henderson, 106–355. Loeb Classical Library. Cambridge, MA: Harvard University Press, 1928.

———. *De Ira* (*On Anger*). In *Seneca: Moral Essays I*, translated by John W. Basore, ed. Jeffrey Henderson, 356–449. Loeb Classical Library. Cambridge, MA: Harvard University Press, 1928.

———. *De Providentia* (*On Providence*). In *Seneca: Moral Essays I*, translated by John W. Basore, ed. Jeffrey Henderson, 2–47. Loeb Classical Library. Cambridge, MA: Harvard University Press, 1928.

———. *De Tranquillitate Animi* (*On Tranquillity of Mind*). In *Seneca: Moral Essays II*, translated by John W. Basore, 203–85. Loeb Classical Library. Cambridge, MA: Harvard University Press, 1932.

———. *De Vita Beata* (*On the Happy Life*). In *Seneca: Moral Essays II*, translated by John W. Basore, 286–355. Loeb Classical Library. Cambridge, MA: Harvard University Press, 1932.

———. *Moral Letters to Lucilius* [*Epistulae Morales*]. 1925. Loeb Classical Library. Accessed July 5, 2016. https://en.wikisource.org/wiki/Moral_letters_to_Lucilius.

Setaioli, Aldo. "Seneca and the Divine: Stoic Tradition and Personal Developments." *International Journal of the Classical Tradition* 13, no. 3 (2007): 333–68.

Shahābu-d-Dīn 'Umar ibn Muḥammad-i-Sahrawardī. *A Dervish Textbook from the 'Awārif al-ma'ārif, Written in the Thirteenth Century*. Translated by H. Wilberforce Clarke. London: Octagon Press, 1980.

Shaviro, Steven. *Post Cinematic Affect*. Hants, UK: 0-Books, John Hunt, 2010.

Shelemay, Kay Kaufman. "The Ethnomusicologist and the Transmission of Tradition." *Journal of Musicology* 14, no. 1 (1996): 35–51.

Shilling, Chris. *The Body in Culture, Technology and Society*. London: SAGE, 2005.

Sideris, Lisa H. "Fact and Fiction, Fear and Wonder: The Legacy of Rachel Carson." *Soundings: An Interdisciplinary Journal* 91, no. 3/4 (2008): 335–69.

———. "The Secular and Religious Sources of Rachel Carson's Sense of Wonder." In *Rachel Carson: Legacy and Challenge*, ed. Lisa H. Sideris and Kathleen Dean Moore, 232–50. Albany: SUNY Press, 2008.

Slobin, Mark. *Chosen Voices: The Story of the American Cantorate*. Urbana: University of Illinois Press, 2002.

Sloboda, John A., and Patrik N. Juslin. "Psychological Perspectives on Music and Emotion." In *Music and Emotion: Theory and Research*, ed. Patrik N. Juslin and John A. Sloboda, 79–96. Oxford: Oxford University Press, 2001.

Slusher, Howard. "Sport and the Religious." In *Religion and Sport: The Meeting of Sacred and Profane*, ed. Charles S. Prebish, 181–82. Westport, CT: Greenwood Press, 1993.

Smith, Warren Cole. "Unreal Sales for Driscoll's Real Marriage." *World Magazine*, March 5, 2014. Accessed March 6, 2014. http://www.worldmag.com/2014/03/unreal_sales_for_driscoll_s_real_marriage.

Sobchak, Vivian. *Carnal Thoughts: Embodiment and Moving Image Culture*. Los Angeles: University of California Press, 2004.

Solomon, Robert C. *The Passions: The Myth and Nature of Human Emotions*. Garden City, NY: Anchor Press/Doubleday, 1976.

———, ed. *Thinking about Feeling: Contemporary Philosophers on Emotions*. Oxford: Oxford University Press, 2004.

St. John of the Cross. *Dark Night of the Soul*, bk. 2, chap. 13. In *The Essential St John of the Cross*. Translated by E. Allison Peers. Radford, VA: Wilder, 2008.

———. *The Living Flame of Love by Saint John of the Cross with His Letters, Poems, and Minor Writings*. Translated by D. Lewis. London: Thomas Baker, 1919.

Stewart, Kathleen. *Ordinary Affects*. Durham, NC: Duke University Press, 2007.

———. "Precarity's Forms." *Cultural Anthropology* 27, no. 3 (2012): 518–25.

Stoll, Mark. *Inherit the Holy Mountain: Religion and the Rise of American Environmentalism*. New York: Oxford University Press, 2015.

Swimme, Brian Thomas, and Mary Evelyn Tucker. *Journey of the Universe*. New Haven, CT: Yale University Press, 2014.

Takayanagi, Yoichiro, Adam P. Spira, O. Joseph Bienvenu, Rebecca S. Hock, Michelle C. Carras, William W. Eaton, and Ramin Mojtabai. "Antidepressant Use and Lifetime History of Mental Disorders in a Community Sample: Results from the Baltimore Epidemiologic Catchment Area Study." *Journal of Clinical Psychiatry* 76, no. 1 (2015): 40–44. doi: 10.4088/JCP.13m08824.

Taves, Ann. *Religious Experience Reconsidered: A Building-Block Approach to the Study of Religion and Other Special Things*. Princeton, NJ: Princeton University Press, 2009.

Taylor, Bron. *Dark Green Religion: Nature Spirituality and the Planetary Future*. Berkeley: University of California Press, 2009.

Terranova, Tiziana. *Network Culture: Politics for the Information Age*. Ann Arbor, MI: Pluto Press, 2004.

Thoits, Peggy A. "The Sociology of Emotions." *Annual Review of Sociology* 15 (1989): 317–42.

Thomas, Keith. *Religion and the Decline of Magic*. New York: Scribner's, 1971.

Thompson, William Forde, and Laura-Lee Balkwill. "Cross-Cultural Similarities and Differences." In *Oxford Handbook of Music and Emotion: Theory, Research, Applications*, ed. Patrik N. Juslin and John Sloboda, 755–88. Oxford: Oxford University Press, 2010.

Thoreau, Henry David. *Walden: A Fluid-Text Edition*. Digital Thoreau Project. Geneseo: State University of New York. Accessed July 19, 2017. http://digitalthoreau.org/fluid-text-toc/.

Titon, Jeff Todd. "Bi-Musicality as Metaphor." *Journal of American Folklore* 108, no. 429 (1995): 287–97.

———. "Knowing Fieldwork." In *Shadows in the Field: New Perspectives for Fieldwork in Ethnomusicology*, ed. Gregory F. Barz and Timothy J. Cooley, 87–100. New York: Oxford University Press, 1997.

———. "Music, the Public Interest, and the Practice of Ethnomusicology." *Ethnomusicology* 36, no. 3 (1992): 315–22.

Tlili, Sara. *Animals in the Qur'an*. Cambridge: Cambridge University Press, 2012.

Tomkins, Silvan S. *Affect Imagery Consciousness*. Vol. 1, *The Positive Affects*. London: Tavistock, 1962.

———. *Shame and Its Sisters: A Silvan Tomkins Reader*. Edited by Eve Kosofsky Sedgwick and Adam Frank. Durham, NC: Duke University Press, 1995.

Trinh T. Minh-ha. "Documentary Is/Not a Name." *October* 52 (spring 1990): 76–98.

Valavanis, Panos. *Games and Sanctuaries in Ancient Greece: Olympia, Delphi, Isthmia, Nemea, Athens*. Translated by David Hardy. Los Angeles: Getty Publications, 2004.

Vásquez, Manuel A. *More Than Belief: A Materialist Theory of Religion*. Oxford: Oxford University Press, 2011.

Wallace, David Foster. *Infinite Jest*. Boston: Little, Brown, 1996.

———. "Tense Present: Democracy, English, and the Wars over Usage." *Harper's Magazine*, April 2001, 39–58.

Watson, Nick, and Andrew Parker, eds. *Sports and Christianity: Historical and Contemporary Perspectives*. New York: Routledge, 2013.

Werpehowski, William. "Do You Do Well to Be Angry?" *Annual of the Society of Christian Ethics* 16 (1996): 59–77.

White, Lynn, Jr. "The Historical Roots of Our Ecologic Crisis." *Science* 155, no. 3767 (1967): 1203–7.

Widdowfield, Rebekah. "The Place of Emotions in Academic Research." *Area* 32, no. 2 (2000): 199–208.

Will, Udo. "Perspectives of a Reorientation in Cognitive Ethnomusicology." Research-Gate, December 2013. Accessed January 2015. http://www.researchgate.net/publication/259451150_Reorientation_in_Cognitive_Ethnomusicology_(English_Version).

Williams, Raymond. *Marxism and Literature*. Oxford: Oxford University Press, 1977.

Williams, Rowan. *The Wound of Knowledge: Christian Spirituality from the New Testament to Saint John of the Cross*. Cambridge, MA: Cowley Publications, 1991.

Wilson, Elizabeth A. *Affect and Artificial Intelligence*. Seattle: University of Washington Press, 2010.

———. *Gut Feminism*. Durham, NC: Duke University Press, 2015.

Winston, Brian, ed. *The Documentary Film Book*. London: Palgrave Macmillan on behalf of the British Film Institute, 2013.

Womack, Mari Rita. "Sports Magic: Symbolic Manipulation among Professional Athletes." PhD diss., University of California, Los Angeles, 1982.

Woodhead, Linda, and Ole Riis. *A Sociology of Religious Emotion*. New York: Oxford University Press, 2010.

Zentner, Marcel, and Tuomas Eerola. "Self-Report Measures and Models." In *Handbook of Music and Emotion: Theory, Research, Applications*, ed. Patrik N. Juslin and John Sloboda, 187–222. Oxford: Oxford University Press, 2010.

DIANA FRITZ CATES is Professor and Chair of the Department of Religious Studies at the University of Iowa. She works primarily at the intersection of religious studies, ethics, and moral psychology, with a focus on the study of virtue and emotion. She is the author of *Choosing to Feel* (1997); *Aquinas on the Emotions* (2009); and many journal articles and chapters that treat the role of emotion in a good human life.

JOHN CORRIGAN is the Lucius Moody Bristol Distinguished Professor of Religion and Professor of History at Florida State University. His books on emotion include *Emptiness: Feeling Christian in America* (2015); *Business of the Heart: Religion and Emotion in the Nineteenth Century* (2002); and *The Oxford Handbook of Religion and Emotion* (2006).

ANNA M. GADE is Vilas Distinguished Achievement Professor in the Gaylord Nelson Institute for Environmental Studies at the University of Wisconsin–Madison. Professor Gade's published work centers on Islamic studies and theory and method in the academic study of religion, along with environmental studies and ethics from a humanistic perspective. She has been researching religion and emotion for two decades, including extensive research in mainland and island Southeast Asia.

M. GAIL HAMNER is Professor of Religion at Syracuse University where she teaches religion and culture through film, media theory, Continental philosophy, and feminist theory. She is the author of *American Pragmatism: A Religious Genealogy* (2002); *Religion and Film: The Politics of Nostalgia* (2012); and numerous essays on religion, film, and affect theory. She currently is writing *Religion and Public Affect*, which looks at Hollywood films, global public affects, and the figure of the religious feminine.

JESSICA JOHNSON is a Lecturer in the Departments of Anthropology and Gender and Women and Sexuality Studies at the University of Washington. She has published several articles and chapters based on her ethnographic research on Mars Hill Church. Her monograph entitled *Biblical Porn: Affect, Labor, and Pastor Mark Driscoll's Evangelical Empire* is forthcoming.

ABBY KLUCHIN is Visiting Assistant Professor of Philosophy and Religious Studies at Ursinus College, where she also teaches Gender and Women's Studies. She holds a B.A. from Swarthmore College and a M.A., M.Phil., and Ph.D. in philosophy of religion from Columbia University. Abby specializes in Continental philosophy, psychoanalysis, poststructuralism, and feminist theory. Abby is also cofounder and associate director of the Brooklyn Institute for Social Research.

JUNE MCDANIEL is Professor of the History of Religions in the Department of Religious Studies at the College of Charleston. Her research areas include mysticism and religious experience, religions of India, psychology of religion, women and religion, and ritual studies. She did field research in West Bengal, India, for two years, funded by Fulbright and the American Institute of Indian Studies. She has written three books on Indian religion and recently coedited a volume on mystical perception.

DAVID MORGAN is Professor of Religious Studies at Duke University and chair of the Department of Religious Studies. Morgan's scholarship has focused on the history of religious material culture in the modern era. His books include *Visual Piety* (1998); *The Sacred Gaze* (2005); *The Embodied Eye* (2012); and, most recently, *The Forge of Vision: A Visual History of Modern Christianity* (2015). Morgan is an editor of the journal *Material Religion*, coedits a book series on media and religion, and another on the material culture of religion.

SARAH M. ROSS is professor of Jewish music studies and director of the European Center for Jewish Music at the Hannover University of Music, Drama, and Media in Germany. She is author of *A Season of Singing: Creating Feminist Jewish Music in the United States* (2016) and coeditor of *Judaism and Emotion: Texts, Performance, Experience* (2013). Her main fields of research are Jewish music, ethnomusicological gender studies, and music and sustainability.

DONOVAN SCHAEFER is Assistant Professor of Religion at the University of Pennsylvania. After completing his doctorate at Syracuse University, he held a Mellon Postdoctoral Fellowship at Haverford College and, while there, cofounded the Religion, Affect, and Emotion group at the American Academy of Religion with Professor M. Gail Hamner. He is author of *Religious Affects: Animality, Evolution, and Power* (Duke University Press, 2015).

MARK WYNN is the author of *Emotional Experience and Religious Understanding: Integrating Perception, Conception and Feeling* (2005); *Faith and Place: An Essay in Embodied Religious Understanding* (2009); and *Renewing the Senses: A Study of the Philosophy and Theology of the Spiritual Life* (2013). He is the editor of *Religious Studies*, and in 2015 he gave the Wilde Lectures in Natural Religion at the University of Oxford.

11, 29, 143, 211, 250–51; as a definition of religion, 3, 82–83, 85; and environmentalism, 17, 176, 181–82, 186–92; and French existentialism, 6; as a heuristic of religious experience, 7; morality of, 23–26; and music, 16, 161–64; of non-Western religions, 118–19; problems in the research of, 2–4, 161–62; psychology of, 3–4, 9–10, 78, 249, 252; and secularism, 14, 81; and sport, 18, 222–37; and the study of religion, 1–2, 5–19, 82–83, 167–68. *See also* affect theory
Evans-Pritchard, E. E., 2
evolutionary biology. *See* Darwin, Charles
*Experiences in Groups. See* Bion, Wilfred

Facebook, 97, 208
Fatimah, 131–35
feeling. *See* affect theory; emotion
Fevre, Lucien, 5
Fischer, Becky, 109–10
*For the Bible Tells Me So*, 99, 111; presentation of conservative Christian emotion in, 106–8
Foucault, Michel, 77, 98
Francis of Assisi, Saint, 177–78, 184–86
Frank, Adam, 78
Freud, Sigmund, 12, 100, 245, 249, 252
Friedmann, Jonathan, 146
Fuller, Robert, 8, 86

Galloway, Alex, 96
Gandhi, Mohandas, 138, 180
Garner, Eric, 97
Geertz, Armin W., 82
Geertz, Clifford, 7, 229; and the definition of religion, 178, 200, 202; and emotion, 200–201, 213
Gershwin, George, 145
Gibbs, Anna, 230
*God Delusion, The. See* Dawkins, Richard
*God Loves Uganda*, 99

Goodman, Mark S., 148
Grady, Rachel, 108
Grierson, John, 97, 99
Guattari, Félix, 201, 248
Gunew, Sneja, 12

Haggart, Ted, 109
Hajdu, Andre, 144
Hall, G. Stanley, 3
Harding, Susan, 208–9
Hardt, Michael, 101
Harpham, Geoffrey, 3
Harris, Sam, 82, 86
Hedges, Chris, 85–86
Hinduism, 126, 130, 136; *bhava* and *rasa* in Indian literature of, 16, 119–30, 135–37; importance of emotion in, 119–21, 127, 185
Hitchens, Christopher, 82, 86
Hochschild, Arlie, 7
Hood, Ki Mantle, 157
Hubbard, G., 165
Huntington, Samuel, 86
Husayn, 130–35, 138
Huxley, Thomas Henry, 75–76

*Infinite Jest. See* Wallace, David Foster
Innes, John Brodie, 84
Islam, 16–19, 73, 86–87, 137, 204; and cassette sermons, 246–47, 255; emotional views of the environment in, 176, 194–95; Qur'anic inspiration for environmentalism in, 186–94; and rhetoric of emotion, 213–14; Shi'ah mourning literature in, 109, 117, 130–32, 136, 138
Islam, Kazi Nazrul, 120, 122, 126

Jakobsen, Janet, 14, 70, 81
James, William, 3, 5, 82, 229; and analysis of emotion in religious conversion, 63, 65; on diversity of religious feeling, 178, 247
Jameson, Fredric, 101

CPSIA information can be obtained
at www.ICGtesting.com
Printed in the USA
JSHW020034251120
9804JS00007B/189